Studies in American Popular History and Culture

Edited by
Jerome Nadelhaft
University of Maine

A Routledge Series

Studies in American Popular History and Culture

Jerome Nadelhaft, *General Editor*

The Literature of Immigration and Racial Formation
Becoming White, Becoming Other, Becoming American in the Late Progressive Era
Linda Joyce Brown

Popular Culture and the Enduring Myth of Chicago, 1871–1968
Lisa Krissoff Boehm

America's Fight over Water
The Environmental and Political Effects of Large-Scale Water Systems
Kevin Wehr

Daughters of Eve
Pregnant Brides and Unwed Mothers in Seventeenth-Century Massachusetts
Else L. Hambleton

Narrative, Political Unconscious, and Racial Violence in Wilmington, North Carolina
Leslie H. Hossfeld

Validating Bachelorhood
Audience, Patriarchy, and Charles Brockden Brown's Editorship of the Monthly Magazine and American Review
Scott Slawinski

Children and the Criminal Law in Connecticut, 1635–1855
Changing Perceptions of Childhood
Nancy Hathaway Steenburg

Books and Libraries in American Society during World War II
Weapons in the War of Ideas
Patti Clayton Becker

Mistresses of the Transient Hearth
American Army Officers' Wives and Material Culture, 1840–1880
Robin Dell Campbell

The Farm Press, Reform, and Rural Change, 1895–1920
John J. Fry

State of 'The Union'
Marriage and Free Love in the Late 1800s
Sandra Ellen Schroer

"My Pen and My Soul Have Ever Gone Together"
Thomas Paine and the American Revolution
Vikki J. Vickers

Agents of Wrath, Sowers of Discord
Authority and Dissent in Puritan Massachusetts, 1630–1655
Timothy L. Wood

The Quiet Revolutionaries
How the Grey Nuns Changed the Social Welfare Paradigm of Lewiston, Maine
Susan P. Hudson

Cleaning Up
The Transformation of Domestic Service in Twentieth Century New York City
Alana Erickson Coble

Feminist Revolution in Literacy
Women's Bookstores in the United States
Junko R. Onosaka

Feminist Revolution in Literacy

Women's Bookstores in the United States

Junko R. Onosaka

Routledge
New York & London

Published in 2006 by
Routledge
Taylor & Francis Group
270 Madison Ave,
New York NY 10016

Published in Great Britain by
Routledge
Taylor & Francis Group
2 Park Square,
Milton Park, Abingdon,
Oxon, OX14 4RN

Transferred to Digital Printing 2010

International Standard Book Number-10: 0-415-97596-4 (Hardcover)
International Standard Book Number-13: 978-0-415-97596-4 (Hardcover)
Library of Congress Card Number 2006000051

Library of Congress Cataloging-in-Publication Data

Onosaka, Junko R.
Feminist revolution in literacy : women's bookstores in the United States / Junko R. Onosaka.
p. cm. -- (Studies in American popular history and culture)
Includes bibliographical references (p.) and index.
ISBN 0-415-97596-4 (acid-free paper)
1. Women booksellers--United States--History--20th century. 2. Women in the book industries and trade--United States--History--20th century. 3. Feminist literature--United States. 4. Lesbians' writings. 5. Women--Employment--United States--History--20th century. I. Title. II. Series: American popular history and culture (Routledge (Firm) III. Series.

Z473.O64 2006
381'.450020820973--dc22 2006000051

ISBN10: 0-415-97596-4 (hbk)
ISBN10: 0-415-88260-5 (pbk)

ISBN13: 978-0-415-97596-4 (hbk)
ISBN13: 978-0-415-88260-6 (pbk)

Visit the Taylor & Francis Web site at
http://www.taylorandfrancis.com

and the Routledge Web site at
http://www.routledge-ny.com

For my parents, Onosaka Isao and Sawako

Contents

Acknowledgments

How does a person properly thank so many wonderful colleagues, acquaintances and mentors? There are many people who have provided me with aid, encouragement, and support during the course of this study, and it is indeed impossible to thank them all. Yet I will make an attempt to single out those particular persons and institutions whose help and guidance have proved fundamental to my research on the history of women's bookstores.

In my "fieldwork" for this study I have especially made use of personal contacts with several pivotal figures in the women's bookstores movement, and I would just like to make a note of heartfelt thanks. Linda Bubon, Ann Christophersen, Mary Ellen Kavenaugh, Carol Seajay, Mev Miller, Trudy Mills and Kate Randall kindly shared their experience and information of women's bookstores with me. Indeed, it's the last of these who has proven to be not just arguably the most influential woman in the history of women's bookstores, but who has given most charitably of her time and energy to help enable me to gain a clearer understanding of her own experience as well as that of others in the movement. Carol Seajay has been most gracious, and a veritable encyclopedia of information about and perspective on women's bookstores. I am most grateful for her help. And I also would like to thank the many women who were willing to answer my questionnaires.

The start at a series of archives have been most kind to me in the course of my work, providing access to their materials, sometimes on-site and sometimes by mail—but invariably offering me their utmost cooperation. These institutions have included: the Special Collections Library, Duke University; The Lesbian Herstory Archives, New York, NY; Gay and Lesbian Historical Society of Northern California (San Francisco Public Library); Schlesinger Library, Radcliffe Institute, Harvard University; Greater Cincinnati Women's Resource Center; Cincinnati Historical Society

Library; and Rare and Special Collections, University of Illinois, Urbana-Champaign.

Although all of these individuals and institutions have been indispensable to the completion of this book, it has been my mentors who have principally guided me academically toward success. Indeed, I wasn't even originally aware of the existence of women's bookstores, and it was only through the guidance of Professor Susan Cahn of SUNY Buffalo that I took notice. Of course, it has been the perfect guidance of my main advisor at SUNY Buffalo, Professor Maxine Seller, that has ensured that I conduct my study with the highest of academic standards and the greatest attention to detail, but also that I think seriously about the larger historical contexts for the very development of phenomena like women's bookstores. I am singularly indebted to her for her ongoing support and sagely advice—every step of the way. I would also like to thank Professors Monica Jardine and Myles Slatin (Emeritus) for their respective guidance and friendship. In particular, my friendship with Professor Slatin, which started when I arrived in the States in 1994, has been a well of encouragement. There are also many friends whose existence has turned Buffalo into a "warm" place for me. I'd just like to mention, among my friends, Yoko Nishimura, Junko Kanamura and Atsuko Nishida. They have all been supportive along the way, and I couldn't have stomached the long process of research without them.

I would also like to thank Mr. Benjamin Holtzman, my editor at Routledge, who not only "discovered" my dissertation and wrote to me originally about the possibility of transforming it into a book, but who has also been patient with me at critical stages of my completion of the work. My mother, Sawako Onosaka, has always supported me in my pursuit of my dreams, even at those points when she may have not completely understood the nature of the academic's life. My brother, Makoto Onosaka has not said anything about my decision, but I have always felt his support. And lastly I would like to thank my husband, Brian O. Ruppert, without whom this book would arguably have been impossible; his academic insights and encouragement helped me to find the perseverance and the historian's devotion to detail that hopefully make this work truly worth reading.

Chapter One

Introduction

This study attempts to establish that women's bookstores constituted political and educational organizations by examining the history of women's bookstores from the 1970s to the 1990s. "Women's bookstores" (also called "feminist bookstores") refers to bookstores established by women and which serve women as their customers.[1] Such bookstores emerged in the United States contemporaneously with the women's movement and flowering of women's culture associated with cultural feminism in the early 1970s. Following their crescendo in popularity between 1985 and 1994, their numbers decreased significantly.

"Cultural Feminism," according to Linda Alcoff, refers to "the ideology of a female nature or female essence re-appropriated by feminists themselves in an effort to revalidate undervalued female attributes."[2] Thus a large number of feminists from the 1970s on created a variety of literary and theoretical works and engaged in a variety of activities to do just that—to validate their female identity.[3] As part of this movement, women's bookstores were owned and operated by women, especially feminists and lesbian feminists. Since cultural feminism takes a more or less essentialized view of the differences between men and women and, as a result, assumes a separatist stance to gender relations, it is claimed that cultural feminism depoliticized and weakened feminism as a result, and eventually hastened its increased invisibility.[4] The view that feminism was no longer a vibrant social movement as of the 1980s has, at least in part, an historical basis, since anti-feminist organizations gained increasing political power after the defeat of the Equal Rights Amendment in 1982 and a larger shift to the right occurred in the Reagan and first Bush administration, which made it more difficult for feminists to make new political strides. Organizations supportive of women such as women's clinics, rape crisis centers, and women's shelters were forced to close their doors due to a lack of government funding, and the number of feminist organizations decreased. Feminism or feminists became largely invisible to the general public, and members of the media often declared its failure by the late 1980s.

This study of the history of women's bookstores, however, challenges the notion that cultural feminism necessarily undermined the feminist movement. It does so, centrally, by exploring the following questions: When did women start their bookstores, and why? What kinds of women were involved in these bookstores? What was the character of the publishing industry at the time, including publishers, the selection of books for review, and the distribution system? How did women operate them? What were the obstacles they confronted? In particular, how did they overcome such impediments, and what helped them to survive and even flourish during the1980s, the era of backlash against feminism? Furthermore, by focusing on the development of women's bookstores in the late 1970s and 1980s, this study demonstrates how it was that women's bookstores came to play an indispensable role in the larger women's movement: through enabling the dissemination of multiracial and multicultural voices—and thus helping to both sustain and enrich the feminist movement. Before turning to examine that history, however, we should first consider the research that has previously been conducted on or in connection with women's bookstores

There is a series of studies that are relevant to the examination of women's bookstores in the United States. Initially, we can note that three major studies and two important articles have been written that are directly concerned with the history or organization of women's bookstores. In addition, some twenty journalistic articles have been produced about women's bookstores, among which one is particularly informative for this study. Otherwise, a book and two articles examine identity, culture and social movements; one of the articles is particularly important because it examines bookstore culture as the medium for diffusion of social movement ideology at the level of individual actors. The others explore the strong relationship between cultural feminism and women's movements. Four additional studies discuss women's bookstores in the context of the study of feminist publishing. Finally, although it is directly related neither to women's bookstores nor to feminism, one study analyzes the role of bookstores as a crucial political site by examining African Americans' bookstores and their ideological dimension. Interestingly, all three major studies were doctoral dissertations written in 1985, when women's bookstores were becoming increasingly visible. Since the establishment of the first woman's bookstores in the early 1970s, the number had at that point reached over one hundred, and were especially prominent in urban centers such as state capitals and campus environs. These studies clarified the interconnection between the women's movement and women's bookstores on the local level. However, since each of the studies focused on just one women's bookstore, we need a larger analysis of the development of women's bookstores across the nation; in particular, it is important, in doing so, to examine how their informal and formal national network helped feminist booksellers to continue as a part of the women's movement as well as both sustain and enrich the movement.

There are in fact no major studies that examine in detail the birth and the development of women's bookstores and their interconnection over three decades from the 1970s to 1990s. Moreover, none connects their informal and formal national network with the larger women's movement in the U.S. In particular, preceding studies did not explore the relationships between women's bookstores or their connections with the larger feminist publishing community which played a crucial role in the women's movement. Although such studies have suggested that women's bookstores were born as part of the women's movement, an in-depth study of the contexts surrounding their genesis and development is warranted. In particular, analyzing women's bookstores both locally *and* nationally—and, in doing so, focusing on their relationships with other women's bookstores, writers, presses, publishers, and distributors—will enable us to understand the larger meaning of their existence as well as their contribution to feminism, especially to the realization of what might be called the feminist revolution in literacy.

Members of the book industry routinely referred to it as the "gentlemen's profession." What, of course, did they mean precisely by "gentlemen?" Since the early 20th century, a large percentage of its employees were in fact women, the vast majority of whom were very well-educated. However, these women had limited authority in crucial aspects of the industry such as wage determination, editorial and financial decision-making processes. Before analyzing the historical context in which women started their bookstores, Chapter Two examines how publishing and bookselling industries developed by the 1960s along with analyzing the status of women within those industries, and briefly considers the history of women in the publishing industry. In doing so, I explore the relationship between social movements and alternative publishing, and proceed to analyze the historical context in which women started their bookstores by exploring the latter's relationship with the women's movement and publishing industry in the late 1960s. The women's movement of the 1960s and early 1970s promoted dialogue not only between women and men but also among women. Such dialogue stemmed from women's profound desire to speak of their own accord and about themselves; moreover, it provided those involved with knowledge concerning feminist activities nationwide and women's issues in general, informing them of what had been accomplished thus far, what other women were thinking, and in what direction the women's movement was heading. Given this context, the years from 1968 to 1973 witnessed the most rapid proliferation of women's works of various forms including manifestos and poetry. Chapter Two also shows how it was that women were eventually able to publish some five-hundred-sixty journals and magazines for female audiences.[5]

Chapter Three further delineates how feminists helped and cooperated with each other to disseminate women's words—particularly, through passing women's written words into other women's hands. Politically and socially controversial materials such as lesbian feminist works were likely to become targets for rejection at the time of publication or distribution. Therefore, they needed their own press and distribution system, that is, their own network for distributing women's works. Eventually, women established the first national conference for women in the publishing industry—the Women In Print Conference in Omaha, Nebraska, in 1976. Women's cooperation, sharing, and caring played a significant role in developing the network of women in print, especially women's bookstores. Since then, by the mid-1990s, the number of women's bookstores reached roughly one-hundred-forty;[6] in the history of women's bookstores to the present, it is thought that there have been somewhere between 600 and 800 women's bookstores opened altogether.[7]

Chapter Four turns from the analysis of the historical context to examine how women started to develop bookstores and to determine what made the rapid growth of women's bookstores possible. I focus on lesbian feminists in the publishing industry, especially women's bookstores, and explore their significant roles in establishing the network of women's bookstores, taking into consideration the split between heterosexual women and lesbian women in the early stage of the women's movement as well as that between lesbians and gays. Moreover, I examine the *Feminist Bookstores Newsletter* (later *Feminist Bookstore News (FBN)),* one outgrowth of the Women In Print conference. *FBN* played a pivotal role in the construction of the women's bookstores' community by weaving together the women's bookstores toward a common goal—disseminating feminist ideas while the type, manner of operation, and the scale of each store differed in part according to their different physical environs: from metropolitan areas to small campus towns. I particularly explore the role of Carol Seajay, who was publisher and editor of *FBN* from 1976 to the end of its publication, and who founded Old Wives' Tales, which later became one of the oldest and most flourishing women's bookstores.

Chapter Five examines criticisms made inside and outside feminism that emerged from the late 1970s and effected tremendous changes both in feminism and in feminist enterprises such as women's bookstores. Women's profound desire to express themselves took multifarious forms and promoted the development of a variety of feminist publishing enterprises. These enterprises, especially women's bookstores, started to help each other through networking activities such as the second and the third "Women in Print" Conference as well as the development of *FBN*. In the meantime, the number of women's bookstores steadily rose. This chapter, in addition, makes clear the ways in which women of color began to express their frustration toward what they experienced as the "separatism" that many women's bookstores exercised, criticizing internalized racism and other forms of discrimination; internal conflicts arose in women's bookstores and often caused their collapse. Finally, this chapter also attempts to clarify the ways in which the economic and political conditions were increasingly unfavorable to feminists.

Chapter Six considers how women involved in the operation and patronage of women's bookstores built their feminist identity and political activism while simultaneously making their bookstores successful as businesses to maintain their activism. In fact, the women involved as operators and patrons experienced virtually continuous conflict in connection with their chosen, alternative mode of working: operating as a collective to ensure the practice of participatory democracy and egalitarianism. In other words, this chapter examines the conflict that ensued with the effort to "enact" feminist philosophy in bookstore operations on the ground. The chapter additionally focuses on the creation and development of women's studies programs, because the rapid increase in purchases of materials by and for women in this connection helped enable women's bookstores to both survive and thrive. Given this was the case, the founding and the development of Women's Studies as a discipline should not be overlooked because the demand for materials to be used in teaching and in supporting Women's Studies curriculum enabled women's bookstores not only to survive but also to increasingly function as an educational center.

Through considering women's bookstores, feminist journals, store records, their correspondence, and articles that appeared in various media in terms of their educational aspect, Chapter Seven attempts to show women's bookstores as referral centers, places for meeting people, for alternative artistic work and information, for the promotion of feminist identity and a sense of community among women as well as for the education of women. Moreover, I analyze them as a part of the ecosystems of feminist publishing communities. A case study of Women & Children First in

Chicago examines it from its beginning as an establishment (1986) to the end of the 1990s. The history and activities of Women & Children First demonstrate the way in which it developed as a prominent alternative educational site for women.

What, at the same time, eventually happened to women's bookstores? Chapter Eight analyzes the larger historical context for the economic and cultural problems that women's bookstores increasingly faced over the course of the 1990s. Due to the rapid expansion of women's bookstores, the number of women's bookstores reached more than 140 by the mid-1990s. However, they began to collapse under the collective weight of continuing sexism, racism and heterosexism as well as the rise of super-bookstore chains like Borders Bookstore and Barnes & Noble Bookstore—and on-line bookstores like Amazon.com. Moreover, generational changes among feminists offered an additional blow. As of 2002, only six years after the number of women's bookstores reached a record high, roughly 75% of them were out of business.

Based on the findings of this study, the last chapter will summarize the role and the accomplishments of women's bookstores in the United States from the 1970s to the early 21st century. I would like to emphasize that women's bookstores were and continue to be political because they have emerged out of the literary, cultural and political contexts brought about by the women's rights and lesbian and gay rights movement, and have disseminated the voices of large numbers of women, and made new perspectives available on everything from politics to everyday life. They not only carry women's works and sell commodities but also offer or organize political, cultural and educational programs and events for women. Armed with knowledge of women's literature and of their own community resources, women operating the bookstores have also provided social services/information to their communities, and played the figurative role of community librarian. In addition, by providing these services, women's bookstores have constituted bridges that mediated between the cultural, educational or political purposes of the women's movement and local female patrons. By socializing in women's bookstores as customers, volunteers, or workers, women have experienced political and cultural transformation. Moreover, women's bookstores not only brought women and groups for women into mutual contact, but also mediated between writers, publishers and readers. They have in doing so enriched not only the feminist publishing industry but also the American publishing industry as a whole. The visibility of women's bookstores has thus ultimately offered legitimacy to the feminist movement; they have become "sanctuaries" for feminists and sustained feminist activities in the communities.

This study argues that women's bookstores have operated as valuable bases for political actions and lifetime learning as well as for nurturing and sustaining women's lives in the communities. The day-to-day operations in women's bookstores were constructed in large part through the deliberate considerations and persistent political missions of feminists to improve women's literacy—their abilities not only to read and write but also to publish and thereby distribute new images of women's, their voices, and their visions. In other words, feminist booksellers helped to bring about a "*feminist* revolution in literacy" at great financial cost and personal effort over four long decades.

Chapter Two

The Days When We Had No Women's Bookstores

In order to understand fully why and how women started publishing operations and bookstores, we need to explore how the publishing industry developed by the 1960s. Analysis of the environs of the larger world of publishing can help us understand the historical context in which women began to construct their own publishing community. We turn first to the social and economic contexts surrounding the larger American publishing industry up to the 1950s, while tracing the history of the publishing industry before the beginning of this radical transformation. Then, in the latter part of this chapter, we consider the history of women in the publishing industry in general: their role and status. And this chapter also examines the historical position of the small press, the so-called "underground," "alternative" or "independent" press in the late 50s and the early 60s. These small presses emerged within developing social movements such as the civil rights, peace, anti-nuclear movements and various other counter-cultural phenomena. By doing so, we can gain an understanding not only of the character of the small press' connections with such movements but also of seminal issues of minority concerns—and we can clarify the motives of many American women in starting their own print media.

GENTLEMEN'S PROFESSION: THE BEGINNING AND DEVELOPMENT OF THE PUBLISHING INDUSTRY

Many publishing houses emerged, especially on the East Coast, in the nineteenth century.[1] Most of them first specialized in educational and religious books and only later addressed themselves to the general public.[2] During the period, some books had enormous sales, and at the same time they exercised powerful influence.[3] For example, *Uncle Tom's Cabin* sold 300,000 copies in its first year, which were the equivalent of 6 million today. It is considered the book that galvanized public opinion against slavery.[4] People in the publishing industry, in this way, came to view publishing not merely as a commercial but also a cultural responsibility. At the same time, they were quite willing to sometimes refer to it as the "worst business in the world" because of its status as "the least profitable of all the professions, except preaching and teaching."[5] On the other hand, most of those in charge of publishing houses were not poor insofar as they were from affluent families: they could afford to sacrifice financial reward by thinking of themselves not as merchandisers, but as businessmen of letters—engaged in the "gentlemen's profession."[6]

Well-known publishers such as Doubleday, Random House, Scribner's, and Harper, on the East Coast—particularly in New York—were established by men from affluent families, and for a long time, these publishers dominated the book trade. They have played an important role in shaping the culture of the publishing industry since they represented what was essentially a group of high status; writers were dependent upon the critical judgment and patronage of the blue bloods—the "cultural elite."[7] Publishing houses were, moreover, for the most part family-owned and small. In economic terms, the industry had for a long time been a minor one in the US, and it was not generally regarded as a prime object for investment. Beginning in the 1920s and 30s some publishers attempted to broaden their publications and seek new readers, and also tried to sell books in greater volume. They founded alternative means to achieve their ends—for example, one was The Book-of-the-Month Club, founded in 1926, and another was New American Library, the American branch of British Penguin, a mass-market publishing house.[8] People in the industry were becoming more enthusiastic in their efforts to create "blockbusters."[9] Such innovations were reflective of but also had some influence on the market conditions surrounding publishing industry. However, the social and economic upheaval caused by World War II, especially the educational boom and the general prosperity in the post-war period, also had great impact on developments in the publishing world.

World War II itself had perhaps the greatest influence on the history of the publishing industry, leading to a huge demand for books. Under the G.I. Bill, veterans flocked into colleges, and purchased a great many books with government funds. However, some scholars claim that what had the most profound effect on the entire book industry was the 1957 shock of the

Soviet's Sputnik launch. The US government urged the growth and upgrading of education at all levels, and in the following year The Library Services Act was enacted, which provided federal funding for the extension of library services.[10] Publishers benefited from the massive infusion of federal funds. Between 1963 and 1969 publishing industry sales increased by 59 percent, from $1.7 billion to $2.7 billion annually. However, ironically, such success presented financial problems.[11] This is because investors saw book publishing as a sound investment with future growth potential, and continuous merger and acquisition activity in the publishing industry began—in 1968, forty-seven mergers occurred, estimated to be 4.7 times the national rate for all industries.[12] Responding to those who might lament the end of the so-called "golden era" of publishing, Patricia Holt says:

> But surely I'm not alone in thinking there has never been a golden era in American publishing. . . . Even in the much heralded "gentlemen's profession" era, publishers were so insulated that only a handful of books from African American, Asian American or Latino American writers got published. . . . Books from women ran into the prejudices of such an exclusive industry. . . . The big problem with the Gentlemen's Profession, of course, was that it was only for gentlemen. The ones who decided what made a person qualify as a gentleman were . . . other gentlemen . . . [they] liked to say the racism and sexism (not terms he used) didn't exist in literature, that books were chosen for their merits alone. . . . But so many publishing houses were run in that clubby uptown atmosphere of the privately wealthy that when someone at the top said there was nothing exclusionary about choosing a book on its merits, he was usually speaking from a vacuum.[13]

In this way, Holt questioned the notion that a clear absence of women and minorities in the "gentlemen's profession." should be seen as a "golden era."[14] In 1981 Mary Gaver indeed noted that "the percentage of women in financial, administrative, sales and managerial jobs in publishing is entirely under-representative of their abilities . . . [upward mobility of women in the book trade] is very miniscule."[15] Even in the 1990's, women's voices were still under-represented within the publishing industry. Statistically, women made up 60% of the total employees in publishing, but this was concentrated in clerical, secretarial and administrative positions with little opportunity for promotion. In fact, only 40% of those made it to managerial positions compared with 60% of the male sector, and 22% to board directors compared to 78% of the men.[16]

WOMEN IN THE PUBLISHING INDUSTRY

Women throughout the world have been active in the publishing industry since as early as the 14th & 15th centuries—from Pre-Gutenberg to the present.[17] Although historically most publishers selected successors from among their male heirs, women actually operated presses themselves as well as legally owned and/or operated printing establishments.[18] Their names appear in the earliest records of typographical history: like Ann Smith in Newport, Rhode Island, in 1735, many women took over their husbands' printing shops upon the latter's deaths.[19] When printing establishments grew in size and importance, women's roles became severely curtailed, although women were never excluded entirely because small publishers in particular needed their wives and daughters as informal familial assistance.[20] However, as Leona M. Hudak points out, no single volume has ever been compiled in any language that chronicles their endeavors.[21]

During the years 1865 to 1919, when the general organization of the industry developed, women were prevented more and more from active and formal participation in the industry while they were increasingly to "comprise a large part of the behind-the-scenes support staff."[22] By the eve of World War I, a growing women's movement was demanding that the larger publishing industry open its doors to women. For example, in 1914 textbook and dictionary publishers employed the largest numbers of female college graduates, with their numbers ranging between 20 and 30 percent of all employees.[23] In December 1917 a group of 15 women booksellers—excluded from membership in the all-male Bookseller's League—met in Sherwood's Book Store, 19 John Street, in downtown New York to honor and recognize women's role in the world of books, and formed the Women's National Book Association (WNBA). The organization still exists in the early 21st century.[24] However, women were still deemed suitable not only for lower-level editorial work but for the developing specialties of children's book publishing and advertising, promotion, and publicity, while many were still consigned to lower-level positions.[25] Even in the 70s, women in the publishing industry were suffering from lower status than men in terms of policy-making decisions and wages.[26] As a result, the labor force in the publishing industry consisted of 75–80% "overeducated," underpaid white women, who were concentrated in the lowest ranks, a few in managerial and sales positions and virtually none at the top.[27] The anthology written by women in the publishing industry in 1974, *Rooms With No View: A Woman's Guide to The Man's World of the Media,* shows whatever growth in the industry brought to the formal structuring of occupations and their career ladders, women remained outside the major lines of authority.[28]

Publishing has crucial power in making decisions of what to print. Men's sole control of the media has had "enormous implications for the power structure of society, patterns of thinking."[29] "WHIMM"s (White, Heterosexual, Insider, Middle-class Males) have been particularly prominent.[30] Those who have different views and ideas from WHIMMs have thus had few opportunities to get published.[31] Publishers often refrain from publishing works and genres that have not been published in some form or forum previously, since it is not able to prove its commercial success. Women's works, like other works by minority authors, were more likely to be rejected by being told that they were not qualified or appropriate to publish due to so-called "objective" standards although, according to Adrienne Rich, objectivity is the name that men have given to their subjectivity.[32] Quoting Anne Finch, Countess of Winchilsea, "Alas, a woman that attempts the pen. Such an intruder on the rights of men," Lynn Spender claims that there has been an "unpublished heritage of women's words and truths."[33]

At the same time, it should be noted that many middle-class or moderately wealthy white women indeed had comparatively more access to the publishing industry than they did to other professions. Moreover, they had greater privileges compared to African-American women and other women of color—indeed, people of color—in terms of status, opportunities of career development and networking in the publishing industry.[34] Although eventually only men became editors or sales representatives, such women could learn about publishing during their stint, and while many women stayed others were brave enough to leave the publishing houses and start their own.[35] Furthermore, even outside of established publishers, some white women had opportunities to apprentice in small presses run by white men. For example, Judy Grahn and Anne Leonard were apprenticed in New England Free Press (white male socialist press) in Boston, and then went back to San Francisco and started their press, the first all-women press, Women's Press Collective, in Oakland in 1974.[36] Even as recently as 1998 the demographic representation of editors has been largely that of relatively affluent whites, while African, Latin, and Asian-Americans are generally not well represented in the industry, while the white gay and lesbian community fares better.[37]

In any event, what so-called WHIMM publishers in the United States present as "American voices" have obviously represented only a part of American people's experiences. Consequently, "the voice of women," as Dale Spender points out, "has been admitted to print only in terms acceptable to men . . . and a history of male dominance in this industry thus implies that society has been shaped by the thoughts and actions of privileged men."[38] It might indeed be said in short that the experiences, values and conceptions of women and other social minorities have been consistently excluded from the media in general, resulting in an unequal and biased cultural heritage.[39] Moreover, for racial and ethnic minorities gaining voice and a sympathetic audience was a matter of survival in a society still dominated by WHIMMs. This is because these minorities could not only express their own voices, but also had to struggle against distorted images. African-Americans especially had to fight against racist stereotypes and negative messages about them that were rampant in mass media.[40] Consequently, together with the growth of the civil rights movement, African-Americans established a number of their own small presses.

THE BIRTH OF WOMEN'S PUBLISHING

The impressive gains in the publishing industry after World War II completely changed both the organizational culture and the actions of publishers. A craze of merges and acquisitions occurred along with a large number of new readers and a huge demand for books. However, they also created a potential niche for readers who were previously ignored by the book industry, a "group of cultural elite." These changes of the industry also created a niche for small publishing houses, so-called small presses since established publishers, academic or commercial, did not always introduce important new knowledge to people. It was particularly the case when highly controversial materials are involved. These small presses were often willing to take the risk of publishing.[41] The late 1950s and 60s saw an explosion of small presses and small print media.[42] Starting especially with the Free Press in 1964, partly in connections with the political and social ferment of that decade, a small press movement emerged. Standing up to "mainstream publishing," which was heavily capitalized and commercialized, and which distributed its products most widely, the small press was considered "the last desperate assertion of the individual against the giant machine—social, military, academic, cultural, spiritual."[43] According to Henderson, "they try to represent the American spirit of happy, cranky individualism."[44] Small presses were also often called the "underground press," "alternative press," or "independent press."[45] They often covered issues such as the so-called "unholy trinity of revolution, sex, and drugs."[46] For example, according to Armstrong, celebrating sex or unrepressed sexuality was for them one way to challenge what media activists saw as the Puritanical taboos and laws of an uptight America, and radical by their definition. Consequently, members of dissident political groups, avant-garde artists and authors found these small presses to be a crucial place for their self-expression. David Armstrong says, "Their readers were overwhelmingly young (in their late teens to early thirties), white, and middle class. It was to them that the underground directed its coverage of the unholy trinity of revolution, sex, and drugs."[47] Therefore, nudity and four-letter words were frequently found in underground papers.[48] More and more people started to publish in special interest fields.[49] However, the small press movement would not have occurred without technological change, which opened the floodgates of new presses with relatively little capital.[50] This is because prior to the 1960s, setting a Linotype machine required technical training as well as great financial means. Armstrong says:

> But the widespread introduction of offset printing in the early years of the decade [1960s] made papers cheap, easy, and quick to produce. In offset printing, a competent typist can use a standard typewriter to prepare copy, which is then pasted down on flat sheets, photographed, and duplicated. The offset revolution made it possible for virtually anyone so inclined to produce a newspaper. In the middle sixties, with a few dollars, a pot of glue, a typewriter, and a handful of volunteers to write and lay out stories, several thousand copies of an offset tabloid newspaper could be printed.[51]

The offset printing "revolution" helped create a number of small presses. By the end of the sixties, the number of these small presses reached over 400.

Furthermore, the press became an important communication tool among groups with similar interests or goals. This is because publishing was unquestionably more affordable than other forms of media. It is said that those who had dissident voices in the civil rights movement, the new Left's activism against the Vietnam War, and the larger counterculture movement built their activism through using small presses. Kirkpatrick Sale refers to "the profound impact on the national life that the alternative press was able to effect."[52] Carol Seajay, co-founder of Old Wives' Tales (women's bookstore in San Francisco, California) and publisher and editor of *Feminist Bookstores Newsletter (FBN)*, notes that "The socialists and the leftists knew that if you want to change something, you start a newspaper and distribute it. You give the ideas to the people and they'll take the ideas and run with them."[53] Millions were inspired to activism by the words and ideas delivered by such rapidly emerging alternative organs. Joining these social movements, those in the women's movement later greatly benefited from their experiences in the social movements. Similarly, women as a minority in the public sphere had historically been receivers of what images and information the mass media produced;[54] the mass media was the primary influence to send women their images of themselves and of the presumed validity of traditional roles.[55] In fact, since the mass media could easily send and change the messages, women received differing images depending on the historical period; particularly during the period of World War II, the mass media had encouraged women to try nontraditional jobs, represented by the figure of Rosie the Riveter.

However, in the postwar years the mass media replaced this image with that of the dutiful homemaker. The Presidential candidate Adlai Stevenson even told the 1955 graduating class of Smith College, "Your task is to influence man and boy through the humble role of housewife."[56] Women were told that "true feminine fulfillment" could only be achieved through their relationships with husband, children, and home. Large-circulation women's magazines such as Ladies' Home Journal, McCall's, Woman's Day, and Good Housekeeping in the 1950s, and 60s led the way, and a woman without a husband and a child was represented as outside of the norm, if not "abnormal." The coverage in these magazines for women was dominated by "domestic" issues, with little or no reference to other social, national, or international problems. Consequently, women increasingly identified themselves as "just a housewife."[57] On the other hand, women also discovered a disturbing aspect of the underground papers. The free media envisioned by radicals were not exceptional in terms of demeaning stereotypes of women. In the 1960s, a byproduct of underground papers' non-judgmental messages about sex eventually allowed for the influx of sexual or pornographic advertisements, which brought in some $5000 a week to the proprietor of one such paper.[58] "No longer was sex being presented as the free medium or[sic] exchange that radicals had envisioned," says Armstrong, "but as a commodity being sold for the profit of a few."[59] They perpetuated some of the same stereotypes of women as those often portrayed in the mass media. For women, underground papers such as the Free Press and the Berkeley Barb were no longer radical and progressive in this regard. At the same time, this also increased women's awareness of the discrimination they faced and also of the need for their own media.

From the outset women actively participated in the civil rights movement, the new Left movement, and the student movement. However, in many ways women did not participate equally in the movement. Most women were assigned clerical jobs, and very few were in the positions of decision making. Women were feeling increasingly frustrated in these predominantly male-led movements.[60] In 1965, Mary King and Casey Hayden issued "a kind of memo" to stimulate a communication network to protest the inferior status of women in the organization. They circulated this paper on women in the civil right movement based on their experiences as the Student Non-Violent Coordinating Committee volunteers:

> [Women] seem to be caught in a common-law caste system that operates, sometimes subtly, forcing them to work around or outside hierarchal structures of power which may exclude them. Women seem to be placed in the same position of assumed subordination in personal situations too. It is a caste system which, at its worst, uses and exploits women . . . having learned from the movement to think radically about the personal work and abilities of people whose role in society has gone unchallenged before, a lot of women in the movement have begun to apply those lessons to their own relationships with men. Each of us probably has her own story of the various results.[61]

It clearly describes a problem in which the lack of status of women even in these political movements led them to think they needed a "revolution within the revolution." This "memo" written by two women is regarded as one of the first documents of the emerging women's liberation movement as it succinctly represented women's voices against sexism in the male-led organizations.[62]

Betty Friedan was one of many frustrated women in the male-led progressive political movement. She questioned the gender roles prescribed by society and women's images produced by the mass media, and her questions became a book, *The Feminine Mystique*, in 1963. It was an immediate and "controversial" bestseller offering a "powerful indictment of the ideology that forced women into the role of fulltime housewife and description of the psychological costs of such a limited life."[63] However, unlike Friedan, most women's words were ignored and never got published. Even though they tried to raise women's issues, they often received ridicule, catcalls and sometimes verbal abuse.[64] It became increasingly clear to women that if they wanted their ideas in print they would have to put them there themselves. Seajay said "We established our own so that no man could ever again tell women what was true, what was relevant to our lives, or what we could publish and read."[65] Thus, women learned again that "freedom of the press belongs to those who own it."[66] Therefore, many women left male-dominated papers, and started their own newsletters or papers. A few, however, did not—instead they took over.[67] For example, Rat, a N.Y. underground press was taken over in January 1970 by women staff members who were awakened to sexism in their own work environs because of the new wave of feminism. They ejected editor Jeff Shero, and the Rat became a women's paper. A poet and journalist Robin Morgan wrote "Goodbye to All That" in the first issue.

> Goodbye to the inaccurate use of the phrase "male chauvinism." Male chauvinism is an ATTITUDE—male supremacy is the OBJECTIVE REALITY . . . Goodbye to the Conspiracy who, when launching with fellow sexist bastards Norman Mailer and Terry Southern in a bunny-type club in Chicago, find Judge Hoffman at the neighboring table-no surprise: IN THE LIGHT, THEY ARE ALL THE SAME. . . . Goodbye to Hip Culture, and the so-called Sexual Revolution, which has functioned toward women's freedom as did the Reconstruction toward former slaves—reinstituted oppression by another name . . . Let it all hang out. Let it seem bitchy, dykey, catty, frustrated, crazy . . . nutty, frigid, ridiculous, bitter, embarrassing, manhating, libelous, pure, unfair, envious, intuitive, low-down, stupid, petty, liberating. We are the women that men have warned us about.[68]

Morgan bid farewell to what men, whether conservative or liberal, offered to society and claimed women needed their own voices and visions to change the latter. Her strong message must have encouraged numerous women who were afraid to be called "bitchy, dykey, catty, frustrated, crazy," etc and, simultaneously, women thus recognized more fully the importance of establishing their own papers.

Since then, such "memos" were written by numerous women, and they quickly evolved into manifestos proclaiming the birth of the women's movement. In these and related writings, women began to talk to each other about their lives and to exchange ideas. Later, a collection of articles first produced on mimeograph machines was eventually published as *Sisterhood is Powerful*, which became the classic of classics of feminist literature. In the early days, however, such mimeographed papers *were* feminist publishing.[69] As June Arnold says, "very early [in the modern women's movement] women saw the need to write down for clarification and make available to other women what feminism stood for." Seajay notes that in doing so, they found that when they shared their "most horrible moments or revealed [their] most shameful secrets, they discovered that other women had had similar experiences." She stresses "that many women had had those kinds of experiences. Something went 'click' and the personal became political."[70] The "click" of understanding that *Ms.* magazine made so famous was the engine of the so-called Consciousness-Raising (CR) groups.[71] As Alisa Klinger points out, "turning the slow dawning of consciousness . . . into a larger conversation among women about their cultural and social roles was the inspiration that undergirded the feminist alternative press."[72] Thus, papers became a "movable, newsprint CR group, expanding participation in that patient, primary, grass-roots form of activism to anyone who reads its pages."[73] As Charlotte Bunch, who is considered a founder and leading thinker in the women's movement and lesbian feminism, says, it was "therefore vital that feminists get our materials into public."[74] "The more we talked, the more we had to say," says Seajay.[75] These papers became newsletters and newspapers and eventually circulated among thousands of women. Moreover, among the existing media, printed media were cheaper and easier to produce, and also to distribute.

Women's papers were also a central force to form networks among women's groups by disseminating "ideas and plans as women were going along."[76] For example, Jo Freeman, who published and distributed *Voice of Women's Liberation Movement* free at bookstores, noted:[77]

> Its purpose was to reach any potential sympathizer in order to let her know that there were others who thought as she did and that she was not isolated or crazy. It also functioned to put women in contact with other like-minded women in the same area and thus stimulated the formation of new groups.[78]

Accordingly, the first large purchase of the Washington, D.C. Women's Liberation group in 1968 was a mimeograph machine.[79] It should be noted that the new women's groups were formed and facilitated not only through emerging women's papers, but also a women's network formed through previous social movements. At that time, universities and colleges witnessed an influx of women attending college for the first time or returning to finish their education. These early groups of women were already actively networking on campus, on a person-to-person basis or in student organizations such as "Students for a Democratic Society."[80] For example, Betty Friedan sent her questionnaires to her classmates of Smith. Then she realized "she was not isolated or crazy," and wrote *The Feminine Mystique.*[81] As a result, her book stimulated the formation of numerous women's groups struggling for women's liberation, most notably the National Organization for Women (NOW), founded in 1966. There were already local women's groups near campus-towns in small cities, but between 1968 and 1969 the number of women's groups rapidly increased, and simultaneously they discovered that they had to have their own independent means of communication, and often put out a newsletter or a magazine as their own tool for communication.

For example, *NOW Acts,* which was one of the first distinctly feminist publications and the first regular periodical of NOW, was founded in 1966. In 1970 alone, 73 different newsletters were started, although about a quarter of them were affiliated with state or regional NOW chapters.[82]

National newspapers, specifically devoted to feminist news and commentary, sprang up. *Voice of Women's Liberation Movement* was issued in 1968 along with *Lilith, No More Fun and Games,* and *Notes from the First Year.* In 1970 *It Ain't Me, Babe* and *Off Our Backs* appeared. However, among the feminist publications *Ms.*, published in 1972, was the most successful in terms of the number of readers, although it was more politically moderate than papers like *Off Our Backs.*[83] Local women's newsletters, newspapers, magazines, and journals were published also in hundreds of cities.[84] By the 1970s, women saw an explosion of writings—mostly newsletters by and for women across the nation. As Adams points out, they meant that the movement had arrived because the first step toward joining the women's movement started with finding it in these papers.[85] They also "served as a mailing address for the movement," and connected women across the nation.[86] These publications, often described as marked by "anger, flair, irreverence, and determination,"[87] covered a wide range of subjects and created new outlets for communicating information, concerns and ideas about the decade's resurging female liberation movement. Thus publications that started from a memo eventually exposed women around the nation to the full range of issues of women's concern. As time went on, women also started to focus in such publications on specific topics like health, education, politics and economics.

It might be noted that, starting with position papers, manifestos, or announcements, their publishers often included poetry. They connected women and these issues to express understanding of the women's movement as a whole. Particularly at the beginning of the women's movement, the power of words was often effectively expressed through poetry. Among genres of writing, poetry is mostly short, easy to read, and also easily memorized. "The written word is," as Audre Lorde says, "which is the most secret, which requires the least physical labor, the least material, and the one which can be done between shifts, in the hospital pantry, on the subway, and on scraps of surplus paper."[88] These words became "political" poetry, which "challenges the paradox" or contradiction between what society says and what people actually experience.[89] Women used poetry as a tool to challenge the paradox. Moreover, women accomplished a fundamental change in the concept of "acceptable poetry."[90] Judy Grahn, who self-published an anthology of women's poetry and drawings, *Woman to Woman* in 1970, says,

> I discovered that some of what had been acceptable as women's poetry, women couldn't even understand and I eliminated some of the more academic or formally accepted poets because my criteria were that ordinary women, my own neighbors and my own friends and people on the bus and so on, had to be able to read it and get something from it. So on that basis we did the anthology.[91]

Grahn suggests that criteria that women thought they created by themselves were actually not their own but created to accommodate to authority—"more academic" or formal. She went against common practice by setting the criteria herself and thereby, creating a totally new type of anthology. Thus many anthologies of poetry by previously unknown women were published and became popular. It was later said that feminist presses "challenged the book world by inventing and popularizing anthologies of previously unpublished and largely political works."[92] Grahn also says, "Particularly in the 1970s, poetry was leading with the ideas. The poets were mapmakers, going out first and laying down the dimensions of the terrain and what the landscape (and the future) could possibly look like."[93] Poets such as Susan Griffin, Audre Lorde, Judy Grahn, Adrienne Rich, and Pat Parker were influential enough to be called by Jan Clausen the leaders of "a movement of poets."[94] Polly Joan points out, although every revolutionary movement has had its poets and its poetry, poetry was "the medium" of the women's movement.

> For a woman to publicly confront her own rejection of female inequality was to call for revolutionary change in both human consciousness and institutions. This invocation to change came out of a woman's soul, the poems of the spirit . . . Women's consciousness-raising groups vocalized their pain and anger in poetry. Women's poetry readings were the focal points for spurring political action. Art and politics blended, personal experience and art converged. There was no separation between a woman's self and her art.[95]

In other words, poetry helped conceptualize the women's movement, and moved women. Poetry readings were among the most popular events in women's bookstores and, in fact, at least a couple of women's bookstores named their stores after Judy Grahn's poem or anthologies including her work. Two "Common Woman" and one "Woman to Woman" bookstores existed in Austin (TX), Edmonton (Alberta, Canada), and Denver (CO). Carol Seajay found a piece of poetry among some books she brought back to her home in Michigan from the West Coast Lesbian conference in Los

Angeles in 1973. She said to her friends, "Look, this is going to change everything!" This is because she had never heard poetry like *Songs to a Handsome Woman,* which said "women were wonderful."[96] Then Seajay moved to California where she thought she could share this excitement more, and established Old Wives' Tales bookstore and published *FBN* in San Francisco. Many women similarly found women's words in the women's papers, and moved to where they thought they could find a group of like-minded women, and together started to build their own community to disseminate the message—women are wonderful.[97]

Through these papers, women throughout the country learned about what other women's groups were doing, where major feminist conferences were being held, and about what issues were being discussed. Thus women's publications steadily constructed their communication networks to expand the women's movement throughout the country. In fact, these publications reached a regular readership of over 300,000 women by 1977.[98] The number of articles about the women's movement, for example, in the *New York Times,* reached 1,814 in 1974, a dramatic increase from 168 in 1966. Louis Gould wrote in *The New York Times Magazine* in 1977, "It is astonishing to learn that such bursts of forward motion are happening at a time when the regular news media are filled only with the token advances of a handful of women 'stars' in corporate jobs and politics, or else with elaborate hand-wringing over the 'movement's' death or dismemberment, all accompanied by rueful sighs or rude yawns."[99] Thus periodicals created by women and for women used words in print to give women new outlets for communicating the information, concerns, and ideas of the resurging women's movement.[100] As Bunch noted, "We believed with a religious fervor that getting more copies ['Why Women's Liberation?'] into more women's hands would ensure that change would happen."[101] Their fervor established a solid base for feminist publishing was to build complex and extensive communication networks among women and to construct feminist communities. Above all, these small publications became irreplaceable communication tools for women as they used the printed word as a "tool of revolution to create social change."[102] They also made the women's liberation movement visible and accessible for women. Most women's periodicals did not last long; however, they certainly paved the way for succeeding publications. That is, women learned that using words helped them to "figure out what they want to do and how things could be different."[103] Namely, the women's liberation movement became "a print movement out of necessity."[104] The more information on women and women's rights available to women, the more women became involved in the women's movement. Carol Seajay says, "they had this idea that if you just published all this information about women together in one place, something incredible was going to happen. And it did."[105]

CONCLUSION

After World War II, money flooded into publishing, and it changed what had been typically a family business, handed down from a father to a son, into an object for investments for businessmen. At the same time, even with such changes, the industry remained controlled by white men of privilege. Extant documents of the US publishing industry indicate that it neglected people of color and women. Although women were always actively participating in the publishing industry, they nonetheless played a largely unacknowledged role, continuing to possess inferior status and power.[106] However, thanks to new technological developments in printing, those with small capital were increasingly able to enter the publishing industry with greater ease. Individuals and organizations, which had previously been excluded from the conventional publishing houses, started their own presses to disseminate their voices to a larger public. Women were not, in fact, in this regard exceptional, as a variety of dissident groups developed their own presses. They felt frustrated in predominantly male-led movements and thought that revolution, even if successful, would only exchange one group of male rulers for another. They soon realized it was the time to produce their own publications to send messages directly from women to women; otherwise their voices would not have been heard at all. Women learned to use the printed word to create social change as a tool of feminist revolution. This is because the printed word was also "still the cheapest, most available form for all women to use, as both writers and readers," and also one of the most practical ways to get their works out in society, where women have an "unpublished heritage."[107]

By the end of the 1960s, many women who had joined social movements, together with millions of other women, followed Betty Friedan in questioning prescribed gender roles, and hundreds of women established their own presses to value their voices—some 500 periodicals appearing from 1968 to 1973 in all but seven states.[108]

Chapter Three

The Birth of Women's Bookstores

By the early 1970s, hundreds of women published their own newsletters, magazines or journals, and disseminated their voices to other women. Although the publications were mostly newsletters, the number reached over 500 with a regular readership of over 300,000 women by the late 1970s.[1] However, most mainstream publishers in these years were still reluctant to publish women's works since they considered that works by and for women were not profitable, or that their subjects were too controversial. For example, Celeste West wrote an article about sexism in the publishing industry, but it was rejected by nearly every one of the mainstream press and library journals.[2] June Arnold, co-founder of Daughters, Inc., referred to the male-controlled mainstream presses, such as Harper & Row, W.W. Norton, Charles Scribner's Sons, and Simon and Schuster, collectively and indiscriminately as "Random House."[3] Thus women became their own publishers. They also started to create their own review media, distribution companies, and bookstores, in other words, a whole network of feminist publishing. This network became a crucial role to support each other and worked as a "feminist publishing ecosystem" over decades. In this chapter, we consider why it was necessary to produce this network, examining the obstacles they faced when they tried to distribute their materials and how this led to the creation of women's bookstores.

THE RISE OF FEMINIST PUBLISHING HOUSES AND THE WOMEN IN PRINT CONFERENCE

Women's belief that women's words in print would change the world surely affected many of their lives. At first, so-called "personal/private" issues appeared in women's papers—issues including domestic violence, family, health, abortion, rape, divorce, and sexuality, as most of such contributions were rejected as inappropriate for publication because it was thought that they should be kept in private. Carol Seajay says:

> There were a number of cases where women's newspapers did articles on the self-help movement—you know, a woman actually looking at her [vagina] and being able to evaluate her own vaginal health. And when these articles started coming out, there were a number of women's newspapers whose printers called photographs of a woman examining herself, using speculum or looking up her vagina, 'pornographic' and refused to print them. At the same time, the mainstream media, when it did cover women's liberation issues, frequently distorted or trivialized them, or resorted to lesbian-bashing. So that made it clear to us that if we wanted to circulate this information, we had to buy the presses and print it ourselves. We had to control the typesetting; we had to do all the printing processes-the stripping, the photographing. Binderies refused to bind lesbian and feminist books, so we had to do the binding ourselves.[4]

In this way, by describing such "private" issues, women started to correct what they perceived as "inaccurate" information about themselves that especially had been produced by the larger media and male authorities.

For example, on information about women's bodies, women in Boston thought male physicians "mystified" health care for power and profit.[5] In 1969 women actually started to discuss "women and their bodies" there, developing their own research and produced papers, deciding to "revise our initial papers and mimeograph them so that other women could have copies as the course expanded."[6] Eventually, they had the pages printed and bound together. In this way, a small woman's discussion group, Boston Women's Health Collective, published the book *Our Bodies, Ourselves* in December 1970 (first edition published by the New England Free Press).[7] Named for the popular abortion-rights slogan, "our bodies, ourselves, our right to decide," it was intentionally produced at a low price so that ordinary people could afford its purchase; unlimited copies were also sold at cost for free distribution by health groups, and a special discount price for clinics. In its first year in print, it sold 250,000 copies.[8]

> Our society adds insult to injury by demanding that the truly "womanly" woman be soft, somewhat weak and awkward—in short, physically unfit. We contribute to this by, for example, wearing high heeled shoes that keep us in our place (we can't run). Our physical limitations are more apparent than real, however, and exist today because we don't

> have the opportunity to defend ourselves, and men and the pressure exerted by our male-dominated society tell us what is good, what is bad (a strong woman is considered "masculine" and undesirable as a woman). We want to become physically healthy and strong and enduring, through exercise, proper eating, and training (like karate), and proud of our bodies. Proud because we feel good ourselves, not because we look good for others.[9]

Our Bodies, Ourselves encouraged women to be themselves and control their own bodies. It also meant they had their own "choice" with their sexuality. As Carol Seajay noted, it is considered that many lesbians worked in women's health clinics because these clinics embodied women's rights to control their own bodies, including their sexuality.[10]

By 1980, *Our Bodies, Ourselves* had sold two million copies and been translated into thirteen foreign languages.[11] As Armstrong points out, it was not only the most practical book to emerge from the women's movement, but also "its voluminous sales—and, particularly, its concrete effects on women inside and outside the women's movement, on an international scale, make *Our Bodies, Ourselves* the single most successful effort of any kind to emerge from the alternative media."[12] Belita Cowan, executive director of the National Women's Health Network, said "I truly believe *Our Bodies, Ourselves* has touched the life of every woman in the country, whether she realizes it or not . . . It allowed a national network of groups to develop . . . It gives women that sense of entitlement that they have a right to know."[13] The success of *Our Bodies, Ourselves* showed enthusiasm to pursue their "rights to know" and to control their own bodies as well as their own words.[14] It also proved that print media was one of the most powerful vehicles to move women beyond geographic boundaries and, practically, the center around which new feminist agendas could be inaugurated. One of the most progressive slogans, "the personal is the political," would be realized through the books by and for women.

As we have seen, feminist publishing houses published works by women that would not have been printed elsewhere, including memos and manifestos that were otherwise easily lost. They also contributed to the history of women by printing older works such as forgotten nineteenth-century feminist works that were out of print or never previously published.[15] Consequently, anthologies by feminist publishing houses became one of the most popular forms of writings. Judy Grahn, who founded the all-woman press The Women's Press Collective in 1970, which published her works as well as anthologies of unknown women's poets or original works, says, "I thought I had to hold the press together . . . because who on earth would publish it?"[16] Women collected unknown women's voices, and published them as part of history. These anthologies had tremendous impact on women's lives. For example, a mimeographed issue of 1000 copies of *Woman to Woman: A Book of Poems and Drawings by Women,* which included poems by Ann Sexton, Judy Grahn, Pat Parker among others, was published in California.[17] Within three months, it was circulated among women in Michigan.[18] The second edition of *This Bridge Called My Back: Writings by Radical Women of Color,* included a letter from a nineteen-year-old Puerto Rican woman reader that stated, "The writings justified some of my thoughts telling me I had a right to feel as I did. It is remarkable to me that one book could have such an impact."[19] Feminist publishing houses challenged the book industry "by inventing and popularizing anthologies of previously unpublished and largely political works."[20] In addition to these works, they published nonsexist children's literature, political theory, and self-help books. In this way, feminist publishing houses have always been integral to one of feminism's major tasks: "bringing women together and spreading the word."[21]

Deborah Snow, one of the founders in 1976 of Persephone Press, said, "We must control our means of communication and support each other as we do it." She also claimed that "if the first wave feminists had created their own publishing houses, feminism would have been much further along."[22] In other words, women tried "to build a publishing network that would provide women with an alternative" to the male-dominated establishment press.[23] In some ways, the feminist press has done far better than the mainstream press. For example, Diana Press, which was established in 1972 focusing on writings by black, working class and lesbian women, published *Songs to a Handsome Woman* and sold 5000 copies in two years.[24] Charlotte Bunch sold sixty thousand copies of a women's liberation anthology as a special issue of a magazine, and later published it with the mainstream publisher Bobbs-Merrill. However, the publisher "let it die without beginning to tap its market."[25] According to June Arnold, the usual mainstream press publishes an author's first work in printing of 2500 copies accompanied by a big promotion, so that all the bookstores order it. If it does not immediately sell well, the bookstores return it in three months and the finishing press gets rid of all unsold copies selling at cost or less to secondhand bookstores. Some books are remaindered even before the publication date.[26] Bunch's book might have been such a case. In contrast, feminist publishing houses "keep the book in print until it finds its audience."[27] For example, Daughters, Inc., established also in 1972, has gone back to press (sold out the first 3000 copies) on every one of its novels; the Women's Press Collective and Diana Press have sold out the first printings of almost all their titles.[28] Furthermore, many feminist publishing houses, including Feminist Press, which was established in 1970 in Baltimore by Florence Howe and a group of feminists, have also supported and encouraged women to write, to edit, to design and produce their works.[29] Most well-known feminist writers at present had their works first published in these feminist publishing houses. Feminist writers were vitally encouraged not only by their audience, but also the press itself.[30] Thus feminist publishing houses are not just a stepping stone for women who cannot publish elsewhere, but a critical part of the women's movement and its vital institutions that creates a "wellspring of women's words, thoughts, and action,"[31] and organizes radical political activism "by speaking the unspeakable."[32]

However, most of these presses "eked out a hand-to-mouth existence," and those involved rarely got paid because the costs of the publications often barely covered the production expenses.[33] Judy Grahn, a founder of The Women's Press Collective, says, "We had no sense of spending money or time on ourselves and barely stopped to eat. I was often living on cigarettes and coffee and booze."[34] Bertha Harris as a writer of many books including *Lover,* says:

> Hardship [in the feminist publishing houses] was the rule, burnout was the norm; but the staying power was in some cases enormous, and it was almost exclusively fueled by the adamantine convictions which had got the presses going in the first place: that well-wrought words on a page could, by speaking the unspeakable, create and organize radical political activism.[35]

Following the explosion of women's papers, the women's enormous "staying power" made possible of the birth of 136 feminist publishing houses in the years up through 1983 to meet the demand for a wider exchange among them of information for and about women.[36] A conservative estimate is that every copy of books published by feminist publishing houses is read by five women; one woman's press book that has "caught on" has already sold 50,000 copies and has therefore probably been read by 250,000 women. By the middle of 1970s, the combined titles of the Women's Press Collective, Diana Press, and Daughters, Inc. had already sold over 150,000 copies and most of the titles continued to sell month after month.[37] Consequently, feminist publishing came to serve as a solid base of communication among women for the coming two decades of the women's movement. Therefore, as Polly Joan and Andrea Chesman have noted, "Feminism, more than any other historical movement, has been identified with publishing."[38]

Furthermore, feminist publishing was not merely an alternative to male publishing. Given its roots in the women's movement, it is clear that women were trying to remove the gap between feminist theory and its practice in their publishing enterprises. At first, they attempted to achieve to break "a tradition of dichotomy of writer-reader in a society where there is a sharp hierarchy between experts and passive recipients of information."[39] Many anthologies of unknown women writers published by feminist publishing houses exemplified this. It told readers that they were also writers. Secondly, in their workplace, considering hierarchies as well as competition part of what they termed "patriarchal culture," they also experimented with collective organization: revolving control, investing authority in the community or eliminating authority altogether.[40] For example, the statement of purpose of a collective of women published *Off Our Backs* in 1970 declared:

> [W]e are attempting to build non-exploitative ways of relating to one another based on trust and concern rather than political expediency. We have serious personal/political intentions in breaking down hierarchical and elitist structures, and for experimenting with leaderless groups and collective decision-making. In dealing with the media these revolutionary principles and practices are destroyed.[41]

The collective of *Off Our Backs* was one of many such groups, with work and responsibilities dispersed, which were established in the 1970s. Their attempt as a collective "breaking down hierarchical and elitist structures" is still continuing in the 21st century. Therefore, every woman involved in a collective was encouraged to participate in decisions. This way no single editor, programmer, or director could be accused of monopolizing status or authority. Simultaneously, it means "there were supposed to be no stars in feminist media—only low-profile leaders validated by and responsible to their colleagues."[42] Many women who were accustomed to "patriarchal culture" found the new feminist theory attractive or exciting, but they often also found them difficult to transform into successful action. For example, such experiments to create and sustain a feminist workplace often proceeded, not surprisingly, at the expense of efficiency.[43] Eventually, given financial and other difficulties, the collective ideal often boiled down to the core partnership of a couple of people. For example, Jean Mountaingrove noted, "we found that we were the only ones left to make the necessary decisions . . . we wanted to be a collective but in practice we were a partnership."[44] Later illusions and conflicts among women became apparent in various feminist institutions.

Recognition of the importance of developing an independent publishing network thus energized women to take another step toward getting women's words out—through creating a feminist publishing community. They believed that they could have the potential for greater mass outreach if they could work together in a conscious effort to build their community. As David Armstrong points out, compared to male-dominated media, women focused on building community rather than on reinforcing individuality.[45] For example, examining contributions of women's writers and their works to literature in North Carolina, Ginny Daley emphasizes the importance of the women's publishing community in North Carolina for their advancement.[46] A 1975 Diana Press's brochure noted, "Diana Press sees itself as part of the growing women's communications network of periodicals, presses and bookstores."[47] Celeste West also points out that new women's literature could not exist "without such community with a marvelous base of support and talent."[48] Cooperating rather than competing, and sharing information and building their own community, constituted the core spirit among them.

A crucial event enabled women to get involved in searching another level of communication and building a feminist publishing community: the first Women in Print Conference (WIP Conference), held in Omaha, Nebraska, in 1976. The Women in Print Conference and *Feminist Bookstores Newsletter* evolved into the first great women's publishing movement in American history—the Women In Print movement that made possible feminist revolution in literacy. June Arnold named it the Women in Print conference. She and other women who met at a Bay Area meeting of feminist publishing houses in January 1976 created the conference from scratch. It was her "most ambitious stab at achieving movement esteem," and it was a "landmark" for all women in print. [49] Arnold explained:

> I had been touring and had done a program at A Woman's Place in Oakland, California. . . . A bunch of people went off afterwards to the Bacchanal, a lesbian/feminist bar, and came up with this idea of "Wouldn't it be great to get all the women who are working on feminist magazines and newspapers and bookstores, and the printers and the publishers, and get them all together in one place."[50]

Arnold would make the idea a reality.[51] At first, in January 1976, Arnold wrote "Proposed National Conference of Women's Presses, Publications, Distributors, and Bookstores," which suggested that book publishers, bookstore people, press operators, and magazine producers should all get together in one place to trade information, to distribute their books and newspapers, and to ask each other questions.[52] The "Proposed National Conference" says:

> A number of women from feminist publishing houses, journals, and bookstores have been discussing the advantages of having a national conference through which we could share skills and problems, get to know each other, and strengthen our political network of feminist communication-already an extraordinarily complete control of our voices. This announcement is going to every known independent women's press, journal, bookstore, or distributor in the United States. . . . It is intended to be a serious working conference concerned with political strategy and skill sharing. To accomplish most and waste the least time, most women think the conference should be carefully structured beforehand.[53]

This proposal demonstrates Arnold's enthusiasm to carry out the conference "concerned with political strategy and skill sharing" as well as her determination to make it valuable and simultaneously successful both in political and business terms. In fact, she "put a fair amount of her own money and enthusiasm and quite a lot of time into it."[54] Soon after, she also sent out a series of mailings leading up to the conference, starting with a six page "Second Mailing: 1976 Conference Women in Print" in March, which described its missions and goals, and addressed questions whether "older boys" or "Third World feminists" working on their publishing projects with men were permitted to attend or not.[55] It also noted the schedule would go from 8:00 AM to 5:45 PM, six days running. The third mailing was a ten-page-long statement of the detailed contents of over 140 workshops, and the fourth (and final) mailing was a list of groups attending by category with addresses and brief descriptions.[56] It was natural that this list of groups itself was a base from which to expand their network.[57]

The first Women in Print Conference (WIP), the conference for workers in feminist publishing, was held from August 29 to September 5 in 1976 in Omaha, Nebraska. Omaha was chosen as a place for the conference because it was an equal distance from both coasts so that everyone could drive from either coast. Seajay said, "In those days, everyone drove; no one had money for plane tickets."[58] Altogether, 127 women from 74 organizations involved in publishing—including presses, journals, newspapers, bookstores, and distributors—came together and discussed "what we had learned and how we could cooperate more."[59] Feminist booksellers talked about skills such as ordering, inventory, and bookkeeping as well as political strategy—from the definition of profit to separatism, political and community responsibility, collective problems.[60] Furthermore, they also noticed that they were clearly in a transitional period in their efforts: from the stage at the beginning of their ventures to the second stage, where they had to keep their operations alive.

Since the independent women's communications network began early in the women's movement in the form of mimeographed newsletters and position papers, women had supported all these activities by volunteering their labor, time and money for the cause. However, they realized, looking at the problems discussed at Omaha, while it was not easy for women to establish publishing houses or publish papers to begin with, it was even more difficult to keep maintain them. The participants in the conference came to understand that "volunteering labor, time and money" would not be enough to enable them to survive. Charlotte Bunch stated:

> We had a lot to learn about publishing. Unless the women's movement does support those, most of them will not go on existing. Many are, in effect, subsidized by a small group of people giving volunteer labor and money, and by their staffs having other jobs or receiving low salaries. But to live off those salaries, one has to have some savings or friends who are willing to help you out. So there's a number of ways we are indirectly subsidizing women's publishing. But we have to decide if it's important enough to become more systematic about support.[61]

Feminist publications would not survive on volunteer works or even sales—either financed through advertising or subsidized by interested universities or organizations They needed to be "more systematic" to support themselves, and that "no matter how high you price a journal" they "still couldn't make it financially."[62] The WIP Conference was in this way held precisely at the point when women in publishing started to look for a means of survival as a community, and the conference rightly facilitated the needs of this growing field.

The Women In Print Conference came to mean controlling the entire production through building a community of women in print, and also making their network and community visible: it enabled those women or small groups of women who felt geographically and psychologically isolated to network with each other, and encouraged them to see how large the women in print movement was and to start new ventures in print. It also gave them "a magnificent feeling. . . . a sense of finding each other."[63] Carol Seajay recalls that the conference was "quite heady and exciting and powerful."[64] It was said that the feeling and "the connections, both creative and personal, realized there greatly influenced feminist publishing and writing for years thereafter."[65] In fact, *Feminist Bookstores Newsletter,* one of the products born on the occasion, lasted more than 20 years. Marie Kuda says with fond remembrance, "The dust and grasshoppers are faded memories and I can almost look a lentil in the eye again, but the enthusiasm and good feelings generated by the WIP conference are still with me."[66] Thereafter the WIP was held on an infrequent basis in various states.[67]

Bookstores as well as booksellers, compared to writers or publishers, have never been prominent, instead usually supporting the latter behind the scenes. However, many women from publishers, who already noticed that it was far more difficult promoting and distributing their works widely rather than publishing them, soon realized and assured in the conference how bookstores and booksellers played an important role to promote and distribute them. This was because "booksellers know so much that is useful and essential to those who are further removed from community contact."[68] Therefore, with regard to feminist booksellers from twenty women's bookstores in the WIP conference, the conference turned them from being passive players in the feminist publishing into active ones.

DISTRIBUTION: OBSTACLES TO THE GROWTH OF FEMINIST PUBLISHING

Myra Marx Ferree and Beth B. Hess noted in 1985, "As more books are published and reviewed, as more magazine articles appear, as more mention is made on radio and television, as newspaper coverage expands," the women's movement itself becomes "institutionalized"; that is, it becomes a "'normal' part of the social landscape."[69] However, until it became a "'normal' part of the social landscape," women had to make every effort to get women's words out—to get published and get reviewed, and more importantly get them into women's hands. At first, women were more concerned with getting the words into print than with distribution. As Polly Joan says in *Guide to Women's Publishing* published in 1978, women writers were, in order "to overcome years of patriarchal rejection . . . angry enough to say I AM I AM by publishing a book."[70] Such emotion helped efforts in the women's press to prosper. Nevertheless, women soon found there was another obstacle to dissemination. Joan said:

> [I]t wasn't until the small of a new pot of coffee had blended sensually with the sweet smell of printer's ink that the victory of publishing dissolved into the realities of "How are we going to distribute them?[71]

After finding ways to publish their own books, and holding books by and for women in their own hands, they had no idea as to how to distribute them and realized that to get a book out was even a far more difficult task. Thus many women who founded feminist publishing houses gradually realized that this was only the first stage in the process. An extensive distribution system for feminist publishing houses was desperately needed if women's books were to reach their desired destination.[72] From its inception, the distribution system in publishing had flaws.[73] By 1976, scholars had already drawn attention to the fact that book publishing was handicapped by serious weaknesses, especially in the retail distribution system.[74] Bookstores often offered only very limited title selections to their clientele, thereby alienating the special interest customers because specialized titles can at best only be delivered by special order.[75] Feminist publishing houses lacked experience with both the distribution system and its "specialized" titles. As for channels for the distribution of new titles, mainstream publishing executives (then and now) use several: direct mail sales to consumers, bookstores, including national wholesalers and local salespersons. Heavy advertising or promotion makes distribution of new titles easier, but small publishers like feminist publishing houses did not have the means to do so. They were understaffed and underfinanced: "dedicated but poorly paid women do the work of many without sufficient backing or support, which can cause delays and conflicts with authors."[76] Therefore, women in the feminist publishing houses felt distribution and promotions to be particularly acute problems.

As Philip Altbach points out, the existence of book reviewing media has been quite important to publishing and can greatly facilitate the distribution of books and help to create a general "book consciousness" in society.[77] For those who could hardly put any capital into advertising or promotions, getting new titles reviewed was more crucial than any other form of promotion.[78] While "signaling to busy audiences what is worth buying and what is not,"[79] reviews beforehand provide publishers with invaluable evaluations of the worth of what they publish, and simultaneously serve as "the single most effective promotional device for publishers."[80] According to Anthony Curtis, American book reviewers are "literary salesmen disguised as critics," and he considers a book review to be most conscious of its role as a book-selling medium.[81] Moreover, book reviewing is a principal way we have of talking to each other about what we do and how we do it, opening up self-reflection and inviting others' response.[82] However, it is not an easy task for publishers, in particular small publishers to get their books reviewed. For example, as Donald F. Joyce's *Gatekeepers of Black Culture* demonstrated in 1983, most black book publishers encountered difficulties in getting African-American books reviewed by the major white reviewing media.[83] He noted that it eventually hampered the growth of African American publishers as well as the American publishing industry. In the same way, although a woman author was sometimes praised or analyzed in the review media, generally unknown women authors from small publishers still had difficulties getting reviewed. Their books, moreover, tended to get shorter reviews if they were labeled "feminist," and they did not rate as highly in the eyes of literary editors.[84] As June Arnold noted,

> A finisher-published book is much easier to review. Its dust-jacket categorizes it for you, finishing reviews establish its existence (validate it?), other woman are talking about it, and by the very fact that the finishing press published it, its subject, theme, and language are somewhat familiar. In contrast, a simple, unvalidated, dust-jacketless volume by an unknown name, on a subject not always immediately clear (because it is not yesterday's idea), in language which reaches out to explore new territory, puts the burden on the reviewer to decide by herself what the book is about, what it is trying to say.[85]

A fate of an "unvalidated" book full of new perspectives by "unknown" women or people of color seemed to be clear—virtually no space in book review sections of mainstream journals for their writings.

Meanwhile, since the vast range of new materials by and for women was available since the late 1970s, women felt overwhelmed by the volume, and these made it difficult for women to keep up with the new materials. Women, who were conscious of the small amount of space available for such reviews even in women's periodicals for such a volume of women's writings, eventually published *The Women's Review of Books* in 1983, which still appears currently. The pilot issue said,

> With minor and occasional exceptions, the existing book review publications have effectively ignored the flood of new works by and about women; and while many feminist journals and newspapers have sprung up over the last decade or so, few of them can devote a substantial part of their space to reviewing books.[86]

For this reason, women decided to start their own review media, circumventing the whims of reviews and their employers in the larger publishing industry.

Although women publishers were confronting problems of distribution, the energetic spirit behind the women's movement sometimes helped carry it a long way. For example, Judy Grahn says, "I have sturdy shoulders now because of the hundreds of times that I've gone out on the road with 40 and 50 pounds of books strapped to my shoulders—and carried them block upon block . . . We didn't have books and we needed them."[87] Given there was virtually no systematic distribution system of women's books, in the name of sisterhood, friends carted these books across the country to other friends who in turn sold or gave them to other friends.[88] Carol Wilson loaded her van with women's books of all kinds, and drove it to Iowa City, Chicago, Detroit, Washington, DC, Boston, and San Francisco. Later she became one of the founders of A Woman's Place bookstore in San Francisco.[89] Women were literally carrying books and distributing them to bookstores from coast to coast. However, feminist booksellers, corresponding by mail with dozens of different small press operations, and witnessing the upsurge of various women's products such as books, calendars, periodicals, records and posters, found out how labor intensive it was to get a single title from a single press. Keeping the bookstore shelves stocked was time-consuming and expensive.[90] Then women soon realized that crucial for selling materials effectively is a distribution company which warehouses books, handles orders, and arranges for shipping, and plays the role of so-called "middlemen" in the transit of books from publishers to consumers.[91]

In 1974, seeing women publishers' distribution problems, three women from Olivia Records (recording company) formed an all-women's distribution company, Women in Distribution (WIND).[92] The WIND brochure of 1975 said that despite the multifarious challenges:

> Women still publish and still record. They go to small independent presses and record companies. And 99% of the time they put out products of equal if not better quality than the large publishers. It is a fact that more tears, more sweat, and more care is placed in the production of these works. Women in Distribution was created to distribute those products.[93]

Since WIND served as a central clearinghouse for these small presses and journals, women's bookstores could routinely make one major order to WIND at a time rather than multiple orders to dozens of individual presses.

Each year between 1975 and 1978 WIND's sales doubled. The list of titles, including books, records and cards by women, increased from 30 in 1975 to over 700 titles by 180 publishers—less than a dozen of which were mainstream publishers—in 1978.[94] Yet less than one year later, in July 1979

WIND had to close its doors. WIND explained that the problem was partly the big trade publishers, with which WIND did not deal. In the late 1970s big publishers started to publish women's works aggressively because they saw a market there, recognizing their potential profitability because women in feminist publishing had first opened up this new niche. Witnessing the flourishing of women's writings, mainstream publishers started to cover "the area of 'women's books' and 'alternative lifestyle books'" and take it over.[95] WIND's lack of human and financial resources also contributed to the demise.[96] Moreover, Judy Grahn suggests that the closing of WIND was primarily caused by their strong commitment to feminist publishing as feminists and to feminist values. Grahn says:

> They went under partly because they were doing more than was possible, and partly because they were carrying *every* book that the women in print movement had published . . . If they cut the list to a third of the books, the third that sold enough to support themselves, then they might have made it. But that would have been too contrary to our values then—our commitment to stocking every book by every woman . . . but the third that sold well couldn't carry the rest of the publications.[97]

These three different explanations of the closing of WIND—(1) lack of capital as well as human capital, (2) the rise of big trade publishers appropriating the profitability of women's writings (i.e., a victim of their own success), and (3) the conflict between feminist values and capitalism—can also be applied to the analysis of the later closing of feminist publishing houses and bookstores nationwide. However, the challenge of WIND did not signal the end of feminist distribution networks. By 1983, over 22 smaller distributors of women's works existed handling books, films, videos, albums, cassettes and artworks.[98]

On the other hand, in spite of the existence of the distributors of women's works, bookstores in general have been reluctant to deal with small presses because of the amount of paperwork required. Furthermore, they did not see that dealing with women's "controversial" materials from unknown small publishers could prove profitable. As a result, women felt frustrated with their unfulfilled searching for materials in their local general bookstores, and hoped for another way to acquire them. As part of the solution, presses usually put their advertisements in periodicals. This is because distribution is easier when books are aimed at a well-defined group. Specialized periodicals helped the press's messages reach a book's most likely purchasers. Feminist publishing houses also appropriated this solution. Diana Press wrote to women's periodicals:

> We at Diana Press are terribly dependent on women's periodicals for spreading the word about us. We are still in the slow and painful process of building up a women's distribution network which can get the word out. Women's periodicals are a crucial link in that distribution network. Reviews, notices and short descriptions in your periodical are often the only way thousands of women outside the large cities ever know that we exist.[99]

In this way, Diana Press and many other women's press relied on women's periodicals. At the same time, for women's periodicals, distribution had also become a problem—most general bookstores were reluctant to stock periodicals since they often took space, were easily worn out, and moreover, only made a small profit.[100] For example, although *The Women's Review of Books* is full of reviews of new materials by and for women, it is a newspaper-type periodical printed in a sheet of brown papers. It is apparent it could not be easily stocked in general bookstores.

Women, in fact, found the solution in their own women's bookstores. In fact, after two years in operation, only 40 percent of WIND's accounts were with women's bookstores, but in terms of the quantity of books ordered, women's bookstores constituted over 60 percent of the sales volume.[101] Although women's bookstores were confronted with a lot of paperwork, they dealt with more than 80 women's small presses at that time and also stocked a variety of periodicals. Not only these small publishers but also women's music labels found that one of their few outlets was women's bookstores. Distribution of the music as well as printed materials was crucial to the "success" of the artist, and until 1979, when WILD (Women's Independent Label Distribution Network) was formed, distribution was done by the women who engineered the record, by volunteers dedicated to this new musical venture, or by word of mouth.[102] For example, Lavender Jane recorded an album, "Lavender Jane Loves Women," and released 1000 copies. All of them sold in three months with no formal distribution system other than mail order and women's bookstores. [103]

Margie Adam, a musician, mentioned Carol Seajay and women's bookstores in her acceptance speech for The Lifetime Achievement Award at the National Women's Music Festival. She said:

> First, let me take this public opportunity to thank Carol Seajay and the network of feminist bookstores for the essential role they have played in disseminating our beautiful Women's Music all these years. Without bookstores like her Old Wives Tales in San Francisco, we would not be here tonight. In the critical early years of Women's Music, its core of

> distribution was situated directly in her loving hands and in the hands of many other women like her all over this country.[104]

Consequently, to establish more women's bookstores seemed a logical next step, a final but quite important aspect of disseminating women's words and constructing a feminist publishing community.[105]

Arnold Toynbee considered a bookstore a "real seminar for self-education." He pointed out that a bookstore offers people opportunities not only to buy books, but to browse a hundreds books.[106] Browsing in the bookstore means "to meet other people's minds, minds that are disputable to their own minds, not only in space but in time" and gives people "the opportunity of creating an opinion for himself and to see both sides."[107] The physical space of bookstores gives people different opportunities to "create an opinion for" and educate themselves. Bookstores are a place to meet not only books but people. Without exceptions women's bookstores in the US were an educational place for people's face-to-face interactions.

In the 19th century, bookstores also often operated printing shops, both producing and selling books.[108] In a similar way, the first women's press, the Woman's Press Collective, was also the first feminist women's bookstore in Oakland, A Woman's Place in 1972.[109] Due to a lack of outlets for women's books, many women started their own bookstores given their unfulfilled searching for materials in their communities. At the same time, of course, their "women's bookstores" were not necessarily "stores." Most of them started selling them in the early 1970s at women's gatherings or feminist conferences. Materials brought back from the gatherings or conferences were also sold at their own rooms or the front yards of women's houses, from their vans. They also started selling them in the corners of local women's centers or lesbian resource centers. Later many women in these community centers found selling materials could pay the rent. As Seajay noted, women's bookstores did not "arise from a vacuum."[110] A function of women's bookstores as local women's community centers originated from their inseparable relationship with previously existing community centers and feminist collectives. Carolyn Dellenbach Virginia was one of those who wanted to open a bookstore to serve "as a community center," as well as to "provide an outlet for the burgeoning feminist literature movement.[111] She sent a letter accompanying an advertisement, writing, "You'll be able to obtain books by and about wimmon [sic], wimmon's music, non-sexist children's literature, wimmon's posters and t-shirts."[112] Virginia was 27 years old, "filled with feminist idealism," and convinced of the need of a women's bookstore in Cincinnati, OH. She named the bookstore Crazy Ladies and began operations in 1979.[113] In the early 1970s many women's bookstores originated as feminist collectives, which were involved in the broader women's movement and then turned to selling women's writings. For example, New Earth Bookstore in Kansas, MO, was started as one of many collectives of the Women's Liberation Union which flourished in the late 1960s.[114] Moreover, Carol Seajay has also noted that most of the women's bookstores were collectively run, saying,

> Choosing a collective was a conscious attempt to remove a gap between theory and practice. Therefore, not imitating male-model capitalism, they were trying to create a non-exploitive and non-hierarchal way of operating their ventures—participatory democracy, equality and community.[115]

Working as a collective was generally a way of practicing feminist ideology in feminist institutions. Organizationally, many women's bookstores created structures and practices that valued collective consensus decision-making. Many women were attracted by the prospect of working as part of such a non-exploitive and non-hierarchical group. As of 1976 the three principal women's bookstores, whose monetary support made possible the first three issues of *FBN*, were Womanbooks, NY, New Words Bookstore, MA, and Amazon Bookstore, MN, all of which were also collectives. Womanbooks in New York City was a collective cooperatively owned and managed by three partners when it was founded in 1975. New Words was established in 1976 in Somerville, MA, as a collective of four women. It issued a statement saying,

> New Words is a feminist bookstore. Our primary goal is to fulfill a need within the local women's community for access to the writings of the feminist movement and to the art, music, and literature that women have created. New Words was begun by the four of us. . . . We made a commitment to work cooperatively as a group and to share equally the responsibility for the decision-making and overall running of the bookstore.[116]

A letter from Amazon Bookstore to *FBN*, which announced its 10th anniversary, indicated that by the fall of 1973 Amazon had a "collective structure" which "was very loose and the number of workers varied from 5 to 25."[117] Furthermore, since women often had little capital, they typically felt that if they did it collectively, they would have a better chance to survive, and it seemed to be a good way for them to work together as women. For example, after two women who started Amazon Bookstore in 1970 sold its inventory to Karen Brown and Cindy Hanson in 1972, a collective was formed because women in Amazon Bookstore thought it would prevent a certain responsibility from "falling on the shoulders of a few."[118]

Women often started with financial support from their respective communities, although the amount varied. For example, A Room of One's Own, a collectively run women's bookstore, started in 1974 with $5000 in donations and loans raised by the women's community in Madison, Wisconsin. New Words in Boston and Womanbooks in New York started at about the same time with about $8000-$10,000 each.[119] At the same time, many women's bookstores started with a small, sometimes miniscule, amount of money. A Woman's Place Bookstore in Oakland started with just $400—equivalent to one month of rent—and a line of credit from a distributor, although it later became one of the largest women's bookstores. As Seajay points out, "Their idea was that you declare a bookstore, and then, little by little, build the stock."[120] Many early women's bookstores shared spaces with other women's collectives or rented corners of women's centers. Amazon shared a space with the Lesbian Resource Center. Margaret Johnston has described the almost symbiotic evolution of the two institutions, as follows:

> They were highly mimetic. As women had a safe place to explore the politics of feminism, they began to write about it. When they wrote fiction and lesbian nonfiction, publishing companies owned by feminist collectives evolved to fill the need, as did women's bookstores and printers. Women's centers were having a hard time paying the rent and thought selling books would help.[121]

At first, women's bookstores in the early 70s did not have enough materials to sell and make profits. When Mary Lowry and other collective members opened New Words in Cambridge, Massachusetts, in 1974, she remembered a large number of people telling her, "There aren't enough books to have a whole store." She was also told by one bookstore owner, "Yuck, it makes me want to throw up to think of a store with nothing but women's books," although his own enterprise later went under.[122] In 1989, celebrating its 15th anniversary, *Publishers Weekly* reported that New Words was "the highest-grossing women's bookstore in the US. and one of the most successful collective enterprises in business."[123] Thus New Words eventually proved there were enough books to have a whole store and a market for them because it was able to thrive for more than 28 years.[124] Since many women bought newsletters, pamphlets, or books only available at women's conference or various women's events in the early 70s, and a number of feminist publications had attempted to reach out to potential subscribers through single-copy sales in the network of women's bookstores across the country, the creation of women's bookstores immediately helped the market.[125] For many feminist publications, women's bookstores were one of the few reliable outlets, and as a result, supported the existence of these publications and the feminist presses.[126]

CONCLUSION

Women's belief that getting women's words into more women's hands could change the world created an explosion of feminist publishing, which built communication networks among women to promote the women's movement. While undertaking the effort to publish women's materials, women in feminist publishing were keen to take control of all aspects of publishing—from typesetting, photographing, printing, and binding, to selling—if they were to successfully circulate their information and disseminate feminist values.[127] Their concern led to the convening of the Women In Print Conference in 1976. Over 120 women came from around the country. They together affirmed that their vision was right, and they simultaneously faced the fact that they would not survive without the help of other women in feminist publishing as well as the women in their communities. The Women In Print movement emerged not just to produce materials by and for women, but to produce and sustain feminist ideologies and practices disseminating women's words through these materials, and it embraced all women involved in feminist publishing such as distributors and booksellers. In the conference, it became apparent that they needed to have their own bookstores.[128] Their awareness that establishing a woman's bookstore was crucial for building and sustaining a feminist publishing community made the explosion of women's bookstores possible. Therefore, it should be noted that they did not see their ventures as "businesses" to support themselves, as they were not primarily motivated by possible profit. A collective member of Labyris Books said, "We are movement women, "and the "movement women" opened Labyris Books in 1972 in New York City.[129] Three women gave up their separate apartments to move in together due to their financial uncertainty. They explained that their privacy was important, yet it was obvious that Labyris was more important to them.[130] This is because, as the advertisement for Labyris Books notes—borrowing Susan B. Anthony's famous words—they were feminist booksellers to "Educate All Women to Rebel."[131] Thus, like women in Labyris who "considered themselves not merchants, but movement women," the motivation of feminist booksellers for starting their stores was mainly political rather than financial.[132] In December 1974, New Words sent a letter asking for a correction in the title of an article about New Words, claiming that the title was not "Cashing in on Capitalism," but "Coping with Capitalism." This is because New Words functioned "within and for the women's community" as "part of a mutually supportive network of women committed to eliminating exploitation." They claimed their intention was not to make profits from the women's movement, and rather to invest their energy in work which benefited themselves and other women in their community.[133] In another instance, in 1978, A Woman's Place in Portland developed a coalition policy called "Basis of Unity," which said, "We have come together fighting oppression as women in our lives, in our work and in our culture. . . . We are here to serve the community, not to provide income to a few individual women."[134] Later in the 1980s women's bookstores, even if they were not "non-profit" organizations, did not consider their ventures simply as "businesses." For example, according to Lynette Secombe-Eastland, Abby Maestas, a co-owner and founder of Twenty Rue Jacob, a women's bookstore in Salt Lake City, Utah, often joked with customers, "What! Do you think I am in this to make money? . . . The reality of it is that you don't do this to get rich, but it would be nice."[135]

In this way, witnessing the burgeoning interest in women's books and virtually no place available to sell them, it was no wonder that many "movement" women grasped at the idea of opening a bookstore for and by women. In fact, women's bookstores seemed a logical next step to "fight oppression"—to control and disseminate women's words in constructing and supporting a larger feminist community. Thus in 1973, as Grimstad and Rennie reported in their *New Women Survival Catalog,* when the ICI (Information Center Incorporated)—A Woman's Place, a women's bookstore in Oakland, CA, published *Starting a Bookstore: non-capitalist operation within a capitalist economy,* there were 168 orders for this item within three months of the publication announcement.[136] In 1975 they noted, "We would like to think we had something to do with the bookstore boom," pointing out that the number of bookstores rose from 9 in 1973 to 44 in 1975.[137] However, the boom had actually not yet come, because the number of women's bookstores had only just begun to rise.[138] The 1980s would witness a veritable explosion of women's bookstores.

Chapter Four

Women's Bookstores in the 1970s: Lesbian Feminists and *Feminist Bookstore News*

By the early 1970s, a small, yet increasing number of women's bookstores had emerged in the US. As of 1975 the number had reached over forty and, by September 1980, seventy-one women's bookstores existed across twenty-eight states. As more women became involved in women-only enterprises, lesbian feminists grew increasingly visible in feminist publishing ventures, including the women's bookstores. Yet precisely how and in what way did these lesbian feminists become involved in establishing women's bookstores and in feminist publishing ventures more generally? This chapter examines what made the flourishing of the women's bookstores in the 1970s possible, and analyzes the historical context in which lesbian feminists emerged as participants in feminist publishing ventures. In doing so, we will explore the role of the *Feminist Bookstores Newsletter* (later *Feminist Bookstore News* (*FBN*)), published by Carol Seajay, which proved a fundamental player in the explosion of the women's bookstores.

THE POWER OF LESBIAN FEMINISTS: THE EXPLOSION OF ARTS BY LESBIAN FEMINISTS

Not merely feminist publishing enterprises but also women-only businesses, events and activities increased in the 1970s. These included a number of small groups in feminist presses, publishers, printers, binders, distributors, and booksellers. When they gathered together for the first time at the initial Women in Print (WIP) conference, many women in attendance were lesbian feminists. Among them were Dorothy Allison, Parke Bowman, Tee Corrine,

Harriet Desmoines, Barbara Grier, Bertha Harris, Marie Kuda, Donna McBride, Catherine Nicholson and Carol Seajay.[1] The official planners of WIP were June Arnold, co-founder of the pioneering lesbian feminist press Daughters, Inc., Coletta Reid (a member of the lesbian feminist press Diana Press), Nancy Stockwell (a member of Plexus, a lesbian feminist journal) and Charlotte Bunch, who joined Rita Mae Brown to form the Furies, a lesbian feminist collective.[2] Moreover, it should be noted that some started or joined these publishing ventures, including women's bookstores, as a means to "be themselves"—not only openly feminist but also lesbian. Issues of sexuality as well as feminism produced hundreds of papers as well as books.[3] Many of the women's bookstores' founders were lesbian feminists so that women's bookstores functioned as one of the safe spaces for lesbians as well as feminists more generally. There were no other places to sell or acquire such materials nor were there similarly open spaces for lesbian feminists; they found both in the women's bookstores in their local communities.[4]

Alisa Klinger points out that the terms "women in print" and "lesbians in print" may have been readily interchangeable, if not synonymous. She says:

> In an effort to sustain themselves in the homophobic cultural climate both of mainstream society and of the women's liberation movement, especially during the 1970s and early 1980s, lesbian booksellers and publishers have consistently employed the more socially acceptable (albeit closeted) term 'women in print' rather than 'lesbian in print' to refer to their ventures.[5]

Women may have in this way employed the term "women in print" because they needed their ventures to be more socially acceptable or reluctantly chose to be "closeted." According to Seajay, up to 40% of the total sales of many women's bookstores have consisted of materials by and for lesbians.[6] At the same time, it is evident that they have been selling these products primarily because of their feminist orientation rather than lesbian content. Indeed, lesbian feminist booksellers employed the term "feminist" rather than "lesbian" not essentially because they were more acceptable in social terms, but because they perceived their bookstores to be "feminist bookstores" rather than "lesbian bookstores." When they decided to publish their newsletter at the first Women In Print conference, they entitled it *Feminist Bookstores Newsletter.* In *FBN,* they defined their operations as "feminist bookstores," and repeatedly emphasized that their primary focus was feminism, not lesbianism.[7]

They saw themselves as feminists and their ventures as not only for lesbians or lesbian feminists, but for all women. If lesbians in the women's bookstores had seen their ventures solely as a part of "lesbians in print movement," their efforts toward building and promoting inclusive feminist publishing communities would not have made possible the prosperity of women's bookstores from the late 1970s to the 1980s and early 1990s—and many women would not have benefited from their significant contribution. They made tremendous efforts toward building a "feminist" community for all women—feminists, non-feminists, and even anti-feminists.

It might be said that women in the women's bookstores seem to have often employed the more socially acceptable term "women's bookstore" rather than "feminist bookstore" in public. For example, in 1991, when they started a national advertisement campaign to improve their visibility for the first time, the advertisement said "Support Your Local Women's Bookstores!" Such usage suggests they thought that the term "feminist" was still not a socially appropriate one to promote their bookstores, and also they wanted to attract all women in their communities. When Linda Bubon and Ann Christophersen opened their bookstore and named it Women & Children First in 1979, they were warned by many women not to do so.[8] The latter were of the view that the store might thereby implicitly exclude anti-feminists as well as non-feminists (women in general), and would unduly limit their clientele in the community. In the late 1970s, "Women & Children First" was regarded an offensive name for a retail store. Because of this inclusiveness, the lesbian presence in women's bookstores was often ignored by both the mainstream media and the feminist one. For example, *Publishers Weekly* (March 1991) covered Old Wives' Tales as a successful bookstore and gave some recognition to the phenomenon of feminist publishing in the books industry. However, while it covered the feminist presence, it ignored lesbian involvement.[9] In a similar vein, when Carol Seajay appeared in *Ms.*, it "[produced] what appears to be a profile of *FBN* and [Seajay's] work—but just happens to omit the word 'lesbian' from every context." [10]

To begin with, how were lesbian feminists situated in the women's movement? A major move toward expanding the women's movement began with the establishment of the National Organization for Women (NOW), started by its first president, Betty Friedan, in 1966. NOW was, of course, one of many women's liberation groups that appeared during the late 1960s and 1970s; they were primarily college educated, middle class white women.[11] Women in NOW believed that changes assuring women an equal position in society would be brought about by "social and legal reform through politics designed to create equal opportunities for women," and repeatedly filed formal petitions against "discriminatory regulations."[12] For example, in 1967 NOW campaigned for a Presidential Executive Order to ban discrimination in federal employment and by companies doing business with the government, and within a year the Order was enacted. This was the first major victory by NOW. Having started as a group of twenty-eight women with a $140 budget in June 1966, by 1970, its membership had reached over three thousand with an annual budget of about $38,000.[13] Since NOW promoted "social and legal reforms," its members were generally called "liberal feminists." On the other hand, others who sought not only "reforms" but the end of patriarchy, which they saw as the defining characteristic of society, were referred to as "radical feminists." The issue that divided both groups of feminists most starkly at that time was the issue of homosexuality.

"Radical" women by the late 1960s insisted that fully embracing lesbianism was absolutely fundamental to their movement. Estelle Freedman says:

> In the movement, in an atmosphere that supposedly encouraged women to be themselves and to speak honestly, lesbian feminists were marginalized and stifled because some feminist leaders wished to avoid any suggestion that women's rights were connected to homosexual rights. Rebelling against such control, lesbians asserted their own voices and demanded recognition that their cause-like that of other feminists-was also one of sexual subordination and oppression.[14]

When many women gradually learned and were encouraged to speak out in public and love what they were, lesbians started to establish connections for social change. However, like many other Americans, "liberal" women in NOW also saw lesbians with disdain. They tended to see homosexuality "as a pathological aberration at worst, or a private matter of no political consequence at best."[15] They considered lesbianism to be a "side issue" of a "special interest group," and a "continuing source of embarrassment to the [women's] movement."[16] Friedan referred them as the "Lavender Menace" in 1969 and 1970. Some leading feminists, who were concerned about the possibly negative impact of the image of "men-hating lesbians" on the women's movement as a whole, also sought to keep the issue invisible. Many other feminist institutions followed the steps of NOW and "purged" lesbian feminists. For example, women's clinics at that time, which gained great energy from the Supreme Court ruling on abortion, Roe v. Wade, attracted many lesbian feminists. Carol Seajay, who used to be one of the workers in a women's clinic in Michigan, claims, "I'd be willing to bet that 2/3 of those active in the abortion movement at the time were lesbians."[17] Finding "a clear connection between freedom from pregnancy and the freedom to be a lesbian, the freedom to make your own choices about what you do with your body," lesbian feminists saw women's clinics as sites to apply their energy.[18] However, Seajay, already an open lesbian, was purged by a colleague at the clinic who raised the issue of Seajay's lesbianism.[19] In the late 1960s, being out of the closet and living openly as a lesbian meant "certain exclusion."[20] Throughout the period from 1969 to 1971, a central issue was thus to recognize whether or not "women's rights were connected to homosexual rights." The women's movement was beset with a crisis known as the "gay/straight split," which occurred in varying degrees throughout women's organizations across the country as more women "came out" as lesbians. At the same time, however, this split became one of the main motivating factors behind the creation of lesbian feminist spaces and institutions. It was not long before NOW established a task force on sexuality and lesbianism; however, lesbians who faced denials of their very existence within the women's movement became disenchanted with heterosexual feminists. When lesbian feminists struggled to gain back their pride as lesbians, the Stonewall Riot occurred in 1969. This incident transformed lesbian feminists, who had been oppressed as women by men and as lesbians by heterosexuals, into essential assets for the women's movement for the foreseeable future. Thus the period during and after the "gay/straight split" and lesbian and gay rights movement witnessed a flourishing of lesbian feminist culture.[21]

Many scholars consider the Stonewall Riot of 1969 the birth of the lesbian and gay rights movement. Although there were already many lesbians and gays in the 1950s and 60s who were active in claiming their rights, the Riot served as the main catalyst instigating the formation of the modern lesbian and gay civil rights movement as well as the corresponding politicization of lesbian and gay identities.[22] On Friday, June 27, 1969, a group of Manhattan police officers raided the Stonewall Inn, a gay bar in the heart of Greenwich Village. It was not a rare incident, but the patrons of the Stonewall Inn refused to comply with officers' requests. When officers tried to haul them, a crowd started to throw bricks and bottles as a protest against the bar raids and related police harassment. The riot continued for three days. Afterwards, many lesbians and gays transformed themselves into a more active political movement, forming organizations to seek justice for themselves.[23] As a result, a number of similar groups were spawned across the country, and they determined not to be silenced and isolated from each other. The Stonewall Riot became the symbol of their resistance to compulsory heterosexism—heterosexual hegemony—ushering in a "counter ideology which repudiated the strongly negative ideology of straight society."[24]

Despite these developments, NOW and other feminist institutions continued to ignore lesbians' claim that lesbianism was a crucial feminist issue and that women's rights were necessarily connected to homosexual rights. As a result, these institutions were losing many talented and energetic lesbian feminists. For example, D.C. Women's Liberation "purged" Marilyn Webb in 1969. It led her to establish *Off Our Backs,* the renowned national women's newspaper, which is still in operation. Rita Mae Brown, who became one of the most influential lesbian feminist writers, also left the New York City chapter of NOW in 1970 and started to work as part of the Furies. Like Brown, many lesbian feminists were angered at their marginalization in feminist institutions, and so they formed lesbian-feminist groups of their own, "fashioning in the process both a political agenda and a theory to sustain their efforts."[25] At a May 1969 conference of women's liberation groups, seventeen women wore lavender T-shirts with red lettering that read "Lavender Menace." The word "Lavender Menace," painted luminous on their shirts, suddenly became visible when the lights in the auditorium were turned off.[26] Lesbian feminists aggressively started to express themselves in public.

Indeed, most feminist publications took radical-feminist positions with regard to the issue of lesbian participation. In the first place, many lesbians were in the feminist publishing enterprises and lesbians in these publications were often not in the minority. For example, in early 1972, the entire staff of *Ain't I a Woman?* was composed of lesbian feminists, and the paper announced that it was being published by "a collective of 16 women functioning as a world-wide conspiracy of Radical Lesbians—and don't you forget it!"[27] Lesbians, who were purged or silenced, or who left without a word from feminist institutions, increasingly refused to be invisible. The number of gay and lesbian publications produced in 1970 surpassed 150, with a combined circulation of at least 250,000.[28] These periodicals voiced outrage and demanded social justice.[29] At the same time, they also offered a space to exchange political agendas and theories, and created their own network. Through 1983 more than 92 lesbian periodicals were published.[30] Numerous lesbian feminist writers nurtured their own perspectives and grew as writers and leading political activists for their own rights as women and lesbians.[31] The large number of lesbian periodicals also signified "how large a part their networks were in the total and how important lesbians viewed the need to communicate their perspectives" and constituted space in which to do so.[32] These publications in this way started to engulf the women's movement as well as the lesbian and gay rights movement.

As we can see, lesbians energetically published their periodicals. Yet even before the flourishing of lesbian periodicals, a crucial publication for lesbians, *The Ladder,* was published by the Daughters of Bilitis (since 1956). The Daughters of Bilitis (DOB) was founded in 1955 in San Francisco to provide an "alternative to the limited social outlets available to them [lesbians]."[33] One year later, it started publishing *The Ladder,* which was the only lesbian publication at that time in the US. However, *The Ladder* was a lesbian yet not an explicitly feminist publication since it stressed accommodative strategies. It emphasized that "lesbians rather than heterosexual society [are] responsible for reducing homophobic prejudice and discrimination."[34] Namely, it was suggesting that lesbians change their behavior through, for example, wearing skirts instead of pants in public. Nevertheless, *The Ladder* was sold in a plain brown wrapper at newsstands because of the conception that all lesbians were perverse prevailed at that time. "You hid your face when you bought it," Judy Grahn says.[35]

With the drastic changes brought by the women's movement and the lesbian and gay rights movement, *The Ladder* became in 1970 a feminist magazine documenting the injustice suffered by lesbians and supported their rights without accommodating to anyone. And in 1972, while it still had a circulation of 3,500, *The Ladder* folded. Charlotte Bunch later noted:

> Those [from 1956 to 1972] were years when very little existed for lesbians to read, but they kept that alive for all of us. They could go out of existence in 1972 because of the present wave of feminist and lesbian writing. History and our own work ebb and flow, but keeping alive the core of what we are about through those hard times has been done by women in our past, and their example can serve as guideposts for us in facing the future.[36]

In this way, the impact which *The Ladder* had on lesbian feminists was enormous. Barbara Grier was one of the most enthusiastic contributors to *The Ladder,* and would later found one of the most successful lesbian feminist publishing houses, Naiad press.[37] Grier's long-time efforts to support the lesbian feminist publishing community starting from *The Ladder* gave her a "standing ovation" at the first Women In Print conference.[38] This is because before the women's liberation movement *The Ladder* was everything for many lesbians. *The Ladder* enabled lesbian feminists to engage in dialogue among themselves, educate themselves, to articulate definitions of their experience and to create an incipient sense of community.[39] It certainly became the seed of the explosion of lesbian feminist publishing ventures that was later to come.

Following *The Ladder,* new lesbian feminist journals appeared across the nation. The year 1971 witnessed the birth of *Siren* (Chicago), and *Killer Dyke* (Chicago), *Lavender Vision* (Cambridge), *The Lesbian Tide* (Los Angeles), *Proud Woman* (Stanford), *Reach Out* (Detroit), *Spectre* (Ann Arbor), *Scarlet Letter* (Madison), *Purple Rage* (New York), *Sisterhood* (New York), and *Lazette* (Fanwood, New Jersey). And the next year, *The Amazon Nation Newsletter* (Chicago), *The Furies* (Washington, DC), Atlanta: *Newsletter of the Atlanta Lesbian Feminist Alliance* (Georgia), *Echo of Sappho* (Brooklyn, New York), *Gay Women's Newsletter* (Champaign, Illinois), *the National Lesbian Information Service Newsletter* (San Francisco), and *Lesbians Fight Back* (Philadelphia) came into existence.[40] Although *The Lesbian Tide* (1971–1980) used to be the journal of the Los Angeles branch of DOB, it severed its relationship by taking "a more radical stance."[41] *The Ladder* (1971–1980) was the first lesbian feminist publication using the term "lesbian" in its title, and later became the "Bible of lesbian feminism."[42] Every year the number of lesbian feminist papers increased, and eventually reached over 92 through 1983.[43] Martha Allen, pointing out the importance of periodicals for racial and ethnic minority women, and lesbians, says:

> [These periodicals] contributed particular perspectives not only essential to the whole picture of American women, but critical in providing other women with their unique insights gained from their very different life experiences. These perspectives, too, were rarely found in other media and were therefore especially needed.[44]

These periodicals provided not only particular perspectives, but also crucial information to those who constituted one part of the whole American women. For example, Carol Seajay, who was living in Kalamazoo, Michigan, heard about the West Coast Lesbian Conference through these periodicals. At the conference held at UCLA in 1973, there were over 200 lesbians whom she "never had seen in one place at one time."[45] This experience drew her to the west coast where she knew some women were starting a woman's bookstore called The Full Moon. Eventually she co-founded Old Wives' Tales bookstore and also published *FBN.* In the late 1960s, Carol Seajay also found that "none [of the early lesbian novels] had a happy ending. I just never read the last chapter—that was the advice everyone gave you," she says. This is because these lesbian novels "inevitably ended in double suicides or dramatic conversions."[46] Until the late 1960s, for many lesbians there seemed to be "no options other than to become alcoholic or jump off a bridge before reaching the age of 30."[47] As a result, "there was a time when 'happy endings' were rarely, if ever, found in books by or about lesbians."[48]

Then the great wave of the lesbian and gay rights movement started, promoting lesbian feminist counter-culture and stimulating the creation of lesbian culture. Lesbian novels emerging in the early 1970s started to provide quite different images of lesbians from previous lesbian novels.[49] The lesbian writer Lee Lynch emphasized:

> I have been through years of self-destructive behavior, therapy, and recovery. I've experienced the damage of all that negativity. I want to create an alternative literature; to embrace where we were, but to deliberately flood our culture with the positive images which will make a better future.[50]

Thus individual lesbians were trying to bring "positive images which will make a better future" to lesbians through their writings. Then the first major breakthrough began with the word-of-mouth bestseller, *Rubyfruit Jungle*. For the first time, it offered a lesbian heroine (Molly Bolt) with a "happy ending." The heroine's non-traditional, independent, courageous deeds and humorous observations on heterosexual norms made *Rubyfruit Jungle* completely different from early lesbian novels, making growing up as a spirited lesbian a source of pride rather than a cause of shame.[51] Accordingly, it generated enormous excitement and enthusiastic admiration from large numbers of lesbians. After the publication of *Rubyfruit Jungle*, numerous "new" lesbian feminist writers began to emerge. However, mainstream publishers were not about to rush women's writings in general, let alone lesbian ones, into print, so lesbians had to publish them themselves. New lesbian feminist publishers such as Daughters, Inc., Diana Press, and Persephone Press then simultaneously appeared in the early 1970s. Although these prominent examples all closed by the early 1980s, Naiad Press, Seal Press, Spinsters, Aunt Lute, Cleis Press, Firebrand, Kitchen Table: Women of Color Press, and many other lesbian feminist publishers followed their footsteps. Their writings were read widely not only by lesbian feminists but also by heterosexual feminists. Through these writings, heterosexual feminists increasingly recognized that lesbian issues were not so very different from feminist issues, and also could find sustenance. The issues covered by lesbian papers and magazines "were bedrock issues of the women's liberation press as well."[52] This is because lesbian perspectives, which were nurtured and developed within these periodicals as well as books, provided valuable insights to the larger women's movement. For example, works by Adrienne Rich and Audre Lorde have "contributed powerfully to forming many cultural resources."[53] Large numbers of women actually read their writings and were affected in some way by them—enabling them to transform their own way of thinking or behavior. Thus, the development and the explosion of lesbian feminist writings became extremely important for the entire women's movement.

The women's movement created women-only events and activities. In these activities, it was natural that more women's expressions were nurtured, encouraged, and promoted without the presence of men. As a result, throughout the 1980s and into the 1990s women witnessed the flourishing of women's arts such as music, painting, theater, and film. Although participants in women-only events and activities remained decidedly mixed in sexual orientation, lesbians were highly visible. Like print, these other forms of arts were quite successful in promoting communication among lesbian feminists. According to Jan Laude, lesbians developed their own way of speaking, wearing costumes, accessories, as well as bodily rhetoric as tools for communication. Through them, they could recognize each other, and communicate with each other.[54] Moreover, they created their own symbols such as the labyris, double women's symbols, or the color of purple. All were part of an emerging lesbian counterculture generated from the grass roots level.[55] Furthermore, they attempted to utterly alter the image of lesbians by sending completely opposite messages through arts—that lesbians are not perverse, that they live happily, with strength and beauty. Lesbian feminists often proudly wore jewelry with labyris or double women's symbols, lavender T-shirts, or buttons with lesbian slogans, like "A Woman Without a Man Is Like a Fish Without a Bicycle." Within lesbian counterculture, music was, next to print media, one of the most available communication tools for them. However, in the early 1970s, women recognized that their ability to produce and sell music in mainstream music markets was extremely limited. This was, of course, primarily due to the fact that lesbian musicians faced exclusion from dominant hegemonic structures that traditionally valued and commodified heterosexual relationships in music. Therefore, feminists—especially lesbian feminists—were eager to produce and engineer music solely for themselves. They needed to change the music industry just as they needed to transform the publishing industry. Women who had left the Furies collective founded Olivia Records in 1973, the first national all-women's record label and a novel collective of lesbian feminists. The next year, the First National Women's Music Festival was held on the campus of the University of Illinois at Urbana-Champaign, as an effort to build an alternative culture in response to under-representation of women in the music industry.[56] Margie Adam, lesbian feminist singer and songwriter says:

> I came to the first National Women's Music Festival in Champaign-Urbana, Illinois . . . hearing Meg Christian play on Wednesday night. After the third song, I found my self putting my head in my hands, crying my eyes out . . . saying to my self . . . She is singing my life. My world was changed forever in that moment when I realized I was not alone.[57]

In this way, many women's worlds were changed by listening to others singing their lives.

Among 800 performers in the first festival were Margie Adam and Meg Christian, as well as Cris Williamson, who recorded and released "Changer and the Changed" the next year (1975) from Olivia Records.[58] "It changed everything," says Scott Alarik. It sold 50,000 to 80,000 copies its first year and went on to become one of the best selling albums ever produced by an independent label, proving there was a viable market for women's music.[59] "Changer and the Changed" became a "symbol of lesbian identity."[60] The audience was mushrooming, and the National Women's Music Festival became an annual event and continued in Champaign-Urbana, Illinois for the next six years.[61] Since 1976 the Michigan Womyn's Music Festival (MWMF) has succeeded the National Women's Music Festival. In 1982, Meg Christian, one of the most popular performers, and Meg Christian came together to perform in two sold-out shows for over 5,600 women at Carnegie Hall, the largest single grossing event since the Hall's creation in 1891.[62] These concerts promoted the value and emphasized the significance of women's music, women's material culture and women's relationships with one another.[63] Simultaneously, they provided women with not only the access to music by women and for women, but also opportunities to express themselves as feminists as well as lesbians, and also to network them. Dorothy Dean, who started Women's Sound Publishing in 1974, set forth goals similar to the characteristics found in feminist publishing. As Dean said:

> We are forming a network of communication, setting up contacts between interested women's centers and women musicians. . . . This is one way to assure that our culture keeps spreading and means that we will have to rely less and less on the patriarchal culture. . . . We must encourage and support each other. What we are saying and how we say it are important to each and every woman both inside and outside the movement.[64]

In this way, developing a network of communication and communities among women was also one of the main goals of women's music as with lesbian feminist papers. Cris Williamson says these concerts were "also social events," and the "buzz was tremendous." The concerts, moreover, doubled as a political gathering: "Tables everywhere for this cause or that, sign up here, vote for this."[65] The "buzz" and the "tables" in the concerts were also a "network of communication," crucial for women to find out what was going on and what was to happen next for their advancements. Concerts became "like town meetings of the feminist movement, rippling with the vibrant, often tumultuous energies of people discovering themselves by discovering others like them."[66] Kathy Rudy noted that upon listening to Holly Near's music she found her way into the lesbian community and her lesbian identity. She said:

> [T]he moment I listened to her [Holly Near's] articulation of alternative sexualities, I was hooked. Her resistance to heterosexual norms, her presence as a strong independent woman who loved other women, the fierceness of her politics—these things called to me, pulled me out of my cloud of unknowing, and helped me identify my true self.[67]

Thus, many women found their identities as lesbian feminists and, even more importantly, they found a network and community based on new social bonds about which they would usually have otherwise never found out.

Community is sometimes used in a territorial sense to refer to a geographic locality. In this case, searching for a community seemed to be easy. However, community is also commonly used to describe a particular quality of human relationships, and its construction in this case was an extremely difficult task. Lesbians who lived in areas other than Castro in San Francisco and a few major metropolitan sites had to identify a community that provided them with "affective ties and mutual support."[68] Phyllis Chesler says women, especially lesbians, were "immigrants who left the old patriarchal country in the late 1960s and early 1970s to clear a path in History for the generations to come," and like other immigrants who "always form infrastructure or self-help groups and title themselves, lesbians need to have their own space."[69] It is apparent that women, especially lesbians, needed such a community, a safe space created by women and for women—where only women came together and women-loving women were visible and welcomed. In this way, women-only events became such a place. Among them, music concerts or festivals were particularly successful in providing a safe space for women to enjoy a variety of music not available anywhere except for a few, but also because the space was easily identified and accessed by all women, especially lesbians, and promoting women's and lesbian identities. The Michigan Womyn's Music Festival (MWMF)'s mission statement indicated their cry for a space for themselves. It said: "[At the MWMF] we create and experience a unique culture here . . . knowing that we have an opportunity to create community that can reflect the values and priorities that are truly important to us . . . our community welcomes all womyn. . . ."[70] Nevertheless, no matter how enthusiastically women formed a warm and supportive space and shared their joy and excitement at such concerts, they only lasted for a few hours. Women needed a space that was less temporary, if not permanent.

Entering the 1960s, feminists were involved in building feminist institutions in their communities—from local branches of NOW to women's clinics, shelters for battered women, and women's centers. Feminist institutions would have presumably become safe spaces for all women, including lesbians. However, many feminist institutions including NOW pushed out lesbians because of their sexual orientation.[71] Furthermore, women's centers, which were emerging in communities across the nation at that time and literally became "center," for local women, were increasingly affiliated with colleges and universities; then the focus of the centers at first included women who were interested in returning to school, but later it specifically came to concern on younger female students typically resident on campus.[72] This shift might have secured the existence of women's center, however, for many women, women's centers were not a place to be easily accessed.

In this period women's bookstores were emerging in the context of lesbian feminist cultural and commercial enterprises. It would be almost unimaginable for women to start to operate women's bookstores without knowledge of or interest in lesbian feminism, which was exemplified in increasingly prominent writings, music and culture. Given the great demand for lesbian information and culture, it is clear that feminist booksellers of the 70s and the following decades needed a strong commitment to both general feminism and lesbianism. It is revealing that feminist authors increasingly used women's bookstores as the setting in which their protagonists were lesbians. For example, one of the most popular lesbian cartoons *Dykes To Watch Out For* by Alison Bechdel featured a women's bookstore as its setting.[73] The women's bookstore in the cartoon, called Madwimmin Books, was based on the Amazon Bookstore Cooperative in Minneapolis, Minnesota. Bechdel focuses on lesbian feminist protagonist Mo's daily struggle, which is mainly in the bookstore. In another case, the real-life Sisterhood Bookstore in Los Angeles was depicted in Terri de la Pena's lesbian feminist novels as a place to lift the heroine's spirits up and to meet a woman who was to become her best friend for years to come. "Her eyes shone as she pointed out well-remembered titles—novels by Katherine V. Forrest, Jane Rule and Ann Allen Shockely; poetry by Judy Grahn, Audre Lorde and Adrienne Rich; non-fiction by Gloria Anzaldua and Cherrie Moraga . . . 'Whenever I feel discouraged, alienated, I stand here and look at all these books, remember these writers and my spirits rise.'"[74] De la Pena also wrote:

> In May 1983 we met at Sisterhood Bookstore in west Los Angeles. We had gone there for the same reason: to see and listen to local Latina writers read from their work . . . Up to that point, neither of us had ever met another Latina writer, much less another Latina *lesbian* writer. We continued to huddle, whisper and joke between ourselves.[75]

Interestingly, Adele Wallace, co-owner of Sisterhood Bookstore happened to find herself reading about Sisterhood Bookstore in her story. Wallace says, "I try to think of how many women's lives Sisterhood changed in the course of its 27 years-and how those women's lives affected others. . . ."[76] As a place to offer a variety of women's voice which was not heard anywhere else, Sisterhood Bookstore kept sending messages to women in the community that "you are not alone."

Of course, it goes without saying that women's bookstores have been a safe space for all women including heterosexual women. For example, Reger Jo says:

> The women's bookstore became an important place for me, a place important in the construction of my self. Emotionally I was connected to this space and the women who worked and shopped there. It felt like a secure relationship. . . . the bookstore was a place of personal exploration and safety.[77]

In this way, the women's bookstore became not only a valuable outlet for feminist writings including hard-to-find lesbian materials in local bookstores, but also a safe site for all women to find their feminist or lesbian feminist identities. For example, comic artist Roseanne Barr also received encouragement through working in a large collective bookstore, Woman to Woman Feminist Bookstore, where the women understood and supported her humor.[78] She has written:

> There came a time in my life that I, thinking myself a writer, walked into a space called Woman to Woman bookstores on Colfax street in Denver, Colorado. . . . I thought I would find books by women writers,

> and I was looking specifically for books about women writers by women writers. It had just dawned on me that I was a woman and a writer, and each and both of these words were huge masses of veins and hair to me, all tangled together, needing to be sorted, cleaned, defined. . . . There was a sign on the coffee table in front of the couch that said this is a safe place for women.[79]

In the first issue of *FBN*, the mission statement clearly says, "We envision feminist bookstores as a network of 'woman's places' and information centers across the country (feminist shelters?)."[80] Creating a women's bookstore directly meant building a safe space for all women. Yet within this framework, Alisa Klinger has noted that women's bookstores, "more than any other cultural, community or commercial women's institutions" also exemplified the viability and endurance of lesbian politics and culture in the period from the early 1970s to the middle of the 1990s.[81]

WEAVING WOMEN'S BOOKSTORES: CAROL SEAJAY, OLD WIVES' TALES AND *FBN*

For Carol Seajay, who arrived in San Francisco in December 1973, her first encounter of the women's bookstore in San Francisco began with a flyer in the women's bathroom of the San Francisco Public Library; the women's bathroom was/is commonly a place to get information on women-only events and activities. It also announced the opening of the Full Moon, a women's coffeehouse and bookstore. Seajay says,

> I think that one of the major successes of the women's movement is that it's created a literacy revolution among women. Now women expect to go out to a bookstore, and we know what we want to read and it better be there! But if it's not, we'll desire it and our desire will call it into being. . . . the desire pulls us into doing the next thing and to knowing where to go, and then we go there and are responded to. And that sparks the next desire—which pulls something new into being. [82]

Such was the beginning of her life-long commitment to building and expanding feminist bookstores network and starting a "literacy revolution among women."[83] Feminists' efforts to make the revolution happen and sustain it strongly linked to the history of women's bookstores: their emergence and development of women's bookstores across the nation. Seajay quickly joined the collective of the Full Moon, which was conceived by middle-class lesbian feminists who were introduced to feminist ideology in women's studies at a local university. It was as an extension of this literary and cultural context that the collective was formed and the coffeehouse and bookstore ultimately established.[84] They started to work toward opening the coffeehouse and bookstore that they envisioned, laying a new cement floor and handling all drainage and plumbing themselves.[85] On International Women's Day, March 7, 1974, the Full Moon opened, although the bookstore constituted only a small section.[86]

During this time, Seajay had two life-changing opportunities. First, she came to know A Woman's Place bookstore in Oakland. She happened to meet Gretchen Milne, who had started A Woman's Place bookstore with other collective members such as Carol Wilson and Alice Molly in 1972.[87] Compared to the Full Moon, A Woman's Place bookstore had two whole shelves of lesbian books. Seajay began to commute there once or twice a week, even though it took three hours by bus; she read all of the lesbian books and then every work by Black women.[88] She also met Paula Wallace working in A Woman's Place. It did not take long until both of them decided to open a women's bookstore as co-owners in San Francisco. She knew there were probably other women who wanted another women's bookstore in San Francisco, and who made a pilgrimage to Oakland once or twice a year. Although there were already four women's bookstores in the Bay Area (The Full Moon in San Francisco, A Woman's Place in Oakland, The Oracle in Hayward, and Rising Woman in Santa Rosa), she thought that having four women's bookstores in the Bay Area did not suffice.[89] However, she needed to figure out whether it was possible to open a bookstore with $6,000. She knew A Woman's Place started with $400, the equivalent of a month's rent, so "starting with $6,000 didn't look like doing it the difficult way."[90] She wondered, though, if such a business could support two people (Seajay and Wallace) in San Francisco. Then she had another life-changing opportunity—to attend the Women in Print conference. Seajay brought a simple question with her to the conference: was it possible to open a bookstore with $6,000? As part of her introduction during that first session, she asked the question to a group of women. The next day, Karyn London of New York's Womanbooks, which was one of the most successful and largest women's bookstores at the time, answered, "Yes, it was possible. We did it in New York, with about that much money."[91] It was the Women In Print conference that provided Seajay with exactly what she wanted to hear—and precisely from those she hoped to hear it.

Since receiving advice and encouragement in the Conference, Seajay and Wallace had no hesitation to pour all of their energy to open their bookstore. The $6,000 was borrowed from the San Francisco Feminist

Credit Union, one of a group of credit unions inaugurated in the early 70s.[92] Two of the three people on the loan committee of the San Francisco Feminist Credit Union were a feminist bookstore owner from Hayward, CA and a lesbian feminist who published poetry. It should be noted that such cooperation and organized efforts among women in the community made feminists' start-up of their own ventures without money possible and successful in the 1970s.[93] Later, with an additional $2,000 loan borrowed from Paula Wallace's parents, they started Old Wives' Tales bookstore at Valencia and 16th Street in San Francisco on Halloween, 1976—less than two months after returning from the conference.[94]

Since there were very few women running women's bookstores with any experience in bookselling, they had much to learn. Like Seajay, most women booksellers were young and full of energy; yet their lack of capital and experience was clearly a major obstacle to successfully carrying out their ventures. WIP Conference gave tremendous opportunities to the representatives of roughly 20 women's bookstores to ask and learn many things regarding women's bookstore's operations—so much so that "nobody wanted to stop talking."[95] Toward the end of the conference, women strongly felt they had to continue their dialogue and exchange information on everything related to running women's bookstores. Seajay has noted: "We worried about how we were going to keep talking to each other after we went home. We thought about phone calls, but none of us could afford that. We thought we could write letters. . . . [but we] already have too much to do. . . . Finally we came up with the idea of a newsletter for the bookstores. . . . But no one wanted to take it on. . . . I thought, "well, maybe I could do it."[96] Thus Seajay started the *Feminist Bookstores Newsletter* (*FBN*) in October 1976, just seventeen days before opening her Old Wives' Tales. She was a part-time editor and publisher at first, but later became full-time until it folded in 2000. The first three issues were created with financial support (loans) from Womanbooks, New Words, and Amazon Bookstore. In addition, other bookstores agreed to donate money on a sliding scale. With Andre from Rising Woman Books, which had a Gestetner printer, Seajay started "to collect information, type it onto stencils, crank it out on the printer" and mail twenty or twenty-five copies out respectively to the bookstores.[97]

Then, what were the roles of *FBN* for the owners and patrons of women's bookstores? First, *FBN* provided a key networking medium for women's bookstores. Anthony Beckles, in his study of political Black bookstores, points out that their lack of a sustained network was fatal, particularly given the added geographical distance between them. As a result, Black bookstores in the US lost vigor soon after a major backlash against the Black civil rights movement.[98] The Women in Print Conference was an opportunity for feminist booksellers to network with each other, but without *FBN*, the network would not have endured, because *FBN* became a powerful vehicle to keep the network alive and an effective medium for women's bookstores' surviving and success. Furthermore, the network was extended to the larger feminist publishing community. Many pages of *FBN* were devoted to exchanging dialogues among feminist publishers, distributors, presses, librarians, and bookstores. Over the decades *FBN* sustained and enlarged a network of the feminist publishing community that had began with the first Women In Print conference in 1976. For example, *FBN* encouraged women in the bookstores to give publishers feedback from their storefront. Often, such feedback prevented important, but slow-selling books from going out of print, so that the books were reprinted or were made into paperbacks.[99] *FBN* also encouraged feminist booksellers to "pay the feminist publishers first and let the straight [establishment publishers] wait!"[100] The support system based on the network, borrowing from Seajay's phrase, a "feminist publishing ecosystem," would not have worked well without *FBN*.

Second, *FBN* offered information on everything of feminist publishing communities from book reviews from small presses to main publishers, book lists on specific subjects, discussions, debates, searches for out-of-print books, announcements, profiles of women's bookstores, tips on new product lines, conferences, trends, trouble with publishers and distributors, as well as outreach programs.[101] Moreover, publishers, distributors, or presses often used *FBN* as a place to announce their changes of policy, give information about their financial situation, and advertise their new ventures. The up-to-date listings of new books by and for women from both mainstream and feminist presses were among the special assets of *FBN* since such information never appeared in the pages of *Publishers Weekly* or the *American Bookstores Association Newsletter.* For example, a listing of feminist books on specific subjects such as Black women, third-world women, reproductive rights, child sexual abuse, battered women and almost out-of-print or imminently-printed feminist paperbacks were available only in *FBN*.[102] Since many women's bookstores also started to sell records, T-shirts, buttons, bumper-stickers, jewelry, and cards, *FBN* soon collected information on these products and published such product news annually in the form of a special issue of "Sidelines."

Many feminist booksellers looked forward to receiving the latest issue, and made the most of it with vehemence. Lynn Taylor of The Women's Store said, "*FBN* is a goldmine of information and helps us in innumerable ways."[103] A woman worker at Sister Moon said, "I read you

[*FBN*] front to back then begin the 1 to 4 hours of work I've marked you for follow- up."[104] Lori Louise of ClaireLight Bookstore needed two copies so that she "could underline, and make notes in [and] otherwise mess up!"[105] In this way, *FBN* offered irreplaceable means to keep their bookstores stocked with feminist materials without spending hours to look through dozens of publishers' catalogs for titles. Furthermore, as a core of the feminist publishing network, *FBN* helped women's bookstores operate effectively, often saving them from getting into financial danger or bankruptcy. For example, when WIND, distributor for 180 small publishers, declared bankruptcy in 1979 after five years in operation, many feminist bookstores and presses were left in immediate financial danger. This is because WIND specialized in distributing feminist and lesbian press books and periodicals to them. Kathryn Adams describes, "A distribution company, if it fails, can bring down a lot of the small presses whose books it handles, as well as create havoc in the operations of all the bookstores that rely on them for ordering."[106] Since WIND had stocked every title of every press it did business with, it became indispensable for many feminist bookstores and presses. Therefore, apparently, "its failure was potentially disastrous."[107]

Seajay and Sherry Thomas, working closely with Helaine Harris and Cynthia Gair of WIND, published *Emergency FBN* to let feminist booksellers know how to do WIND's work in its absence. Seajay also published "listings of every lesbian and feminist publisher that WIND did business with, explaining the differing terms and transactions that each bookstore would confront when they began ordering from dozens of publishers rather than a single source."[108] Seajay wrote:

> How can we say what the last few weeks have been like? In the bookstore [Seajay's Old Wives' Tales] at 11:30 at night looking up yet another of WIND's 180 publishers and seeing with relief that this one gives 40% with no minimums . . . it has for us been quite graphically and clearly a time of national questioning, crisis, mild chaos, pulling together, going on. For all of you it must have been some version of the time.[109]

As a co-owner of Old Wives' Tales, Seajay made the most of her knowledge, and shared deep concerns and sense of crisis among other women in feminist publishing community. As a result, *FBN*'s timely and critical intervention saved not only women's bookstores, but also small feminist publishers that greatly depended on WIND's distribution. *FBN* encouraged feminist booksellers to continue to order directly from these publishers.

Seajay knew how booksellers were exhausted from dealing with daily operations and managing a shoe-string budget, and it was natural for them to avoid ordering from different small presses, which required extensive paperwork. However, if women's bookstores had been too reluctant to do so, the survival of many small publishers would have been put in question. Seajay says in the *Emergency FBN:*

> The next priority is to begin (or continue) to order directly from the publishers as soon and as often as possible. Making the effort now to get books from presses that have only one title. To not let those books vanish from our shelves, our stores. To remember that without small presses, our stores are terribly vulnerable. To believe that "the boys" will publish us a moment longer than it suits and profits them, is to be optimistic in the extreme. It is our own presses that we must depend on. And they will continue to be there only as long and as well as we support them. Now (as always) is the time to take time to educate the women in our stores about which are the women-made books, how and where they've come from, why they cost what they do. $5.00 for *The Wanderground* is a sure investment in a feminist future.[110]

Seajay stressed the importance—to invest their money in feminist publishing is to assure a "feminist future."

Even more important is the fact that she was able to persuade not only feminist bookstores but also the entire feminist publishing community that without mutual help and cooperation among them, they could not work successfully. At the end of the special issue, she added a passage from Judy Grahn's *The Common Woman Poems,* writing:

> This issue of this newsletter now is my form of a love letter to each of us in feminist publishing—from the writers to the publishers to the printers to the distributors to bookstores who will take on the workload WIND's absence leave us and will continue to go on as Judy Grahn writes in *Vera.*
>
> . . . the common woman is as common
> as good bread
> as common as when you couldn't go on
> but did.
> For all the world we didn't know we had in common
> all along
> The common woman is a common as the best bread
> and will rise
> and become strong.[111]

She thus concluded the special issue with a positive message implying they would together become stronger and prosperous after overcoming the current crisis. Her "form of a love letter" presumably would have opened up many feminist booksellers' eyes and assured that their work was a part of the women's movement.

The mission statement of *FBN* said, "We want a feminist bookstore newsletter to share information and to help create a communication network based on cooperation rather than (you guessed it) competition."[112] *FBN* constantly emphasized the necessity of women's mutual help and cooperation. Rodger Streitmatter, in his study of gay and lesbian press, points out that while men's presses were competitive, women's, on the contrary, have embraced the concept of sharing rather than competing.[113] Anthony Beckles, in his study of Black bookstores, also pointed out that most Black bookstores in the 1960s and 70s were established solely for economic opportunity, and the few political Black bookstores in existence tended to be competitive.[114] For example, according to Seajay, women's bookstores in the Bay Area of California, although they were relatively geographically close together, worked cooperatively and helped each other by ordering materials together to get them discounted from publishers.[115] Seajay says, "Because we knew that the more stores there were, the more books we could sell altogether."[116] Consequently, women saw each other not as competitors but as partners to grow together and to grow a whole feminist publishing industry. Responding to *FBN,* many feminist booksellers generously gave valuable information on almost everything about ordering and selling materials. They reported their successful or sometimes failed promotions and programs in their bookstores to *FBN*. They commonly also presented their own ideas on operating bookstores effectively. A Room of One's Own Bookstore, for example, created a form for problems and errors of publishers; Paula Wallace in Full Circle Bookstore also presented a sample letter regarding returning books smoothly to publishers on *FBN*.[117]

Over the years, the number of letters *FBN* received increased. They were not only from booksellers but also publishers, distributors, writers, and librarians. Since many of them had little money but a lot of passion and hard work, they often spoke of how to deal with "LICE (Literary Industrial Corporate Establishment)" and exchanged ideas about how to confront them. Thus women's bookstores combined with *FBN* to operate as bridges between readers, writers, publishers and distributors. Eventually, the letters to *FBN* came to constitute an "information bank" to share with all women in the feminist publishing community.[118] Such a development was made possible because, as Seajay said, "[Women] believed in the power of sharing resources as well as supporting each other."[119] In 1989, Seajay received the Publisher's Service Award of the 1989 Lambda Literary Awards, which was established especially for lesbian and gay literature. In an interview, she said:

> I have consistently re-chosen to make FBN my priority. For me, it's been a pretty clear reality that unless there is a network of feminist bookstores to be selling lesbian work, there's no point in writing it, and no point in publishing it, because that's whether it gets sold. And unless we have this world we created for ourselves to support lesbian writing and see it into print and sell it and promote it and circulate it, then there's not a lot of value in writing it.[120]

As a communication network based on sharing and cooperation, *FBN* also provided emotional support to women.

As a co-founder and worker of Old Wives' Tales, Seajay could fully understand what women working everyday in the bookstores most wanted. When women were discouraged, low in confidence, and exhausted, *FBN* would arrive in the mail. Sadhbh Neilan of New Leaf Books wrote, "Your newsletter made me feel I was not in this book business alone, that I have caring and sharing colleagues dotted across the land."[121] Karyn London at Womanbooks said, "On harried days, *FBN* is one more piece of paper, something else to feel guilty about not having done but when it arrives it's a life line of communication and support."[122] Seajay noted,

> You can sit working in Toronto or Calgary or Tallahassee and get *FBN* in the mail and remember that there are other women doing this work and that you're part of a network which is easy to forget when you're the only women's bookstore for hundreds of miles. It's important to get that kind of encouragement, to hear what other women are doing around the country and around the world and to support them by telling them what you're doing.[123]

As a result, in addition to providing a network of feminist publishing communities and practical information on bookselling, *FBN* played the role of a regular and valuable cheerleader by giving care, compassion and encouragement to feminist booksellers. Her belief that women could share "lives, adventures and knowledge through the books that women read and write and buy and sell" carried *FBN*. However, without numerous positive letters sent from women across the nation, such roles of *FBN* as Seajay tried to realize would have been impossible. In return, women helped Seajay to keep up with the crushing double workload: the Old Wives Tales Bookstore and *FBN*. The newsletter started with 20 to 25 copies, but later the number reached 500, and was sent to feminist and feminist-inclined bookstores in the US, and Canada as well as feminist booksellers in England, Europe, Australia, New Zealand, India and Japan. Subscribers included booksellers, libraries, Women's Studies teachers, book reviewers, publishers and feminist bibliophiles. *FBN* literally created a transnational network of women in feminist publishing communities, laying the foundation for sharing resources, promoting cooperation, and caring among women, and helping women's bookstores to grow healthfully and steadily over a quarter-century.

CONCLUSION

The women's movement also brought new messages to lesbians—questioning marriage, family and home, and especially their gender roles in the society—although heterosexism in feminist institutions eventually disillusioned many energetic and talented lesbians. Then the Stonewall riot occurred, in 1969, and the lesbian and gay rights movement gathered greater energy. Originally, novels in which lesbians appeared typically "ended in double suicides or dramatic conversions."[124] Having learned to speak out and be honest to themselves in social movements, lesbians refused to be silenced and invisible, and started to speak out about what was wrong with the larger society rather than with themselves, and to write novels they truly wanted to read. Mushrooming lesbian papers and writings became their most crucial tool of communication with each other. Their writings and art forms emerged in their new publications, which also nurtured numerous talented lesbian feminist writers. Eventually, they added invaluable insights and power to the women's movement as well as the feminist publishing community. In addition to words in print, various types of arts such as music helped define lesbian feminist identity and often their communities. Building a safe space based on "affective ties and mutual support" became a life-giving and life-altering activity. Carol Seajay has said, "Many, if not most, of the women who felt the need for a bookstore strongly enough to get involved, raise funds, build bookcases, and do volunteer shifts week after week after week were lesbians."[125] This is not to say that lesbians are responsible for the creation of all women's bookstores. Yet lesbian feminists were central figures in their birth and development. Without lesbian feminists, disseminating women's words might have been extremely difficult, if not impossible.

The cooperative ideal—sharing rather than competing—bore fruits with the creation of the Women in Print Conference (WIP), and the WIP enabled women's further creation of bookstores and of *FBN*. *FBN* provided not only practical information crucial to operate women's bookstores, but also offered a network of feminist publishing communities as well as emotional support. Even more importantly, *FBN* assured women that their work was political by reminding women who felt under pressure from their daily activities at the bookstores, "Oh, but this is also a political body of work; your work is very important in a larger context" and "You did extraordinarily well!!"[126] In this way, Carol Seajay helped promote the cooperative ideal ("Sisterhood is powerful") by continuing to publish *FBN*. However, entering the 1980s, women's bookstores like other feminist institutions experienced internal conflicts and challenges that shook their beliefs, requiring renewed efforts to find out if "sisterhood is (even) possible." In addition to such conflicts, with the election of Ronald Reagan and failure to ratify the Equal Rights Amendment, the New Right as well as Religious Right became more powerful. The next chapter will examine how women's bookstores dealt with challenges from women and internal conflicts in their operation, and how they countered political and social backlashes against feminism.

Chapter Five

Women's Bookstores in the 1980s Part I: Backlash and Challenge

In the mid-1970s the women's movement underwent rapid expansion. Feminist questions and issues often rose to the forefront of the national agenda. Feminist organizations grew, entered the political arena, and gained some legislative victories. Along with the expansion of the women's movement, the number of periodicals, books and music by and for women was increasing. Many women thus launched feminist publishing ventures as well as women's bookstores. It seemed that organizations expanded, membership grew, and substantial funds continuously poured in from outside sources. However, by the late seventies, America had entered a period of backlash such that many of the progressive social changes advocated by the alternative and underground media were increasingly under political attack.[1] At the same time, conservative commentators in the mass media such as television commentator Phyllis Schlafly became more prominent.[2]

With the election of Ronald Reagan in 1980, the national political agenda shifted markedly toward the New Right along with the rise of a grassroots Religious Right movement.[3] In 1982, failure to ratify the Equal Rights Amendment constituted an additional blow to many feminists. Much was written in the 1980s about the decline of the women's movement and the onset of a "postfeminist" era, and the Eighties proved to be harder times for feminists than the previous two decades.[4] During the decade, given the political positions of the Reagan and Bush administrations, many of the accomplishments feminists made previously were under almost unceasing attack. These administrations cut back social services and reduced the real income of welfare recipients and low-wage workers while providing major tax cuts for businesses and wealthy Americans. Accordingly, the gap between rich and poor widened, and the basic economic survival of many women was placed at risk.[5] Fueling such problems, the Reagan and Bush administrations continued also to reduce revenues available for social programs, and were "indifferent to the needs of real families and real children, while trumpeting support for 'family values' and 'unborn children.'"[6]

Many feminists had to confront the loss of social programs and institutions for women's advancement. Anita Bryant, as a born-again Christian mother, launched the lesbian-and-gay- bashing "SAVE OUR CHILDREN" campaign in 1977. The AIDS epidemic also started to plague gay communities around the nation, so right-wing politicians started to use the issue to exacerbate homophobia. Additionally, feminists had to face internal conflict. Women generally believed that the "politics of trust grounded in interpersonal relationships" supported interpretations that reduced these conflicts among women to a matter of individuals' act, intentions, and capabilities.[7] Many undoubtedly hoped that workers' mutual political commitment to feminism would have fostered a sense that a common feminist identity transcended other differences. Unfortunately, however, since such a view tended to ignore issues of discrimination and related inequality based on differences among women, it clearly could not work. Kathleen M. Weston and Lisa B. Rofel, for example, pointed out conflicts that stemmed from these differences even in a lesbian workplace.[8] As Joan Gibbs and Sara Bennett noted, subtle forms of racism and classism were evident in meetings and in styles of work in lesbian feminist institutions. They wrote:

> [W]hite or middle-class women, empowered by their privileged education or selective experience, frequently dominate meetings, feel the need and do rephrase everything said, and/or act as if all of us come from the exact same background as they do and have the exact same privileges.[9]

Furthermore, when a separatist discourse came from the idea of improving women's condition through the activism of a women's community separate from the oppressions of and distinct from others, it was questioned and criticized especially by women of color.[10] Since women's bookstores also consisted of predominantly "white or middle-class women," they were not immune to such conflict.

BACKLASH: THE BLOWS OF REAGAN, BUSH AND AIDS

The growth and success of the women's movement during the 1970s greatly contributed, tellingly, to the rejuvenation of right-wing activism, although the backlash against women's bookstores had already begun in the late 70s, before the Reagan Administration era began. For example, Pam Wilson, an owner of The Open Book, Salt Lake City, Utah described her backlash experience after the 1977 Utah International Women's Year convention. Some Mormon women were for the ERA, and some against it, and that conflict erupted bitterly at the convention. Organizers planned it for 3,000 people. But 10,000 showed up after getting marching orders from the Church—and the nearly hysterical mob voted down every proposal regarding the ERA. Wilson notes,

> It was a scary experience. I think the answer from many of us was to get out of the public eye & just LIVE our feminist beliefs, not preach them anymore. I felt that way, and so, apparently, did many women, and my feminist business dropped off dramatically. . . . a policeman said "apparently someone thinks you've been selling pornography." . . . *The Joys of Fantasy* and *Men Loving Men*, both are available at other bookstores in town, but the Vice Squad denies that the bookstores admit it!. . . . Since other non-feminist stores sell the same books I was busted for, I certainly DO think it was because of the feminist nature.[11]

Her statement alludes to a change in treatment by the public authorities and religious institutions in Salt Lake City, which led to questions about The Open Book's "feminist nature." The next year, The Open Book closed its doors. Presumptions about their "feminist nature" often hindered women from borrowing money from governmental agencies. The Small Business Administration (SBA) denied Donna Loercher a loan to expand The Feminist Book Mart, her mail order business to include a bookstore outlet. She sued SBA on First and Fifth Amendment grounds, saying in her suit:

> Mr. Elbaum [the district counsel for SBA] by telephone said he was concerned over the Book Marts' use of the word 'non-sexist.' He said this could be interpreted as 'political.' On July 2, 1975, the Central State Bank received SBA's final rejection letter. The only stated reason for determining that I was ineligible was that I sell books directed to the female or the so-called Feminist Movement."[12]

Although the District Court ruled on June 1, 1977 against the SBA, Donna Lercher had by this time—over two years after she had applied for a Small Business loan—gone out of business for lack of the loan.[13] However, the situation became worse because the Reagan administration completely terminated the Small Business Administration (SBA)'s programs for women and minorities.[14] The shift in policy severely hit feminist ventures like women's bookstores. For example, in 1987 the SBA denied loans to Sally Owen and Carol Levin who planned to open Judith's Room, a woman's bookstore in New York City. They noted afterwards, "'[Materials which Judith's Room was going to sell were presumably] too specialized [to receive a loan],' . . . the bank officer was angry. [This is because] rarely does the SBA refuse to guarantee a loan after it is approved by the bank."[15] SBA then denied a loan to Grand Books in Wyoming in 1988. According to Seajay, "Grand Books [is] a general bookstore for feminist . . . and educational materials. Concerning about their intention to carry educational materials, the SBA felt it was 'the state's right to decide.' SBA's letter justified their refusal to grant a loan for fear of 'interfering with First Amendment rights.'"[16] Furthermore, the Reagan administration tacitly condoned and often successfully promoted many New Right activities. The administration put leaders of various New Right organizations into high-ranking positions in their administrations. This made New Right organizations legitimate, viable, and growing.[17] In particular, two antifeminist organizations, Eagle Forum and Concerned Women for America, scored major victories in the 1980s. Phyllis Schlafly, long active in Republican Party politics, started the STOP ERA movement in 1973 and founded Eagle Forum in 1975.[18] Concerned Women for America was founded by Beverly LaHaye in 1979, reportedly after she heard Betty Friedan's "anti-God, anti-family rhetoric" in a televised interview and became infuriated at Friedan's claim to speak for American women.[19] Although Schlafly's background was primarily conservative politics and LaHaye's religious, both of them were part of a larger conservative agenda that "opposes government spending, supports a strong defense, condemns media and school promotion of individual decision-making, and favors reinstitution of absolutist moral principles."[20]

Cheryl Hyde has analyzed the diverse effects of attacks by the New Right on nine feminist organizations across the nation during the 1980s. She finds three types of New Right strategies commonly impacted these organizations: resource withdrawal, legislative activities and direct action.[21] First, within the first year of the Reagan administration, key federal programs upon which feminist organizations depended for fiscal resources were drastically cut or eliminated.[22] Second, on the legislative front, during Reagan's first term, "countless 'Human Life' and 'Family Protection' measures were proposed."[23] For instance, members of Congress allied with the administration attempted to re-criminalize abortion (or otherwise weaken the "right to choose") and re-institute "'traditional' (patriarchal) values in families, schools, and places of employment."[24] In particular, the anti-gay-rights campaigns focused on explicitly allowing employment discrimination and preventing AIDS-related treatment and education. Third, among the most "virulent antifeminist right-wing activities" were the direct-action campaigns against abortion clinics and other local clinics—they were picketed, vandalized, and fire-bombed.[25] As a result, Congress passed the Hyde Amendment, which excluded abortion from the comprehensive health care services provided to low–income people by the federal government through Medicaid, and public funding was gradually withdrawn from abortion services across the nation.[26] According to Susan Faludi, "in 1988, United Way stopped funding Planned Parenthood, and in 1990, under pressure from the Christian Action Council, AT&T cut off its contributions too (after twenty-five years), claiming that shareholders had objected to the agency's association with abortion—even though 94% of its shareholders had voted in favor of funding Planned Parenthood."[27] Memberships in many feminist organizations dropped drastically, and a large number of the organizations became defunct.

The New Right wing and the Reagan administration were thus hostile to not only feminists but also gays and lesbians. According to Rita Ciolli, Patrick McGuilgan of the conservative Institute for Government and Politics stalled the grant for a women's shelter when he announced, "I don't think pro-lesbian, hard-core feminists should be getting a grant from the Reagan Administration."[28] The U.S Department of Justice even refused to include the words "lesbian" and "woman abuse" (arguing that men are also abused) in their publications.[29] The early onset of the anti-gay and lesbian climate had actually occurred in the late 1970s. One of the emerging vocal opponents of lesbian and gay rights was Anita Bryant, a runner-up in the 1958 Miss America Contest, a Southern Baptist, as well as a gospel and pop singer. When a gay rights ordinance was passed in January 1977 in Dade County, Florida where she lived, she rose up as a born-again Christian mother to launch a campaign for its repeal.[30] Her attack symbolized the beginning of a backlash, the conservative political climate of the AIDS-Reagan era—1981 to 1988. Susan Cavin has noted,

> Led by Jerry Falwell's Moral Majority, virtually every fundamentalist, conservative religious group scapegoated lesbians and gay men. Some called for outright "extermination of homosexuals," others for "quarantine" in concentration camps. . . . Violence against lesbians and gays increased in every US city that kept records on homophobic assault.[31]

In the name of God, conservative religious groups propelled the backlash of hatred and anti-gay violence that spread throughout the nation.

As for feminist publishing, attempts to censor books in the nation's libraries had more than tripled since the Presidential election of 1980, according to Judith Krug, director of the office of Intellectual Freedom of the American Library Association.[32] She was struck by the increasing numbers of complaints about books by people who typically said that they were members of the Moral Majority—or if they were not card-carrying members, said they sympathized with its aims. Presumably well-meaning and concerned, they often introduced the subject with, "I'm not a censor, but . . ."[33] *Our Bodies, Ourselves,* which was published in 1970, specifically targeted for attack from the Moral Majority. A "confidential" letter from the Moral Majority in January 1981, says:

> We have only begun to fight. If the liberals and advocates of pornographic sex education think that, by swearing me, they can stop the Moral Majority's campaign to remove offensive sex education materials from our public classrooms . . . The book is entitled *Our Bodies, Ourselves*. . . . I tell you, my friend . . . the little bit of this book that we have read is not only disgusting, it is shocking. . . . Believe me. You and I are slowly losing control over what our children are being taught! . . . Then, I encourage you to sit down right away and write me a check for the largest amount you can possible sacrifice and send it back immediately. Please let me hear from you soon. Each day counts when a small child's mind and morals are at stake. I will be anxiously awaiting your reply.[34]

As this letter indicates, groups of the New Right started to eagerly to search for any possibility to destroy what feminists had gained since the early 1970s. The targets, as can be seen, included feminist (as well as lesbian and gay) publishing. Feminist or lesbian and gay publishers in *FBN* reported increasing incidents of censorship since the late 1970s.[35] Simultaneously, women's bookstores often experienced complaints or harassments from "highly concerned citizens" and unfriendly neighborhoods. Some were simply uncomfortable and commented that there were "too many books by women."[36] Others explicitly expressed their hatred against women's bookstores, which were carrying "disgusting" and "shocking" *Our Bodies, Ourselves* or other "controversial" materials. Having received an unusually large number of damaged and opened packages, seven bookstores on the East coast including the women's bookstores Djuna Books, Woman Books, Womankind, Bloodroot Restaurant & Books, and Herizon Books formed a coalition to fight against such harassment.[37] The telephone of Djuna Books was also bugged, and there was evidence of a break-in.[38] Furthermore, harassment continued and escalated, and some women's bookstores were set afire or bombed. On October 14, 1980, Vancouver Women's Bookstore was set ablaze after being burglarized twice in the preceding weeks. The fire was believed to be a hate crime.[39] It was reported that over a period of several years Womanfyre Books of Northampton, MA, was the target of anti-lesbian and anti-feminist attacks, including telephone and mail threats and, later, bomb threats.[40] Womanfyre Books closed its doors in 1989.[41] In particular, women's bookstores strongly and openly associated with gay and lesbian rights as well as women's rights were targeted. The Closet Bookstore in Lancaster, PA, was bombed soon after it opened, and again bombed later. Nancy Helm, owner of The Closet Bookstore thought that the store became target for a hate crime because she was an active supporter of a gay and lesbian rights ordinance. *FBN* reported that Emma, a women's bookstore in Buffalo, New York, had been targeted by the so-called "League for Moral Decency" and "concerned citizens" since the end of 1979. They harassed the women working at the store about the stock they carried and asked the "sexual-affectional preferences of collective members."[42] According to Cavin, in the late 1980s the number of anti-gay violence incidents rapidly increased. *The Response of the Criminal Justice System to Bias Crime: An Exploratory Review* reported in 1987 that "the most frequent victims of hate violence today are Lesbians, Gay Men, Blacks, Hispanics, Southeast Asians, and Jews. Lesbians and gay men are probably the most frequent victims."[43] In addition, in 1992 Alaska Women's Bookstore was faced with a new censorship law. The ordinance made it unlawful for any person (or store) "to exhibit obscene materials for the purpose of selling." The definition "would include nearly everything at the store's sexuality and lesbian sections."[44] In the same year, Little Sister (women's bookstore) in Vancouver, Canada, was also bombed.

FBN reported that sales in women's bookstores decreased partly because of the harassment, which continued even into the 1990s and included—borrowing Seajay's words—"other kinds of right-wing madness/or general vandalism."[45] Thus, over the decades most women's bookstores suffered harassment to greater or lesser degrees while managing on a shoestring budget. Nevertheless, many women's bookstores survived, and even flourished. Vancouver Women's Bookstore, a volunteer-based collective whose whole building was demolished because of arson, was able to recover and continued to thrive as one of the oldest women's bookstores for a long time. After the arson, without large-scale free labor and the continuing support of volunteers, it would never have reopened its doors.

CHALLENGES WITHIN: SEPARATISM AND RACISM IN THE WOMEN'S MOVEMENT

Many in the women's movement made every effort to build "women-only" institutions, such as women's bookstores. Women regarded separatism as a purposeful activity that offered a place to heal, define, develop, empower and connect women.[46] For them, it promised to provide all women with a space that freed them from oppression. However, such separatist practices often alienated men as well as other "potential sympathizers."[47] In 1977, a transsexual recording engineer named Sandy Stone was working at Olivia Records, which needed a recording engineer with skills and experience to help their fledgling all-women's recording studio. However, separatists threatened a boycott of Olivia products and concerts because they did not regard Sandy Stone as a woman.[48] In 1980, when a Black lesbian musician appeared with a male accompanist, tomatoes were thrown at her.[49] Zuelma, a Black feminist collective, immediately responded to the incident, noting:

> Many white women have the mistaken notion that there is only one women's community and that its needs and goals are a reflection of white society. This premise is not only narrow, [but] it is incorrect. The presumption of separatism is one that we, as Third World women, vehemently object to. On a day-to-day basis we have consistently fought against and been the victims of separatism in the form of racism. Because of our history, we can not afford to separate ourselves from Third World men. . . . To cut ourselves off from Third World men and to turn our backs on the problems of racism in this society would be akin to suicide.[50]

Emphasizing that many white feminists who supported separatism simply assumed that the concerns and objectives were the same for all women, Zuelma claimed that, in doing so, they ignored racism: women of color had to face racial discrimination every day, and separatism did not offer any way to address racism in society—rather, it disguised the fact that women of color had to struggle with racism in addition to sexism. Thus, separatist practice was criticized not only by those outside the women's movement but also by those within. Indeed, some of the strongest anti-separatist voices within the movement emerged among women of color, especially Black lesbian feminists. Making note of recent shootings of five anti-Klan demonstrators in Greensboro, North Caroline, the shootings of four Black women in Chattanooga, Tennessee, and a nine-year-old Black girl in

Wrightsville, Georgia, Joan Gibbs and Sara Benette claimed in 1980 that women of color "are not part of such a lesbian community . . . [of separatists] but instead one which manifests all the problems of the 'US' as a whole."[51] In fact, separatism practice tended to exclude women of color not only as "potential sympathizers" but also as powerful supporters of feminism. African-American women have always held comparatively more favorable views of the movement than have white women: 60 percent versus 37 percent in 1970; 77 percent versus 65 percent in 1980; and 85 percent versus 64 percent in 1989.[52] Moreover, when many heterosexual Black women were still reluctant to identify themselves as feminists, Black lesbian feminists such as Audre Lord, Pat Parker, Margaret Sloan, and Barbara Smith played a crucial role in building the women's movement by providing their voices through their books. Their oeuvre broke significant new ground because "it was explicitly socialist, addressed homophobia, and called for sisterhood among Black women of various sexual orientations."[53]

In 1977 Barbara Smith issued a position paper called "The Combahee River Collective: A Black Feminist Statement," asserting the legitimacy of feminist organizations of Black women and rejecting separatism.[54] It says:

> We believe that sexual politics under patriarchy is as pervasive in Black women's lives as are the politics of class and race. We also find it difficult to separate race from class from sex oppression because in our lives they are most often experienced simultaneously. . . . Although we are feminists and lesbians, we feel solidarity with progressive Black men and do not advocate the fractionalization that white women who are separatists demand. Our situation as Black people necessitates that we have solidarity around the fact of race, which white women of course do not need to have with white men, unless it is their negative solidarity as racial oppressors. We struggle together with Black men against racism, while we also struggle with Black men about sexism. As we have already stated, we reject the stance of lesbian separatism because it is not a viable political analysis or strategy for us. . . . We must also question whether lesbian separatism is an adequate and progressive political analysis and strategy, even for those who practice it, since it so completely denies any but the sexual sources of women's oppression negating the facts of class and race.[55]

Thus, Black feminists started to articulate a clearly feminist and powerfully antiracist political point of view of the women's movement.

Claiming that the history of American feminism had primarily been a narrative about the heroic deeds of white women, Black feminists contended that some white women claimed racial justice as a priority, but many consistently failed to acknowledge the widely different historical, material, and cultural realities between themselves and women of color, and asserted that racial problems within the women's movement were both the reflection and the result of the racism of the larger American culture. Consequently, for the first time, racism within the women's movement began to be seriously and openly discussed. Black feminists also claimed that feminist publishing communities were dominated by white, middle-class women. In the late 1960s, women started their own publications promoting their rights. This was not, of course, the first time. Women had already started their own publishing houses of the women's rights in the early 19th century. However, they might not have served all women. Catherine Mitchell argues that historians must ask whether or to what extent "these newspapers crusaded for the rights of all women, and consider moving toward cultural history, a perspective which could enable them to incorporate the notion of privilege."[56] Louise Michele Newman also emphasizes that Susan Anthony and other white women shared feelings that a great injustice had been done them when Black men received the right to vote ahead of them; such envy and ill-feeling diminished the possibility for interracial cooperation between the groups struggling for civil rights and woman's rights.[57] It is crucial to note who was the primary definer and beneficiary of woman's rights at that time. Even in the 1970s, numerous political, particularly feminist publications were published by predominantly white, middle-class women.[58] Mitchell also suggests that historians should examine the interaction among the white, upper-income editors and American women who were from the working class, who were women of color or otherwise of minorities.[59] Although in the period of 1968–1988, over eighty among fifty hundred women's periodicals were published by and for African-American, Asian, Latina, and Native American women, the establishment of their own periodicals was conditioned by the fact that works of women of color had been generally marginalized by tendencies toward racism and classism of white feminists and their media.[60] At first feminist publishing houses did not seek out writing by African-American feminists and lesbians.[61] Responding to the strongly WASP tone of much early feminist literary history, Barbara Smith contends:

> I think of the thousands and thousand of books which have been devoted by this time to the subject of Women's Writing and I am filled with rage at the fraction of these pages that mention Black and other Third World women. [62]

Black women identified alternative and white-controlled feminist presses as just as likely sites for literary disenfranchisement as mainstream houses because they "had no options for getting published except at the mercy or whim of others."[63] Erlene Stetson, who teaches courses on Black women writers, also points out that Black women's writings are "mostly out of print," and "too many Black women writers have disappeared, and countless others have never been permitted to sing in public."[64] Along similar lines, it has been noted that white women sold books about "inaccurate" or "distorted" Native American spirituality.[65] Furthermore, these sold "more copies than all books by Native writers combined because they have the white privilege and power to make themselves heard at the expense of Native Americans." [66]

In addition to the friction and the distorted images of feminist writings about women of color, women of color had "experienced a lot of negative things trying to get our work published, particularly in a feminist context."[67] Furthermore, Joan Gibbs and Sara Bennett also claim:

> [T]he white, middle class dominated lesbian publications, publishing "special issues" on "Third World Women," or "Racism and Classism" instead of opening up their pages to all of the women in our community all of the time. Another way that racism, in particular, but also classism is exhibited is in the issues we choose to work on or support. Many women in our community for example openly refuse to work on any issue that is not entirely a "lesbian issue." Such issues as public hospital closings, gentrification, police brutality, the rise of the Right, etc, are lesbian issues, in our opinion . . . [68]

In fact, "out" lesbians of color especially found it difficult to get their works printed.[69] It was not until 1974, with the publication of Ann Aller Shockly's *Loving Her,* that the first open and explicitly lesbian novel written by a Black woman appeared in print. Usually, Black women could not be open about their sexual preference for fear of bringing "shame" on their families and finding themselves ostracized by the larger Black community—"both of which they were psychologically dependent upon and committed to from birth, as a means of survival in the hostile white world."[70] Therefore, it was not surprising that Shockly received harsh criticism from African-American male reviewers who, "rather than focusing on the literary problems with the novel, instead vented their sexist and homophobic rage."[71] Thus lesbians of color had to risk the loss of family and ethnic-community support for the less certain support of the white lesbian community.

Claiming that women's rights more generally were intimately connected to lesbian/gay rights, lesbian feminists in this way published a variety of articles noting what they saw as a problem. However, white, middle-class lesbian feminists often failed to connect such lesbian/gay rights to the experiences of women of color—and, by implication, to the rights of people of color and working class people in general. For example, it is reported that the lesbian community in a city where one-third of the population was Mexican-American consisted of predominantly (non-hispanic) white lesbians in the early 1980s.[72] Dana Shugar found that while separatist fantasy novels flourished from the early 1970s to 1980s, of all separatist utopias written between 1960 and 1990, not one was written by a woman of color or envisioned a utopia for women of color.[73]

It should be noted that many white lesbian feminists like Adrienne Rich made efforts to create both a literature and a practice of resistance to racism, and attempted to form substantive alliances across race with women of color writer/activists. There were always questions as to whether the predominantly white feminist publications accurately identified issues of vital concern to Black women's lives, or marketed its books in order to reach this audience successfully. It was clear to Black feminists that, in order to confront racism in white feminist publishing as well as sexism and heterosexism in Black publishing, they had to have their own press. Barbara Smith, Audre Lorde, Cherrie Moraga, Hattie Gosset, and Myrna Bain had a meeting in Boston in November 1980 and then, a year later, they officially founded Kitchen Table: Women of Color Press (KTWC) in 1981 to publish writings by "Third World women," particularly lesbians. Smith says:

> The founding [of KTWC] was partially motivated by our need, as Third World women, to have complete control over both the content and the production of our words—control which is usually not available even when working with feminist and alternative publishers.[74]

In this way, "Third World women" quit waiting for white feminist and alternative publishers' "whim" or "mercy," and began to fill their own needs. Meanwhile, Smith edited her and others' writings in *Home Girls: A Black Feminist Anthology.* Persephone Press, a "white women's press," planned to publish it as well as *This Bridge Called My Back: Writings by Radical Women of Color,* edited by Cherrie Moraga and Gloria Anzaldua. After Persephone Press collapsed into bankruptcy in May 1983, the editors had to struggle to regain the rights to publication. This problem confirmed Smith's belief that women of color need to control the entire process of book publishing.[75]

They chose as their target audience "the most difficult audience to reach."[76] Smith said that they wanted to reach those who were "not white feminists, lesbians, and gay men," but people of color who "may never have related to the women's movement, who may indeed be homophobic," and that they wanted to "shake up."[77] Audre Lorde, one of the founders of KTWC, also tried to "shake up " whole feminist communities by writing and speaking frequently about the racism, classism, and heterosexism that blinded—and continue to blind—the feminist movement. Without truly acknowledging and grappling with the very real, material, often definitive differences between women, Lorde reasoned, the ideal of "sisterhood" would remain an empty fantasy. She believed that dealing with difference would not only sustain connections between women of different nationalities, classes, religions, races, ages, and sexualities but eventually enrich them individually and collectively. In this connection, Carol Seajay reported about the Second Women In Print conference in Washington, DC in 1981 where many women helped fundraising for KTWC:[78]

> This conference was very different from the one five years ago in that women-of-color were a strong and vital force. . . . there was rich and solid consciousness about race, class and disability—you will be feeling and seeing the effects of these conversations over the years to come.[79]

Bearing out Seajay's prediction, KTWC published renowned books by and for women of color one after another. They included works such as *Home Girls: A Black Feminist Anthology, This Bridge Called My Back: Writings by Radical Women of Color, Camp Notes and Other* Poems (by a Japanese American), and *The Combahee River Collective Statement: Black Feminist Organizing in the Seventies and Eighties.* These included books written not only by Black women but also by other women of color such as Japanese Americans. Accordingly, the inclusion of these multi-ethnic and multi-racial writers constituted crucial work to overcome any tendencies for Black lesbians' isolation and to build an inclusive women's community.[80] As Norma Alarcon has noted with regard to one of the books, "There is little doubt . . . that *This Bridge* has problematized many a version of Anglo-American feminism, and has helped open the way for alternate feminist discourses and theories." [81] These works were not only "instrumental in theorizing the complex relationship between different axes of identity oppression, but also permanently demystified literary composition, textual production, and political activism for a class of people whose words and actions have historically been censured or silenced."[82]

Their writings became a revolutionary tool, "a vehicle for shaping ideology which serves as a foundation for making practical social and political change."[83] For example, *This Bridge Called My Back* has since sold in excess of 86,000 copies, and won the Before Columbus Foundation American Book Award for 1986. These writings have literally transformed the conversation on racism, sexism, and homophobia in the classroom over the last decade.[84] Alice Walker published *The Color Purple* in 1982, and became the first Black novelist to win the Pulitzer Prize the next year. Her book went on to become a national bestseller. Later *Seventeen Syllables and Other Stories,* by Hisaye Yamamoto, a Japanese American poet, was published by KTWC in 1988. It was purchased by the Quality Paperback Book Club, which was the first time a lesbian feminist press has sold a title to major national book club. In the same year, Toni Morrison won the Pulitzer Prize.[85]

The emergence of women of color in feminist publishing communities, which was embodied by the creation of KTWC, was successful in bringing forth the voices of a wide range of people of color. Consequently, their works made "a difference in the lives of women of color in the 'real world," and brought "some more understanding of the issues and realities of the lives of women of color."[86] The visibility of writings by and for women of color as well as lesbians of color encouraged all people of color. In "Leaving the Shadows Behind," in a piece in *In the Life: A Black Gay Anthology,* Joseph Beam wrote:

> I was fed by Audre Lord's *Zami,* Barbara Smith's *Home Girl,* Cherrie Moraga's *Loving in the War Years,* Barbara Deming's *We Can Not Live Without Our Lives,* June Jordan's *Civil Wars.* . . . Their courage told me that I, too, could be courageous. I, too, could not only live with what I feel, but could draw succor from it, nurture it, and make it visible.[87]

In this way, even aside from writers who were women of color, Black gay writers were profoundly influenced by the works of lesbians of color in connection with their experience of being both Black and gay. However, not only people of color but also white women were encouraged by "angry, strong, incredible women's voices."[88] The popularity of Black women's materials was clearly reflected in the sale of Black women's materials in many women's bookstores that undoubtedly benefited from the rising prominence of writings by women of color.

In fact, feminism as a movement had already lost much of its momentum since the late 1970s, although its cultural and intellectual influence continued to increase. Writings about feminist politics did not sell as well as they had previously.[89] The 1982 annual birthday statement of Old Wives'

Tales pointed out that since the emergence of "Reagonomics and repression have hit women. . . . we see these changes inside the bookstore too: sales dropping for feminist and lesbian periodicals . . ."[90] On the other hand, the sale of Black women's materials was rising, and it became a valuable vehicle to compensate for the loss as well as a crucial factor contributing to the prosperity of feminist publishing communities. For example, in 1981 Old Wives' Tales had sold over 300 copies of *This Bridge Called My Back* in just four months. Lammas Women's Shop, in Washington, DC, sold 172 copies of *Color Purple* during 1984, and it was ranked first among Lammas' bestseller lists of 20 books that year.[91] Also included on the bestseller list were *Home Girls, Zami: A New Spelling of My Names* by Audre Lorde, and *In Search of Our Gardens* by Alice Walker. At Women & Children First, *The Color Purple* was still ranked first among the best-selling books of 1985, and *Their Eyes Were Watching God* by Zora Neale Hurston was ranked the fourth in fiction.[92] On the other hand, without the earlier creation and development of the feminist book market, the readership for works by Black women would have been unable to sustain such a proliferation of feminist publishing houses. For example, as for *FBN,* two-thirds of the first issue published in 1976 was allocated to information on materials by and about women of color. It also introduced materials in Spanish, bilingual or multicultural books, as well as interracial books for children. Judging from the articles published in *FBN* over two decades, feminist booksellers, at least *FBN,* seemed to try to be sensitive about materials by and for women of color. In particular, *FBN* continuously promoted race consciousness among feminist booksellers, and encouraged them to reflect it in their stocks. Furthermore, from time to time, *FBN* reported on feminist bookstores that were tackling racism in their community. For example, in 1978, *FBN* published an article about racism in the community of A Woman's Place in Portland, Oregon. Noticing racism in the lesbian bar in their community, which discriminated against Black women customers, A Woman's Place in Portland spent "an entire week talking about the issue."[93]

Entering the 1980s, many women's bookstores began to offer materials by and about women of color as one of their missions in their communities.[94] For example, New Words in Cambridge, which was established by white women, released the 1986 annual statement, and it announced that they developed new sections including "Third World and International Women, Jewish Women, Lesbian Fiction, and Spirituality, and Women and Abuse."[95] The 1988 statement also says:

> Sections within the store have expanded from the early ones like fiction, poetry, biography, feminist presses, history, politics, mystery, and

> non-sexist children's book to ones that reflected changes in the women's movement, in publishing, and in our own growing commitment to issues of race, class, and ethnic diversity. . . . Our diverse interests and backgrounds come together in our shared commitment to serve the women's community and to reach as many different women as we can.[96]

Like New Words, many other women's bookstores also started to develop their own sections of works of women of color along with the increase number of their works.

Many women's bookstores also started to support artists and activists who were women of color. From the establishment of women's bookstores, they offered authors' readings as one of the main store events. Numerous known and unknown women artists, especially local artists, were promoted in the stores. For example, from the beginning, Old Wives' Tales was willing to have women of color artists and activists appear at least once a month.[97] Since Alice Walker was one of the local writers, she was invited to read her works as early as 1979 at Old Wives' Tales when she was not a well-known author. Later, Alice Walker became one of the authors most supportive of the store and was a favorite on its shelves.[98] When it faced a financial crisis in 1993, Alice Walker sent a letter and offered to give a reading to reduce the bookstore's debt.[99]

It might be difficult to determine whether the expansion of writings of women of color in women's bookstores can be equated with the expansion of booksellers and customers in terms of race or class. This is because as Cherrie Moraga emphasizes, "One thing about books is that they can get places that bodies can't." Namely, while books written by women of color could get into places such as women's bookstores and, later, general bookstores, the bodies of women of color were rarely found there.[100]

Furthermore, this seemed to be intensified by separatist politics in the women's bookstores. Women who got involved in women's bookstores may not have explicitly subscribed to separatist politics, but their practices were clearly influenced by separatist theory—creating a safe space to promote the sisterhood and solidarity by using the exclusivity. The theory was often regarded as positive at women's bookstores because it did not overtly involve the denial of access to and from men or the withdrawal from "real society." It was, rather, not anti-male but pro-female, and it represented "an authentic attempt to communicate to and with those who care."[101] However, some feminist booksellers tended to be reluctant to make accommodations for men in their stores. For example, in the early 1970s books written by men were shelved under the title of "enemy" or "sensitive male."[102] Furthermore, in some cases, not only husbands or boyfriends of female workers or customers but also male children were not welcome. Women's bookstores in general had only women events. Their flyers announcing monthly store events often described them as for "women-only."[103] Therefore, in some women's bookstores, a male presence was usually regarded as "intrusive."[104] Even at Twenty Rue Jacob in Salt Lake City, Utah where separatism discourse was not used, "When men came in, particularly men who were not perceived as gay, conversation [among workers in the store] usually ceased and the atmosphere was tense until they left."[105] It also never changed the sign on the bathroom door for non-females, which read simply: "others."[106] Nevertheless, most of the women's bookstores did not employ hostile approaches to men, although they had to commonly deal with problems related to the separatist discourse. For example, they received materials that were only made available to "wimmin" or intended to restrict the sales to "lesbians." In *FBN* a woman asked how far feminist booksellers could go in respecting an author's wishes since some authors wanted to sell their materials to "wimmin" or lesbians only.[107] Women's bookstores also needed to decide how to deal with male customers in the area of their lesbian book section; otherwise, the problem might destroy a women's bookstore position as a safe space for women, especially lesbians. Selma, of the Bloodroot Women's bookstore in Connecticut, reported that the store had a small sign that said: "GENTLEMEN—We trust those of you who support women's self-determination will curb your curiosity about lesbian books and limit your browsing to other sections of the store. Thank you."[108] According to her, commonly, when men saw the sign, the effect of an "electric shock-physical recoil [was] evident." They got an argument from the man or from his girlfriend or wife, but they were determined that they did not want women who were browsing in this section to be embarrassed by those men who considered lesbianism titillating, and they thought that some men had made the sign necessary.[109]

However, it was apparent that separatism discouraged not only men but also some female customers in the women's bookstores, in particular, women of color. First, women of color found that some women's bookstores were indifferent or insensitive to racism, even though women's bookstores shelved women of color writings and developed the women of color sections. For example, in 1979 one woman of color challenged racism in the women's bookstores. She wrote:

> People are visually stimulated. Pictures, posters, calendars, and book covers that only portray white women do several harmful things: they

> reinforce the idea that the feminist movement is a movement only of white women that addresses only white women's needs; and the invisibility of women of color in the items in the store does absolutely nothing to encourage peoples of color to use the store as a resource.[110]

Showing the fact that in the bookstore pictures of women of color were rarely seen on posters and calendars, she demanded more materials by and about women and people of color not only be shelved but also displayed. Andy Smith also noted:

> The most disturbing aspect of these racist practices is that they are promoted in the name of feminism. . . . I can't open a feminist periodical without seeing ads with little medicine wheel designs promoting white "feminist" businesses. . . . And I certainly can't go to a feminist bookstore without seeing books by white women promoting Native spirituality. . . . If white feminists are going to act in solidarity with their Indian sisters, they are going to have to take a stand against Indian spiritual abuse. Feminist book and record stores selling these products, and feminist periodicals should stop advertising these products.[111]

In this way, Smith reminded feminist booksellers should be cautious that "not sexist" materials written by white "feminists" should be "not-racist" at the same time.

Furthermore, the "exclusivity" used to promote the sisterhood and solidarity and to "communicate to and with those who care" had its downside.[112] It hindered the diversity of customers as well as booksellers. Regardless of gender, historically, publishing industry including bookstores attracted white, middle-class people despite of the low salary. Women's bookstores were no exception. For example, when New Words started, a collective of four women consisted of "strangers introduced by mutual friends."[113] Yet, while "strangers," they were all very similar backgrounds. Two of them had professional jobs (an optician and a genetic geologist), and the others were pursuing higher degrees in graduate schools like Harvard University.[114] Women's bookstores were invariably a place where homogeneous women got together because of the nature of the bookstore; knowledge of books, moreover, constitutes a form of "cultural capital" of the sort analyzed by scholars such as Pierre Bourdieu.[115] Consequently, members of women's bookstore collectives often consisted of white middle-class and, commonly, well-educated women.[116] As a collective member of Twenty Rue Jacob says, it was unfortunately true that "there was usually more of an effort to include PLUs (people like us) in any casual conversations."[117]

What is worse, "PLUs" in Twenty Rue Jacob often meant only white lesbians. As a result, virtually all of the regular clientele at Twenty Rue Jacob were white lesbians. Gibbs and Bennett also contend:

> Perhaps the most obvious way that racism and classism manifest themselves in the lesbian community is in the ownership and control of our resources. Almost every bookstore, restaurant, bar, magazine, newspaper, etc. that is owned by lesbians is owned by white middle class lesbians. And although a large number of these resources are allegedly for all lesbians, Third World lesbians, in particular, and poor lesbians, in general, have very little access to them. . . . Then too, a lot of the time, most of us are not even considered or around when "all lesbians" or "all women welcome" events occur because a large majority of lesbian festivals, conferences, concerts, for example, are either too expensive, too far away, or require time off work that those of us without jobs or with inflexible ones can't attend.[118]

The "all white lesbian" collective members in the women's bookstores, in this way, were seen as having reflected their customers' race and, presumably, their sexuality as well.

A collective member of Twenty Rue Jacob, also noted, "I want everyone to be, to feel welcome in there. Right now I don't think the Black women feel welcome in there. . . . Because they're not political and they have no reason to be political . . . Black women don't consider themselves lesbian—not the ones in Salt Lake. Because to them—lesbianism is this big white thing."[119] Her view on Black lesbians clearly shows there was a big difference even among lesbians—between white lesbians and lesbians of color. Actually, Gloria Anzaldua writes that "'lesbian' is a cerebral word, white and middle class, representing an English-only dominant culture, derived from the Greek word lesbos . . . ' Lesbian' doesn't name anything in my homeland."[120] Moreover, although women's bookstores' primary focus was on feminism, not on lesbianism, given the visibility of lesbians in some women's bookstores, there were some heterosexual women who also felt isolated.[121] For example, many women's bookstores represented itself as "feminist first," although "some shoppers sometimes refer to them as a "lesbian bookstore."[122] Twenty Rue Jacob was not exceptional in this regard.

This didn't seem to be threatening to them at first since lesbians constituted a decidedly literate consumer niche in women's bookstores. For example in the early 1990s, lesbian books often constituted forty to sixty percent of their sales.[123] However, the generation gap among lesbians was getting wider, and their diversity was also becoming greater. This was partly related to the fact that many young lesbians started to see themselves not solely as lesbians but rather "queers" who were more likely to associate with gay men, bisexual or transgendered people, along with the emergence of so-called "lesbian chic" among young, urban, fashion-conscious lesbians. As Rebecca Cragin points out in her "Post-Lesbian-Feminism: Documenting 'Those Cruddy Old Dykes of Yore,'" lesbian communities have become increasingly diverse and "the 'women's culture' that defined lesbian communities in the 1970's and 80s came to be rejected in activist, academic, and social settings."[124] As a result, in the 1990s many women's bookstores found they could no longer merely add "lesbian" customers, which had historically been core to many women's bookstores. Therefore, most women's bookstores could not have survived in the 1990s, if they were seen solely as "lesbian" sites in their communities. The collective members of Twenty Rue Jacob were well aware that "lesbians are there for a sense of community or connection, but that non-lesbians are there to buy books or food."[125] According to the collective members, "When non-lesbian feminists did come in their presence was greeted with enthusiasm and hope"; however, eventually they were not able to appeal enough to non-lesbian customers, let alone men.[126] Even, however, the "sisterhood" among lesbians they had felt they could count on became questionable among them over time. One member said, "We have a pseudo thing and I'm not really sure of what it is—not really sure. . . . when business is going okay, sisterhood—providing a common connection—emerges as the paramount organizational goal. . . . but when business is poor 'being a business' AS A MEANS OF SURVIVAL BECOMES THE PARAMOUNT GOAL."[127] Twenty Rue Jacob closed its doors after four years of operation.

Receiving criticism from women of color in particular, and later noticing the changes of the women's communities and the importance of appealing to as wide a range of women as possible, many women's bookstores have continued to face a fundamental question—why were there no or only a few women of color or heterosexual women?[128] In the 1980s, to resolve this at least partially, many women's bookstores started to intentionally hire a wide range of women, in particular, women of color. In 1983 New Words in Cambridge, which was started by four white women, had a new collective member, who was African-American.[129] An advertisement for job opening at Old Wives' Tales in 1984 said, "We are particularly interested in applications from third world/women of color."[130] It started as a co-ownership of two women, but later it became a collective, which included at least two women of color. In 1985, among five collective members, there were three women of color (Chinese (Hong Kong),

Brazilian, African-American).[131] Nevertheless, several customers sent letters to them protesting discrimination, including racism, at Old Wives' Tales over the years. One customer says:

> I am African-American. I was made to feel unwelcome by the salesperson . . . she did so with contempt, crudely as though this were invasive! . . . there are many ways whites show contempt for non-whites, body language . . . such as hate-stares and non-acknowledgement . . . the incident I described here is NOT an isolated one, similar incidents happen periodically at Old Wives' Tales . . . I submit this letter for your consideration and discussion.[132]

Later, at least twice, Old Wives' Tales received letters about racism in the store from customers.[133] In particular, in October 1992, an incident regarding a mistaken accusation of theft became the occasion for a boycott by lesbians of color due to the unsatisfactory response of the store. In March of the same year, Old Wives Tales lost an eleven-year collective member, who resigned. Her resignation letter clearly points out racism in Old Wives' Tales. It says:

> I enjoy being a bookseller and always thought that I had found my life's work in this field. However, I am totally burned out. . . . and last but not least the struggles around racism (all issues) but specially the inability of some white women to accept leadership from women of color. . . . the bookstore goal for many years is to have at least 50% of the collective and staff be women of color. I request that you put it in the manual now, so that it won't be forgotten. OWT is and will continue to be an important part of my life and community.[134]

Her resignation was presumably a serious blow to the store that already had a financial crisis.[135] Old Wives' Tales, which used to be one of the most successful women's bookstores and was known for the "outstanding service to the women of San Francisco" for 19 years, closed its doors just before its 20th anniversary, October 29, 1995.[136] As Adam Hochschild of *Mother Jones* points out:

> Despite the sweeping nature of their world views, alternative media still appeal mainly to white, well-educated, middle-class people under forty . . . but one thing we'd probably all agree on is that any American movement for social change that really gets off the ground must include a range of people far broader than the middle-class group of men and women who read this magazine.[137]

Women's bookstores needed to expand their customers not only for social change but also for their survival under such economic and political situations. As Barb Wieser of Amazon Bookstore pointed out, it needed a "broader community to survive" as well as a "broader community resource."[138] It can be difficult to establish a separate space in which to define, develop and establish a women's culture when not enough women support the efforts to make it a viable business entity. Including more women of color, working class women, and all kinds of feminist sympathizers as customers was an absolute and unconditional mission for them. To make it even more difficult, women usually had less money than men, and only a small minority of the latter patronized them with any regularity. Some women's bookstores did not succeed in efforts to appeal to a wide range of women; however, others were able to succeed by negotiating the problems of their clientele and by appealing to as wide a range of women as possible.

CONCLUSION

In the backlash against feminism of the 1980s, women had to face the fact that achievements by women during the 60s and 70s, such as establishments of feminist organizations and women's centers, were at risk. On the other hand, as Thomas Scheff has argued, the maintenance of social bonds is the "most crucial motive" for humans, and threats to social bonds generate intense feelings.[139] Under attack, women's bookstores constituted the space for "the maintenance of social bonds," and a rare and hard-to-find place to allow women such as "an 'out' feminist or lesbian feminist to discuss, explore and acknowledge women."[140]

Women's bookstores also proved problematic as a "women-only space" because the concept of building "women-only space" was tightly bound to the concept of separatism.[141] The most vocal criticism of separatism came from Black feminists. Women's bookstores, which were operated predominantly by white women, needed to focus on differences among women as a way of recognizing the connections among as well as the additive effects of multiple systems of oppression and domination. In the process, Black lesbian feminists came to successfully establish their own press; their works came to be widely circulated, well recognized and praised, while the Left and other feminists steadily lost political momentum in the 1980s. However, understanding the view that race, class, gender, ethnicity, and sexuality form "interlocking systems of oppression" did not always affect feminist institutions' actual practice.[142] At the same time, as Barbara Smith points out, it is conceivable that the women's movement is "one of the few places in this society that people of different racial and nationality backgrounds actually do interact with some commitment above and beyond window-dressing or superficial things."[143]

Women's bookstores needed to expand their customers by opening up to as many kinds of women as possible, not only for social change but also for their survival. The persistent tensions over separatism, racism and desired clientele indicate that women's bookstores were a rare place to negotiate differences, commit to eliminate various kinds of oppression and ensure openness, while they at the same time suffered from problems endemic to social life.

Chapter Six

Women's Bookstores in the 1980s Part II: Conflicts and Growth Beyond Backlash

During the openly hostile administrations of Presidents Reagan and George H.W. Bush, in addition to the loss of social programs and institutions helpful to women, feminist institutions including women's bookstores also received criticism for their internalized racism or classism. Furthermore, over the years, women's bookstores had to face other problems, which arose in running women's bookstores as business. As Myra Marx Ferree and Beth B. Hess point out, these external and internal challenges often brought about individual burnout and organizational collapse one after the other.[1] Since the late 70s, booksellers in general were facing "the greatest financial crisis since the depression of the thirties."[2] Particularly in the 1980s, the increase of postage and book costs made the average bookseller's profit less than 5 percent, putting them in economically harder situations.[3]

In spite of these realities, the number of women's bookstores steadily increased. In 1973 the number of women's bookstores was only nine, but by the end of the 1980s almost one hundred women's bookstores existed across the nation and in Canada. What made it possible for them to flourish? For example, it might be said that national education has played an important role as one of key factors in the growth of the publishing industry. In fact, the creation of the academic field of Women's Studies had a huge impact on the future of feminism as well as on women's publishing and bookselling. This chapter turns to the problem of how feminist booksellers managed challenges arising from the effort to conduct business based on feminist beliefs and examines the ways in which the creation of Women's Studies supported and affected women's bookstores.

CONFLICTS OVER FEMINIST PHILOSOPHY

In general, collectives refer to self-managed groups that have non-hierarchical structures of a few to a few dozen members, and which make decisions by consensus.[4] With work and responsibilities shared by women opposed to authoritative management styles exercised in "male-model capitalism," women attempted to remove hierarchy and pursue egalitarianism in their workplaces. Every woman involved was encouraged to participate in decisions that affected her life so that women could ideally put these central concepts into practice in their work environments. Many feminist organizations tried to "manifest this vision as microcosms of a new social order."[5] For example, *Off Our Backs,* a pioneer national feminist news journal since 1970, was and still is run by a collective. The "Statement of Purpose" of *Off Our Backs* says:

> [W]e are attempting to build non-exploitative ways of relating to one another based on trust and concern rather than political expediency. We have serious personal/political intentions in breaking down hierarchical and elitist structures, and for experimenting with leaderless groups and collective decision-making.[6]

In this way, working as a collective was generally a way to practice feminist ideology in feminist institutions, including women's bookstores, since the early 1970s. Under the slogan of "Sisterhood is Powerful," efforts toward unity among women occupied a central place in the feminist ideology of the 1960s and early 1970s. Working as a member of a collective also gave many of them a sense of unity.

As a result, many women flocked in the 70s to women's bookstore collectives. One collective member of Vancouver Women's Bookstore, which opened in 1973, says, "In the 70s, women fought to get into the collective. We had to split shifts to make room for everyone."[7] For women's bookstores with less capital, the increase of the number of the collective members meant more free labor as well as more loyal customers. However, the alternative working and management style of the collective itself also, ironically, discouraged working-class women from joining the collective in the women's bookstores. Trying to equalize their responsibility, collective members in women's bookstores minimized the division of labor, specialized knowledge, and status differences between participants so that they discouraged institutionalization of major differences in knowledge, status, and power.[8] Their action of rejecting professional status, which thus minimized differences between women, however, discouraged many working-class women or women with dependents from joining the women's bookstore collectives. How so? For many women, lack of assurance of training in specific work skills and potential individual control over their work constituted a problem. The rejection of professional status, from their perspective, was incomprehensible. In particular, like many feminist institutions, most women's bookstores in the early stages could not pay women even minimum wage so that, inevitably, many women could not afford to join collectives or do voluntary work, even should they wish to do so. Furthermore, working-class women were not always welcomed as customers nor were some community members in the women's bookstores. For example, some women in Full Moon collective, predominantly white and middle-class, felt that "'bar women' . . . have less commitment to feminist political identification and therefore do not necessarily view themselves as part of a larger community of women."[9] Their reason for taking such a position was that they tended to view working-class lesbians ("bar women") as following patriarchal culture in playing dual gender roles—and so considered them "politically incorrect."[10] Some collective members in Full Moon thought working-class lesbians did not come to the store and "would not feel comfortable there"—although they also felt that homogeneity (white, middle-class women) among collective members was indeed one of the collective's limitations.[11] Thus, class differences would presumably have negatively affected middle-class lesbian feminists' perception of "butch/fem" lesbians, who were mostly from the working class. As a result, women's bookstores often ended up discouraging working-class women including butch/femme lesbians from socializing at the women's bookstores.[12] Thus even though the collective was a new promising working and management style, it tended to attract women with similar educational and socio-economic level as collective members as well as customers. As a result, the "collective" often intensified the "exclusiveness" of its own members in the women's bookstores as "separatist discourse" did so. Therefore, collective members in the women's bookstores tried to establish them with the idea of offering a safe and free space where women could relax in comfortable, pleasant surroundings, with women's art works available, and removed from male-dominated environments, but for working-class and black women, women's bookstores were not necessarily a comfortable place.

Consensus decision-making was encouraged while any expressions to monopolize status or authority in the work-place were avoided because of its association with "male" capitalism. However, by attempting to create an alternative structure where work and responsibilities were shared equally, without the taint of hierarchy, were women in collectives successful in finding a "feminist" way to operate women's bookstores? In fact, women's bookstores collectives found many obstacles to operating the bookstores by implementing such an alternative working style. Conflicts actually grew out of the very structure of collectives. At first, as Jo Freeman's article, "Tyranny of Structurelessness," emphasized, homogeneity among workers tended to be fostered, and informal power structures which developed without a formal structure were often more difficult to negotiate than formal ones because organizational power accrues through informal mechanisms, particularly interpersonal networks—almost invariably constituted between those of common backgrounds.[13] Therefore, especially once more than two women became involved and the collective membership expanded, "interpersonal networks" controlled the organizational power. As Freeman shows, individuals in the feminist organizations were criticized and even expelled for acting "as if they were leaders," and intense face-to-face relationships among workers personalized conflicts and so made them emotionally painful.

According to Seajay, the reasons for conflict within collectives also varied—from finances, ownership and control, principles of unity, racism, class separatism, anti-Semitism, working conditions, and allowing men to come to bookstore programs to priorities for service and activities.[14] At the same time, such conflict should not surprise us, since the existence of a monolithic feminism or lesbian-feminist identity is impossible nor, presumably, advisable. Women's bookstore collectives could not escape internal conflicts over their members. Some conflicts and struggles emerged as urgent problems, which were often only resolved with the help of a professional feminist mediator.[15] Others remained unresolved or latent issues. However, conflicts between ideological differences tended to be more unresolved and complicated. For example, a conflict between "socialist women" and other women in A Woman's Place collective in Portland emerged when they created their mission statement in 1978. One collective member said:

> [Mostly socialist women]'s intention (privately but not publicly expressed) was to close the collective to women who do not espouse socialism. The original document contained more specifically Marxist rhetoric which was toned down in the final version. I could never assent to the statement paragraph that 'I cannot support any group or individual that does not acknowledge and respect the interdependence

> of these issues,' [this is because] the women who walk in here every day are extraordinarily diverse. Some have only begun to think about and make political choices. I'm not going to automatically withdraw my support from women who do not share some of may own political perspectives.[16]

In all nine "socialist women" would leave the collective. Even after conflicts ended, women's bookstores suffered from the effects. New collective members were usually invited to join the collective to compensate for the loss; however, they invariably needed to learn the operation of the bookstore from scratch. Such turnover often caused a lack of continuity in the operation of the bookstores, which resulted in confusion among collective members as well as customers. Sometimes conflicts resulted in the closing of bookstores due to the sudden absence of experienced workers. For another instance, an "exceedingly bitter, internal collective" dispute that occurred in ICI (Information Center Incorporated): A Woman's Place in Oakland continued over six years. The members disagreed over a number of issues such as ownership and control, racism, classism, separatism, anti-Semitism and more. One side of the collective tried to take control of the bookstore, and the other side filed a lawsuit and filed for a temporary restraining order. Carol Seajay who learned bookselling at ICI: A Woman's Place in Oakland said:

> [ICI: A Woman's Place in Oakland became] one of the six largest feminist bookstores in the country with no experienced staff. . . . During the course of the dispute, shopping in the store was very tense and community members were asked to take sides in the dispute. The collective were plagued with high staff turnover, inexperience, financial problems, and sorely divided customer base. Bridges were never mended, many of the store's previous customers never or rarely turned up to shop.[17]

Eventually all of the collective members left the store, the door of which closed in 1989. At any rate, once conflict among collective members emerged, it tended to be longer, complicated or destructive due to its non-hierarchal, leaderless, "structureless" structure.[18]

Even if collective members managed "non-exploitive, non-hierarchal, leaderless, structureless" structure and dealt with internal conflicts, they "often proceed, not surprisingly, at the expense of efficiency" in the women's bookstores.[19] For example, consensus decision-making may have empowered group members and challenge hierarchical structures of decision-making, however, participation in consensus decision-making was usually very demanding and time-consuming.[20] Over time, many collective members were not always willing to participate in this process, even though they were facing problems that needed immediate resolution. Common Woman Books, established in 1978, suffered from dysfunctional operations for a long time, and its collective disbanded in 1986. One former member of Common Woman Books says, "We formally were a large collective-run store which was great in many ways . . . but has the drawback in that if a decision was needed we could wait up to four weeks for the next collective meeting to finalize anything. . . . it's amazing how few people in the non-hierarchical world can grasp this group process!"[21] What is worse is that "while many wanted to take part in the decision-making process, not everyone wanted to take responsibility." As a result, the form of a bookstore might be collective, but in truth, it was "never really a collective."[22] The inefficiency also ended up forcing many women to overwork. Accordingly, many women became exhausted and left the stores. Every issue of *FBN* reported stores' opening and closings, but often explained that the reason for the closing was not so much financial failure as women's "burnout." In 1982 feminist booksellers held workshops about "Burn-Out." Seajay said:

> One of the exciting and passionate workshops I attended was the one on Burn-Out. We laughed (sometimes hysterically), told a few of our deepest, darkest secrets. The sharing was immense. This workshop 'changed my life' and is also changing the dynamics in my collective.[23]

Like other feminist organizations, almost all women's bookstores would not have been able to survive without "constant fundraising, donated labor, and donated supplies" supplied by their communities.[24] Karen Voltz of Sistermoon Feminist Bookstore & Art Gallery (Milwaukee, Wisconsin) reported that most volunteers in her store stayed one to two years and were extremely responsible.[25] Full Moon always had new volunteers who were recruited from among regular customers.[26]

While benefiting from free labor, heavily volunteer-run stores often experienced a high degree of turnover because volunteers who were unhappy with the way in which the collective was run easily dropped out. For example, Womanfyre Books gave as reasons for closing the store problems such as "severe staff burnout, high support volunteer turnover."[27] Toni Armstrong also points out, "[Volunteer turnover] creates a logistical nightmare when you're trying to run a business in a responsible way."[28] Although Common Woman, a women's bookstore in Alberta Canada had "a lot of volunteers," it closed doors in 1992 after 13 years of operation. In addition to "undercapitalizing, recession, and staffing problems," "there wasn't anybody willing to take on the management role for nothing," said Andrea Harbour, an early volunteer and later paid-manager of Common Woman.[29] However, as a collective member of Amazon Bookstore said, "Without [volunteer] support, our struggle would have been more difficult."[30] Without volunteers, no women's bookstores could have survived or, for that matter, have even been opened. Over the years, many women's bookstores increased or reduced their volunteers and respective numbers of collective members. At the same time, most of them preferred a "closed" or "core" group, in other words, a small number of collective members; yet they requested the help of volunteers in their community from time to time when they moved to a new location or had major store events.[31] It was, in fact, partially to avoid the prospect of relying too heavily on volunteers that many women's bookstores remained a collective. For example, the Amazon Bookstore, founded in 1970, came to be managed by a "closed" collective of ten women in 1980 after realizing that "working toward consensus [decision-making] could be hell."[32] Later, additional help was provided by women who volunteered of their time and energy.[33] In 1986 it was incorporated as a for-profit business with a manager. The store was owned by those who earned shares of stock as part of their compensation. The various managers and co-managers have changed several times since then.[34] Vancouver Women's Bookstore was also a volunteer-based collective from the start; however, after 14 years, it had a "core collective of three (Gloria, Kathleen, and Miriam) and a larger "fringe' of members who come and go."[35] After being in existence as a collective for eight and a half years, Common Woman Books dissolved the notion of the "collective as such," says a former collective member. Eventually, two or three women made the store's operational decisions, while many more gave support with ideas for specific projects and/or time as volunteers to sell books there on a regular basis.[36]

However, such a shift to a different operational style or sale into the hands of other women was not always made smoothly. For example, the battle over ownership of Womanbooks became a long and difficult legal struggle among the three founders. Eventually, one of the founders took over and was able to make Womanbooks one of the most thriving women's bookstores of the time.[37] Even when lovers started women's bookstores, they were not always successful.[38] Carol Seajay and her partner, Paula Wallace, founded Old Wives' Tales in 1976; however, they later broke up.[39] Wallace left, and Seajay formed a collective. Then, around 1982, Seajay invited another lover to join the collective, followed by another breakup a few years later. It affected daily bookstore operations and the other collective members negatively. "In the wake of this situation, Seajay was exhausted, burnt out, and eventually resigned the collective."[40] While the members changed from time to time, the collective survived and flourished until 1994.

Announcements of new women's bookstores in *FBN* in the 80s also clearly showed an increase in other forms of operational system. Lucille Pauline Frey's study of women's bookstores shows many of the women's bookstores of the 80s started from partnerships owned by a couple of women—"two co-owners who were not lovers, never were, and never planned to be," in a single proprietorship.[41] Karen Voltz of Sistermoon Feminist Bookstore & Art Gallery (Milwaukee, Wisconsin) says, "My clarity about who owns the store, what is expected, what will be tolerated and what they'll get in return is so 'clear' that hardly ever do bad feelings or misunderstandings result."[42] On the other hand, as Old Wives' Tales exemplified forming a collective sometimes offered a way for women's bookstores to recover from various crises such as burn-out and financial difficulties. When the women's bookstore called Thirty-first Street Bookstore in Baltimore was for sale by the owner, it was purchased by a collective consisting of 650 women, mostly lesbian feminists; what they held in common was their mutual interest in purchasing it "rather than seeing it going out of business."[43] Likewise, Alaska Women's Bookstore, owned by two women, was sold to women who formed a cooperative that gave people a way to support the bookstores by buying 100 shares for $100 each.[44] Thus, many women's bookstores that began as non-collective enterprises were later transformed into collective ventures, and survived as core communities for women.

Individual women sometimes went so far as to purchase bookstores to save them from closure. For example, in 1980 Edie Rosen bought Antigone Bookstore, which was founded in 1973 by three women.[45] Carol Seajay reported in *FBN* that Edie Rosen "had been a customer who finally realized that if the bookstore closed, it would be CLOSED . . . and so she ended up buying it, so as to run it and keep it open. She gets this month's *FBN* award for courage!" Rosen "expanded" it, and two years later Sue Sturtz bought it and then operated it "with careful management."[46] In 1987 Trudy Mills, formerly a sociology professor at University of Arizona, bought it, and "brought her academic connections with her," and Kate Randall joined it as a partner in 1990.[47] Mills says, "Each owner contributed something to help Antigone Books grow into what it is today."[48] In 2006, Antigone Bookstore still thrives as one of the oldest women's bookstores in the U.S.

These transformations of women's bookstores also evoke the trials-and-errors of feminist practices in the 70s and 80s. Most of them have thus in the process moved away from purely consensus-based decision-making among all collective members; in doing so, they have established hierarchical relations to some extent while developing flexible divisions of labor that provide women with some level of skills and responsibilities. By the mid-1980s, as Carol Seajay points out, "fewer of the new bookstores were being started by collectives and more were opened by triads, partners and/or lovers, and sole proprietors."[49] Lucille Pauline Frey's 1985 study of women's bookstores also demonstrated that only one-third were run by collectives, whose numbers ranged from three to twenty-two women.[50] Women's bookstores thus modified their operational style over the years. As the operational changes of Amazon Bookstore—which has now thrived for more than thirty-three years—demonstrate, the longer women's bookstores were in operation, the more they faced problems that demanded their transformation. If they did not have the capacity and flexibility to change, many of them would not have survived. Indeed, for similar reasons, other feminist institutions operated by collectives also started to modify the latter. As Schechter describes it, women's shelters increasingly became some form of modified collective or modified hierarchy.[51] In a sense, it is clear that the "*collective* was the way to be, or at least the name to have" for feminist institutions in the 70s.[52]

At the same time, even after entering the 1990s, the collective remained an option for operating women's bookstores. For example, women's bookstores such as In Other Words in Portland, OR (1993), and The Bluestocking in New York City (1999) started as collectives.[53] In spite of various and sundry tribulations, many women still found the collective to be a fundamental idea for feminist practice and, in this case, for the operations of women's bookstores. From this perspective, a collective still embodies an alternative method to challenge the traditional hierarchical structure of organizations.

A cartoon by Marian Lyndbrooke in *Rumbles* in 1980 describes one woman who is "sick of working in a collective" because "everybody seems to hate each other much of the time"—but when she then starts to see "Beauty Aids for You" advertisements on television, whispers, "By tomorrow, the collective will seem like a joyful alternative." As the title of the cartoon says, she realizes "We are not perfect yet."[54]

As changes and modifications in operational style demonstrated since the late 1970s, many feminist booksellers started to individually or, with a partner, own their bookstores. In fact, in the 1970s women in general were becoming self-employed at three to five times the rate of their male counterparts and launching businesses three times as frequently. The number of firms women owned jumped to 2.1 million in 1979 and 2.3 million in 1981—representing an increase of sixty-four percent in just nine years.[55] Sales at women-owned firms increased three times faster than those owned by men from 1977 to 1983.[56] They were generating a total of $98.3 billion in 1983.[57] However, many feminists could not help feeling reluctant to "make profits from women," or at least they disliked to be thought to do so. Actually, many early feminist publications, as forerunners in the feminist publishing communities, did not start their enterprises to make any profit and did not charge for their publications. For example, *Voice of Women's Liberation* was initially free. The price of *Our bodies, Ourselves* was reduced from 35 cents to 25 cents because of the conviction that it was wrong to make a profit from women.[58] Many feminists may have actually felt something "IMMORAL" about money so that money was a "much greater taboo than sex" in the women's community.[59] In fact, in the late 1970s some feminists such as Brooke William and Hannah Darby criticized such feminist ventures. They claimed:

> There is no such thing as a "feminist" business. What we have is female capitalism . . . . we cannot allow businesses to represent the women's movement or to advertise themselves as feminist any longer. What is necessary is that "feminist" businesses be seen (and advertised) for what they are—as businesses like any other—not as feminism or as any sort of solution.[60]

They said that "money stands between feminists" and that such operations were "no more than 'female capitalism.'"

Strong criticism, and sometimes hostility against "female capitalism" also led to violent incidents. Diana Press exemplified the controversy about money. In 1977, after having moved out to California, Diana Press met disaster after five years of successful publishing. Vandals destroyed thousands of copies of its books and poured paint, ink, chemicals and solvent into their machines, presses, and typesetting composers, making it impossible to do commercial work.[61] A press release from Diana Press says:

> In October 25, 1977. 5000 copies of *Plain Brown Rapper* by Rita Mae Brown were destroyed. They poured gallons of solvent and every other chemical available on the 5000 books plus ink and solvent on 4500 copies of the first page of *LESBIAN LIVES.* Pasted-up copy from early works like *Songs to a Handsome Woman* by Rita Mae Brown was

> destroyed. . . . The vandals were women. Because of their footprints—government agents, women in the movement who were opposed to Diana Press and a combination of agent provocateurs and women who felt they were saving the movement from "feminist capitalism."[62]

Even today, it is not known who the vandals were and why they destroyed the copies by Diana Press. A letter from Amazon Reality, a distributor of feminist materials, criticized the press, saying that "Diana Press did not conscientiously answer [the accusations about] the alliance with the Feminist Economic Network (escaping from valid criticism)," indicating that the disaster at Diana Press might be attributed to its involvement in "feminist capitalism."[63] Before the vandalism, criticism and hostility between Diana Press and women in the community were already reported in the local feminist press. It was apparent that women in the community saw Diana Press's involvement in Feminist Economic Network not only as an association of women's businesses aimed at sharing skills and resources but also at promoting "capitalism."[64] However, it should be noted that Diana Press was started by a group of working-class women in Baltimore, Maryland. From the beginning, they wanted to make their "business" both financially successful and feminist, and they became involved with many other feminist businesses around the country. They said, "We wanted the movement to include the kinds of jobs that ordinarily working class men have."[65] Unfortunately, their "business" was not welcomed in the Bay Area in California. Their idea, which stemmed from their identity as working class women, was not understood by some middle-class women in the community. Two years later, the press suspended publishing. Given cases like this, women involved in feminist ventures were, generally, extremely cautious about how they were viewed by the surrounding community of women.

Since feminist booksellers already knew that because "women's culture" has never been perceived to be "important enough, or valuable enough" to be given government funds.[66] Therefore, financial support as well as the physical help of women in their community was crucial to their survival. According to Seajay, collective members often wrote personal checks for books or magazines they wanted to see in the bookstore if the bookstore couldn't afford to buy them; in other words, "long-term financial planning had more to do with raising money or saving it out of sales to pay the rent than anything else."[67] Although talking about money might be a taboo, if women in the institutions did not ask for monetary support, it was apparent that their enterprises could not survive.[68] For example, in

1975 Bonnie Blush wrote "Empty Shelves at Labyris " in *Majority Report,* a feminist newspaper, about Labyris's lack of money to buy books, and asked for help from women in the community. Blush lamented the situation:

> The unfortunate truth is that their [women in Labyris] feelings of sisterhood have backfired. They will not hassle women to buy books, magazines, newspapers. So women come to the store. They eat lunch. They rap. They discuss their problems. They use the phone. But when it come to buying books, to putting money in a jar that sits on the front desk, sisters forget. But why? A feminist bookstore may not just be a bookstore but still it pays rent. And shelves have to be stacked with books.[69]

In a similar way, many women's centers, shelters, and health clinics also took seriously the need for grassroots community fundraising. Claire Reinelt points out that the considerable costs of running a shelter for battered women made "fundraising a high priority."[70] These feminist institutions could turn to foundations, corporations, or local and state governments to fund their programs.

Most women's bookstores, however, could not turn to these sources of funding because they were not non-profit organizations. Many feminists who started women's bookstores had to continue drawing on their personal finances to keep the operations afloat. In spite of their efforts, they often had to close their bookstores without getting back their initial investment. When Carol Seajay left Old Wives Tales, she could not recover her original investment, but some women were even left with great debts after closing their bookstores.[71] For example, Common Woman was left with a $20,000 debt. Unlike failed corporations that received bail-outs by the federal government, the two women at Common Woman "left holding the (empty) bag" and "took out personal loans to cover the losses."[72] Likewise, Moonyean Grosch closed Womansplace Bookstore in Phoenix, AZ, with $11,000 in debts.[73] She said, "[I] found a job managing a bookstore in Gainsville, Florida, which pays "real money—three or four times what I've ever earned before—so I should be able to pay off all my bookstore debts in a year or so. . . . I'm going to pay the women's and small presses first, naturally."[74] Once the price of *Our Bodies, Ourselves* was reduced from 35 cents to 25 in order not to make a profit off women, it was clear that outside financial support for the publication would be necessary. Eventually, the publication rights of *Our Bodies, Ourselves* were sold to a mainstream publisher, Simon and Schuster. Judy Norsigian, co-author of *Our Bodies, Ourselves* and one of the collective's founding members said, "Going to a capitalist publisher was one of our biggest struggles, but it was the only way to reach a mass audience."[75] The move proved to be successful. The book sold 11,000 hardcover and 850,000 paperback copies—eventually selling more than two million copies and undergoing translation into at least thirteen foreign languages.[76] At the same time, it was apparent to everyone involved that the move was not for purposes of "making money," because the book was sold at cost for free distribution by health groups, and at a special discount price for clinics.

Entering the 1980s, most feminist enterprises "were forced to confront the chasm between philosophical and political desires as feminists and economic need."[77] Although moral ambivalence about money was strong among feminists, they gradually realized they would not survive if they did not take care of their businesses themselves nor did not change their attitude toward "money" and reevaluate their understanding of the business. They not only needed money to feed them but also to buy new materials and pay rent. As a matter of fact, after *FBN* was published for just one year (1976), its expenses far exceeded its total income. Three years later, Carol Seajay could get only 35 of the 80 feminist bookstores to subscribe to the publication. Nett Hart, in her study "Taking a Slide," points out that the sliding-fee scale failed simply because "seldom is the scale realistic" and so often did not work.[78] Yet *FBN* was actually able to use the sliding-scale system for its subscription because of the advertising revenues of the literary industrial corporate establishment, which feminist booksellers referred to as LICE. However, before taking advertisements from LICE, *FBN* was continuously facing financial crises; Seajay reports that she had difficulties even printing *FBN,* let alone paying herself the minimum wage. Although those at the Women in Print conference had decided that whoever published *FBN* should be paid a salary, it was apparent that feminist booksellers (subscribers) alone could not support the operation.[79] Before Seajay started to take advertisements, she asked the opinion of subscribers, but there was seemingly no strong opposition. One woman, however, strongly recommended this step, saying:

> Contrary to popular belief, there is NOTHING IMMORAL about advertising . . . that is to say, communication between producers and consumers is essential to the success of feminist enterprises. There is nothing wrong with taking MONEY for printing advertising. Printing and mailing a publication COSTS a lot of MONEY . . . Too, remember that being paid MONEY $ does not mean that getting MONEY is your MOTIVE for your work.[80]

Seajay started to take advertisements from LICE, such as Doubleday and Harper & Row, in the same year. The rapid increase in the number of feminist publishers and mainstream publishers, which started to enter the new market in the early1980s, helped *FBN* to survive. For example, in 1985 subscription revenue was $7115 and advertising revenue $5600; the overall loss ($2250) was covered by loans. One year later, advertising revenues ($11200) exceeded subscription ones ($9000) and the loans were paid. Eventually, advertising revenues came to make up about 70 percent of all annual budgets. Consequently, *FBN* was able to sustain itself well enough to witness the flowering of women's bookstores in the late 1980s. If *FBN* had not taken advertisements from LICE, it would not have survived nor offered the sliding-scale system for its subscription. It was clear to feminist booksellers that getting financial help was a far more difficult task than getting physical help.

Thus, they became more aware of the "business" aspect of operating women's bookstores, even if their mission remained the same. Some had, of course, been aware of this aspect even earlier, as a 1975 March newsletter of *First Things First: Books for Women* in Washington, D.C, had noted:

> We seek viability—an income through sales that allows us to be self-supporting rather than dependent upon outside grants. We don't believe in volunteerism. For women to build a realistic economic base, we must realize our skills are not "for free," i.e. worthless. We shall support ourselves as workers![81]

Theresa Corrigan of Lioness Books in Sacramento, CA said, "I'm not in the business to make money. I need money to stay in business. I need money to expand my business. But my purpose is to change the world, to end sexism, racism homophobia, ageism, classism and all those 'isms' that threaten us."[82] A Woman's Place in Portland which declared not to pay women in its official statement, the "Basis of Unity," was criticized in that it did "not deal adequately with the issue of volunteerism" as a "volatile one." Rebecca, a worker at A Woman's Place said:

> There has been a real lack of continuity in the operation of the bookstores in part because we're not able to pay most of our workers. This in turn affects our ability to serve the community, because a new group of women are constantly relearning what's already known about running the store. . . . I'd personally like to see the bookstore set the hiring of more paid workers.[83]

Eventually, all of the women who had created the "Basis of Unity" left the bookstore in 1978. Moreover, when a collective member of Oracle in CA closed it in 1980, she left a message to FBN, which said, "We don't have enough womanpower, since no one is paid. . . . We're tired. Must give ourselves credit for maintaining a financially healthy, non-traditional business, want to close while we still feel good."[84] Seconbe-Eastland also shows in her study that women began to develop means to succeed by essentially bypassing the need to directly confront the apparent contradiction between feminist ideology and business practices/needs.[85] Thus by the end of the 1970s it became clear that feminist ideals and necessity were at odds with one another many feminist collectives. As we will see, they modified their methods of operating bookstores—and in the end, not only kept their bookstores open but also made their efforts healthy financially and psychologically.

Some feminist booksellers who opened bookstores tried not only to serve the needs of their community but also their own—to support themselves financially through operating the bookstore. Carol Seajay and Paula Wallace started Old Wives' Tales together with their own money, based in part on a loan from the Feminist Credit Union. While the enterprise was their own, and they hoped to be able to support themselves, they nevertheless had to deal with potential criticisms for doing so. Seajay, in an official statement concerning the store, noted:

> No one has any "capital" invested in the store. All the money came through a loan from the Bay Area Feminist Federal Credit Union. Neither of us feels she "owns" Old Wives' Tales, more that it is a community resource. Our agreement is that neither of us can take any of the store's assets if and when she leaves. . . . We are not geared to making lots of $ as a commercial profit-making enterprise. We find many contradictions in running a small business (service) under the present system. In trying to provide a service to the community and support ourselves, we are forced into a legal and political structure that defines us as owner, profit-making and capitalists, which is the opposite of our intentions. . . . How to deal best with such contradictions and the criteria for decision making is not always clear. We need and want discussion in these areas.[86]

It was apparently difficult for them to communicate to women in their communities that they were neither obsessed with profits nor operating as a collective. Since they were not "non-profit," they needed to verify that their intention was solely to pay themselves a "livable wage."[87] For example

Womanbooks in New York, one of the largest and strongest women's bookstores in the US for a decade, was sold to a new owner; after making changes in personnel in store policies and personnel, she was criticized for being "profit-minded," and faced boycotts and pickets by women in the community.[88] The store, which "any would call the flagship store of the women's bookstore movement," closed doors after only two years under new ownership.[89] In spite of such examples, women were increasingly comfortable with seeing their bookstores grow into "viable" businesses that could pay women.[90] For example, in 1980 Amazon Bookstore decided to pay regular members of the collective $64 monthly (for, minimally, 2–4 hours' work weekly) and two of the members a part-time rate of $4/hour.[91] In an *FBN* issue in 1981, Carol Seajay, reporting about the second Women In Print conference in Washington, DC, said, "All in all, it seems that the bookstores are sturdiest and have the most paid positions."[92] New Words also concluded, "We wanted a non-hierarchical work situation that would be supportive of our individual needs. We agreed that women should be paid for their work and so never used volunteers."[93] In one case, Common Woman, which started as a collective, incorporated in 1981 and eventually disbanded the collective in 1986. Then Andrea Harbour took on the task of managing the store for pay ($6/hour).[94] Thus, over time, women's booksellers started to pay wages to their workers and were usually proud to do so.[95] From their perspective, the ability to pay wages was evidence of good management and, moreover, it meant that their venture was successful. Women were required to gear the store towards a "business orientation."[96] Accordingly, *FBN*, which was devoted exclusively to information on books and the book industry in the 1970s, gradually started to focus more on "training & skills sharing" to get business "savvy" in the early 80s.[97] In 1985, it featured an article about purchasing computers to enhance business.[98]

In 1990 Women & Children First in Chicago became the first women's bookstore offering health insurance with a pension plan to their employees. This change presumably had some connection with their success, which continues in 2006. The bookstore, which was established in 1979 by Ann Christophersen (who has served as president of American Booksellers Association since 2002), and Linda Bubon, now carries more than 30,000 titles, and had become one of the most successful and thriving women's bookstores as of 2003.[99] Karen Mey, owner of Paradigm Women's Bookstore in San Diego, says, "[We] have learned through the 70s and 80s that things that are collective don't necessarily survive and although that would be ideal, nobody seems to be wanting to take it away from me as a business."[100]

Once women's bookstores proved themselves a "viable" business, many women who had left the women's bookstores for varying reasons came back, began their own ventures, or joined related enterprises. For example, Moonyean Grosch returned to Claire Light Women's Books in Santa Rosa, CA, after working for a year in a general bookstore to pay off her debts.[101] According to Seajay, "old [women's] bookstore workers never die" but they "just fade into another aspect of the [book industry] trade." Her old colleague, Pam Hicks, a manager of A Mind of Your Own Bookstore in Des Moines, IA, became a press operator in the offset press.[102] Kiriyo Sponner in Womanfyre Books in Northampton, MA, found a job in Crown Books.[103] Many others became librarians. It clearly shows that working experience in women's bookstores provided many women with job skills they could use in the book industry. More importantly, since many feminist booksellers could prove that women's bookstores are not economically unstable ventures, they provided a wide range of women with opportunities to join them. Thus improving the "business" aspect of women's bookstores may have modified their feminist principles to further accommodate capitalistic methods. This transformation allowed women's bookstores to offer competitive wages and benefits, and also provided working-class women, women of color, and women with dependents opportunities to work in women-only spaces. As a result, as Seajay says, "Women's bookstores in the 80s had less volunteer labor and more paid workers, and more books and fewer coffeepots."[104]

THE GROWTH OF WOMEN'S BOOKSTORES IN THE 1980S: THE CREATION OF WOMEN'S STUDIES PROGRAMS

Although feminist booksellers modified their structure and working style to serve women's communities better and stay alive, the 1980s were not generally kind to small independent bookstores. While the cost of books soared, booksellers' profit became less than five percent, and moreover the cost of freight and shipping soared. "The one thing that happened that we certainly hadn't planned on is the unbelievably high cost of books that hit in the very late seventies," says Bill Davis, of Bookstacks in VA, which went out of business in 1984.[105] Despite this problem, the number of women's bookstores was increasing, and many survived or even thrived.[106] In such politically and economically difficult times, it was no doubt that most women who were actually involved in the daily operations of bookstores and in the women's communities supported women's bookstores. Nevertheless, without stable financial resources, almost all women's bookstores—like other feminist organizations—would have closed their doors sooner or later. With the exception of fundraising efforts, the strongest financial support for women's bookstores seems to have been the expanding materials by and for women and the audience for these materials.

In the 1980s feminist publications moved from the margins to virtually the mainstream of the publishing industry. The feminist intellectual revolution had become successful in realizing audiences large enough to make it a financially viable area of the book industry. Black feminists successfully established their own press and developed a new audience in feminist publishing. Materials by and for women of color, international women, and Jewish women were constantly increasing. Along with the explosion of lesbian feminist publishers, lesbian materials including mysteries, romances, and works on lesbian and gay politics emerged. As *FBN*'s bestseller lists show, while in the 1970s women read the same books in women's bookstores throughout the country, with the increasing diversity among feminists and lesbian feminists in the 1980s the bestsellers at many women's bookstores increasingly had very little in common with each other, with the exception of works such as *This Bridge Called My Back* and *Color Purple,* which were popular in virtually all women's bookstores. Many women's bookstores also expanded categories on their own and in response to their communities; thus they added new categories in the 1980s that reflected their personal and social concerns, including book sections on violence and sexual abuse among heterosexual couples as well as homosexual ones, recovery from alcohol and chemical abuse, lesbian mothers, and AIDS, to name just a few.[107] However, it should be noted that the direction of national education constituted the key factor in the growth of the publishing industry.[108] As Anthony Collins noted, Black bookstores, which sold materials by and for African-Americans, prospered together with the rise of the Civil Rights movement and the establishment of African-American Studies.[109] Historically, publishers as well as bookstores have benefited from such developments. The creation of Women's Studies programs around the nation, which feminism inspired as a new academic program in the colleges and universities, came to provide golden opportunities for many publishers as well as booksellers.

While in the 1970s women witnessed the explosion of feminist publishing in forms that varied from pamphlets and newspapers to books, in the 1980s feminist publishing gained energy from different directions. Feminist publishing previously emerged from grass-roots organizations and small groups of women; however, entering the 1980s, it particularly flourished in academe with the development of Women's Studies programs.[110] This time, materials by and for women were mainly used not only as tools of communication among women, but also as tools for educating women in the colleges and universities. In 1964, forty percent of college-age Americans attended college. During the 1960s, on the heels of Sputnik and with the war in Vietnam (and the Baby Boom), colleges and universities underwent a rapid expansion. Like men, many women took advantage of these new opportunities through programs like Sarah Lawrence College's Center for the Continuing Education of Women established in 1960 as the first of its kind in the US.[111] By the end of the decade, institutions for returning students were established at most co-educational colleges and universities.[112] Moreover, by 1976, over 45% of college and university students were women.[113]

Women, witnessing or experiencing the rise of the women's movement off-campus, began to enter universities and colleges and form their own organizations there as well.[114] They also started to write a proposal for what they called a "Women's Studies" program in their respective academic institutions. This development also reflected women's ongoing desire to establish free spaces of their own. Although female teachers lacked institutional support as well as administrative power, they started to establish Women's Studies programs with the "cooperation of large numbers of equally determined and enthusiastic students."[115] In 1970, only two such kind programs existed in the US.[116] Florence Howe reports that by 1976 there were more than 270 programs and 15,000 courses spread across the campuses of 1,500 institutions.[117] By the end of the 1970s, a huge number of female students were eager to learn and to participate in the programs. It was not unusual for the first courses to attract more than one hundred students, and even those courses that began as small seminars often expanded rapidly beyond all expectations. For example, at the State University of New York at Buffalo, according to Elizabeth Lapovsky Kennedy, 1,400 female students enrolled in the Women's Studies program within a year of its inception.[118] Eventually, by the mid-1970s, between 10 and 33 percent of all women undergraduates enrolled in Women's Studies courses.[119] This development altered the curriculum and style of teaching and produced research that has shifted the paradigms and changed the content of most disciplines.[120] By the mid-1970s, some 850 teachers were already actively designing comprehensive interdisciplinary curricula for courses such as "Image of Women in Literature," "Sociology of Sex Roles," and "History of Women in the US."[121] As the Black Studies movement caused growth in interest among African-Americans in books by and for themselves, the creation of Women's Studies programs also produced a huge demand for books by and for women. Similar to the situation with the inauguration of Black Studies, for teachers of Women's Studies, most challenging in the beginning was the effort to find textbooks because Women's Studies is not simply the study of women but analysis of women that places women's own experiences at the center of study. Their frustration was due to the fact that neither male nor female scholars had as yet written any such work.

Soon many textbooks grew out of the classes taught by teachers in the early Women's Studies classes. One example was *Women: A Feminist Perspective,* one of the first major introductory textbooks, which was edited by Jo Freeman in 1975 and issued in its fifth edition in 1994. The first two editions of *Women: A Feminist Perspective* (1975, 1979) each sold some fifty thousand copies; with three subsequent editions, the total sales come to about two hundred thousand, making this probably the most widely used introductory Women's Studies text.[122] In 1983, a group of faculty at Hunter College in New York City published *Women's Realities, Women's Choices: An Introduction to Women's Studies* as a basic textbook for introductory Women's Studies courses. It covered "from the *Song of Solomon* by Toni Morrison to Judy Chicago, from the stages of labor in giving birth to the patterns of women's political participation around the world."[123] Eventually, it sold more than thirty-five thousand copies.[124] *This Bridge Called My Back* was originally compiled as a class reading in 1981. According to Marilyn Boxer, it also "exerted a major influence in Women's Studies."[125] Thus, many of the early textbooks were anthologies featuring largely unknown women's writings and were published by small publishers including independent, feminist, or university publishing houses. A steady increase in sales of books for use in programs of Women's Studies made this relatively new discipline a profit-maker for these small publishers. However, after small publishers took the initial risk, worked hard to prove there could be a healthy and profitable market for women's studies materials, and propelled the growth of the market, mainstream publishers started to eagerly publish them. As South End Press editor Ellen Herman points out, after small presses laid the ground work, "Mainstream publishers decided it was okay to publish Women's Studies materials."[126] Since many publishers found it a profitable business, the market as a whole has rapidly expanded.[127] As a result, today women will find a shelf devoted to women's issues; whereas in 1970, "the category did not even exist."[128]

Many university presses also started to establish a Women's Studies series, however, unlike mainstream publishers, they were not solely seeking profits in creating these series. For example, Indiana University Press had a political commitment to publishing in paperback and thus tried to keep prices down by taking consideration of women's traditionally low incomes.[129] Parallel with this development university-based feminist academic journals were born: *Signs: A Journal of Women in Culture and Society* (University of Chicago Press), *Feminist Studies* (based at the University of Maryland), and *Frontiers: A Journal of Women's Studies* (housed at the University of Colorado at Boulder). They played a crucial role in the development of feminist theory by providing a tool for women in academia to exchange ideas. Soon books about sexuality as well as gender flourished as well. It is no surprise that specialization in research has led to specialization in books, and in turn, to specialization in publishing programs. Consequently, according to Linda Garber's *Lesbian Sources,* published in 1993, 50 lesbian periodicals existed in the US of which twenty-nine were affiliated with universities.[130]

The market for textbooks also benefited women's bookstores. Not only did some of them become bestsellers but textbook sales came to constitute a crucial part of many feminist bookstores' revenues (15–30%),[131] and they also boosted cash flow during two of the stores' slowest months—September and January.[132] Sandi Torkildson of A Room of One's Own in Madison, Wisconsin, says in *FBN,* "You do make a lot of money [by selling textbooks]."[133] She was willing to share her strategies over five pages of *FBN:* from ordering and selling textbooks by showing her original order form for an instructor in an educational institution to building good relationships between stores and instructors.[134] Furthermore, textbook sales brought in not only cash but also students, professors and librarians who sometimes became the store's most loyal customers. Many students who came to buy the textbook learned for the first time of the existence of the women's bookstore in their community and, occasionally became part-time workers or dedicated volunteers.[135] Some professors, especially in Women's Studies, took students to tour the women's bookstores and, when doing so, taught them of the history of such bookstores and their connection with the women's movement; others gave students opportunities to work in the women's bookstores by offering class credit for their working experience. For example, Sara Luce Look, co-owner of Charis Books & More in Atlanta, "first discovered Charis when her Women's Studies teacher took the class on a field trip to visit the store, learn about its history, and its activist role in the early days of Women's Studies. Before that field trip, she was actually afraid to visit the store!"[136]

On the other hand, it was not surprising that there were many, especially conservatives, who did not like to see faculty members supporting women's bookstores. For example, a professor who picked *Oranges Are Not the Only Fruit* as a textbook, and placed the textbook order at Antigone Books in Tucson, AZ, was criticized by an "Arizona constituent" who made "vociferous complaints after her daughter was asked to read a novel with a lesbian character in Jeanette Winterson's *Oranges Are Not the Only Fruit,*" and to "go off campus to buy their course books at Antigone

Books" which was "outside the university bookstore," and "catering to lesbians."[137] Although textbook orders at Antigone fell by 50 percent due to the incident, sales later rose to about 75 percent of their former condition because a determined core of faculty members renewed their commitment to supporting Antigone and academic freedom. It kept the store's textbook sales alive.[138]

However, the flourishing of Women's Studies programs did not go unchallenged, even among feminists. Critics started to raise questions about the institutionalization of Women's Studies, criticizing academic feminists and seeking alternative forms of support and validation for feminism. For example, in 1984 Audre Lorde challenged the assumptions of white feminism, particularly within academic contexts.[139] Some feminist booksellers also point out that by the early 1990s a distance had developed between "common people's lives" and Women's Studies, particularly because books about feminist theory used as texts were increasingly inaccessible to women not initiated into abstruse theoretical perspectives.[140] Even today "the institutionalization of Women's Studies" still remains a controversial issue among feminists. Nevertheless, Women's Studies enabled large numbers of students in colleges and universities across the nation to read the writings of women. Presumably, many of these students would never have read the writings of women, in particular women of color and lesbians, if the Women's Studies programs did not assign them as textbooks. The "legitimization" of Women's Studies also helped the expansion of the existing publishing market for such works because university presses as well as commercial presses entered the market, which was both profitable and stable. Accordingly, they started to publish a variety of feminist textbooks including writings by women of color and lesbians. Among them, some bestsellers were also created. If Women's Studies programs had not been emerged, feminist publishers as well as women's bookstores would have almost invariably had more difficulty surviving in the 1980s.

In the 1970s commitments by teachers to Women's Studies were also crucial because they created "avid book buyers" who "vowed to buy every book ever published."[141] A 1986 Ford Foundation Report revealed the number of courses offered in Women's Studies programs grew from only seventeen in the academic year 1969–70 to more than thirty thousand in the 1980s. In 1985, Donna Dorian reported in *New Directions for Women* that books exhibited in the National Women's Studies Association conference had burgeoned.[142] Accordingly, women witnessed a huge boom of materials by and for women. Most were no longer able to keep up with the readings or even to read the piles of brochures announcing new publications.[143] All in all, as Myra Marx Ferree pointed out in 1985, "What had been esoteric in the late 1960s was widely available in the mid-1970s and is today a well-established sub-field in American commercial and university publishing."[144] It was clear by the 1980s that the market was big enough to support women's bookstores throughout the country. Correlated with this growth, from 1982 to 1985 sales in women's bookstores in the U.S doubled to reach $8 million.[145] By the end of the 1980s, the more than one hundred women's bookstores in the U.S. and Canada together grossed an estimated $30 million of sales.[146] In 2001, textbook sales were generally 15 to 30% of women's bookstores revenues.[147]

CONCLUSION

Women's bookstores in their early years had drawn political strength and energy from defining their existence in opposition to patriarchal and hierarchical institutions. This development was in response to the fact that women needed a "women-only space" to challenge the cultural devaluation of women and to experiment with and to create new organizational forms.[148] In the effort to transcend rather than imitate male-model capitalism, valuing feminist ideology, participatory democracy, and equality empowered women to form collective structures in their bookstores. They tried to create non-exploitative and non-hierarchical ways to operate their ventures. However, women had to confront various conflicts within the collectives, and sometimes these conflicts became bitter. Eventually, most women's bookstores' operations had to modify their structure and accept a complex economic reality "as the condition of their activism."[149] By going through external challenges and internal conflicts, women's bookstores acted as physical spaces that allowed for continuing negotiation of difference between women. Although some women's bookstores could not bear the full brunt from external attacks and internal conflicts and closed their doors, many others grew, and new women's bookstores were continuously born. As Seajay says, thriving women's bookstores had "broad-based stock reflecting the needs of the class/age/ race/sexuality/politics and priorities of the diversity of women that used the stores."[150]

Nevertheless, in an era unfavorable to feminism and marked also by continuous challenges within women's bookstores, they would not have survived without the creation and steady development of Women's Studies, which helped create a larger feminist audience and aided the publishing of feminist textbooks in which the diversity of women's voices was promoted. The prosperity of Women's Studies programs promoted small publishers like feminist or university presses as well as mainstream presses to produce more books by and about women. At the same time, it has been noted that "whatever is newest, groundbreaking and close to the cutting edge of feminist thinking is published by the feminist publishers."[151] Such has generally been the case because feminist publishers were part of the feminist movement and thus born out of necessity. As Seajay pointed out, they were "much more in touch with grassroots feminism in this country than New York City corporate publishers can ever hope to be."[152] It was the dynamic and symbiotic relationship between women in Women's Studies and those in feminist publishing communities that originally formed the contest for the flourishing of books by and for women, and it was also these women that made long and continuous commitments to feminist writings and created a whole new market by nurturing numerous women authors and cultivating a new readership beginning in the late 1960s.

Chapter Seven

More Than a Bookstore: Books and Visions

In the early 1970s, androgyny and the minimizing of gender differences was increasingly the trend among feminists. However, Mary Daly, Adrienne Rich and others later started to focus on femaleness. Works by Nancy Chodorow, Carol Gilligan, and others suggested that women's personalities, ethical thinking and language—all important elements of culture—differ from men's and, by implication, that women as a group might have a common culture.[1] Figures like Linda Alcoff later argued against such views, claiming that Rich's and Daly's work constituted part of a growing trend within feminism toward essentialism. Accordingly, their writings were criticized because of "their denigration of masculinity rather than male roles or practices, by their valorization of female traits, and by their commitment to preserve rather than diminish gender differences."[2] Alice Echols named this trend "cultural feminism," and inferred that cultural feminists' emphasis on building a free and safe space and women-centered culture constituted a form of essentialism. While many feminist booksellers tried to create and maintain a safe space for women free from masculine values, the effort in and of itself could be criticized as "cultural separatism." Echols says:

> By equating feminism with the so-called reassertion of a female identity and culture, cultural feminism seems to promise an immediate solution to women's powerlessness in the culture at large. Its growth is attributable to the frustrating fragmentation of the women's movement and the erosion of feminist gains in the recent past. Cultural feminism represents a retreat from the difficulties of political struggle into the self-validation that community-building offers.[3]

In Echols' view, women's bookstores symbolized "cultural feminism" and simultaneously "essentialism," and, moreover, that they were places "offering us little more than the illusion in the difficult period ahead."[4] Brooke William and Hannah Darby directly criticized women's bookstores of being "more insidious than outright reformism." From their standpoint, such bookstores had "pretensions to radicalism" since they "seek to build an alternate women's culture" defined as "pseudo-movement busywork that distracts women from political realities of women's oppression" and a way to "avoid the grim realities of life."[5] While they did not regard feminist newspapers as "feminist business" because their primary function was not business—in other words, making money—but disseminating political messages, they described women's bookstores as "feminist business" because they "exist for primarily business purposes."[6]

It is clear that this characterization of women's bookstores and women's culture does not fully describe the "position." This chapter examines how women's bookstores served their respective communities. By examining their activities, I will show that women's bookstores served as crucial vehicles to sustain the women's movement as well as the feminist publishing system—that is, indispensable parts of the "ecosystem" of a feminist publishing community, which developed in order to disseminate feminist values. To do this, I focus on one women's bookstore in Chicago, Women & Children First, in order to demonstrate how we can say that women's bookstores were more than *merely* "bookstores."

SAFE SPACE, BOOKS AND VISIONS FOR ALL WOMEN

Unlike general bookstores, women's bookstores emerged as crucial conduits of feminist writings, music and arts that were ignored by mainstream companies. Accordingly, they gave opportunities for women to encounter materials full of new perspectives that were not available anywhere else. In general, customers in bookstores can sample and enjoy without the obligation or expectation of making a purchase, or having any expectations of activism.[7] Women's bookstores, since the early stages of their development, were unique insofar as they offered more individual freedom to browse or look over materials than comparable mainstream bookstores—a feature that still marks them. This was because many women's bookstores were equipped with comfortable sofas and sometimes coffeepots in the cozy corners. This atmosphere encouraged women to browse materials comfortably and educate themselves by exposing themselves to these materials, which were not available anywhere. Although later chain bookstores such as Borders and Barnes & Noble Booksellers imitated these practices, their purpose was completely different from that of women's bookstores. Some women's bookstores even had a rental system, and others allowed women to pay later.[8] For example, at Full Moon, women sometimes asked to take books they wanted home, promising to pay later, and they usually did so.[9] On the other hand, chain bookstores let customers browse because they found that the longer the customers stay in the bookstore, the more likely they are to buy goods from it.

When New Words in Boston was planned, many women told them there were not enough books by and for women to fill an entire store.[10] Fifteen years later (1989), however, it became "the largest feminist bookstore in the US in terms of dollar sales" and stocked 8,000 titles in 1143 square feet of space, which turned over 3 to 4 times a year. In addition to books, New Words had an extensive collection of journals, which general bookstores were always reluctant to have because they made less profit and were easily worn out. However, the journals were regarded as a "consciousness-raising" aspect of New Words. It carried works from as far away as India, England, Mexico as well as Canada, the US and continental Europe.[11] Women's bookstores gradually expanded their categories of books to include mysteries, lesbian fiction, biography/autobiography, works by and about women of color, Jewish women, history of women, violence and sexual abuse, and feminist politics, to name just a few. By the 1980s, subjects also included lesbian and gay politics, substance-abuse recovery, lesbian mothers, and AIDS. In the 1990s, more subsections, such as bisexuality and queer politics, were added. In addition to printed materials, so-called "sidelines" such as records, videos, pictures, posters, cards, T-shirts, buttons, bumper stickers and other varieties of feminist artistic expression sometimes constituted 30–35% of sales at women's bookstores.[12] Women's bookstores had as their primary policy the commitment to sell women's writings but they also thought, "A poster or a button or a T-shirt is a lot more accessible to many women than books. One button, worn in the right situations may be worth a thousand words. Feminist humor is alive and well in buttons and cards, even if still too rare in other forms of print media."[13] These sidelines encouraged women who were unfamiliar with printed materials and who saw feminist booksellers as "elitists" who had "a lot of education" to actually socialize at women's bookstores, and likewise offered them opportunities to expose themselves to feminist writings.[14]

Over the decades feminist booksellers needed more knowledge from ever expanding feminist works to community resources. For example, Womanbooks created a 10-page "quiz" called "Bookstore Skills Questions."[15] It tested the knowledge of its workers regarding differences in the list and cost price of books, and knowledge of books in order for them to better ascertain customers' questions and recommendations, the "quiz" included items such as:

> Where can "the Combahee River Statement" be found [in the store]? . . . Why do we carry several editions of some 'classics'? Explain in terms of the difference between the New American Library and Penguin editions of *Sense and Sensibility*.[16]

Judging from the contents of the "quiz," feminist booksellers played the role of highly skilled librarians whose specialty was feminism and women's issues in their local community.

The visibility of all kinds of feminist materials from magazines, books, records, videos to pictures, posters, T-shirts, buttons, bumper stickers and other varieties of artistic feminist expression, which filled one shelf at first and later the entire store, undoubtedly had tremendous impact on the community and thus helped to sustain feminism. The visibility gained by feminist booksellers went beyond a women's community and reached the general public, thereby gaining some level of "legitimacy." Thomas Linneman, who describes the introduction of new ideas into the cultural mainstream as one of the roles of booksellers, notes:

> While browsing through the bookstores, the general public many happen upon these movement books and read them, or acknowledge that such ideas are now legitimate topics for discussion. If people do not change their minds about an issue, at least the topic is on their minds and thus enters the public arena.[17]

Thus, the visibility of these feminist materials also gave feminism enough "legitimacy" to avoid being completely ignored and, presumably, also to be discussed in the public arena. Mev Miller also said:

> From my years in bookselling, I know so many women who have been affected—emotionally, politically, and/or radically by finding books that reflect their experiences. . . . Everyday I talk to women (and some men) who talk about how the materials in our store (books and magazines mostly) have helped them make sense of their lives. They come for the comfort of the space. Women have described being able to "breath better" in an atmosphere that clearly values women's work, feeling, thought, ideas. The sensation of "I'm not the only one" has profound meaning.[18]

In this way, materials introduced by feminist booksellers not only offered new perspectives to women but also united and empowered them.

It was clear that women's bookstores originated within the larger literary, cultural and political context of the women's movement and lesbian and gay rights movement. Thus women's bookstores might be interpreted as a politicized community. In fact, they actually organized not only cultural, but also political, social, educational, and consciousness-raising events. For example, according to records of Old Wives' Tales from 1977 to 1979, almost 150 store events were held. Records of 33 months (records of three months are missing) show that Old Wives' Tales had more than four store events per month. They included altogether 58 writers, 20 artists, 21 poets, 51 political activists and others. As the number shows, the most common events were writers' and poets' readings. As Elizabeth Long notes, the conceptualization of reading as a purely solitary activity ignores those not uncommon times that reading is done in group situations. Long points to the many ways in which a relationship between readers and the institutions which produce books and literacy is established.[19] Therefore, these events also played an important role not only to promote authors and their materials, but to build literacy and knowledge among women. Knowledge gained in this way created one path to activism. Political activists who gave talks at Old Wives' Tales included a candidate for the San Francisco Board as well as representatives of a broad range of organizations and concerns such as Women's Coalition for Chile, Women against Violence in Pornography, Lesbian mothers, Lesbian School Workers, Fat Politics, and Anti-Semitism. Along similar lines, many feminist institutions like a local branch of NOW as well as individuals used the bookstores to advertise their efforts.[20] For example, Alaska Women's Bookstore offered space to raise a fund for Sally Elliott, who was battling a lesbian custody case. She noted that the bookstore was "an island of sanity."[21]

Many women's bookstores took seriously their commitment to supporting feminist artists, especially local ones. For example, Judith's Room in New York had a reading series and Emerging Talent Competition for feminist artists. The owners of Judith's Room said that they believed it was important to promote writers whose reputations were not as yet established, and they were counting on the women's community to support them.[22] Jane Addams Bookstore in Chicago co-sponsored the first Chicago Women Writer's Conference with the Artists-in-Residence program of the Chicago Council on Fine Arts in 1980.[23] Similarly, Women & Children First carried on the tradition of supporting local literary communities in Chicago.[24] In 1989, it had a month-long series of programs celebrating its 10th anniversary. The programs celebrated the diversity and breadth of

Chicago's literary community by inviting members of the Chicago Feminist Writer's Guild, and had panels such as Chicago Women of Color: Publishing Ourselves/Publishing Each Other, Chicago Women's Theatre, Chicago Women Writing Non-Fiction, Chicago Women Journalists, Alternative Women's Press: a Chicago History, and Chicago Women Writing Fiction. These events also included workshops and performances, featuring poetry, fiction, playwriting, as well as critics, journalists, leaders from the community of feminist writers along with academicians. Book Woman in Austin, TX organized "Turning the Tables: A Literary Feminist Feast." The annual event supports local women or women of color artists. It was so popular that women in the community needed to purchase the ticket a year in advance.[25] Women's bookstores also offered a variety of slide shows. In Old Wives' Tales they included "Women in prison," "Lives of women and children after revolution in Cuba," "China," and "Young Asian exploited by US corporation." The advertisements for some events noted "Everyone welcome," while others said "Especially for women" which referred to events related to lesbianism or sensitive issues such as rape and domestic violence. By offering a variety of events, Old Wives' Tales promoted feminist writings and arts and encouraged feminist artists, simultaneously raising political consciousness. These Old Wives' Tales' events would, in fact, continue for 19 years. They were titled "Women's Voices" in the early 1990s, and were the basis for the awarding of a Certificate of Honor to the bookstore by the Board of Supervisors of the City and County of San Francisco in 1995. In addition to these events, women's bookstores organized numerous groups for women. For example, Amazon bookstore organized and hosted reading groups such as an international fiction study group and lesbian lives study group.[26] It also developed a program in conjunction with the Minnesota Literacy Foundation for new adult readers who would like to further develop their skills in both reading and, for those for whom English is a second language, in conversational English.[27] In another case, Charis Books and More created programs for girls and young feminists such as "Girls Speak Out," and "The High School Writers," and also created a place where older and younger women could meet together and learn from each other in monthly meetings held in the bookstore.[28]

Women's bookstores also sponsored fundraisers for various causes, including AIDS relief and female congressional candidates.[29] In particular, entering the 1980s, when women's organizations faced drastic losses of funding, women's bookstores often hosted fundraisers for community women's organizations or donated prizes for raffles conducted at the latter's fundraising. Some events and programs were free, although others required donations, especially for nationally known feminist authors or musicians. For example, in the 1980s and 90s Old Wives Tales adopted a sliding scale from $3 to $10, but it did not forget to add the message "No one turned away."[30] Therefore, in almost all cases, the money they brought in did not make up for the basic costs to run the event. Rather, events and programs were financial burdens for many women's bookstores. The "Women's Voices" series offered by Old Wives' Tales, for example, had accumulated $2,027 in losses in six months in 1991.[31] The new owner of Womanbooks tried first to cut these store events and programs, although she met with strong opposition from women who had worked in Womanbooks under the previous owner. Noticing that store events became financial burdens for Charis Books and More, supporters arrived at an innovative solution, organizing the Charis Circle to help underwrite its events. A co-owner, Linda Bryant said, "The Circle has really saved our lives."[32] Thus while Charis Books and More was not a non-profit organization, the Charis Circle, as a non-profit organization, was eligible to apply for grants to support store events and programs separately from Charis Books. In this way, the Circle rented space from the bookstore for events, paid for the staff time spent on programming, and for program-related activities.[33] To inform the community of these store activities, new materials available in the store, and other important information, many bookstores issued newsletters or flyers. For example, Amazon bookstore issued a small catalog twice a year to fifteen hundred women, and Dreams & Swords (Indianapolis, Indiana) issued 6000 newsletters, including three thousand outside Indiana and one hundred outside the US, which cost $3,000 twice a year. Given this financial burden, many women's bookstores eventually attempted to reduce the cost. A Room of One's Own (Madison, Wisconsin) started to issue its newsletter twice a year instead of its formerly quarterly format. The Book Garden in Denver, Colorado, compensated for the financial loss caused by the newsletter by taking advertisements.[34] Accordingly, even though these sundry events and activities did not bring prosperity to women's bookstores, they by varying means enabled them to continue with their operations and outreach.

It is apparent that the sales of materials that originated in the creation and expansion of women's studies in colleges and universities greatly helped women's bookstores. However, it is also true that women's bookstores which offered these materials not available in the general bookstores aided students who were eager to study women's studies as well as teachers who had difficulty finding good textbooks. Moreover, women's bookstores provided educational opportunities to not only women who belonged to the higher educational institutions but also those who did not belong to any educational institutions. Although in the late 1970s women could take

Women's Studies courses offered on virtually every college campus, how could they educate themselves after graduation—especially about issues often considered "controversial" or even "disturbing" by many in the general populace? Many feminist groups from local ones to national ones such as NOW have also tried to offer an educational space for discussing issues like discrimination based on sex, rape, sexual harassment, divorce, domestic violence, abortion, and sexuality. However, when the political climate is not favorable to feminists, many women will not be seen going NOW or other local feminist institutions. Women's Studies departments and libraries in universities and colleges often welcome adult learners. Nevertheless, even if it is not so difficult for adults to gain admission to colleges and universities, the time required to commute regularly after work and the cost of tuition are hurdles difficult for many women to clear—especially working mothers and women in poverty. Moreover, in conservative political situations, public learning places including community centers and churches in general become reluctant to offer information on "feminist" or "controversial" issues.[35] Given the dearth of opportunities for lifetime learning, women's bookstores have offered a variety of activities–unique, original and affordable informal education—to large numbers of women in their respective communities. In the early 1990s almost one hundred women's bookstores across the nation offered some form of informal education once a week.

Various events and programs also provided opportunities for women not only to educate themselves, but also to socialize and work in feminist institutions. It often became a life-changing opportunity—both politically and emotionally. Clearly socializing in feminist institutions is/was a political act. However, if they wanted to socialize with feminists, or lesbian feminists, they had to "join" a local branch of NOW or to "volunteer" in the women's centers or clinics. Moreover, in general many women had been so intimidated by the media's portrayal of "bra-burning," "man-hating" feminists that they were afraid to go into feminist institutions such as women's centers, although "bra-burning" actually never occurred.[36] Instead, women often found women's bookstores to be a safer entryway into feminism. This is because it was the appeal of socializing-while-shopping that proved attractive many.[37] Seajay says, "Women are always going to store, shopping. It is OK for women to go to stores to spend time, socialize people and [spend] some money."[38] In women's bookstores, they had to neither "join" nor "volunteer" to socialize, and did not even have an obligation to "purchase" anything. Yet some women hesitated to enter at first—circling the store three times until they gathered enough courage to enter.[39] A survey by Crazy Ladies Bookstore in Cincinnati, OH, showed 15% of customers agreed with the statement that "some people I know are reluctant to be seen going into the bookstore."[40] But, once they entered the bookstores, at first they had great freedom to "browse" the bookshelves, and any women could browse the shelves "until she found the courage to ask the questions she needed to ask."[41] Many women could ask a variety of questions including materials from books and records to cards and bumper stickers, store events and programs which available for all women who frequented the premises, and seek information on their communities only available from "out" feminists or lesbian feminists in the women's bookstores.

The study of lesbian protest teaches us that the definition of feminist protest must be expanded to include coming out publicly as one's private self. As Susan Cavin points out, celebrating a "woman-identified woman" identity in a male-identified society is a legitimate form of social protest.[42] Breaking lesbian and feminist invisibility was a key aspect of their social protest. Therefore, the very presence of "open" feminists or lesbian feminists working daily in the women's bookstores made women's bookstores "a place of feminist sanctuary."[43] Their visibility was crucial not only for feminists and lesbians but also others. Since it is estimated that in 1994 some 56% of Americans said that they did not have any acquaintances who were homosexual, informing the public about the realities of their lives was paramount.[44] Linda Bubon of Women & Children First says, "People come to see [in our stores] how lesbian feminists are."[45] In another instance, one woman, who almost lost custody of her children because of her sexuality, took them to Meristem, a women's bookstore in Memphis, before revealing to them her lesbian identity. She said:

> Meristem was a great store in the middle of a crappy city where being gay is not acceptable. It was acceptable in Meristem. Before I told them, we browsed the store often and they talked with Audrey and Vickie the storeowners who were also partners. . . . I told them, because if I didn't, who knows what a homophobic "well-meaning" person might say. Even before they were told, they were exposed to gay and lesbian couples. These people were professionals, homeowners, African Americans in committed relationships. The exposure helped them realize how normal and natural my relationships . . . [46]

In cases like these, women's bookstores helped women to resist prevailing social norms concerning femaleness and to reinforce feminist or lesbian identities. Moreover, as a safe space based on "affective ties and mutual support" for all women, women's bookstores also provided them with emotional support they needed. Twenty Rue Jacob in Utah always put forth the supportive message that "I know this is a tough time, but you have us. We're always here" so that it "served a strong and nurturing matriarchal role" in the community.[47]

Community services offered by women's bookstores were also arguably political. The American Library Association (ALA) defines the public library as a community activities center, community information center, formal education support center, independent learning center, popular materials library, pre-schoolers' door to learning, reference library, and a research center, although most libraries focus on a few key areas.[48] Considering the various activities of women's bookstores, they also served the same role as public libraries—namely, social services. Lucille Frey, former co-owner of Alaska Women's Bookstore, described the store's unofficial function as a general information center and clearinghouse for Anchorage's community of women. Frey said, "You're not just selling books, you're doing social work, too. . . . We'd get women who'd just been beaten up. We'd send them to the women's Resource Center and the same thing would happen at the Resource Center, someone would be in counseling, and they'd say, 'you should get this book.'"[49] The overlapping of the two organizations' clienteles eventually convinced them to move into the same building. Later, when many feminist organizations and communities were losing their spaces like the Resource Center in Anchorage (due to lack of financial resources), women's bookstores took on an even more crucial role for women.[50]

Shay Youngblood, who first appeared publicly as a writer at Charis Books and More, said that it was "a kind of home/community for me for over 15 years. . . . I found my first apartment, my first real job, a massage therapist, a dentist, a doctor, and lots of new friends at Charis."[51] For Youngblood, Charis Books and More was an irreplaceable community resources. Women's bookstores were "the first place women turn to find community resources of all kinds."[52] However, what women in the community counted on most was direct referral and information from feminist booksellers. Some bookstores collected and filed community information, and required all workers to answer questions relevant to their community. For example, Womanbooks had Q&As about their community such as "Where do you suggest a woman for career counseling? A woman is looking for a feminist therapist. Where do you call? Where is a cheap place to eat near-by? How about a safe, inexpensive abortion?"[53] As "Resource information and Referrals" of Womanbooks describes "Womanbooks as a woman's center disguised as a bookstore," it is no doubt that women's bookstores were women's centers in their communities and thus served as valuable information resources.[54] Donna

Niles has said that fifty percent of their work at Amazon Bookstore was a retail business, but fifty percent was a combination of hotline and community network.[55] This "social service" in their community became one reason for feminist booksellers' "burn-out" because they spent "all day pouring out energy for other people" in addition to bookstores' day-to-day operations and they "did not have any left" for themselves.[56] Carol Seajay and other feminist booksellers joked about numerous "outrageous basic services" they found themselves providing at the bookstores. The services they offered included:

> Housemate referrals, book & record critic, art critic, tax returns/support, advice, information. Mental health counseling . . . lavatory, phone booth, shower, bank, credit reference, unemployment reference, pick-up point (you can read that goods, if you will!), communication center, out-of towners referral service, dating service, women's center, job referrals, ticketron, sex therapy, fashion advisor (what to wear to interviews), jewelry & gift registry, child care, pet-sitting, gift wrapping, mail order, dyke chamber of commerce, baggage check room, lost and found, map reading, bus and freeway adviser, odd & even gas days almanac, check book balancing, composer of greeting card sentiments . . . library, practice medicine without a license, stationary store (OWT [Old Wives' Tales] gave up & just SELLS pens, now), loaners of everything that moves. Political education, information for first time publishers, informal classes, Consignment 101, Book distribution 101, Book distribution-advance, safe space. . . . official polling place, notary public, art exhibits/gallery. Lonely hearts club, workshop, recommending photographers, selling books, sponsoring sports teams, sharing information with other bookstores, door prizes for every feminist events & fundraiser in town.[57]

The owner of Pandora Bookstore in Kalamazoo, Michigan, said, "If I got paid a consultation fee for all the referrals I do, I wouldn't have to worry."[58] Feminist booksellers thus offered "a multitude of community services" which public institutions could not or did not provide.[59] Furthermore, women's bookstores not only helped women to fundraising in the store, but also made donations to various groups in their communities in spite of their shoestring budget. For example, records of New Words in 1979 also show that the net profit was $3,635, of which $1,117 was donated to others.[60] In 1981, total donations of $1,225 went to Transition house (women's shelter), Rosie's Place (women's shelter), Oral History Project, Women's Center, Aid to Incarcerated Mothers, Women's Educational

Center, and Mobilization for Survival.[61] Women's bookstores were also committed to globally achieving social justice. For example, Women & Children First launched The Balkan Women's Book Drive Project in July in 1994; later, women's bookstores across the U.S and Canada joined the project. Based on their efforts, they shipped fifteen hundred books to Croatia. Thirty First Street women's bookstore sent four boxes to Nona, Zagreb, and two weeks later, to women prisoners.[62] Over the years, many women's bookstores or feminist booksellers were honored or awarded for their community service by their respective communities. In 1993 three women's bookstores, including Herland, Charis Books and More, and Meristem, received awards for their public service. The Oklahoma Pride Network gave Herland the Outstanding Community Organization Award, and The Memphis Women of Achievement Award for Vision went to Meristem founders Audrey May and Vickie Scarborough.[63]

During the Reagan and G.H.W. Bush era of the 1980s, feminist institutions that previously had "outside funding sources" faced drastic losses in funding.[64] They had to close their doors or became "deprioritized" by others for purposes of space.[65] Meanwhile, as Seajay noted, women's bookstores, which were financially independent, were able to relatively "stand firm."[66] For example, New Earth Bookstore, Kansas City, MO, was one of many "collectives" of the Women's Liberation Union (WLU) when the WLU lost its "women's center." New Earth then became even more important after the eventual demise as well of WLU, when many women saw New Earth Bookstore as the remaining cornerstone for the feminist and lesbian feminist community.[67] Contrary to the decrease in the number of other feminist institutions, the number of women's bookstores constantly increased in the 1980s. It shows that women's bookstores became more valuable places than ever for women when various feminist institutions and women's community centers closed their doors.

In 1977, the average profit of trade book retailing business was 25%.[68] In 1984, however, according to the American Bookseller Association, the average seller's profit was down to only 5 percent.[69] Shrinking profits inclined publishers to put more and more emphasis on the "blockbuster, the book that is more likely to be a best seller, the one for which heavy advertising and promotion expenses are likely to justified."[70] However, books by women and for women, especially feminists and lesbian feminists, were outside of this "blockbuster" category with very few exceptions. In contrast to the rare bestsellers, 90% of all books went out-of-print within a year because of the large number of new books and limited retail space. Consequently, most books quickly became absent from general bookstores.[71] Under such a circumstance, the existence of women's bookstores in their local community became more significant for readers as well as writers because women's bookstores were not trying to constantly find new blockbusters, but attempting instead to nurture women's works and keep them alive as long as possible. Readers often found that books unavailable in most stores could still be found in women's bookstores. For example, Mary Kay Blakely, herself a writer, said that 70 percent of the sales of her books was made by feminist bookstores, and noted, "My career only stays alive because of feminist and women's bookstores. . . . People like me stay in print because feminist bookstores are willing to carry back-stock and to reorder."[72] Minnie Bruce Pratt said, "Charis changed my life, as she's changed the lives of countless others."[73] Today, authors who are household names like Alice Walker, Gloria Naylor and Robin Morgan were first promoted through women's bookstores' networks. In many cases, women's bookstores hand-sold their first books as "cultural and intellectual expressions, not merely as commodities."[74] As Ginny Daley has stressed, it is of course easy to see the contributions women have made to literature simply by looking at the writers and their works—however, it is often the publishers, editors or book sellers "who pave the way for writers to develop their art, become published, and gain recognition."[75] Thus, feminist booksellers have been "influential" in part because they have "mediated" between publishers/writers and readers "through a face-to-face relationship that transcends commerce."[76] Without feminist booksellers and women's bookstores, one wonders how many feminist authors would have been able to write their second books, and how many of their books would have remained in print.

Feminist booksellers, moreover, also helped to keep feminist publishers in operation. For example, Mary Ellen Kavanaugh, owner of My Sister's Words bookstore in Syracuse, New York, said that she was "roundly advised by everyone to pay feminist presses first, general indies second, and the big companies last," when she asked at a Feminist Booksellers meeting the method by which others determined how to pay their bills. Many years later, she "has never had an account put on hold, and 'still' uses this triage to decide who gets paid."[77] Many women's bookstores also made special efforts to sell materials published by feminist publishers. Women & Children First, for instance, allotted one month for promoting one feminist publisher and sold books published by the publisher at a ten percent discount.[78] Thus, feminist booksellers and publishers tried to support each other, and to survive under the unfavorable political and economical circumstance. Seajay came to refer to their strong interrelationship as an "ecosystem."[79] In this context, Theresa Corrigan has written:

> When each part thrives, the entire system is healthy. When one part suffers, the rest feel the effect. Feminist publishers are dependent upon feminist bookstores to carry their books; the chains will only order those books they can get at discounts most feminist publishers cannot offer. Without feminist bookstores, one would probably never have encountered the works of Cherrie Moraga, Kitty Tsui, Chrystos, Katherine Forrest, Barbara Wilson, Jewelle Gomez, Dale Spender . . . [80]

In this way, women's bookstores functioned in conjunction with feminist publishers as symbiotic elements in the feminist publishing "ecosystem" that enabled the entire feminist publishing community to grow and expand.[81]

MORE THAN A BOOKSTORE: A CASE STUDY OF "WOMEN & CHILDREN FIRST" IN CHICAGO

The example of Chicago's Women & Children First illustrated how women's bookstores in the US have played an important political role through helping to sustain the larger feminist movement. In 1979, two women, Ann Christophersen and Linda Bubon, launched Women & Children First.[82] The owners had first met as graduate students in literature at a time when it was hard for them to find anything but the most famous of books by women authors in most bookstores. Indeed, the third edition of *The Norton Anthology of English Literature* (1974), a standard text in college English classes, included only eight women writers in its list of more than 170 works.[83] Even in the late 1970s it was hard to find books by women and for women except in the fields based on traditional gender roles such as cooking and nursing in their community. The two owners noted, "It was harder to look for books about women's body, women of color, or lesbians, and violence against women."[84] Bubon recalled an unsuccessful attempt in 1978 to locate a lesbian life-story. She visited six different bookstores, but not only did they not carry the book she was looking for—she could count the number of books by women authors that they stocked on one hand.[85] Christophersen and Bubon decided "to meld a love for literature with a passion for politics," launching Women & Children First on November 10, 1979 in a small storefront in the De Paul neighborhood.[86]

They said, "We strive to do this in an atmosphere in which all are respected, valued, and well-served."[87] The owners thus envisioned a store that would define "feminist" inclusively, as encompassing the interests and lifestyles of women whether they were heterosexual or lesbian, partnered or single, family-centered, career-centered, or both—regardless, moreover, of their ethnic, racial or religious background. They wanted a place where women's art could be celebrated and where women could come together to talk about issues of their concern. The store emphasized the strengths that made it unique: its outstanding selection of fiction, poetry, and art books authored by women; non-fiction sections on pregnancy and parenting, psychology, spirituality, health, violence against women, international politics, biography, and women's studies. It also created a large children's section which features books from babies' board books to young adult reading, with special emphases on multicultural selection, strong girl characters, and health issues. The store's program series, which began the day the store opened, offered performance and communication space for a diversity of writers whose strong, independent voices brought new dimensions to the chorus of voices asserting and redefining the reality of women's lives.[88] They ranged from local poets to nationally renowned authors, straight white writers, and authors who are women of color, as well as lesbian artists and writers.

Christophersen and Bubon were willing to stock books from small presses like Kitchen Table: Women of Color Press to provide multiracial and multicultural women's voices. They said, "Noticing the truly original, or non-mainstream voices, putting them on the shelf, and pointing them out to customers is our mission."[89] Thus they started the business to make available to readers the broadest possible range of female voices asserting and redefining the reality of women's lives through literature. In doing so, they were willing to take a risk on the new and sometimes "quirky voices" emanating from small publishers. They offered selective readers variety and choice, and often promoted works by offering a discount. In 2006 Women & Children First continues to offer new and alternative ideas and encourages women toward continuous learning and intellectual growth. By introducing expressive arts created by women of color as well as lesbians, they try to create bridges between women in general and feminists, who were easily divided by their race, class, and sexuality. They thus attempt to attract diverse kinds of women, promoting the survival of the women's movement as well as the larger women's culture. "What we are trying to do, whenever possible, is put people in touch with the voices behind the book," they have said. They find it exceedingly important to bring women of all races together, and their efforts resulted in Women & Children First being "one of the few places in Chicago today where women of color and white women regularly find themselves in community."[90]

Answers given to questionnaires I distributed to women frequenting Women & Children First in 1999 demonstrated that customers were strongly attached to the bookstore, recognizing its importance as a community center and as an information center.[91] One woman noted that she was attached to the bookstore "Because of everything it does for women and the women's community." The women's answers to the questionnaire reveal that the bookstore's bulletin board is an invaluable resource for women seeking housing, support groups, conferences, hotlines, organizational meetings, involvement in political activism, and entertainment. The store has received calls from people who want information concerning a whole range of issues—from where they can stay when they visit Chicago to far more difficult issues, such as how to get help for a friend who is living in an abusive relationship. The owners said, "We are in the network of women's services—we refer them to someone who can help." Thus, Women & Children First fosters a sense of community, and is a place many women turn to as an initial site for information, encouragement, or desperately needed help. As one reporter noted, the store has remained "a kind of control center for consciousness-raising, and its customers cut across organizational lines."[92] All female staff are not "just book people," they are "active feminists trained to refer customers to battered women's shelters, rape crisis centers and health centers if need be."[93] Although it is a place where books by and for women are of principal concern, it is also a community center for women. The owners host weekly Wednesday-morning story hours at which Bubon reads new and classic works for an enthusiastic audience of local toddlers and their accompanying adults. They have, in this way, tried to make it a space open to all in its community. The owners have noted, "When you bring all this material together, you also bring people together, a diverse group of women come together here, they talk to each other, they challenge each other."[94] It has been vitally important to them to build a place of inclusion—a common ground where women could both enjoy the things that connected them and discover more about their differences, and where feminist political organizations often fail. Furthermore, they have created an exciting cultural center for women. The bookstore has offered every woman, whether she is interested in literature or not, opportunities to enjoying feminist expressive artworks such as women's music on CD and cassette, videos and audio-tapes for sale or rental, jewelry, cards, posters and calendars, as well as tickets for cultural events and benefits. They stressed, "All this is what Feminism is."[95]

More importantly, they and most of their staff members are intensely involved in outside political, artistic, and literary activities, which enrich the quality and depth of the service they provide their customers. In May 1986, Christophersen and Bubon received the second annual Glynn Sudbery Award that is presented to persons who showed their involvement in independent political activism, especially in human rights.[96] In addition, they also have been involved in electoral politics, organizing a press conference of State Representative Carol Rosen (Democratic, Chicago) as well as speeches by Hillary Clinton and many other feminist politicians. In March 1998, the store moved to a larger space, about 3,500 square feet, making it promise to stock more than 30,000 titles. Women & Children First celebrated its 20th anniversary in 1999. *The Chicago Free Press* made note of the anniversary, saying, "It's a victory for connections built through a strong feminist identity, community involvement, political activism and support for women authors."[97] Thus Women & Children First is a prime example of how a women's bookstore can be far more than a bookstore. In the first issue of *FBN* (October 1976), the mission statement clearly said that "We [feminist booksellers] envision feminist bookstores as a network of 'woman's places' and information centers across the country (feminist shelters?)."[98] Just as Seajay originally envisioned, Women & Children First has offered a "woman's place" along with providing materials that express, support, and further feminist identities and culture. Consequently, women's bookstores make feminists' accomplishments visible and alive, and play a crucial role as an institution within the women's movement.

CONCLUSION

Women's bookstores on the whole never segregated themselves from reality, nor distracted feminists from political activities in order to make profits. Women's bookstores were operated by feminists who attempted to incorporate feminist belief into a business, which strove for goals beyond the immediate accumulation of capital. They gave women not only a safe space but also a social, cultural, educational and political place—by offering materials, events or programs in their stores, and community services. As Theresa Corrigan points out, women's bookstores "helped innumerable women through life crises, not by counseling them, but by empowering them about the choices they have."[99] Saralyn Chesnut and Amanda C. Gable stress that events and programs in the women's bookstores historically made it possible for them to be "much more than a bookstore in their lives."[100] Finally, the existence of women's bookstores assured that feminist publishing communities enjoyed a lively and healthy business. In other words, it played a crucial role as part of the feminist publishing ecosystem, which helped disseminate feminist values and ideas, and simultaneously keep feminism literally visible in their stores where women can breathe intellectually and culturally. All in all, women's bookstores were/are one of the women's movement's vital institutions: a more flexible and broad political site that signaled the legitimization of feminism and women's culture.

However, many women suffered from the effort to put feminist ideology into practice in their women's bookstores, both emotionally and financially. Nevertheless, many women continued to challenge themselves and establish bookstores. *A Labor of Love: A 25 Year History of Feminist and Lesbian Bookstores and Publishing,* a one-hour documentary radio program was produced by Mev Miller, a former collective member in Amazon Bookstore.[101] In the program, fourteen women testified to their "25 years hard works, long nights, financial risk, unwavering commitment, and daily vision by women dedicated to publishing, printing and selling books of feminist or lesbian perspective," which originated from their "labor of love."[102] Sandi Torkildson, owner of A Room of One's Own, said about her efforts to start it:

> I must admit that if somebody came up to me today and asked me to do it, I'd probably say "no" in a second! But having gone through it . . . it's one of those experiences like going on a[n] incredible hiking trip in the mountains . . . And then you get back and every time you talk about it you say "I really had a great time! And other people say, "I remember you wanted to turn back your thing you were dying? You didn't think we were going to survive!" But once you have gone through it . . . you realize that you really are a very competent person.[103]

Feminist booksellers' "incredible amount of hard work" and "labor of love" made possible women's bookstores which exemplified "the viability and endurance of feminist politics and culture as well as lesbian feminists" and which supported these politics and culture over the past 30 years.[104]

Various kinds of women's culture, cultural perspectives, and events presented and held in the women's bookstores gave women visions for the women's community. Such visions gave them hope that feminist politics and culture would succeed in the fight against the backlash of the 1980s, and they sometimes succeeded beyond booksellers' wildest dreams. For example, when Food For Thought in North Dakota and Women's Bookstore in Montana were born in 1986, Carol Seajay said:

> It was the most exciting news I'd heard all month—flashing back to the first WIP conference, I recalled that we'd fantasized wildly about the day when there'd be feminist bookstores in Montana and Idaho and North and South Dakota. . . . .never believing that they would actually come into existence. Happily the future isn't limited by our vision. [105]

In 1993, *FBN* proudly announced that it reached 500 feminist and feminist-inclined bookstores and booksellers in the US, Canada, England, Europe, Australia, New Zealand, India and Japan.[106] During the course of thirteen months twenty-six new women's bookstores were added, and the number reached 124 in the US alone in 1994—a record high. Given such a development, who could have predicted that the whole situation of women's bookstores would change radically within a couple of years? The next chapter will examine the changes that occurred in women's bookstores in the 1990s.

Chapter Eight

Women's Bookstores in the 1990s

This chapter explores sexism, racism and heterosexism as they continued in the 1990s and their implications for women's bookstores. The reverend and Presidential candidate Pat Robertson's observation in 1992 that "The Equal Rights Amendment encourages women to leave their husbands, kill their children, practice witchcraft, destroy capitalism and become lesbians" demonstrated that extreme heterosexism as well as sexism could be expressed even in the public arena. Feminism, given this situation, became in some sense "the F-word of the 90s."[1] Gay-bashing skyrocketed by as much as 80% in some parts of Colorado since anti-gay Amendment 2 was introduced.[2] *FBN* reported in 1993 that similar proposals for new laws were taken by many as sanctioning gay-bashing. The climate in which such proposals were made undoubtedly had a negative impact on book sales at women's bookstores. In addition, women's bookstores, which had embraced "activist, academic, and social settings," were seen by some of those in the new generation of feminists as stagnant or passé institutions.[3] Moreover, chain bookstores such as Borders and Barnes & Noble Booksellers were popping up across the nation, and Amazon.com overhauled the system of bookselling—from storefront to virtual store. They began to alter the landscape of the entire book industry. These and other changes, indeed, would come to sweep away most women's bookstores during the same decade in which their expansion reached its peak.

CONTINUING CHALLENGES: RACISM, HETEROSEXISM, AND CLASSISM

Persistent homophobia continued in the 1990s in the publishing industry.[4] As of 1991, *The Readers Guide to Periodical Literature,* which was a major periodicals guide, still refused to index gay/lesbian periodicals. Moreover, even a feminist magazine like *Ms.* implied homophobia in some articles. In 1990 *Ms.* featured an article about the success of women's bookstores; however, Seajay who was interviewed by *Ms.*, was "truly awed and quite unappreciative of *Ms.*'s ability to produce what appears to be a profile of *FBN* and my work—but just happens to omit the word 'lesbian' from every context."[5]

Racist incidents also continued outside and inside feminist publishing communities as well as women's bookstores. In May 1993, representatives of North America's various feminist-of-color presses—Kitchen Table, Aunt Lute Books, and Women's Press (Toronto, CA)—came together in an alternative session to the usual meeting of feminist and lesbian publishers at the industry trade fair, the American Booksellers Association (ABA). The edited account of their discussion, published in *Sojourner* magazine as "Packing Boxes and Editing Manuscripts: Women of Color in Feminist Publishing" (1993), constituted a watershed in the public airing of racism within feminist publishing, as the representatives of the various presses expressed anger and incomprehension at the increasing careerism and financial expediency they perceived amongst white North American feminist presses.[6] An African American editor even eventually resigned from Aunt Lute Books. While she "was enjoying learning other women's culture . . . Jewish, Latina, Native American . . . and their cultural relationships to the English language," she was also "working on books by upper-middle and middle-class Jewish and white women."[7] She noted:

> I ended up spending a lot of time explaining and policing out racism in the books, correcting inaccurate historical information and editing out the careless and dismissive racist notions of various Jewish/white authors. This work became a chore I did not relish/that I resented. I find it unpleasant spending most of my coalition time sensitizing white women to racism . . . my reprioritizing of alliance is towards a politics between women of color, not a reoccupation with readjusting white women's attitude/behavior towards us.[8]

Thus feminist publishers, let alone mainstream publishers, still produced racially problematic books. Women's bookstores also received letters that pointed out racism in books they shelved. For example, New Words received a letter from students of Lakota Studies, which claimed racism in the fiction written by Ruth Beebe Hill: since "she did not understand esoteric and metaphysical Lakota concepts, she twisted them to fit her fiction."[9] Old Wives' Tales received a couple of letters complaining of racism among workers at the check-out counter.[10] Old Wives' Tales responded to one of those, and said:

> There are some of us who would like to talk with those of you at the store to get the facts, and discuss what, if any, actions will be taken. Please accept this offer in the spirit of acknowledgement that, in community life, we—white womyn—all have committed and/or will commit acts of racism, but can work together to try to right the wrong.[11]

Two years later, an experienced feminist bookseller left Old Wives' Tales partly because of the lack of racial diversity there. She wanted to see more women of color working and socializing in Old Wives' Tales; however, this seemed a difficult task not only in Old Wives' Tales but also other women's bookstores.[12] For example, Feminist Bookstores' Day was set up as a gathering for feminist booksellers in 1990. They took advantage of the American Bookseller Association's annual convention, and decided to have a gathering in the Friday before the day of convention. One picture taken in the 1992 Feminist Bookstores' Day in Anaheim, CA showed that the forty-three feminist booksellers who attended were seemingly all white.[13]

In spite of these challenges and conflicts, feminist publishing communities including women's bookstores found their overall situations were not all bad in the late 1980s to early 1990s. In the early 1970s a few publishers such as Daughters, Diana, the Women's Press Collective, and Shameless Hussy began publishing a small number of feminist and/or lesbian titles. While in 1985 only five university press books specifically addressed lesbian lives, in 1990 the number of such books published by university presses was rapidly increasing. By 1993, the roughly 154 feminist or lesbian presses were producing over 300 titles per year, while 300 to 400 independent publishers produced feminist and lesbian books.[14] In addition, various genres of books such as works on women's recovery from alcohol and chemical dependency sold well. Carol Seajay noted:

> All of our larger [feminist] publishers have good solid lists, and even some of the "newcomers" have three to five book lists, and "occasional" publishers are bringing their new titles out in sync with the larger world of publishing, all of which add up to the largest strongest season ever for feminist publishers. "[15]

On the other hand, some started to raise questions about "feminist writings." As one owner reported that books on feminist politics "sit there like dust," feminist booksellers noticed that "feminist writings" from politics to theory did not sell well.[16] Some feminist booksellers also felt by the 1990s a gap developed between "common women" and feminist writings, in particular, books about feminist theory, which were "either too scholastic or too tepid."[17] Mev Miller says:

> It is my opinion that as feminist writings have moved from the places of activism to the places of academia, feminism has become not only more prevalent but also more difficult to understand-even obtuse. This not only makes feminist theory inaccessible to those women with limited reading skills, but perhaps even irrelevant.[18]

"The institutionalization of Women's Studies" might make feminist writings more and more "scholarly" because many feminist writings were presumably written by women in academia, who needed to publish to stay in academia and whose audiences were mainly other academic women. How were the feminist writings in the 1970s, which mobilized thousands of women, different from those in the 1990s? This will be a crucial topic for exploration in future research.

THE EXPANSION OF SUPERSTORE CHAINS AND THE RISE OF E-COMMERCE

In 1991, when 70 feminist booksellers gathered together on Feminist Bookstores Day, they were glad their national growth rate continued to be in the double-digit percentages. They were literally "soaring and thriving,"[19] despite the recession. For example, sales at Amazon Bookstore were $241,000 in 1985, and reached $360,000 in 1990. Of the seventy-three women's bookstores listed in a 1983 issue of *Ms.*, thirty-nine (54%) were still serving their communities in 1994, and in 1989 New Words reported its sales reached $570,000. Aggregate sales of women's bookstores reached $30 million in total.[20]

As for the number of women's bookstores, in the thirteen months leading up to 1993, twenty-six new women's bookstores were added.[21] In total there were some one hundred thirty-five overall in the US and Canada in 1994. Along with the increase in the number of women's bookstores, the number of feminist booksellers attending the Feminist Bookstores' Day at the American Booksellers Association convention became steadily larger.[22] In 1989, twenty-six feminist booksellers from eighteen women's bookstores attended, in 1990, thirty-eight women from twenty stores and by 1993 sixty-eight women from forty stores did so.[23] These women assembled at the nation's Capitol in June 1993 for the March on Washington for Lesbian, Gay and Bisexual Rights, proudly marching with a banner saying "Feminist Booksellers and Publishers: Entertaining,

Empowering, Emboldening."[24] However, there were also some indications of impending decline in women's bookstores. For example, gay men's bookstores were popping up throughout the country by the late 1970s and were willing to sell lesbian materials, which may have aided lesbian publishers and authors but undoubtedly also constituted new competitors in the book market. Norman Laurila opened A Different Light in 1979 in LA, as well as additional locations in San Francisco and New York City in 1983.[25] In 1991, when Carol Seajay was asked about the competition with gay men's bookstores, she pointed out that women's bookstores served the women's community in a way that gay men's bookstores could not and provided an atmosphere and a collection of literature that was not available elsewhere.[26] It was women's bookstores that were dedicated to selling not only lesbian materials but also gay materials more generally since the early 1970s. Seajay asserted, "Long-term, I see a lot of women who've gone off to wander come home to feminist bookstores."[27] As a matter of fact, before many women came home to feminist bookstores, other and more ominous competitors such as national chains, superstores like Borders and Barnes & Noble Booksellers and the Internet giant Amazon.com intervened. Many feminist booksellers still believed that their bookstores were "actually in a more favorable position" than the other independent bookstores because they were "more specialized" and they had "not had a chain open [nearby]."[28]

However, the moves of chains and superstores were very quick and, moreover, highly aggressive. By the early 90s, the 16 leading chains were B. Dalton, Barnes & Noble, Bookland, Books-a-Million, Books & Co., Bookstar, Book Stop, Borders, Brentano's, Coles, Coopersmith's Crown Books, Doubleday, Scribners, Super Crown, and Waldenbooks. They were, in fact, owned by just four parent companies: Barnes & Noble Booksellers, Books-a-Million, Crown Books, and K-mart. K-mart, for example, owns both Waldenbooks and Borders, with revenues reaching $39 billion in 1992.[29] What were the women's bookstores up against, given the rise of the chains and superstores? For example, the latter typically opened one store after another close to existing regional independent bookstores in short periods of time. In Connecticut in 1992, Encore, a chain bookstore, opened one block from Huntington, the oldest and largest independent bookstore in Hartford, CT. In April, Encore opened a second store, one block from Bookfair, the largest bookstore in West Hartford, CT. In May, Barnes & Noble Booksellers, carrying 60,000 to 70,000 titles in a 9,000 square foot space, opened across the parking lot from Bookworm in West Hartford.[30] Furthermore, these chains started to open stores on or near university campuses throughout the country—many on which numerous women's bookstores had long relied for textbook sales.

Chains and superstores in this way quickly recognized that specialty bookstores such as women's bookstores, gay and lesbian, and Black bookstores had a profitable market. As part of their campaign to launch new stores close to these specialty bookstores, they began to stock feminist titles that had "traditionally been the backbone of the women's bookstores'"—bestsellers by popular writers like Gloria Steinem and Alice Walker.[31] The chains also closely watched "what programs and events the local women's bookstores run."[32] Susan Krikorian, owner of Valley Women Books and Gifts, in Fresno, California, reported chain-store staff members coming into her store, copying down titles, services and programs and duplicating them. One feminist bookseller also said "Book groups, poetry readings, you name it, they've imitated it."[33] Thus they started to offer author readings by "well-established authors including Gloria Steinem and Rita Mae Brown, whose original audiences were built in feminist stores."[34] However, as Stephanie Poggi pointed out, the chains were "leaving out the political analysis and the social change agenda."[35] For example, the chains started "Discovery Series" in order to promote "unknown" authors. Since early 1970s women's bookstores have promoted "unknown" authors. However, unlike these chains that promoted "unknown" authors, just as women's bookstores had long done; however unlike the chains' promotion of "unknown" authors who had previously published, women's bookstores promoted those "who never published their works, or published controversial materials."[36] Furthermore, they also started to discount the popular feminist titles, the "backbone of the women's bookstores." As Theresa Corrigan points out, chains and superstores had a "special arrangement" with publishers to purchase books "wholesale at discounts which independent bookstores can only dream of."[37] Mary Ellen Kavanaugh explained that "Not only do superstores get to buy their books at a better discount, they get paid to promote certain titles. . . . Certain superstores seal such deals with publishers before some 'bestseller' titles are even published. What does this mean about how books are marketed to the public?"[38] It is clear that independent booksellers including women's bookstores increasingly felt threatened by their presence, evidenced by Northern California Booksellers Association's filing of an antitrust suit against Avon publisher's discounts for chain-bookstores in the mid 1980s.[39] In 1988, some 1,000 booksellers again signed a petition against such publishers' discounts.[40] In 1994, the American Booksellers Association finally filed an anti-trust suit against Penguin USA, St. Martin's Press, Houghton Mifflin, Rutledge Hill Press, and Hugh Lauter Levin Associates.[41]

However, in fact, since chains and superstores became so powerful, publishers were also starting to be dictated "the rules of business" by them.[42] They "tend to return books to publishers more quickly than independent, who let books stay in stock longer, even when they're not selling at a significant pace."[43] According to the *Chain Store Age Executive Journal,* the chairman of Bookstop (a superstore in Texas and Florida) said that if a new release did not do well in his stores in its first few weeks, it was replaced. However, he added, "classic works" stayed forever. Theresa Corrigan said about his remarks, "We all know what he means by 'classic,' and he doesn't mean 99 percent of the books carried by feminist bookstores."[44] It is thought that this trend accelerated especially after the emergence of super-chain bookstores such as Borders and Barnes & Noble Booksellers, which were said to be "patterning [themselves after] food supermarkets."[45] The assumption was that, like bagels and apples and eggs, books have a limited shelf life.[46] Seajay also points out that books became "wallpaper" and were "used for decoration to make stores look full and rich."[47] Therefore, publishers experienced heavy returns after selling, as if they were renting their books to the chains. Receiving the books, which became dusty and were replaced with "newer, fresher titles" in their stores, publishers again had to offer their "discounted" new titles. Chains typically returned any book that had not sold within 30 days, and never re-ordered it.[48] Small publishers would soon go bankrupt because "returns counted as credit toward the store's future purchases, which equaled less cash flow for the publisher."[49] For example, Papier Mache Press, which took a huge order from a big chain, was then forced into bankruptcy when the chain returned half of them for full credit.[50] In another expression of their dominance, they demanded more discounts from publishers, which small presses usually could not afford, and promotions in their stores were too expensive for them to carry out. Carolyn Gage described the situation in the following manner:

> If a publisher doesn't like the arrangement, fine, they don't have to do business with the chains. And they will go bankrupt within weeks. So the presses have had to agree to a practice that does not exist in ANY OTHER RETAIL BUSINESS IN THIS COUNTRY. This means trouble for the small press that is operating without huge cash reserves . . . so the small presses are closing.[51]

Chains would only order those books they could get at discounts which most feminist publishers could not offer, or ordered those which would be "wallpaper." Famous authors dominated bookstore shelves, but numerous minor authors' titles were ignored or not permitted to stay there for more than a few weeks.[52] On the other hand, women's bookstores ordered books to carry and sell, and they were more likely to keep books for six months or longer whether they sold or not.[53] Rather than promoting "hot off the press" or "just released" new books, many women's bookstores continued giving priority to the best-selling backlist titles.[54] This was crucial for feminist publishers because it is "backlist sales that keep them alive and solvent."[55] Their survival also depended on women's bookstores.

In 1993 women's bookstores such as Amazon, 31st Bookstore, and My Sisters' Words saw superstore chains open near them.[56] The effects were immediate. For example, while sales of My Sister's Words in Syracuse had increased consistently since it opened in 1987, when the first superstore came to Syracuse, 1993 annual sales of My Sister's Words fell by ten percent.[57] Financial reports of many women's bookstores increasingly showed that the sales were not good, although Seajay pointed out continuous harassment of all kinds of "right-wing madness or general vandalism" should be seen as one of the causes of declining sales at some bookstores.[58] In December1996, *Publishers Weekly* reported that Barnes & Noble Booksellers, Borders, Books-A-Million and Crown took in $3.2 billion in sales for the first nine months of 1996. Barnes & Noble Booksellers opened 59 new superstores during the first three quarters of 1996, and planned to have 440 superstores open by the end of 1998.[59] In 1994, *FBN* reported: "'[Invasions of chains are] not going to happen to me,' has shifted to 'What are we going to do about it?'"[60] A memo to the workers of Southern Sisters in August 1994 says, "Sales are so down. It's hard to get up about the store. The store looks great, but there is no one there—this must change ASAP or it's over."[61] They needed to take immediate and more direct action—not only toward chains and superstores and mainstream publishers but also with regard to their customers.

FEMINIST BOOKSTORE NETWORK: STRATEGIES FOR CONFRONTATION

In order to confront the rise of chain-bookstores and superstores, feminist booksellers needed each other more than ever. Informally, a national network of women's bookstores had been functioning for years. *FBN* was part of the network. However, as a "visible public image for the informal network they already had" a formal national network, Feminist Bookstores Network (FB-Net) was formed in 1992.[62] Feminist booksellers reached group consensus within the membership that a store's primary focus must be on feminism: 51% of the stock must be by/about women, 51% of the workers must be women, and the store must be owned by women.[63] The FB-Net, which consisted of 117 women's bookstores, soon became a powerful tool to fight against the threat from chains. It started a national advertisement campaign promoting them.[64] In addition, it also held a Strategic Planning Conference to discuss their future in May 1993. Strategies included setting up and celebrating National Feminist Bookstore Week as well Feminist Book Awards, and included developing a Feminist Bookstore Catalog, which introduced feminist books and listed bookstores in the US and Canada.[65]

At first, they agreed that they needed to "educate" their communities by letting them know of the "ecosystem" of feminist publishing communities.[66] *FBN* featured a detailed article in 1992 about chains and superstores entitled "Invasions of Chains," which emphasized the importance of networking among bookstores, educating customers, and continuing to raise questions about such "invasions."[67] This is because most customers, even "supporters," didn't notice that "every chain store in the country has a women's section, however badly or insultingly stocked it may be."[68] In this way, educating people in their communities became a major agenda in *FBN*. However, it was apparently not easy. For example, in the May/June 1994 issue of *FBN* Elena Rutter reported in "A Warm Welcome Is Not a Line Item" that a lesbian photographer exhibition was held at a national chain bookstore, to which 200 lesbians were invited. The photographer said to her, "The store took care of everything so it didn't cost me anything and besides they have been terrific to work with."[69] It was clear that the photographer had no idea how her involvement with a national chain bookstore hurt her neighborhood women's bookstore, and might eventually bring about a disastrous result to a whole feminist publishing industry. Carol Seajay said "the question is not whether feminist bookstores are valuable or useful. The question is in an industry where the profit margin is 1 to 3 percent, how will feminist and other political bookstores survive. . . . And the answer is, with education."[70] In this way, issues regarding "educating people in the communities" repeatedly appeared in *FBN*.

From October 22 to 24, 1994, a group of twenty-five feminist booksellers once again had a "brainstorming session dedicated to insuring the survival of the feminist bookstores,"[71] and they continuously discussed their "strength, weakness, opportunities, and threats."[72] That same year, the Feminist Bookstores Network cooperated to publish its *Fall Catalog,* which was in full color, 40 pages, and featured 157 titles from 113 publishers. Of 300,000 copies of the catalog in circulation, 120,000 were mailed to national mailing lists such as the entire *Ms.* subscriber list and a women's list for *Out* and *The Advocate.* It proved a "tremendous success."[73] Many bookstores reported to *FBN* with excitement. For example, New Words found that many women "walked in with the catalog in hand," and some of them "dropped $100."[74] In addition, in 1995 (May 13–20), the first annual National Feminist Bookstore Week was held. Across the nation, women's bookstores had various events: a celebration of mothers and daughters featuring local writers in Memphis, TN, a music event with a singer-songwriter in Houston, Texas, and a reading from *The Woman-Centered Economy* in Arlington Heights, IL.[75] These store events were successful as part of a campaign designed to promote their visibility. *FBN* featured an article about their "success stories" that was over five pages long.[76] In 1996 *FBN* sponsored Feminist Book Awards—proposed by FB-Net—to spotlight books that represented the best of feminist writing and publishing.

Furthermore, the network of feminist publishing communities, noticing the importance of the "ecosystem" began to flourish. At first, women's bookstores received support from feminist writers including Dorothy Allison, Blanche McCrary Boyd, Tee A. Corinne, Jewell L. Gomez, and Alice Walker. As a group, they acknowledged their indebtedness to the feminist and lesbian feminist publishers and women's bookstores and signed the Feminist Writers Pledge. They announced:

> Without independent bookstores and small presses some of us could be silenced and the next generation of authors with important ideas might never be found." When pledging their support, writers vowed to "seek out local feminist and independent bookstores in each city or town to do [their] first reading or book-signing."[77]

These feminist writers thought their vocation as authors had been made possible by the feminist and alternative presses and the feminist and independent bookstores. This is because their first works were published in small feminist presses, many of them were sold by feminist bookstores, and most of them had their first public readings in feminist bookstores. Dorothy Allison, whose first book was published by Firebrand, a feminist press and read in Herstore, a women's bookstore in Tallahassee, Florida, said:

> Without the bookstores, magazines and presses that have encouraged and sustained my imagination, I would not have known what to do with the stories I wanted to tell. At a time when the survival of the independents is so uncertain, I want to do everything I can to make sure that these vital community institutions are there for everyone.[78]

In the same spirit, in 1994, feminist publishers issued a "Women's Presses Resolution" in support of feminist, lesbian and gay, and other independent booksellers. Presses such as Firebrand Books, Seal Press, Cleis Press, and Papier-Mache Press pledged to include in their direct mail catalogues a list of the names and addresses of independent bookstores in order to encourage their authors to give readings and do signings there.[79] Consequently, even though 1996 saw the lowest growth in 20 years (only one new women's bookstore appeared since the previous year), the total number of women's bookstores in the US and Canada reached 143, up from 135 (124 in US) in 1994. Carol Seajay, pointing out that general bookstores' "profitability" was at an all-time low but that women's bookstores created "a much more solid financial footing," reported that promotions by the Feminist Bookstore Network were successful and that fears of women's bookstores' demise were "greatly exaggerated."[80] Seajay said, "I find myself feeling incredibly optimistic. . . . We're here, we're good at what we do, and you haven't seen the end of us 'cause we're not done yet!. . . . *FBN* turns 20 in October. . . . We plan to celebrate all year long."[81]

The battle was not over, however. In July 1995, Amazon.com had opened its "virtual doors." Only two-and-a-half years later, the sales of Amazon.com reached $87.4 million, increasing 446% compared to the same period a year earlier, and its cumulative customers rose to 2.26 million by the end of March, 1998.[82] Amazon.com not only caused confusion with Amazon Bookstore, which perpetually received phone calls from people who confused Amazon Bookstore with Amazon.com, but also became a great blow to women's bookstores as well as other independent bookstores throughout the land.[83]

CHANGE IN THE WOMEN'S COMMUNITY AND THE END OF OLD WIVES' TALES

Sales in the first fiscal year of Old Wives' Tales, founded in 1976, were $41,855. The next year, they doubled, and afterwards they steadily increased. In 1980, they reached $198,000.[84] After the collective split in 1983, sales declined from $294,000 to $285,000.[85] However, they recovered after just one year. In 1991, its collective members proudly claimed that "the sales continued to flourish" and reached $391,000.[86] However, from the next year on sales started to decrease and ended up at $355,000 in 1993.[87] Mondschein of Old Wives' Tales explained that it was "a victim of its own success."[88] She said that Old Wives' Tales was carrying Alice Walker when no one knew her name; however, now Walker's works are carried even at bookstores in small-town malls. Women's bookstores successfully nurtured feminist writers, and created a market for feminist books. Now virtually all bookstores have a section for women's studies or gay and lesbian studies. At the same time, like many other women's bookstores, Old Wives' Tales served as more than just a place to buy books because half of the calls to the store were not about books. As Darlene Pagano of Old Wives' Tales said, "If there was a way to charge 25 cents per inquiry and $1 for the binders [with listings of community information such as available housing and jobs], there would have never been a financial problem. We might even own this building."[89] They had done "what didn't necessarily translate to dollars" for years.[90]

Feminist booksellers believed that due to the greater service role in the community they could depend on the loyalty of their feminist and lesbian customers. Women in the community had traditionally helped women's bookstores open and keep afloat by donating their time and money. After Old Wives' Tales asked women in the community for help in 1992, it "made [it] through the crisis" because of the aid offered.[91] However, it could not halt its increasing debts, which reached $60,000 in the middle of 1993. Old Wives' Tales needed to raise $25,000 immediately, and once again had to appeal to women in the community.[92] It started the Debt-Free By 20th [anniversary] Campaign. The flyer said that "As we near our 18th anniversary, we're looking ahead to our 20th. In order to make that milestone, we have to do some serious fundraising."[93]

Old Wives' Tales must have received numerous offers of support as some letters it received showed. There were letters including an offer of a "$100 no-interest loan for an unspecified period of time" as well as notes of encouragement telling Old Wives' Tales of its importance.[94] For example, Adrienne Lauby, a writer wrote a letter to describe how the existence of Old Wives' Tales was crucial for authors. She said:

> A feminist bookstore still needs to exist, 1. for new writers who haven't found audience or perhaps developed the skill to draw a commercial audience, 2. for the communities of readers and writers who will never (until the resolution or the utopia) be commercially exciting. At this point, these include most women of color, lesbians of color, disabled women, old women, poor women, imprisoned women, sexual outlaws and . . . 3. for readers & writers who haven't found feminism or a place within feminism, 4. for the kind of community building you offer, 5.for me, a writer who will soon finish her first novel and wants to fulfill her dream of a reading at Old Wives Tales.[95]

Her remarks make it clear that women's bookstores like Old Wives' Tales were more than bookstores and crucial for her life.

However, all women in the community did not necessarily feel like her. There were some additional potential problems for Old Wives' Tales, as well as for all women's bookstores, reflecting changes in the women's movement and women's culture since the 1970s. In particular, lesbian communities changed following the outbreak of AIDS in the 1980s. As Daneel Buring has pointed out with regard to lesbian and gay communities in Memphis, the AIDS epidemic brought about in lesbians a "sense of humane community responsibility," and they participated in "everything from fundraising to hospice care." It marked lesbians and gays in Memphis as a community that went beyond their separate institutional structures.[96] Lesbians who used to be excluded from male-dominant gay organizations started not only to participate in various social and political activities with gay men but also played a crucial role in them. Thus young lesbians who came out in the 1980s were more comfortable with working with gay men than had lesbians of previous generations who came out before Stonewall Riot or during the 1970s. Many young lesbians now saw themselves not as lesbians but rather "queers" who were more likely to associate with gay men, bisexual or transgendered people. Although many women's bookstores had sold materials about and by gay men for a long time, they now dealt with the new situation by establishing more AIDs and gay-men shelves. According to Sally Munt, people involved in AIDS activism started "Queer Nation" in New York in 1990, responding politically to a number of incidents of bashing of lesbians and gay men in the East Village.[97] Queer Nation also celebrated sexual freedom, subversion and ambiguity, opening the doors to the marginalized and excluded, especially those who were transgendered, bisexual and/or sadomasochist.[98] Their actions might be seen as rebellion against separatism, and related to queer theory, which emphasizes the socially constructed character of group categories—calling "into question all categories upon which conventional notions of identity rely."[99] As Rosemary Hennessy has noted, queer theory is opposed to identity politics "as a form of expressive pluralism where identity is reified—that is, understood to be represented in a self-evident and authentic way through one's body—and collectivity is reduced to group affiliation defined according to the standard of authentic embodiment."[100] Thus, young lesbians as "queers" started "Queer Nation" together with others in the direct action-protest style such as ACT UP.[101]

The mid-1990s also witnessed the emergence of so-called "lesbian chic." Lesbians became chic in mainstream pulp culture. According to Rebecca Cragin in her "Post-Lesbian-Feminism: Documenting 'Those Cruddy Old Dykes of Yore,'" the term "lesbian chic" describes "the members of a newly emerging subculture of young, urban, fashion-conscious lesbians," and it became "a social phenomenon (a sudden fascination with and glamorization of lesbianism by the dominant culture) and a snowballing proliferation of media images."[102] Lesbian chic became prominent in popular culture of the middle of the 1990s, but in fact primarily featured white, conventionally feminine and beautiful lesbians.[103] Their physical beauty and good fashion sense were contrasted with the "negative" stereotypes of lesbians in the previous generations. According to this view, earlier lesbians' "politically correct uniform was flannel shirts and work boots," signified the "short-haired buldagger," the "hairly-legged, bra-burning angry feminists" and "hard-core separatists" of the women's movement.[104] Young lesbians "integrated feminism into their daily lives," but they seemed to "reject the view that lesbianism is *the* feminist act and the belief that any sexual identity is more authentic and unmediated than any other."[105] Young lesbians were not necessarily attracted by "lesbian community," "lesbian identity," or "women's culture."[106] In this way, women's bookstores championing "women's culture" did not necessarily appeal to the emerging young "queer" generation.

At one point, a woman wrote a letter to Old Wives' Tales and emphasized that "queer community" superseded "women's community," and women's bookstores were not in vogue if not "uncool" with the younger generation.[107] She said, "The power of a multi-age, multi-sexual preference, multi-race women's community is what I can see that could turn this society around."[108] Another sent a fax to Old Wives' Tales, and in a similar way, she stressed the importance of diversity and generational change. She claimed:

> Women, particularly feminists have grown and changed. . . . Remember when all lesbians looked alike?. . . . Now, everyone does what they [sic] want, when they want. Women are having fun with their bodies and clothes, hair and make-up and make changes at will. . . . [B]ut the store looks like its in the past, stuck in a dreary 70's time warp. . . . It won't attract new customers-especially customers that are younger than we are. It won't attract the thousands of straight women, who may feel they won't be welcome (I had felt that way myself) who want to support a woman's or feminist bookstore. It doesn't attract men who have had the courage to evolve, and who would like to support you and continue their growth through the important books you carry. Move your attitude out of the 70's as well.[109]

All women's bookstores were not necessarily a "multi-age, multi-sexual preference, multi-race women's community," although they tried to be by seeing the changing of their communities. These two comments clearly suggested that Old Wives' Tales was failing to sufficiently appeal to enlightened men, heterosexual women, and younger generations, especially lesbians. In fact, in the early 1990s half of feminist booksellers were already over 40, although many of them were in their twenties when they started their ventures in the 1970s.[110]

When Barbara Wilson left Seal Press, which was founded by her when she was twenty-six in 1977, she wrote her reflections about feminist publishing communities. She said:

> Meeting with June Arnold changed my life. Nowadays, if you say her name, only a handful of people will remember who she was. . . . But to some of us, then, June Arnold was a legendary figure; the founder of Daughters, Inc., one of the first of the feminist presses, the discoverer and editor of Rita Mae Brown, and a wonderful lesbian author in her own right.[111]

It was June Arnold who had organized and made successful the first Women In Print Conference. When June Arnold died in 1982, a living "legend" to early feminists became unknown to younger generations. In the early 1990s, *FBN* started to feature "obituaries" soon filled with names of pioneer feminists both in the women's movement and in the feminist publishing communities such as Audre Lorde and Nanci Stern.[112] The divide between two generations of lesbians seemed profound: young lesbians who came out in the 1980s and who were more interactive with other sexual minorities including gay men, bisexual or transgendered people, on the one hand, and lesbians of their previous generations who came out before Stonewall Riot or during the 1970s, and who were more associated with heterosexual feminists, on the other. Roughly half of feminist booksellers, including the women in Old Wives' Tales, belonged to the older generation.

Without specifically "marketing to young feminists," the booksellers could not successfully draw them into women's bookstores. This was because, in the early 1990s, lesbian materials in particular were no longer available solely in women's bookstores. They did not have to go to women's bookstores to get feminist and lesbian materials. In addition, they may not have even known about the existence of women's bookstores.[113] Many women's bookstores' dependence on lesbian and related materials for sales was increasingly threatened by the new competition including national and super bookstore chains, gay bookstores, and later e-commerce bookstores.[114] The Thirty First Street Bookstore Cooperative, which was founded in 1973, closed its doors in 1994. Jennie Boyd Bull, a manager in her 50s blamed the demise on the competition from Borders which also offered feminist and lesbian materials. Moreover, she also noted that the generation gap in the lesbian community negatively affected the store because "younger, queer dykes more identified [themselves] with gay [men] than feminist politics."[115] A Different Light, a gay bookstore founded in 1979 in San Francisco, apparently increasingly attracted younger lesbians who would presumably otherwise be customers of Old Wives' Tales. The National Lesbian & Gay Book Month was initiated in 1992 by the Publishing Triangle, a gay publisher, as a way to bring lesbian and gay books to the attention of a wider reading public.[116] In 1993, the Book-of-the-Month Club launched lesbian and gay entries.[117] Given the size of the market for feminist and lesbian materials, the impact of the incorporation by chains and superstores of such works was felt almost immediately. Many women's bookstores' dependence on lesbian and related materials for sales was increasingly threatened by the competitions.[118] In the mid-1990s, many women's bookstores began to report to *FBN* decreasing or stagnant sales—and constant efforts at fundraising.[119] Among them were pioneers or role models of women's bookstores, which were prosperous for a long time and well-respected not only by their communities but also by booksellers at other women's bookstores. In October 1995, Old Wives' Tales, which used to be one of the most prosperous women's bookstores, closed its doors after 19 years in operation.[120]

Similarly, those which had already became impoverished due to the continuing political backlash, the rise of superstore chains and e-commerce, could not survive—particularly and ironically soon after 1996 when the number of women's bookstores in the US and Canada had peaked at 143.[121] By 1997, sales by independents and small chains fell to 17% of market share,[122] having constituted 32% in 1991.[123] In addition to superstores and chains, Internet booksales grew incomparably fast. Amazon.com's sales grew 838% from 1996 to 1997, from $15.7 million to 147.7 million. Barnesandnoble.com earned $15 million in sales in its first 10 months of operation.[124] Internet sales sealed the fate of many women's bookstores.[125] In 1997 and 1998 alone, 25 women's bookstores closed and in 1999 the number of women's bookstores fell to 85—a 25% drop.[126] In 1999 Sisterhood, one of the oldest women's bookstores, reported:

> As you know, corporate bookstores and online books sales have dramatically changed the business climate. Sisterhood's sales have steadily decreased during the past several years, and are now down about 50 percent from their peak in the late 1980s. We can no longer afford to remain open unless something changes.[127]

As a result, Sisterhood closed its doors the same year, after 27 years of operation. In 2000 it was reported that since the early 1990s two-thousand independent bookstores went out of business.[128] Thus, along with the decrease in the number of women's bookstores, feminist publishers also closed their doors one after another. As Carol Seajay had predicted, chains successfully tailored women's or gay and lesbian's bookstores' inventory to compete with the existing competition and drove them out of business—and they tended to stop stocking feminist or gay books.[129] It caused feminist publishers to lose two customers at once: women's bookstores as their longstanding clients as well as the chains who had recently courted them. In this way, feminist publishers with a long and thriving history, such as Kitchen Table: Women of Color Press, Herbooks, Firebrand, Naiad, and Spinsters Ink, eventually had to close their doors. Nancy Breano, of Firebrand press said:

> As the [book publishing] industry got more and more irrational, I was less and less inclined to enjoy it. It's one thing to love doing books. It's another thing to deal with the Goliaths of the world. . . . I think we underestimated the capitalist maw and we were swallowed up by it.[130]

In this way, "the capitalist maw" swallowed women in the feminist publishing community. As a result, the ecosystem of feminist publishing was also destroyed. The effect was to reduce the amount of feminist and lesbian writings published. Anjula Gogia, co-manager and buyer for Toronto Women's Bookstore said, "There's less variety in our lesbian section and our sales for that section are down. What's more, lesbian titles carried by the big publishing houses are going out of print because they're not selling enough, which is killing the diversity of voices."[131] For example, 85 to 90 percent of lesbian books, which were listed in *the Safe Sea of Women* by Bonnie Zimmerman, were published by lesbian, feminist and other small publishers.[132] When these presses failed, many legendary feminist and lesbian materials went out of print.[133]

CONCLUSION: THE END OF FEMINIST BOOKSTORE NEWS

As a 1999 issue of *FBN* reported, women witnessed "another hard season of bookstore closing."[134] It was not only the women's bookstores, other independent bookstores, and publishing houses that faced financial challenges but also *FBN* itself. That year, *FBN* confronted the same problems since most of its subscribers were independent bookstores. When each one closed, *FBN* lost one of its customers, while *FBN* also suffered from the cut of advertising budgets of independent and small presses as well as the threat of "the ever-consolidating corporate publishers."[135] All of them "put dents in *FBN*'s other primary source of income."[136] In addition to a sharp reduction in the number of feminist presses that placed advertisements, there were "dramatic mergers of mainstream publishers which did feminist books, for example; Schocken and Knopf were both independent publishers, but they were bought by Random House, and then Random House was also bought. Then three or four publishers were consolidated into one imprint."[137] Seajay said, "So, instead of having our lists of 15 books [from] each [publisher] you have one list of 20 books [from one publisher]. . . . So from *FBN*'s perspective, where we used to have 120 mainstream publishers advertising with us regularly that got cut down to 20."[138] The devastating effects of mergers rippled outward to *FBN*. Advertising constituted 70% of *FBN*'s annual revenues (30%, subscribers), including payment made on a sliding-scale determined by their sales—and annual advertising revenues declined by one-sixth.[139] In other words, altogether, *FBN* lost almost 58% of its revenues, and continued losing its subscribers. In 2000 Seajay announced that "it was no longer financially viable for *FBN* to continue."[140]

Her decision to close *FBN* came partly from her eventual personal consideration of "elder care." According to her, she had to raise her income level from subsistence to something that would give her a decent base for Social Security. She said, "At issue was a labor of love versus facing elder care. . . . There is a price to pay for doing what you want in life."[141] This was an issue not only for Seajay but also other pioneers in the feminist publishing communities. Most of them were now over 50 years old. Aging became a crucial issue among them. Nancy Breano of Firebrand press also said:

> I've had a superb 15 years as far as getting to do work that I wanted to do and feeling that I made some significant contributions and meeting terrific people, but I'm 58 now, and I have to figure how to put some money away.[142]

Alice Molly and Carol Wilson were co-owners of a twenty-year-old women's bookstore, Mama Bears. They had also founded A Woman's Place Bookstore in 1971 and left it due to internal conflicts, starting Mama Bears in 1983. As one of the pioneering feminist booksellers, they were carving out their own future in running the women's bookstore for more than thirty-years. They "would have retired 10 years ago, but knowing they wouldn't get any good offers for the business and concerned over the loss of a feminist resource, they hung on."[143] Discouraged by the closing of other women's bookstores, their comrades in pioneering feminist bookselling since the 1970s—helping and caring each other from the beginning, fighting back against political backlash and going through bitter internal conflicts, as well as enjoying their accomplishments in the early 1990s—it was natural for many of them to be concerned about their own future.

FBN, once called the "bible for lesbian and feminist booksellers," ceased after Carol Seajay and numerous women in feminist publishing had devoted 24 years of constant labor to its publication.[144] Sandy Torkildson, co-owner of the twenty-five-year-old bookstore, A Room Of One's Own, said, "It [*FBN*] kept us connected to what was going on. It was also a source of strength and inspiration."[145] Moreover, for the feminist publishing community, Seajay's "political savvy, knowledge of the publishing industry, leadership skills, creative and enterprising ideas and labors, and passionate conviction about the value of feminist bookstores" had made *FBN* more than simply a trade journal, just as many feminist booksellers had made the women's bookstore "more than a bookstore."

In the 1990s, against the rise of chains and e-commerce bookstores, women in the feminist publishing community shared their knowledge, and made the most of their network: they created Feminist Bookstores Network, Feminist Bookstores Week, and Feminist Bookstores Catalog. All of them were successful in the beginning. However, the chains' approaches to women's and lesbians and gays' markets were both shrewd and ruthless. Moreover, the women's community, from which women's bookstores gained their power, was losing centripetal force. For younger generations of feminists, women's and lesbians' materials seemed to be available everywhere. All of these developments swept away many women's bookstores by the late 1990s. Losing *FBN* in 2000, a crucial vehicle to promote the ecosystem of the feminist publishing community, the rest of the feminist booksellers seemed to be lost to the turbulence of the publishing industry. Yet, as will be shown in the Conclusion, some pioneer feminist booksellers still thrive and serve their communities, while others have handed down their torch to the next generation with the dawn of the new millennium.

Chapter Nine
Conclusion

THE FEMINIST REVOLUTION IN LITERACY

As Charlotte Bunch has pointed out, "feminist publishers are not passive receptacles for what is already out there but are actively creating new directions for thought and action," and women's bookstores likewise have not been passive receptacles for selling materials created by women.[1] Serving as separate collectivities of women with distinct sets of cultural and aesthetic values, women's bookstores have been bases for sustaining feminism as well as for enriching women's lives in their communities.[2] By offering or organizing political, cultural and educational programs and events for women, women's bookstores have helped to create a "feminist revolution in literacy"—contributing not only to women's abilities to read and write but also to disseminate their voices. Feminist writers and publishers created books that changed many women's lives as well as, to some extent, the larger American society. In these books, women found new self-images, and American society also found totally different images of women: women who were brave and confident, who loved women or who were women of color—beautiful and strong. This empowered many women, and expanded their world. It was feminists in the publishing community that spawned the feminist revolution in literacy, yet women's bookstores constituted the central sites disseminating new images of women, women's voices, and visions directly to women in their physical spaces. In doing so, they also provided "tremendous pleasures" for women who frequented them.[3] Through women's bookstores, many women found their identities, communities, and sisterhood. The existence of the women's bookstores in their local communities was, for them, a profound *genius loci* of self-enlightenment.

The flourishing of women's bookstores over the decades also demonstrates the demands for materials based on the different historical and cultural realities women experienced, especially women of color and lesbians. Such realities were quite different, not only from men's but also those of white heterosexual women. Without the voices of women of color and lesbians, who rejected the idea of a "universal" female experience, women's cultural expression would be shallow and shaky, incapable of harnessing the power necessary to call into question the structures that reproduce racial, class, gender, and sexual oppressions. Likewise, shelves of women's bookstores would be poor and homogeneous without works by and for women of color and lesbians. Multiracial and multicultural voices were distributed by the women's bookstore network, which spanned the nation, and their cultural expression flourished through acquiring such sites for their performance. Consequently, the women's movement opened itself to a multiplicity of women's voices, many of which had never been heard before.

Patricia Hill-Collins has emphasized that "resistance can occur at three levels, the individual level of consciousness, the cultural level, and the social structure level." Along these spectra, women's bookstores were crucial to raising individual consciousness as well as the cultural level of women in their daily lives.[4] Creating and using a "women's culture" was a strategic choice open to the women's movement, with women's bookstores playing the crucial role of enabling "a wholly women's culture to flourish."[5] In creating "cultural" space, women's bookstores offered a "political" space to realize feminist ideals.[6] The significance of the fact that women's bookstores sustained feminist identity and activism over the long-term cannot be overemphasized, particularly when social, political and economic environs became hostile to feminism. Women's bookstores offered places for "the maintenance of social bonds," providing rare and hard-to-find places to meet, for example, "an 'out' feminist or lesbian feminist to discuss, explore and acknowledge women."[7]

Women's bookstores, surrounded by classic and new materials that legitimated women's voices and demonstrated women's cultural and intellectual accomplishments, offered a place where "culture and education merged into one experience." Proving women's works were not a mere addendum to men's accomplishments, women's bookstores encouraged women to express their own voices, and to educate and explore themselves. Alice Molly and Carol Wilson noted that a major function of these bookstores was that when a woman entered one, she was immediately connected to a whole random network of feminist activism—the "web" women's bookstores wove.[8] They said:

> As Bell Telephone Labs put it some years ago, "a random network, richly redundant, is the most efficient form of communication there is."

> In a random, yet purposeful network such as the women's movement, the women's bookstores are major connective nodes.[9]

A woman entering the women's bookstore witnessed numerous women's steps toward social justice and a fair society, felt a thriving feminist spirit, and heard diverse women's voices that had fallen on deaf ears until a couple of decades ago. Cultural change made visible by women's bookstores was one of the most enduring forms of transformation.[10]

Numerous women, especially lesbians, have been involved in the "feminist revolution in literacy" since the 1970s. Heterosexism in the women's movement disillusioned many lesbian feminists, but their political activism never stopped. Through mushrooming numbers of lesbian papers and writings, they continued adding irreplaceable insights to feminism. The crucial step toward building the feminist revolution in literacy was to have a national network among women in the feminist publishing community; and the central force responsible for the realization of the first Women In Print Conference was the community of lesbian feminists. Women's bookstores, as an important part of the ecosystem of the feminist publishing community, gathered strength centered around *FBN* and its network across the nation. Again, there were large numbers of lesbian feminists who "felt the need for a bookstore strongly enough to get involved, raise funds, build bookcases, and do volunteer shifts week after week after week."[11] They helped transmit women's dissident voices, and simultaneously kept feminism literally visible in their stores. Without lesbian feminists, the feminist revolution in literacy might have indeed been impossible.

WOMEN'S BOOKSTORES IN THE NEW MILLENNIUM: PASSING THE TORCH TO FUTURE GENERATIONS

Theresa Corrigan, who was a collective member of Lioness Bookstore, proudly wrote:

> [Feminist booksellers] were "in the business to educate, to end sexism, racism, homophobia, classism, ageism, and all the other inequalities that threaten our society and survival, and to create a safe place for our sisters and brothers. We are in the business to change the world. That will never be profitable or in vogue. Feminist bookstores are in it for the long haul and proud to be part of a larger movement for social change."[12]

As one of the women's movement's vital institutions, women's bookstores constituted a political and educational site to change the world.

However, any such site invariably evolves or otherwise changes. Thus women's bookstores inevitably changed. As Ann Christophersen of Women & Children First noted in 2000, "women's bookstores are going through a transitional, reorganization phase."[13] In 2001, one year after the closing of *FBN,* the number of women's bookstores decreased to 74. In 2002 when one of the oldest and the most thriving women's bookstores, New Words, closed its doors after 28 years of operation, the number fell to half—only 38 women's bookstores remained.[14] When Amazon Bookstore faced with an unexpected $10,000 property-tax bill in 2002, women in their community successfully raised $35,000 which largely came in small donations. As Barb Wieser said, it "really showed how much people want the store around."[15]

Recognizing that "a goodly number of the old guard is still invigorated and committed [to] our project," Christophersen took hope in the fact that "there are energetic, skillful, young feminist booksellers stepping in" as well.[16] Some young feminists are trying to open women's bookstores. In 2001 Rose Norman interviewed fourteen feminist booksellers, and pointed out there were some energetic young feminist booksellers.[17] 24-years-old Helen Roman bought Brigit Books in St. Petersburg, FL in June 2000 from its founder, Patty Callaghan.[18] In 1999, Kathryn Welsh, who was twenty-three years old, founded Bluestockings in New York City.[19] Catherine Sameh was 28 in 1993 when she and her friends founded In Other Words Women in Portland, OR.[20] According to Catherine Sameh, In Other Words is a not-for-profit store, and it has one full-time employee and thirty-five volunteers.[21] Like many earlier women's bookstores, these bookstores have bulletin boards and several notebooks filled with information about women's resources to connect women. In addition to author readings, they organize and offer political, cultural and educational events and programs, for example, "The Last Word," a monthly open-mike evening for women writers; a nonsexist-parenting lecture series; a women's health series; and "Reading with Writers."[22] 26-year-old Sarah Cohen is an owner of Change Makers Books & More for Women that opened in May 2003 in Oakland. She said:

> California has lost feminist bookstores in Los Angeles, San Diego, Long Beach, Sacramento, Fresno and San Francisco. I'd hate to see that happen here. The Bay Area is this country's poster child for freedom of speech and human rights. Here of all places we should be able to protect independent thinking, free speech and the feminist movement.[23]

As of 2006, Cohen's new women's bookstore, Change Makers Books & More, is thriving and providing irreplaceable space and valuable information to women in the community, "protecting independent thinking, free speech, and the feminist movement." These women's bookstores, opened by those of a newer generation, continue to create what original founders or previous generations of feminist booksellers had envisioned putting their new and provocative insights in their stores. Despite the argument about the generation gap between the second wave feminists and the succeeding generations, feminist booksellers in the new millennium had also been educated by their forerunners, as feminist booksellers, in the importance and necessity of women's bookstores as "part of a larger movement for social change."

In 2004 Women & Children First celebrated twenty-five years in spite of the openings of "seven Borders or Barnes and Noble stores within three miles of the front door" in the past eight years.[24] With the opening of super national chain bookstores as well as Internet bookstores, the number of women's bookstores has decreased. However, as of 2006, there are still over 19 major women's bookstores, and many of them have a long history.[25] Amazon Bookstore, and A Room of One's Own celebrated thirty-five year anniversary. In addition, in May 2005, three University of Wisconsin-Milwaukee graduates, Molly Tennessen, Amy Daroszeski, and Kelly Todd opened Broad Vocabulary, a new women's bookstore in Milwaukee, Wisconsin. They say:

> Broad Vocabulary offers a diverse and complete selection. . . . Additionally, we provide a safe and accessible space for established community organizations and potential store-operated groups, created based on local interest and demands. Broad Vocabulary is also committed to hosting sliding scale or free-of-charge events featuring book and poetry readings, lectures, workshops, local art, music and other performances.[26]

These old and new women's bookstores have demonstrated their ability to persevere in the face of necessity and changing circumstances while keeping their missions as women's bookstores. New Words in Boston and Crazy Ladies Bookstore in Cincinnati reopened, yet each was reborn as a not-for-profit information and cultural space promoting women's artistic and literally expression.[27] Crazy Ladies Bookstore became Greater Cincinnati Women's Resource Center. The announcement said, "We're movin' forward! In the spirit of continued evolution, we are focusing on *building bridges!*" "Figuring out how to thrive," Greater Cincinnati Women's Resource Center serves women in the community by "building bridges with evolving activists."[28] In a similar way, the mission statement of the Center for New Words says,

> Building on the foundation of New Words Bookstore, the Center for New Words is a non-profit organization that serves as a catalyst for

> diverse women's and girls writing, voices, and ideas. Our goal is to be a word-centered programming, performance and meeting space, anchored by a new feminist bookstore—a mission more pressing than ever today, as spaces of and for "alternative" culture narrow and close.[29]

In essence, the Center for New Words will continue to be a window to "a whole random network" of feminist activism, and women's voices and visions. The network is one thread in the "web" feminist booksellers in New Words have woven for 28 years in the community. Carol Gilligan congratulated it upon its reopening and emphasized that its space was more important than ever, saying, "New Words Bookstore has always been a place where . . . one's ideas and one's life are accepted and encouraged to grow. . . . In the coming decades, we will turn to the Center for New Words again and again to inspire and transmit women's voices in ways we have not yet even imagined."[30]

New demands for information, educational and cultural programs and events for women even in this era of Information Technology clearly show a persistent eagerness among women to listen to women's voices, educate and empower themselves. The Internet offers many ways to find information and to educate themselves, yet it is difficult to build lasting relationships or create a sense of community without face-to-face communications.[31] Center for New Words plans to resurrect the bookselling operation because spontaneous communication is harder to come by when it is not a drop-in space anymore.[32] Women have gathered information and strength from such spontaneous communication. In this so-called "post-feminist" era, women still need a safe place to learn what is considered to be "not-feminine," "unpopular," "controversial," "radical" or "too liberal" by authorities, a safe space to acquire knowledge that formal educational institutions cannot provide.[33] Women's bookstores might change style according to the era, but they will not cease being a "word-centered place" for all women. They may indeed be evolving but they will continue to function as sites for women's ongoing learning and enlightenment—the feminist revolution in literacy. Barbara Grier, who established Naiad with Donna McBride, once said:

> I think in five years, or 15, or 25, there'll be another group to come along and suddenly think "I have to go and find the sword in the stone and I'll put it out, and I'll charge up the hill, and people will follow me, and I'll change the world all over again." Now, that's going to happen again in some format. Probably when I'm dead. And I'm sure they won't call to me to do anything. And I'm grateful.[34]

Women's unheard voices and unseen visions were the swords to change numerous women's lives in the late 20th century.

Women's bookstores helped to improve women's literacy and make women's voices heard; they became the physical space within which new visions were realized. The sword of the new millennium will undoubtedly be constituted, at least in part, in the renewed recognition of the significance of feminist literacy, undertaken through efforts such as maintaining and opening women's bookstores and transmitting them to the next generation.

Appendix A

List of Archival Collection

Gay and Lesbian Historical Society of Northern California, San Francisco Public Library: Old Wives' Tales Bookstore collection (OWT)

Special Collections Library, Duke University: Dorothy Cookie Teer papers collection (DCT)

The Lesbian Herstory Archives, New York, New York: Bookstore Subject File (LHA)

Cincinnati Historical Society Library:Crazy Ladies pamphlet (CLP)

Greater Cincinnati Women's Resource Center: Crazy Ladies collection (CLC)

Rare and Special Collections, University of Illinois, Urbana-Champaign (UIUC)

Schlesinger Library, Radcliffe Institute, at Harvard University: New Words Bookstore collection (NWC)

INDIVIDUAL COLLECTIONS

Linda Bubon and Ann Christophersen Personal Archives; Women & Children First (WCF)

Trudy Mills and Kate Randall Personal Archives; Antigone (ATG)

Mev Miller, "A Labor Of Love: a 25 year history of feminist and lesbian bookstores and publishing." cassette recording 1995. (MMC)

Appendix B
Interviews

Anonymous, 2002, Cincinnati, Ohio

Anonymous, 2001, Tucson, Arizona

Linda Bubon, 2000, Chicago, Illinois

Ann Christophersen, 2000, Chicago, Illinois

Mary Ellen Kavanaugh, 1998, Syracuse, New York

May Lui, 2002, Toronto, Canada.

Carol Seajay, 2003, San Francisco, California.

Appendix C

A List of Bookstores That Conducted Surveys and Observations of Customers and Workers

Antigone Books, Tucson, AZ.

Bloodroot, Bridgeport, CT.

Charis Books and More, Atlanta, GA

Crazy Ladies Bookstore, Cincinnati, OH

My Sister's Words, Syracuse, NY.

Toronto Women's Bookstore, Canada.

Women & Children First, Chicago, IL

Appendix D
A List of Questionnaires to Customers and Workers

1. QUESTIONNAIRES TO CUSTOMERS

female, male (Approximate Age:)
Level of Education: K12, BA, MA, Ph.D, Others
Race: White, Black, Hispanic, Asian-Pacific Islanders, Others

1. How many months ago was your last purchase of books here?
2. How many months ago was your last visit of this bookstore?
3. How often do you purchase books through Internet bookstores like Amazon.com
4. Why is "this women's bookstore." Important to you?
5. What other materials and/or services could "this store" provide you?

2. QUESTIONNAIRES TO OWNERS OR MANAGERS—-PART I

(Approximate Age:) Level of Education: K12, BA, MA, Ph.D, Others
Race: White, Black, Hispanic, Asian-Pacific Islanders, Others

1. Why did you start this bookstore? (mission or goal of this bookstore)
2. When did you start this bookstore?
3. What was the greatest impediment to starting it?
4. What has been the greatest impediment to keeping it?
5. How did you survive during the Reagan, Bush era?
6. What was most helpful to the start-up of the bookstore?

7. What has been most helpful to maintaining it?
8. What kinds of customers frequent the bookstore?
9. What does it mean for you to run a women's bookstore?
10. What do you think are the accomplishments of a women's bookstore?

3. QUESTIONNAIRES TO OWNERS OR MANAGERS—PART II

1. Bookstore's name and address, and name of main contact person
2. It was founded in 19______ by______________________
3. At present this bookstore has been operated by (collective, co-operative, single, or two or more ownership, others).

   Please specify____
4. If the operation system changed over the years, please explain the change. (for example, Six women collective for non-profit (first 5 or 6 years), Two women ownership for pro-fit (two years), Three women co-operative for profit (to present))

   ____
5. The number and sex of workers at present

   ______ female workers (including ____part time workers)

   ______ male workers (including ____part time workers)

   ______ transgender workers (including _____part time workers)
6. Age of workers (including part time workers)

   under 20 ______

   20–29 ______

   30–39 ______

   40–49 ______

   50–59 ______

   over 60 ______
7. What is your bookstore's mission or goal? (you might want to attach any store flyers describing your store's mission, if you have any)
8. Sexuality of workers (including part time workers)

   heterosexual ______

   homosexual ______

bisexual ______
unknown ______

9. Race of workers (including part time workers)

Caucasian ______
Black ______
Hispanic ______
Asian and Pacific Islanders ______
Others ______________

10. Level of Education or workers (including part time workers)

K12________
BA__________
MA_________
Others_______

11. Please describe political organization or activity names in which workers get involved, if there are any.
12. Please describe what kind of organizations to which your store makes donations, if there are any.
13. Please describe what distinguished from other bookstores.

____

14. What has been the most helpful to operation of your bookstore? (for example, loyalty of your community, relationship with universities, knowledgeable workers, business skills, etc)

____

15. What has been the greatest impediment to the operation of your bookstore?

____

16. What do you think are the main accomplishments of your bookstore?

____

17. What does it mean for you to operate a women's bookstore?

____

18. Any other thoughts concerning the past and future of women's bookstores?

Appendix E

Women's Bookstores (2005)

This list is primarily based on "Books to Watch Out For (community links: feminist /women's bookstores)" and I added some from other sources (see references below).

A Room of One's Own	307 West Johnson Street, Madison, WI 53703	608–257–7888	http://www.roomofonesown.com
Amazon Bookstore	4755 Chicago Avenue, S. Minneapolis, MN 55407	612–821–9630	http://www.amazonbookstorecoop.com
Antigone Books	411 N. 4th Avenue, Tucson, AZ 85705	520–792–3715	http://www.antigonebooks.com
Aradia Bookstore	116 W. Cottage, Flagstaff, AZ 86001	928–779–3817	
Bloodroot	85 Ferris Street, Bridgeport, CT 06605	203–454–5708	http://www.bloodroot.com
BookWoman	918 W. 12th Street, Austin, TX 78703	512–472–2785	http://ebookwoman.booksense.com
Broad Vocabulary	2241 S. Kinnickinnic Ave.,Milwaukee, WI 53207	414–744–8384	www.broadvocabulary.com
Change Makers For Women	6536 Telegraph Ave, Oakland, CA 94609	510–655–2405	http://www.ChangeMakersForWomen.com

Charis Books & More	1189 Euclid Avenue, NE, Atlanta, GA 30307–1509	404–524–0304	http://www.nghosibooks.com/pages/charisbooksandmore.htm
Herland Sister Resources	2312 NW 39th Street, Oklahoma City, OK 73112	405–521–9696	http://www.herlandsisters.org
In Other Words	3734 SE Hawthorne Blvd.,Portland, OR 97214	503–232–6003	http://www.inotherwords.org
Minnesota Women's Press	771 Raymond Ave., St. Paul, MN 55114	651–646–3968	http://www.womenspress.com
Mother Kali's Bookstore	720 E. 13th Avenue, Suite 102,Eugene, OR 97402	541–343–4864	http://www.motherkalis.com
New Woman Books	213 W. Meeker Street,Kent, WA 98032	253–854–4311	http://www.newwomanbooks.com
People Called Women	3153 W. Central Ave, Toledo, OH 43606	419–535–6455	http://www.peoplecalledwomen.com/
Sisterspirit Bookstore	938 The Alameda, San Jose, CA 95126	408–293–9372	http://www.sisterspirit.org
Wild Iris Books	802 W. University Avenue, Gainesville, FL 32601	352–375–7477	http://www.wildirisbooks.com/
Women & Children First	5233 N. Clark, Chicago, IL 60640	773–769–9299	http://www.womenandchildrenfirst.com
Word Is Out	2015 10th Street Boulder, CO 80302	303–449–1415	http://www.wordisout.net

REFERENCES

Carol Seajay, "Books to Watch Out For Community Links (Feminist/women's Bookstores)" Available Online: http://www.btwof.com/links/search.php

Martha Leslie Allen, "Women's Institute for Freedom of the press (Women's Bookstores)" Available Online: http://www.wifp.org/DWM/Bookstores.html

Rose Norman, "Feminist and Independent Bookstores with Online Ordering" Available Online: http://mortonweb.uah.edu/wip/stores.htm

Off Our Backs, "feminist bookstores"
Available Online: http://www.offourbacks.org/Bookstor.htm

Mother Kali's "Feminist Bookstores"
Available Online: http://www.motherkalis.com/links.htm

American Booksellers Association "directory"
Available Online: http://www.bookweb.org/infohub/

Mev Miller, "Feminist Bookstore Locator"
Available Online: http://www.litwomen.org/WIP/stores.html#stores

Notes

NOTES TO CHAPTER ONE

1. In this book I use "women's bookstores" to refer to bookstores run by women and sold materials for women and by women, which is also a synonym for so-called "feminist bookstores."
2. Linda Alcoff, "Cultural Feminism versus Post-Structuralism: The Identity Crisis in Feminist Theory," in *Culture/Power/History: A Reader in Contemporary Social Theory* , ed. Nicholas B. Dirks, et al (Princeton: Princeton University Press, 1994), 98.
3. In this context, Aptheker, for example, describes the term as referring to women's expressive art that arose coincidentally with and deeply influenced the women's movement in the 1970s. See Bettina Aptheker, "Cultural Feminism," in *The Reader's Companion to U.S. Women's History,* ed. Wilma Mankiller et al (New York: Houghton Mifflin Company, 1998), 205.
4. Alice Echols, *Daring to be Bad: Radical Feminism in America, 1967–1975* (Minneapolis: University of Minnesota Press, 1989), 301. Brooke Williams, "The Retreat to Cultural Feminism," in *Feminist Revolution,* ed. Redstockings of Women's Liberation Movement (New York: Random House, 1978), 79.
5. Kathryn Adams, "Paper Lesbians: Alternative Publishing and the Politics of Lesbian Representation in the United States, 1950–1990," 1994, 29.
6. According to Nelle Oosterom, one hundred and thirty-five women's bookstores existed in the North America in 1994. Nelle Oosterom, "Are Women's Bookstores Getting Squeezed Out," *Herizons* (July 31, 1994): 16. Women's Books Online by Lee Anne Phillipe reports the number in the U.S reached 147 in 1996. Available online: http://www.igc.apc.org/women/bookstores/bookmain.html. In the same year, *FBN* reported 143.
7. The author's interview with Carol Seajay.

NOTES TO CHAPTER TWO

1. Many big established publishers such as Doubleday, Random House, Scribner's, Harper are still often called publishers in "Madison Avenue [in Manhattan]."
2. For example, Harper & Row (1817), G & C. Merriam (1831), Houghton Mifflin (1832), Little Brown (1837), and G.P. Putnam's Sons (1838).
3. For example, the tremendous growth of reading audience occurred after the Civil War, and also libraries increased from 2500 to 4000.
4. Andre Schiffrin, *The Business of Books: How International Conglomerates Took Over Publishing and Changed the Way We Read* (New York: Verso, 2000), 8.
5. John Tebbel, *Between Covers: The Rise and Transformation of Book Publishing in America* (New York & Oxford: Oxford University Press, 1987), 84.
6. Richard W. Clement describes how the book industry changed in *The Book in American with Images from the Library of Congress* (Golden, Colorado: Fulcrum Publishing, 1996). Tebbel, 85.
7. Michael Gabriel, "The Astonishing Growth of Small Publishers 1958–1988," *Journal of Popular Culture* 24 (Winter, 1990): 60.
8. The modern paperback was responsible for the creation of some, such as Pocket Books (1939), Bantam Book (1946), New American Library (1948), and Fawcett World Library (1950).
9. For example, reflecting the impact of World War II, Ernest Hemingway's *For Whom the Bell Tolls* sold a million copies by 1946. Tebbel (1987), 18.
10. The Library Services Act of 1958 also provided federal funding for the extension of library services. In 1965 Primary and Secondary Education Act provided major funding for public schools in some schools and up to $200 million for library materials for all schools, public and private. See Everette E. Dennis, *Publishing Books* (New Brumswick & London: Transaction Publisher, 1997), 4–5.
11. The growth of the market meant that publishers needed to invest fully to meet its demands and capital resources had to be boosted so that many small houses which ran out of money either went bankrupt or were absorbed into a larger group.
12. Merger and acquisition activity in the publishing industry beginning first in the 1960s, occurred again in the mid 1970s, and enjoyed resurgence in the late 80s and mid-1990s, but these mergers and acquisitions have had a profound effect upon the book field. This is because in many cases they also placed the power of ultimate decision and policy-making in the hands of people unfamiliar with books, their peculiarities, and their markets. As a result, these mergers changed both organizational culture and the actions of publishers because of the priority given to return on investment. For them, an absolute necessity is to look for a book that sells in huge numbers and that guarantees that any future writings by its author will automatically draw a large audience. See Everette E. Dennis, Craig LaMay, and Edward Poare eds., *Publishing Books* (New Brumswick & London: Transaction

Publisher, 1997), 5. John P. Dessauer, Paul Doebler, and Wayne Nordberg, eds., *Book Industry Trends* (Darien, CT: Book Industry Study Group, 1978), 7.

West and Wheat also pointed out earlier in 1970 that merger brought about publishing became a commercial rather than a cultural activity, and big corporations patterned books in their marketing approach after food supermarkets, and stressed the rise of the "chain bookstores" such as Walden Book Company and B. Dalton. In a similar way, Ben Bagdikian warned that mergers and acquisitions (573 during the period) would hurt the whole publishing industry, particularly, in terms of its diversity, the number of titles produced. Although there were 12000 small publishers in 1985, compared to approximately 1000 in 1958, brand name authors have actually dominated bookstores' shelves in general, so that numerous minor authors' titles (such as those by feminists or people of color) are at least removed from the shelves within a few weeks. It is considered that this trend accelerated especially after the emergence of super chain bookstores such as Borders and Barnes & Noble. For national percentages, see Kendrick J. Noble Jr, "Assessing the Merger Trend," in *The Question of Size in the Book Industry Today: A Publishers Weekly Special Report,* ed. Judith Appelbaum (New York: R.R. Bowker, 1978), 14. For discussions about mergers in the publishing industry, see Maxwell J. Lillienstin, "Concentration and Other Threats to the Book Industry," *American Bookseller* 4, no. 2 (1980): 22–25, Ted Solotaroff, "The Paperbacking of Publishing," *The Nation* 253, no. 11 (1991): 399–404, Thomas Whiteside, *The Blockbuster Complex: Conglomerates, Show Business, and Book Publishing* (Middletown, CT: Wesleyan University Press, 1981), George Woodcock, "Books as Literature vs. Books as Commodity," *Sewanee Review* 90, no.2 (1981): 240–250. See also Celest West and Valerie Wheat, *The Passionate Perils of Publishing* (SF: Booklegger Press,1978), 1–2, 6; Ben Bagdikian, *Media Monopoly* (Boston: Beacon Press, 1983). For discussions over super chain bookstores and e-commerce like Amazon.com, see Laura Miller (1997), (1999), and Audrey Eaglen, "Book Publishing: Past & Present" in *Buying Books* (NY & London: Neal-Schuman Publishers, INC, 1989).

13. Patricia Holt, "No 'Golden Era,' Please," *Holt Uncensored* (February 2, 2001). Available online: http://www.holtuncensored.com/members/column213.html.
14. West and Wheat, 6.
15. Mary V. Gaver, 1974–76 president of the women's National Book Association. Catalyst *Publishing* (NY: Catalyst, 1981), 9.
16. Georgia Bushell, "Women in Publishing: How the Culture of the Publishing Industry has created barriers" (1996). Available Online: http://apm.brookes.ac.uk/publishing/culture/1996/BUSHELL.HTM#LINK1
17. It is considered that the smallness and agility of a woman's fingers made her particularly adept as a compositor. In colonial North America, at first in New England, the demand of printing brought women into this

profession, mostly typesetting and binding as it involved small and delicate handwork, such as in sewing and needlework. Lois Rather, *Women as Printers* (Oakland, California: the Rather Press, 1970), 30, 69. UIUC collection.

18. Hudak, ix.
19. John Tebbel, *A History of Book Publishing in the United States, Volume I: The Creation of an Industry 1630–1865* (New York: R.R. Bowker, 1972), 74–5, 77. Tebbel shows various examples of women's taking over printer: Mary Katherine Goddard succeeded from her brother, and became the official printer of the Declaration of Independence.
20. In the latter half of the nineteenth century, according to Abbott, the printers union instituted a mandatory four-year linotype apprenticeship and effectively excluding women from the industry. Abbott (1910), 258–260, and Madisons (1966): 277,284. Five of six women were widows of printers who assigned business responsibilities upon their husbands' death. For early women printers in the southern states, see Martha Joanne. "Making an Impression: women printers in the southern colonies in the revolutionary era," 1992.
21. There were even some female printers who appeared from 17th to the early 19th centuries. (Leona M Hudak, *Early American Women Printers and Publishers 1639–1820* (Metuchen, NJ & London: The Scarecrow Press, Inc., 1978, ix.) Hudak's study is primarily concerned with individuals who actually operated presses themselves or who legally owned and/or operated printing establishments significant in printing history.
22. John Tebbel, *A History of Book Publishing in the United States, Volume II: the expansion of an Industry 1865–1919* (New York: R.R. Bowker, 1975), ix. For example, a survey conducted in 1890 by the *New York World* revealed a respectable number of women publishers in NY. However, most of them were involved with publications of special interest to women, or publications concerned specifically with church or school.
23. Gayle Johnson, "Women in Publishing," in *Perspectives on Publishing,* ed. Philip G. Altbach (Lexington, MA: Lexington Books, 1976), 259. On February 17, 1914 George H. Plimpton of Ginn and Company gave one of the first detailed reports on the subject of college women in publishing in a speech before the Conference on Literary Work of the Intercollegiate Bureau of Occupation in NY. The Women's Suffrage Parade of October 27, 1917 featured a section of women from bookstores and publishing.(Ibid., 259)
24. Women's National Book Association, *Women's National Book Association Honors Book Women: 70 Who Have Made A Difference, on the occasion of its 70th Anniversary 1917–1987, and the Year of the Reader* (New York: Women's National Book Association, 1987), 3, 5. The association's memberships was open to women in all facets of the book world-publishers, booksellers, librarians, authors, illustrators, agents, production people-the only criterion being that part of their income must come from books. See also the Women's National Book Association's website: Available online: http://www.wnba-books.org/history
25. Tebbel (1975), 174–77. Tebbel has noted that the years during World War I and the suffrage movement signified a leap forward for women in

publishing, Tebbel (1978), 583- 584. However, a 1917 survey showed 826 of a total of 1406 women in publishing were in clerical and stenographic job. 259 were in editorial positions and 321 were in publicity and promotion. According to Margery Davies, a number of educated women were attracted to the book publishing industry in the early 1900s when 38075 male graduated from high school, compared to 56,808 females. This is because teaching jobs were limited and they were looking for positions that demanded literacy and suited their abilities and in which they could take pride. Margery Davies, *Woman's Place Is At the Typewriter: Office Work and Office Workers, 1870 to 1930* (Philadelphia: Temple University Press, 1982), 283–284. In 1914, college-educated women numbered between 20 and 30 percent in the industry. Tebbel (1975),176. In fact, the industry found it easy to employ women who were well educated and to pay them less than men in comparable positions.

26. According to Greco, even in university press, long known for their firm vocal commitment to affirmative action principles, males comprised less than one-third of the total university press universe, but they held sixty-eight of the directorships (80.68%), women filled the remaining eleven jobs (13.92%). Women have had rather limited authority in four key areas: wage determination, editorial decisions, financial decision-making, and general policy. Albert N. Greco, *The Book Publishing Industry* (Boston: Allyn and Bacon, 1996), 5.13. Caplette also notes that significantly women comprise a large in-house staff that exerts much influence over the publishing of individual books but publishing was becoming a "women's business" just as the industry is subsumed by the larger, more powerful entertainment and communications industries. Furthermore, women hold few line positions of authority where they make publishing policy. Michelle Kathleen Caplette, "Women in Book Publishing A Study of Careers and Organizations," 1981, 15, 71.
27. West and Wheat, 6.
28. Ethel Strainchamps, *Room With No View: A Woman's Guide of The Man's World of the Media* (New York: Harper, 1974), xxv. One woman in NBC News told herself "coffee-snack-meal-getter, personal maid, details-organizer, mail-opener, morale-booster," in "Corporate Handmaidens: NBC News," in *Room With No View: A Woman's Guide of The Man's World of the Media* (New York: Harper, 1974), 11. Some scholars note that career success in publishing depends upon a network of informal ties and a sponsorship system. This is because, as Tebbel emphasizes, publishing was a "unique kind of business . . . like a small town where everyone knew everyone else and felt a kinship that was not to be found in ordinary commercial enterprises." (Tebbel, 462–463).
29. Dale Spender, "Electronic Scholarship: perform or perish?" in *Women, Information Technology, Scholarship,* ed. Jeanie Taylor, et al, (Urbana, Illinois: Women, Information Technology, and Scholarship Colloquium Center for Advanced Study, 1993),33.
30. Ibid., 33. Lynn Spender, *Intruders on the Rights of Men: Women's Unpublished Heritage* (London: Pandora, 1983), x.

31. For example, Spender was told there was no market all for "women's series." Dale Spender, *The Writing or the Sex? Or Why You Don't Have To Read Women's Writing To Know It's Good* (NY: Pergamon Press, 1989), 54. Dale Spender, "The gatekeepers: a feminist critique of academic publishing" in *Doing Feminist Research,* ed. Helen Roberts (Boston: Routledge & Kegan Paul, 1981), 186–202. She also argues that those who make decisions an active role in shaping a discipline or area and thus raises legitimate cause for concern for those attempting to work in ways which challenge mainstream orthodoxies.
32. Adrienne Rich, *On Lies, Secrets and Silence* (New York: Norton, 1979).
33. Lynn Spender, ix.
34. Even in 1930, women executives of publishing houses and creative artists banded together to form the "Club of Printing Women of New York," which is still in existence today (Hudak, ix.) See also Catherine Mitchell "Historiography : A New Direction for Research on the Women's Rights Press" in *Journalism History*19 (Summer 1993): 59–63.
35. Strainchamps, xxv.
36. Carol Seajay, "Some Beginnings: An Interview with Judy Grahn. Part II," *FBN* (August 1990): 53–61. Seajay says, such socialist presses also published early women's pamphlets, and the New England Free Press or KNOW, Inc were one of the first distribution networks among feminists. Ibid., 53.
37. Arnold, 3.
38. Dale Spender (1993), 33, 36.
39. According to Bushell, women in 1996 made up 60% of the total employees in publishing, they were still concentrated in clerical, secretarial and administrative positions with little opportunity for vertical promotion. See Georgia Bushell, *Women in Publishing: How the Culture of the Publishing Industry Has Crated Barriers for Entry in Career Development,* Available online: http://apm.brookes.ac.uk/publishing/culture/1996/BUSHELL.HTM
40. Calvin Reid, "Third World Press: 25 years fighting for empowerment," in *Publishers Weekly* (Jan, 1993): 22. For example, in 1967 the third world press was started by Haki R. Madhuburt (the Chicago based, black owned press). Although African American journalism already began with the 1827 publication of *Freedom's Journal,* and started their first newspaper, *New York Sun*). From 1865 to 1900 almost 1200 new African American newspapers and magazines were born, however, although a black editor in the 1850s noted that they needed a press of their own, Lauren Kessler pointed out "it is no less true today." Lauren Kessler, *The Dissident Press: Alternative Journalism in American History* (Beverly Hills: Sage Publications, 1984), 47. For further study about Black publishing, see Colin Anthony Beckles, "Pan African Sites of Resistance: Black Bookstores and the Struggle to Re-present Black Identity," 1995; Donald F. Joyce, *Gatekeepers of Black Culture: Black-owned Book Publishing in the United States, 1817–1981* (West Port, Connecticut: Greenwood Press, 1983); and David Armstrong, *A Trumpet to Arms: Alternative Media in America* (L.A., California: J.P Tarcher, Inc., 1981).

41. Philip Altbach, "Publishing and Intellectual System" in *Perspectives on Publishing* (Philadelphia: American Academy of Political and Social Sciences, 1975), 9.
42. They organized the Committee of Small Magazine Editors and Publishers (COSMEP) in 1968.
43. Len Fulton and Dick Higgins, *Whole COSMEP Catalog* (CA: Dustbooks,1974), 5, 6.
44. Henderson, 103.
45. Fulton and Higgins, 5,6.
46. Ibid.
47. David Armstrong, *A Trumpet to Arms: Alternative Media in America* (LA: J.P.Tarcher, Inc., 1981), 32.
48. Armstrong, 51.
49. However, such small presses were not a development new to the twentieth century. For instance, in the second half of the nineteenth century, hobby printers all over the country published "amateur newspapers." Historically, small presses acted as seedbeds for the literary avant-garde in the US. *The Dial* (1840–1844), for example, never had more than three-hundred paying subscribers, but it was regarded as the most influential utopian periodical and read by influential American and European thinkers and writers. The first editor was Margaret Fuller, then Ralph Waldo Emerson. Henry David Thoreau was first published in *The Dial.* A number of writers who later achieved great fame-such as James Joyce and Upton Sinclair were forced to publish their own books because no "reputable" firm was willing to issue them. Furthermore, politically, morally and socially controversial materials that commercial publishers would not accept were brought out to small presses by many writers like Paine, Whitman, and Crane. Bill Henderson, "Independent Publishing: today and yesterday," *Annals of the American Academy of Political and Social Science* 421 (September 1975): 101.
50. On the other hand, political enthusiasm always drove people to overcome difficulties. According to David Armstrong, in 1912 alone there were 323 avowedly Socialist periodical publications issued in the US. He also points out "during the Socialist Party's happiest days," at least 600 periodicals were published. Armstrong, 37.
51. Ibid., 32.
52. Kirkpatrick Sale, "A Matter of Influence" in *The Sixties Without Apology,* ed. Sohnya Sayres, Fredric Jameson, and Anders Stephason (Minnesota: University of Minnesota Press, 1984), 331–332.
53. Seajay (August 1990): 54.
54. There have been some exceptions, although many women's periodicals in the late 19th and 20th centuries were not usually run or owned by women, and their presses were short-lived, and circulated among a limited number of people. Elizabeth Cady Stanton and Susan B. Anthony launched a weekly journal, *The Revolution,* in 1868. Interestingly the rise and fall of *The Revolution* is strikingly similar to one of feminist small publications of

later eras. At first they used to work for a previous movement promoting civil rights—the abolitionist movement. They likewise learned from their experience with male-run alternative organizations' publications. *The Revolution* covered not only suffrage but also equal pay for equal work, divorce and prostitution, but it folded in 1872 because of a lack of capital. Such a lack of capital was often the cause of the closing of many presses throughout women's publishing history. See Martha Allen, *The Development of Communication Networks Among Women, 1963–83* (Available Online: http://www.wifp.org/tableofcontents.html), and Susan Albertine, *A Living of Words: American Women in Print Culture* (Knoxville: The University of Tennessee Press, 1994) about women in print in the 19th century.

55. As important as what women and minorities did not get published was the kind of information the public received as a result. As Susan Faludi shows mass media bias against women in her *Backlash,* and describes certain media truths and cultural narratives are not necessarily constructed in accumulations of the evidence, but defiance of the evidence. Susan Faludi, *Backlash: The Undeclared War Against American Women* (New York: Crown, 1991). See also, Susan Douglas, *Where the Girls Are: Growing Up Female with the Mass Media* (Random House: New York, 1994), Gaye Tuchman, *Making News: A Study in the construction of Reality* (New York: Free Press, 1978).
56. Kessler, 82. According to Kessler, a 1950 *Atlantic* article stated "women must boldly announce that no job is more exciting, more necessary or more rewarding than that of housewife and mother."
57. William Jay Jacobs, *Women in American History* (New York: MacMillan Publishing Company, 1976), 259. Rosalyn Baxandall, Linda Gordon, and Susan Reverby, eds., *America's Working Women* (New York: Random House, 1976), 302. The mass media sent messages portraying women "either as a sex object or as a contented homebody, often flighty and irresponsible." Lois W. Banner, *Women in Modern America: A Brief History* (New York: Harcourt Brace Jovanovich, Inc., 1974), 215.
58. These papers were usually supported by record and concert ads, but sometimes by explicit sex ads, and created by volunteer or low-waged staffs. This arrangement caused the largely volunteer staff of the *Berkeley Barb* to walk out and form the *Berkeley Tribe* when it was revealed that the *Berkeley Barb*'s owner had made substantial money from sex ads. For discussions about alternative papers and sex ad, see Armstrong, 54–55, 163–166.
59. Ibid., 55.
60. Sara Evans, *Personal Politics: The Roots of Women's Liberation in the Civil Rights Movement and the New Left* (New York: Random House, 1980), 98–101.
61. Armstrong, 226–7. Evans, 112.
62. In the September 1967 founding meeting of the National Conference for New Politics in Chicago, a group of women including Jo Freeman and Shulamith Firestone formed a radical women's caucus and formulated a resolution. Nevertheless, it was described as "trivial," and one man said to the

woman in the conference, "Calm down, little girl," and he patted her on the head. Judith Hole, *Rebirth of Feminism* (New York: Times Books, 1973), 113–114. Later, Freeman and Firestone became leading journalists and writers in the women's movement.

63. Barbara Deckard, *The Women's movement: Political, Socio-Economic and Psychological Issues* (New York: Harper and Row Publishers, 1979), 343.
64. Quoted in Martha Allen, "*The Development of Communication Networks Among Women, 1963–83,*" Available Online: http://www.wifp.org/tableofcontents.html
65. Seajay (1992), 79.
66. Ethel Strainchamps found that women's view points were not only reflected but also distorted in the media because of its chauvinism. See discussions about discrimination against women in the media Ethel Strainchamps in her *Room With No View: A Woman's Guide of The Man's World of the Media* (New York: Harper, 1974). However, many women were not satisfied to "reform" the media and the presses regardless of the size.
67. At least one publication, *Liberation News Service* (LNS), decided in 1970 that its collective should be two-thirds women, both to allow women to learn nontraditional skills like printing and to make sure that women had a voice in the organization's meetings. Ellen Gruber Carvey, "Out of the Mainstream and into the Streets: small press magazines, the underground press, zines, and artists' books" in *Perspectives on American Book History,* ed. Scott E. Casper (Amherst: University of Massachusetts Press, 2002), 394.
68. Robin Morgan, *Sisterhood Is Powerful: An Anthology of Writings from the Women's Liberation Movement* (New York: Random House Trade Paperbacks, 1970).
69. Carol Seajay, "Feminist Publishing in the US" in *250: An Introduction to a World of Women's Books,* ed. Feminist Book Fair Group, (London: Feminist book Fair Groups, 1984), 30.
70. Ibid., 77.
71. Alisa Margaret Klinger, "Paper Uprisings: Print Activism in the Multicultural Lesbian Movement," 203.
72. Ibid.
73. Ibid.
74. Charlotte Bunch. *Passionate Politics: Feminist Theory in Action* (New York: St. Martin's Press, 1987), 218.
75. Seajay (1992), 77.
76. Cadman, 43.
77. Kathleen L. Endres and Therese L. Lueck, *Women's Periodicals in the United States : Social and Political Issues* (Westport, Conn. : Greenwood Press, 1995),414
78. Jo Freeman, *The Politics of Women's Liberation : a case study of an emerging social movement and its relation to the policy process* (New York: McKay, 1975), 110.
79. Bunch (1987), 218.

80. According to Seajay, free lectures on feminism, lesbianism or Marxism by female students were available on campus. They were teaching these issues each other so that it was not surprising some of them started to form local women's groups. Author's interview with Carol Seajay.
81. Betty Friedan, *The Feminine Mys*tique (New York: Norton, 1963).
82. In 1973, *The New Women's Survival Catalogue* listed hundreds of feminist organizations, however, in the 1975 edition could not list all because the number of such organizations reached over a few thousands.
83. In addition to *Feminist Bookstores Newsletter* which introduced numerous feminist writings, many of women's periodicals also introduced women to feminist writings. According to Kathryn Adams, the editors of *It Ain't Me Babe* printed in every issue a boxed sidebar entitled "read," and inside the box there was a short bibliography of books, pamphlets, articles, and journal titles. Kathryn Adams, "Paper Lesbians: Alternative Publishing and the Politics of Lesbian Representation in the United States, 1950–1990," 214.
84. They were from New York, Chicago to Los Angeles and in college towns from Iowa City to Eugene, Kalamazoo, Sacrament, Houston, Pittsburgh. Ibid., 194
85. Ibid.
86. Anne Mather, "A History of Feminist Periodicals," *Journalism History* 1, no.3 (1974):82.
87. McDermott, 29.
88. Audre Lorde, *Sister Outsider* (Ithaca, NY: Crossing Press, 1984), 116.
89. Karen Brondine, "Politics of Women Writing" *The Second Wave* 5 (1979):11.
90. Seajay (May/June 1990): 21.
91. Ibid.
92. Carol Seajay, "Feminist Presses, Publications, and Bookstores," in *The Reader's Companion to US Women's History.,* ed. Wilma Mankiller, (Boston: Houghton Mifflin Co., 1998), 224–226.
93. Seajay (August 1990):61.
94. Jan Clausen, "A movement of poets: thoughts on poetry and feminism, 1970–1981 and beyond," *New Women's Times Feminist Review* (November/December 1981): 9.
95. Polly Joan and Andrea Chesman, *Guide to Women's Publishing* (Paradise, C.A: Dustbooks, 1978), 3.
96. Seajay (May/June 1990): 19–20. Rita Mae Brown, *Songs to a Handsome Woman* (Baltimore: Diana Press, 1973).
97. According to Allen, the more than 620 single-issue periodicals, and 237 special-identity periodicals (race, ethnicity or sexuality) also provided both depth and breadth crucial to the development of the women's movement between 1963 and 1983. Martha Allen, *The Development of Communication Networks Among Women,* 1963–83. Available Online: http://www.wifp.org/tableofcontents.html. In a similar vein, rooted in the surge of Women's Studies programs and feminist organs, from 1972 through 1975 feminist scholarly journals were created, including *Feminist Studies*

and *Women's Studies* in 1972, *Frontiers* in 1975, and *Signs* in 1975.(McDermott, 37)

98. Louis Gould, "Creating a Women's World," *The New York Times Magazine* (Jan, 1977): 35.
99. Ibid. *Off Our Backs* became one of the most respected newspapers of the women's movement, and is still operating at present.
100. Bunch (1987), 218.
101. Ibid., 219.
102. Ibid., 218.
103. Frances Doughty, "Frances Doughty Talks to Charlotte Bunch about Women's Publishing," *Sinister Wisdom* 13 (Spring 1980): 71.
104. Carol Seajay, "Our Words in Our Hands: a brief history of women's presses and bookstores," *Ms.* (July/August 1992), 77.
105. Kate Brandt, "Carol Seajay: Spreading the Word," in Kate Brandt ed., *Happy Endings: Lesbian Writers Talk About Their Lives and Work*. (Tallahassee, Florida: The Naiad Press, Inc., 1993): 141.
106. As early as 1930, female executives of publishing houses and artists banded together to form the Club of Printing Women of New York, which is still in existence today. See Hudak, ix.
107. Bunch, 218.
108. Patrice McDermott, *Politics and Scholarship : Feminist Academic Journals and the Production of Knowledge* (Urbana and Chicago: University of Illinois Press, 1994), 28.

NOTES TO CHAPTER THREE

1. McDermott, 28. Louis Gould, "Creating a Women's World," *New York Times Magazine* (Jan, 1977): 35.
2. Celest West, *The Passionate Perils of Publishing* (SF: Booklegger Press, 1978), 6.
3. Bertha Harris, *Lover* (NY: New York University Press, 1993), xxii.
4. Kate Brandt, "Carol Seajay: Spreading the Word: Keeping Connected with Feminist Bookstore News," in *Happy Endings: Lesbian Writers Talk About Their Lives and Work,* ed. Kate Brandt, (Tallahassee, Florida: The Naiad Press, Inc., 1993), 143.
5. The Boston Women's Health Book Collective, *Our Bodies, Ourselves* (New York: Simon & Schuster, 2nd ed., 1976), 11.
6. Ibid.
7. In 1973 *Our Bodies, Ourselves* was published by Simon & Schuster instead of the New England Free Press, whose staff was strained by the growing volume of requests. It sold 11,000 hardcover copies and 850,000 in paperback.
8. In 1975 the publication rights were sold to Simon and Schuster, which issued a revised and expanded edition. Judy Norsigian explained, "going to a capitalist publisher was one of our biggest struggles, but it was the only way to reach a mass audience." The move was successful. It was ini-

tially sold for 35 cents per copy. The price was later reduced to 25 cents because of their political conviction that it was wrong to make a profit off women. Ibid, 11.

9. Ibid.
10. Elizabeth Sullivan, "Carol Seajay, Old Wives Tales, and the Feminist Bookstore Network: I came to San Francisco with a ray of hope about living life as a lesbian woman," Shaping San Francisco on the Web. Available online, http://www.shapingsf.org/ezine/womens/bookstrs/main.html
11. The Boston Women's Health Book Collective, 14.
12. David Armstrong, *Trumpet to Arms: Alternative Media in America* (LA: J.P.Tarcher, Inc., 1981), 235
13. Ibid.
14. However, this success was not, of course, welcomed by all. Particularly given the religious Rights and conservatives in the early 1980s, *Our Bodies Ourselves* was under heavy attack from the Moral Majority, which said the book was "offensive," "disgusting" and "shocking," and claimed it should be banned. "Confidential" (January 1981). NW collection, Box 4.
15. Kay Ann Cassell, "Women in Print, An Update," *Library Journal* (June 15, 1977): 1353.
16. Carol Seajay, "Some Beginnings: An Interview with Judy Grahn.Part II," FBN 13, no. 2(August 1990): 57.
17. *Woman to Woman: A Book of Poems and Drawings by Women/from SCUM*. (Women's Press Collective, 1970).
18. Carol Seajay, "Some Beginnings: An Interview with Judy Grahn. Part I," *FBN* 13, no.1 (May/June 1990): 22.
19. Cherrie Moraga, and Gloria Anzaldua, *This Bridge Called My Back: Writings By Radical Women of Color* (Berkeley, CA: Third Woman Press, 2002).
20. Carol Seajay. "Feminist publishing houses, Publications, and Bookstores," in *The Reader's Companion to US Women's History,* ed. Wilma Mankiller, (Boston: Houghton Mifflin Co., 1998), 224–226.
21. Bunch (1987), 220.
22. "Persephone Sells Above Industry Norm; Goal: Strong Feminist Communication," *Media Report to Women* (September 1980): 5. Molly Lovelock, "Successful Persephone Press Closes Up; Molly Lovelock Interview Asks Reasons," *Media Report to Women* (May/June 1984): 15–16.
23. Carol Seajay, "The Backlash and the Backlist" *The Women's Review of Books* 12 (1994): 18.
24. Rita Mae Brown, *Songs To A Handsome Woman* (Baltimore: Diana Press, 1973).
25. Bunch (1987), 221.
26. June Arnold, "Feminist publishing houses & Feminist Politics," *Quest* (Summer 1976): 18.
27. Ibid.

28. Ibid.
29. *Baltimore Women's Liberation Newsletter* (September 1971): 7.
30. Celeste West, *Words In Our Pockets: The Feminist Writers Guild Handbook on How To Gain Power, Get Published & Get Paid* (Paradise, California: Booklegger Press, 1985).
31. Bunch (1987), 221.
32. Harris, xxx.
33. Ibid.
34. Seajay (May/June 1990), 25
35. Harris, xxx.
36. Jenny Wrenn, *Guide to Women Book Publishers in the United States for 1988/89* (LA: Clothepin Fever Press, 1990).
37. Arnold (1976), 20.
38. Joan and Chesman, 1–3.
39. Cadman, 81.
40. Suzanna Downing, "A Community-Based Medium: The Story of the Pittsburgh Feminist Network News" in *Communications at the Crossroads: the Gender Gap Connection,* ed. Ramona R.Rush and Donna Allen (Norwood, N.J.: Ablex Publishing Corp, 1984), 99.
41. Nancy Ferro, Coretta Reid Holcomb, and Marilyn Saltzman-Webb, "Statement of Purpose," in *Women in Media: A Documentary Source Books,* ed. Maurine Beasley and Sheila Silver (Washington, D.C.: Women's Institute for Freedom of the Press, 1977), 117.
42. Armstrong, 231.
43. Linda Steiner, "The History and Structure of Women's Alternative Media" in *Women Making Meaning: New Feminist Directions in Communication,* ed. Lana F. Rakow (NY: Routledge, 1992), 126.
44. Kathleen L Endres, and Therese L. Lueck, *Women's Periodicals in the United States: Social and Political Issues* (Westport, CT: Greenwood Press, 1995), 457–88.
45. Armstrong, 231. According to Rodger Streitmatter, when women writers who had different opinions on a subject disagreed, they were likely to adopt a non-attack approach that allowed opinion to be expressed without name-calling or personal animosity. To the contrary, neither gay or straight male journalists of any era tended to fail to replicate a healthy and enriching dialogue. Rodger Streitmatter, *Unspeakable: The Rise of the Gay and Lesbian Press in America* (Boston: Faber & Faber, 1995),181.
46. Ginny Daley examined local feminist media such as *Feminary* (female liberation newsletter) published in 1969, Lollipop Power Press founded in 1970, Carolina Wren Press in 1976, *Sinister Wisdom* in 1976, Women's Book Exchange in 1983 (a membership library), and Southern Sisters Bookstore in 1988. She shows how these feminist media institutions became an advocate of community involvement not only in disseminating information but also in promoting literature and literacy among women in a wide variety of genres. Ginny Daley, "Women and Publishing in North

Carolina," (March 1992) Available Online: http://scriptorium.lib.duke.edu/women/ncwwpub.html.

47. "Diana Press Publications Brochure (1975)," NW collection.
48. *West, 1985.*
49. Harris, ixx; Bunch (1987), 223
50. Brandt, 141.
51. Ibid.
52. "1976 Conference Women in Print," NW collection, Box 3.
53. Ibid.
54. Brandt, 141.
55. The majority of attendance "felt strongly that Third World feminists working on Third World projects with men but who are feminist-identified should be included," and also "having older boys (seven or older) is putting the older girls into an oppressive situation that we ourselves would not like," and the conference planners "the question of providing for children at women's conferences as a means of insuring the presence of mothers, but that if it is possible to make other arrangements for boys seven or older, that every effort should be made to do so, mainly out of respect for the girls coming." "Proposed National Conference of Women's Presses, Publications, Distributors, and Bookstores," NW collection, Box 3.
56. However, the conference did not plan to invite writers. Seajay explained it came from Marxist ideas that laborers should control their own labor, and the conference should be a "conference for workers" so that the conference didn't "put the writers on a pedestal." Elizabeth Sullivan, "Carol Seajay, Old Wives Tales, and the Feminist Bookstore Network: I came to San Francisco with a ray of hope about living life as a lesbian woman." *Shaping San Francisco on the Web*. Available online, http://www.shapingsf.org/ ezine/womens/bookstrs/main.html
57. June Arnold noted, "Women have created a circle of media control with every link covered: a woman writes an article or book, a woman typesets it, a woman illustrates and lays it out, a woman prints it, a woman's journal reviews it, a woman's bookstore sells it, and women read it-from Canada to Mexico and coast to coast." June Arnold, "Feminist publishing houses & Feminist Politics," *Quest* 3, no.1 (Summer 1976): 18.
58. Brandt, 141.
59. The number of women who registered the conference was 132 but, in fact 127 women attended. "A note of budget, and documentation dated in October 15, 1976 and Women In Print Newsletter 1, no.3/4 (January 1997), NW collection, Box 3. Bunch (1987), 223.
60. They also discussed "How to keep the Man from making as little money off us as possible," and "How to deal with the male book industry." 1976 Conference Women in Print," NW collection, Box 3. Women's Bookstores which attended the 1976 conference were Alexandria (Philadelphia, PA), Amazon (Minneapolis, MN), Common Woman Bookstore (Austin, TX), Coventry Books (Cleveland, OH), Everywoman Books (San Raphael, CA), First Things First (Washington, D.C.), ICI: Woman's Place (Oakland, CA),

Lesbian Feminist Bookcenter (Chicago, IL), Mother Kali's Books (Eugene, OR), New Earth Bookstore (Kansas City, MO), New Words (Somerville, MA), Rising Woman Books (Santa Rosa, CA), Room of One's Own (Madison, WI), Sister Bear Bookstore (Liverpool, NY), Sisterhood Bookstore (LA, CA), Womanbooks (NY, NY), Woman's Gallery (Albuquerque, NM), Woman's Place (Portland, OR), Women's Cultural Trust (Philadelphia, PA), Woman to Woman Feminist Bookcenter (Devner, CO). At a mid-Thursday meeting during the conference it was also decided that a newsletter be established to keep open the lines of communication begun at WIP. Therefore, *1976 Women in Print Conference (almost) Newsletter* was published in November 1, 1976. It said that "Pledges were offered for the necessary seed money and Womanpress offered to do the first few issues leaving the future of the newsletter to be decided by the WIP participants. This is an attempt to pass on the information gleaned to date and enlist your support in clearing up a number of loose ends." However, it did not last. Marie Kuda, *1976 Women in Print Conference (almost) Newsletter* 1, no.1 (Nov. 1976):1. NW collection, Box 3.

61. Bunch (1987), 223.
62. Ibid.
63. Ibid.
64. Brandt, 143. Bunch says, "There wasn't any single result to point to—particularly because the emphasis of the conference was 'networking' and developing resources for improving cooperation—women affirmed that "the vision of producing our own institutions, and particularly the importance of publishing as a tool for communication and for developing ideas, has not failed, and the vision that [they] would be able to do it better if [they] controlled it ourselves is still true." Bunch (1987), 227.
65. Brandt, 144.
66. Marie Kuda, *1976 Women in Print Conference (almost) Newsletter* 1, no.1 (Nov. 1976):1. NW collection
67. The second Women in Print Conference was held in the National 4-H Center, Washington, DC in 1981, and the third was held in 1985 at the University of California, San Francisco.
68. Seajay (August 1990), 58.
69. Myra Marx Ferree, and Beth B. Hess, *Controversy and Coalition: The New Feminist Movement* (Boston: Twayne Publishers, 1985), 76.
70. Polly Joan and Andrea Chesman, *Guide to Women's Publishing* (Paradise, CA: Dustbooks, 1978), 2.
71. Ibid.
72. Dale Spender, *The Writing or the Sex? Or why you don't have to read women's writing to know it's no good* (NY: Pergamon Press, 1989), 48.
73. Sievers also describes problems of distribution which affect academic libraries. Arlene Moore Sievers, *Issues in Collection Management: Librarians, Bookseller, Publishers* (Greenwich, CT: JAI press, 1995).
74. Martin Lightfott points out the lack of empirical research on the distribution system. Martin Lightfott, "The Distribution of Books: weak link in the

publishing chain," in *Perspectives on Publishing,* ed. Philip Altbach (Lexington, MA: Lexington Books, 1976), 71–79.

75. John P. Dessauer, "Pity Poor Pascal: some sobering reflections on the American Book Scene," in *Perspectives on Publishing,* ed. Philip Altbach (Lexington, MA: Lexington Books, 1976).
76. Bunch (1987), 221.
77. Altbach, 5.
78. George Zinkhan, "The Role of books and book reviews in the knowledge dissemination process," *Journal of Marketing* 59 (Jan. 1995):106.
79. Alan Wolfe, "the Solemn responsibilities of book reviewing," *The Chronicle of Higher Education* 44 (Apr. 1998): B4-B5.
80. Bruce Macphail, "Book Reviews and the Scholarly Publisher," in *Literary Reviewing,* ed. James Hoge (Charlottesville: University Press of Virginia, 1987), 101–111. For example, Ann Haugland examines the significant role of the *New York Times Book Review* in both the commerce and the culture of book publishing through advertisements, bestsellers lists, reviews, and other editorial features, and finds the tension between them. Ann Haugland, "Books as Culture/Books as Commerce" *Journalism Quarterly* 71 (Winter 1994): 787–799.
81. Anthony Curtis, *Lit Ed: On Reviewing and Reviewers* (U.K. Manchester: Carcanet Press, 1998).

    Presumably, reviewing is never a "neutral enterprise" since a reviewer's own prejudices and assumptions can never be wholly avoided. For example, as Alan Wolfe points out, in the case of books dealing with contentious political themes, reviewers frequently fail to honor books, and tend to review everything except the book itself. Similarly, O'Sullivan points out a book review section is not above the biases which shape the dissemination of news in this country. He describes where controversial authors of subjects are involved, reviewers and review editors can be just as bellicose as any op-ed writer or reporter, and this is particularly true where political agendas stand to be set or defended. For example, Foster points out the *New York Times* published "insulting reviews to Kate Millet or Adrienne Rich" at a meeting of the Writers guild. However, as a matter of fact, "bad reviews are better than no reviews at all." This is because most of books have never been got reviewed anywhere. This is especially true for unknown writers and works from unknown publishers, that is small publishers. According to Champion, who analyzed the contents of 2378 book reviews in the past 20 years period (1949–1971), he found nearly 70% of the reviews for these years expressed positive attitudes toward the books, less than 20 % were negative, and the remainder received no criticism. Furthermore, according to Hirsch and Potter-Efron, book reviews seem to influence the formal rewards and subsequent careers of the authors of books and, furthermore, book sales. In the 1960s, more and more people published in special interest fields from small publishers. However, book review media are taken up by a disproportionately high percentage of books published by companies that can advertise heavily in those book review media journals. See Walter Hirsch and Ronald Potter-Efron, "Book reviews and the Status of Authors and reviewers," *Contemporary Sociology* 9 (July 1980). 520–522: Dean Champion, "A Content analysis of book reviews in the AJS,ASR, and Social Forces," *American Journal of Sociology* 78: 1256–1265, Alan Wolfe, "The solemn responsibilities of book reviewing," *The Chronicle of Higher Education* 44 (Apr. 1998): B4-B5, Gerry O'Sullivan, "Against the Grain," *Humanist* 50 (November 1990) : 43–45, Margaret Foster, "Women in Publishing," in *Reviewing Reviews: A Woman's Place on the Book Page* (London: Journeyman), 82, Pierre Van den Berghe, *Academic Gamesmanship* (New York : Abeland-Schuman, 1970).

82. Steven Stowe, "Thinking about Reviews," *The Journal of American History* 78 (1991): 591–595.

 Also it is said book reviewing is one of a few places where conversation about cultural matters occurs. Jay Parini, "The Disappearing art of reviewing books," *The Chronicle of Higher Education* 45 (July 1999): B4-B5. For example, James Hoge thinks the intellectual community should regard reviewing seriously since book reviewing is to analyze a book, explain its argument or its methods, highlight and illustrate its most significant contributions or shortcomings, and initiate its absorption into the whole body of the field. It ensures the lively and healthy interchange of ideas in fields. James O Hoge, *Literary Reviewing* (Charlottesville: University Press of Virginia, 1987), 88–100. Furthermore, as Steven Moore says, "the real job of reviewing is to see that great books are bought now, not years and years after publication." This is because "forgotten masterpieces will be rediscovered but complacent confidence is damaging to both writers and our culture." Steven Moore, "Introduction," in *Fire the Bastards,* ed. Jack Green (Normal, IL: Dalkey Archive Press, 1992), xiv.

83. Donald F. Joyce, *Gatekeepers of Black Culture: black-owned book publishing in the United States, 1817–1981* (Westport, Conn.: Greenwood Press, 1983).
84. Foster, 79. Margaret Foster monitored twenty-eight publications for the year 1985.
85. June Arnold, "Feminist publishing houses & Feminist Politics," *Quest* III (Summer, 1976): 19–26.
86. *The Women's Review of Books: Pilot Issue* (Summer 1983): 3.
87. Seajay (May/June 1990): 36.
88. Joan, 2. Seajay, (May/June 1990): 22.
89. Ibid.
90. Adams, 222.
91. Ronald Zboray, Ronald and Mary Saracino Zboray. *A Handbook For the Study of Book History in the United States* (Washington, D.C.: Library of Congress, 2000). 51.
92. "Press Release, Women in Distribution," (November 1974). NW collection
93. "Women in Distribution Autumn 1975 Catalog," NW collection
94. Seajay, (May/June 1990), 36. "How Easily Publishers Can Destroy Important Part Of Our Communications System," *Media Report to Women* (August 1979): 9.

95. Ibid.
96. According to Bunch, the failure of WIND was not to have brought "new blood to revitalize and inspire them" in it, and also not to have been able to "see any way of becoming financially viable without major contributions of energy and money from a significant number of women." Bunch (1987), 223.
97. Seajay (May/June 1990): 36.
98. Martha Allen, "The Development of Communication Networks Among Women, 1963–83": Available Online: http://www.wifp.org/tableofcontents.html According to Allen, Pomegranate Productions in New York distributed books, albums, notecards, posters and buttons. Women's Resources Distribution Company in Philadelphia also published and distributed them. Calliope Distribution in Atlanta distributed women's records and songbooks throughout Georgia. Serious Business Company in Oakland, California, was a distributor for independent women filmmakers. Amazon Reality, located in Oregon, distributed a variety kind of feminist works, specializing in Northwest and West coast distribution. Genevieve Productions in Seattle distributed women's records, cassettes, songbooks and local-area books in Washington, Idaho, Oregon, Montana, and Vancouver, B.C. Many of these items were distributed to women's bookstores.
99. Press Release, Diana Press, "Calendar and Date Book," (December 1975). Quoted from Martha Leslie Allen, "The Development of Communication Networks Among Women, 1963–83," Available Online: http://www.wifp.org/tableofcontents.html
100. Quoted in *Media Report to Women* (October 1975), 1. Ragwomen Distributors was founded to distribute feminist periodicals and serviced nearly 300 newsstands, bookstores and record stores.
101. Polly, 244.
102. Karen Peterson. "An Investigation into Women-Identified Music in the US," in *Women and Music in Cross Cultural Perspective,* ed. Ellen Koskoff (Urbana : University of Illinois Press, 1989), 208.
103. Mary Alice Gebhart, "The Michigan Womyn's Music Festival," MA thesis, Michigan State University, 1998,102.
104. "Margie Adam's Lifetime Achievement Award Acceptance Speech" at the opening evening concert of the 22nd National Women's Music Festival, May 31, 1997. Available in Margie Adamas, "Women's Music, Bookstore, Space," http://www.margieadam.com/info/nwmfs.htm
105. Joan, 241.
106. Philip Altbach, *Perspectives on Publishing* (Philadelphia: American Academy of Political and Social Sciences, 1975), 9.
107. Ibid.
108. According to John Tebbel, women's greatest achievements in the early 20th century had been in book-selling. In Europe, many American women, alone or in partnership with their husbands, were noted for their bookshops and related publishing ventures. For discussions about women in publishing industry, see John Tebbel, *A History of Book Publishing in the United*

States, Volume III: The Golden Age Between Two Wars 1920–1940 (New York: R.R.Bowker, 1978). The most famous was Sylvia Beach, who published James Joyce's *Ulysses* in 1922. Her bookstore in Paris served as a "club" for the American writers Ernest Hemingway, John Dos Passos, F. Scott Fitzgerald, and others. Sylvia Beach owned Shakespeare and Company, a bookstore in Paris. See also Charles Anderson, *Bookselling in America and the World: Some Observation & Recollections* (NY: Quardrangle/The New York Times Book Co.,1975). In the US, many small personal bookshops in NY, were owned by women. In a 1922 Madge Jenison, one of the founders of the Sunrise Turn, wrote that women "have overrun bookselling . . . the number of women at the National Bookseller's Convention increases markedly each year. One half the attendance of the convention last year was women." John William Tebbel, *Between Covers: The Rise and Transformation of Book Publishing in America* (New York & Oxford: Oxford University Press, 1987), 277. *Publishers Weekly* reported that by 1928 the entry of women into the field of bookselling was significant. Women headed 36 percent of the new bookshops that were started between 1919 and 1928. Marion Humble, *Publishers Weekly* (Oct 1928):1552.

109. According to Caplette, historically, more common in the publishing industry were the women who achieved some measure of esteem and recognition as small-scale booksellers. Michele Caplette, "Book Publishing: A Study of Careers and Organizations," 48.
110. Carol Seajay in Mev Miller's A Labor of Love (one-hour documentary on cassette tape).
111. Karen Phebe Beiser, Susan Freeman, Linnea Lose, and Betsa Marsh, *Crazy Ladies: Vision and Venture* (Cincinnati, OH: Crazy Ladies Center, Inc., 1994), 2.
112. Ibid.
113. When Carolyn Virginia was thinking about the name of the store, she heard a story about a woman who was dubbed a "crazy lady" because she chose to follow her own path. She chose the name "in honor of that crazy lady and all the other crazy ladies out there who are brave enough to fight the traditional roles assigned to us," Ibid.
114. *FBN* 9, no.6 (1987):
115. Seajay also points out the structure of women's bookstores were as diverse as the women's communities. Seajay (1995), 79.
116. "New Words statement," NW Collection, box 3.
117. "Amazon bookstore collective: Her Tenth Year," *FBN* 4, no.1 (1980):7.
118. Zahniser, 116.
119. Seajay (1995), 83–84
120. Carol Seajay, "Some Beginnings: An Interview with Judy Grahn Part II Summer Supplement," *FBN* (1990): 59.
121. McKey Koivisto & Elise Matthesen, "Honoring women who Honor women: Amazon Turns 25!" *FBN* 18, no.4 (1995):25.
122. Judith Rosen, "New Words: The Collective Works," *Publishers Weekly* (April 21, 1989): 56.

123. Ibid.
124. Women's bookstores usually adopted a sliding-fee scale in store events, the policy being that those who could pay more simply paid more, and those who found it difficult to pay simply paid less—a feminist ideal. For example, Carol Seajay set the regular price of FBN, but repeatedly said to booksellers to "just send whatever you can afford." She maintained this position throughout the course of its publication.
125. For example, according to Kathleen Endres, *Woman Spirit,* published in Oregon, was mailed directly to women's bookstores.
126. Endres and Lueck, 414.
127. Lamenting that the United Kingdom had only one women's bookstore (Sisterwrite in London) in the late 1970, Cadman pointed out British women's lack of enthusiasm for building a solely feminist distribution network combined with a feminist publishing enterprise. Cadman, 88,
128. Brandt (1993), 143.
129. Bonnie Blush "Empty Shelves at Labyris," *Majority Report* (April 5, 1975) no page number available. LHA collection. According to the flyer, "Labyris" means "the sacred double ax of Crete, symbol of the goddess and of matriarchal rule." Labyris Books flyer (April 1974) LHA collection. Bookstore subject file.
130. Ibid.
131. Labyris Books flyer (no dated), LHA collection.
132. Bonnie Blush, "Empty Shelves at Labyris," *Majority Report,* April 5, 1975. LHA collection.
133. Untitled letter (1974 December 16), NW collection, Box 3.
134. "Basis of Unity," *FBN* 2, no.2 (1979):
135. Secombe-Eastland, 252.
136. ICI-A Woman's Place, "Starting a Bookstore: Non-capitalist operation within a capitalist economy," in *The New Woman's Survival Catalog,* ed. . Kristen Grimstad and Susan Rennie (New York: Berkley Publishing Corporation, 1973), 23.
137. Grimstad and Rennie (1975), 139–145. In 1976 the number of women's bookstores reached 25 to 30. Seajay (1995), 83.
138. By the end of the 70s, there were over 70. Grimstad and Rennie (1975), 139–145. Even between years 1992 and 1994, 25 new women's bookstores opened, until by 1997 they numbered over 140.

NOTES TO CHAPTER FOUR

1. June Arnold, "Proposed National Conference of Women's Presses, Publications, distributors, and Bookstores," (January 15, 1976). NW collection, Box 3.
2. June Arnold, "Second Mailing: 1976 Conference Women in Print," (March 1976). NW collection, Box 3.
3. For example, it is considered that *Rubyfruit Jungle* was, like *The Feminine Mystique,* one of the most enduring and influential books during the era.

According to Klinger, Brown's work touched the life of apparently every lesbian feminist at the time. In the wake of the work's publication, a whole world of lesbian feminist writings exploded into birth—bringing forth what have been called "paper uprisings" by "paper lesbians" who developed their own network, and a sense that they were entitled to live happily, beautifully and with strength. Alisa Margaret Klinger. "Paper Uprisings: Print Activism in the Multicultural Lesbian Movement." Tracy Kathryn Adams. "Paper Lesbians: Alternative Publishing and the Politics of Lesbian Representation in the United States, 1950–1990."

4. Carol Seajay says: "Once they made it through the doorway [of the women's bookstore], the book what they found changed their lives—— [they] left abusive relationships, found new self-images, came out, [and] found sisterhood and a community." Carol Seajay, "Our Words in Our Hands: a brief history of women's presses and bookstores" in Loraine Edwalds and Midge Stocker ed., *The Woman-Centered Economy: Ideals, Reality, and the Space in Between* (Chicago : Third Side Press, 1995), 77–86.
5. Klinger, 81.
6. Author's interview with Carol Seajay.
7. For their emphasis on feminism, not lesbianism in running women's bookstores, see following pages of *FBN; FBN* 1, no.1 (1976): 1, *FBN* 14, no.2 (1981): 25, *FBN* 15, no.2 (1992): 19.
8. Author's interview with Linda Bubon.
9. "*Publishers Weekly* Covers a Feminist Bookstore in Bookselling and Marketing Column," *FBN* 4, no.6 (1981):4–5.
10. "Notes from the computer, " *FBN* 13, no.5 (1991): 2.
11. Toni Carabillo and Jidith Meuli, *Feminist Chronicles, 1953–1993* (Los Angels: Women's Graphics, 1993), 48.
12. Margaret Anderson, *Thinking About Women: Sociological Perspectives on Sex and Gender* (New York: Macmillan Publishing Co., 1988), 297. The purpose of NOW was to take action to bring American women into full participation in the mainstream of American society *now,* "exercising all the privileges and responsibilities thereof in truly equal partnership with men." Barbara Deckard, *The Women's Movement: Political, Socio-Economic and Psychological Issues* (New York: Harper and Row Publishers, 1979), 347.
13. Carabillo and Meuli, 55.
14. D'Emilio and Freedman, 244.
15. By the end of the 1980s some organizations had included lesbian issues in their agenda, however at the same time some organizations like NOW lost credibility with the general public and even their own members because of NOW President Patricia Ireland's "confession" of bisexuality. Mainstream media utilized the conflict within NOW. When Kate Millett's acknowledgment of bisexuality, articles about her bisexuality "discredited her as a spokeswoman for her cause, cast further doubt on her theories, and reinforce the views of those skeptics who routinely dismiss all liberationists as

lesbians." See Roberta Spalter-Roth and Ronnee Schereiber, "Outsider Issues and Insider Tactics: strategic tensions in the women's policy network during the 1980s," in *Feminist Organizations: Harvest of the New Women's movement,* ed. Myra Marx Ferree and Patricia Yancey Martin (Philadelphia: Temple University Press, 1995), 123–124. John D'Emilio and Estelle Freedman, *Intimate Matters: A History of Sexuality in America* (New York: Harper Collins Publishers, Inc., 1988), 245, 246.

16. Karla Jay, "The decline and fall of an idealist or why ain't I marching anymore," *Lesbian Tide* (August 1983): 177. Yolanda G. Retter, "On the Side of Angels: lesbian activism in Los Angels, 1970–1990."
17. Sullivan, http://www.shapingsf.org/ezine/womens/bookstrs/main.html
18. Ibid.
19. According to Seajay, the colleague raised her sexuality in order to secure the job for herself.
20. Sullivan, http://www.shapingsf.org/ezine/womens/bookstrs/main.html
21. For example, in the year of 1971 alone, more than 10 lesbian journals were emerged throughout the country. In addition, after the appearance of the breakthrough bestseller *Rubyfruit Jungle* in 1973, numerous lesbian feminist writings were published.

    In 1975 the first National Women's Music Festival was held, and the song "Changer and the Changed" by Cris Williamson became a symbol of lesbian identity. Two national cultural events were then held the next year for the first time; the first Women In Print Conference and the first Michigan Womyn's Music Festival. Both of them attracted a number of lesbians around the nation, and were huge successes.

    Seajay explained women in the WIP conference were highly energetic and up-lifted. She said, "We weren't going to depend on anybody for anything! Nobody was going to stop us! That was the energy that was at the first Women In Print Conference." Carol Seajay, "Some Beginnings: An Interview with Judy Grahn Part II Summer Supplement," *FBN* (August 1990): 58.
22. For discussions about the Lesbian and Gay Liberation Movement, see Margaret Cruikshank, *The gay and lesbian liberation movement* (New York: Routledge, 1992), Martin Duberman, *Stonewall* (New York: Dutton, 1993), John D'Emilio, *Sexual Politics, Sexual Communities: The Making of a Homosexual Minority in the United States, 1940–1970* (Chicago: University of Chicago Press, 1983), Lillian Faderman, *Odd Girls and Twilight Lovers: A History of Lesbian Life in Twentieth-century America* (New York: Columbia University Press, 1991), Eric Marcus, *Making History: The Struggle of Gay and Lesbian Equal Rights 1945–60* (New York: Harper Collins, 1992), Eric Marcus, *Making Gay History: The Half-century Fight for Lesbian and Gay Equal Rights* (New York: Perennial, 2002), Jeffrey Weeks, *Sexuality and its Discontents' Meanings, Myths, and Modern Sexualities* (New York: Routledge, 1985), Jeffrey Weeks, *Making Sexual History* (Malden, Mass.: Blackwell, 2000).

23. The Stonewall riot also invented Gay Pride Days since 1970 in New York, Washington, DC., Philadelphia, and other cities throughout the nation during the months of May and June.
24. John Howard, *The Cutting Edge: Social Movements and Social Change in America* (Philadelphia: Lippencott, 1974), 129.
25. D'Emilio and Freedman, 246.
26. Jan Laude, "Folklore as an instrument of stigma; Folklore as an instrument of liberation: the case of Lesbian coding," 38.
27. Friedan made her statement on March 4, 1973; see Leigh W. Rutledge, *The Gay Decades: From Stonewall to the Present* (New York: Plume, 1992), 54–55.
28. Rodger Streitmatter, *Unspeakable: The Rise of the Gay and Lesbian Press in American*(Boston: Faber and Faber, 1995), 117. Yet by the end of 1972, it seemed that their radicalism had almost faded from the political landscape, but then in 1978 gay San Francisco supervisor Harvey Milk and Mayor George Moscone were assassinated by Dan White, and lesbians, gays and supporters united in a massive march protesting this incident.
29. They were, for example, *Gay Times, Com Out!, Gay Sunshine, The San Francisco Gay Free Press,* and *Killer Dyke in Chicago.*
30. Papers published in 1971 include *Focus: A Journal for Gay Women [The Maiden Voyage]* in Cambridge, Massachusetts; *Sisters: By and For Gay Women* in San Francisco; *The Lesbian Letter* in New York, and *Purple Star: Journal of Radicalesbians* in Ann Arbor, Michigan.
31. Susan Brownmiller describes the weaknesses, disappointments, and differences of feminists as well as their drive, their prophetic vision, and their commitment to their ideals, and jealousies among feminists often worked to the detriment of the movement. According to her, Marilyn Webb was told to scale back to give other women a chance to write, and Webb's gift of writing was greeted with resentment at "*Off Our Backs,* " and her colleagues ejected her from "*Off Our Backs.*" Susan Brownmiller, *In Our Time: Memoir of a Revolution* (New York: Dial Press, 1999). For discussion about feminists' competition with each other for fame, leadership, and prestige, see Valerie Miner and Helen Longino, eds., *Competition: A Feminist Taboo?* (New York: The Feminist Press, 1987); Ruth Rosen, *The World Split Open,* particularly Chapter Seven: The Politics of Paranoia (New York: Penguin Books, 2000); for in particular "public trashing"—-allegation to Gloria Steinem with a link to CIA by feminists, see Carolyn Heilbrun, *The Education of a Woman: The Life of Gloria Steinem* (New York: Ballantine, 1996) and Caroline Lazo, *Gloria Steinem: Feminist Extraordinaire* (New York: Lerner, 1998).
32. Martha Leslie Allen, "The Development of Communication Networks Among Women, 1963–83," Available online: http://www.wifp.org/tableofcontents.html
33. Salvatore John Licata, "Gay Power: A History of the American Gay Movement, 1908–1974," 142.

34. Rose Weitz, "From Accomodation to Rebellion: The Politicization of Lesbianism," in *Woman-Identified Woman,* ed. Trudy Dart and Sandee Potter (Palo-Alto, CA: Mayfield Publishing Co., 1984), 238.
35. Carol Seajay, "Some Beginnings: An Interview with Judy Grahn Part I," *FBN* (May/June 1990): 20.
36. Charlotte Bunch, *Passionate Politics: Feminist theory in action, essays, 1968–1986* (New York: St. Martin's, 1987), 228.
37. According to Linda Rapp, later Grier worked as *The Ladder*'s poetry and fiction editor from 1966 until 1968, when she assumed the general editorship. Linda Rapp, "Barbara Grier," *glbtq: an encyclopedia of gay, lesbian, bisexual, transgender & queer culture:* Available online: http://www.glbtq.com/literature/grier_b,2.html
38. Quoted in Adams, 224.
39. D'Emilio, (1998), 110.
40. According to Faderman, *The Lesbian Tide* had been the journal of the Los Angeles branch of DOB, severed from its mother organization in 1973 because it felt the need to take a more radical stance. *The Ladder* stopped publishing in 1972, not only because of internal difficulties with the publishing staff but also because they had failed to appeal to younger women, who were more interested in the numerous militant gay and lesbian-feminist magazines. Lillian Faderman, *Odd Girls and Twilight Lovers: A History of Lesbian Life in Twentieth-century America* (NY: Penguin, 1992), 197. Streitmatter also points out, for many pioneers, the lesbian and gay presses not only donating huge quantities of time with zero financial reward, but also becoming victims of hate crimes such as Phyllis Lyon in *The Ladder,* Sasha Gregory-Lewis in *the Advocate,* George Mendenhall in *the Bay Area Reporter,* and Jeff McCourt in *the Windy City Times.* Rodger Streitmatter, *Unspeakable: The Rise of the Gay and Lesbian Press in America* (Boston: Faber & Faber, 1995), 342.
41. Faderman (1991), 197.
42. Streitmatter, 160. See also Faderman (1992), 204–209.
43. I calculated it based on the number reported in Andrea Clardy's *Words to the Wise: A Writer's Guide to Feminist and Lesbian Periodicals and Publishers* (Ithaca, N.Y.: Firebrand Books, 1986), 44.
    In 1970 Daughters of Bilitis (DOB) and *The Ladder* split, since then newsletters of DOB chapters continued to appear during the 1960s.' According to Allen, in1975 the Lesbian Herstory Archives was established, and started a tri-annual newsletter to report archive activities, new acquisitions, research queries, bibliographies, and announcements. Martha Allen, *The Development of Communication Networks Among Women, 1963–83.* Available Online: http://www.wifp.org/tableofcontents.html
44. Ibid.
45. Carol Seajay, "Some Beginnings: An Interview with Judy Grahn: Part I," *FBN* (May/June 1990): 35.
46. Elizabeth Sullivan, "Carol Seajay, Old Wives Tales, and the Feminist Bookstore Network: I came to San Francisco with a ray of hope about living life

as a lesbian woman," *Shaping San Francisco on the Web,* Available online, http://www.shapingsf.org/ezine/womens/bookstrs/main.html. Seajay points out until the late 60s the choice was strictly New York or San Francisco for lesbian and gay people who want to live out of closet.

47. Sullivan, http://www.shapingsf.org/ezine/womens/bookstrs/main.html
48. Kate Brandt, *Happy Endings: Lesbian Writers* (Tallahassee, Florida: The Naiad Press, Inc., 1993), 1.
49. They are, for example, Anne Aldrich, *We Walk Alone Through Lesbos' Lonely Groves* (Greenwich, Conn. : Fawcett, 1955), Ann Bannon, *Beebo Brinker* (Tallahassee, Fla.: Naiad Press, 1986), and Claire Morgan, *The Price of Salt* (Tallahassee, Fla.: Naiad Press, 1984).
50. Lee Lunch, "Cruising the Libraries," in *Lesbian Texts and Contexts Radical Revisions,* ed. Karla Jay and Joanne Glasgow, ed (NY: New York University Press, 1990), 47.
51. National Museum & Archive of Lesbian and Gay History, "Lesbians in Literature," in *Lesbian Almanac* (New York: Berkeley Books, 1996), 271.
52. Streitmatter, 180.
53. Myrna Marx Ferree, and Beth B. Hess, *Controversy and Coalition: The New Feminist Movement* (Boston : Twayne Publishers, 1985), 214.
54. Laude, 41.
55. Ibid.
56. Margie Adam, "Women's Music, Bookstore, Space," in Margie Adam's Lifetime Achievement Award Acceptance Speech, at the opening evening concert of the 22nd National Women's Music Festival, May 31, 1997. Available online: http://www.margieadam.com/info/nwmfs.html. In 1982, the festival was officially incorporated as a nonprofit org called Women in the Arts: National Women's Music Festival, Inc., and moved to the Indiana University Campus in Bloomington, Indiana.
57. Ibid.
58. Olivia Records was established by a group of five women on January 19, 1973 as the first independent label only dedicated to recording women. The formation was crucial because it meant that entire process of producing music was made solely by women. After the creation and successes of Olivia Records, a number of protest-oriented women's music labels were started. It produced nearly fifty albums, hundreds of concerts and reached millions of women with music made by women. Gebhart points out, "Olivia Record also signified a move toward the commodification of women's music. As the brainchild of a collective of women who were searching for a way to implement their lesbian-feminist politics, Olivia had the distinction of being the first collective attempt at being an integrated organization devoted to the production, distribution and promotion of women's music." For discussions of the development of women's music and Olivia Record, see Mary Gebhart, "The Michigan Womyn's Music Festival," MA thesis, Michigan State University, 1998, 90–106. For discussions over "commodification" of lesbianism, see Danae Clark, "Commodity Lesbianism," in *The Lesbian*

and Gay Studies Reader, ed., Henry Abelove et al. (New York: Routledge, 1993), 186–201.

59. Scott Alarik, "Two music pioneers remember the struggle," *Boston Globe Correspondent* (Oct 1, 2000): no page number.
60. Christopher Seeley, "Two Foremothers of Lesbian Folk rock combine voices for Histories," *Southern Voice* (October 25, 2000): Available online: http://www.criswilliamson.com/news.htm
61. Adam, http://www.margieadam.com/info/nwmfs.htm.
62. Meg Christian was instrumental not only in promoting women's music, but became the representative of the lesbian community, performing hundreds of shows all over the country for audiences that were starved for music that mentioned lesbians or lesbian relationships. Olivia, "Olivia Timeline": Available online http://www.olivia.com/about/timeline.html
63. Since then, every year more than 5000 women continue to travel from all over the world to spend a week camping in the woods of north-western lower Michigan. Gebhart, 1.
64. Debbie Charles, "Revolution NOW! Alternatives in Music," *Paid My Dues* (October 1974): 10–11.
65. Alarik: http://www.criswilliamson.com/news.htm
66. Ibid.
67. Kathy Rudy, "Radical Feminism, Lesbian Separatism, and Queer Theory," *Feminist Studies* (Spring 2001): 194.
68. Joseph R. Gusfield, *Community: A Critical Response* (NY: Harper & Row, 1975), xv-xvi.
69. Phyllis Chesler, "All We Have Is Each Other," in *The Woman-Centered Economy,* ed. Loraine Edwalds and Midge Stocker (Chicago: Third Side Press, 1995), 105.
70. Ibid., 4.
71. Certainly there should be cases that heterosexual women were pushed off by lesbians, or if not pushed off, there were heterosexual women who left because of the predominant presence of lesbians. For example, Jill Diane Zahnizer showed that there were heterosexual women who were "always a minority," and "sometimes felt isolated, mistrusted, or dismissed" in the bookstore collective because of her sexuality. Zahnizer, 119.
72. Flora McMartin, "The Institutionalization of women's centers and women's studies programs at three research universities,"26. According to McMartin, the number of women's centers was also increasing in the 1970s. By 1974 there were 215 women's centers, but by 1979 it reached 360.
73. Linda Steiner points out that the underground women's comic strips not only attempts to "bridge the gap between academic and popular views of feminism," but also to "touch quite large audiences" by creating images of women quite different conventional popular ones. Linda Steiner, "The History and Structure of Women's Alternative Media," in *Women Making Meaning: New Feminist Directions in Communication,* ed. Lana F. Rakow (NY: Routledge, 1992),134. See also Dolores Mitchell, "Humor in California Underground

Women's Comics" in *Women's Culture,* ed.Gayle Kimball (Meuchen, New Jersey: The Scarecrow Press, Inc.,1981.)

74. Quoted in Alisa Klinger, "Writing Civil Rights: the political aspirations of lesbian activist-writers," in *Inventing Lesbian Cutlures in America,* ed. Ellen Lewin (Boston: Beacon Press, 1996), 68.
75. Terri De La Pena, "Eco deuna Amistad/Echo of a Friendship," in *Lesbian Friendships: For Ourselves and Each Other,* eds., Jacqueline S. Weisntock and Esther D. Rothblum (New York: New York University Press, 1996), 32. May Sarton wrote a novel called *The Education of Harriet Hatfield* (NY: W.W. Norton & Company, 1989) in which the lesbian feminist protagonist ran a women's bookstore, although the bookstore ended up closing due to hate crimes against lesbians in her homophobic neighborhood.
76. "GOING, Going, Gone . . . ," *FBN* 22, no.3/4 (1999): 20.
77. Jo Reger, "Emotions, objectivity and voice: an analysis of a "failed" participant observation, " *Women's Studies International Forum* 24, no.5 (2001): 607–608.
78. Seajay (1995), 81.
79. Roseanne Barr, *Roseanne: My Life as a Woman* (NY: Harper & Row, 1989), 153, 154.
80. Andre, "(frontpage)," *FBN* 1, no.1 (1976): 1.
81. Klinger, 68.
82. Seajay (1990), 35.
83. Ibid.
84. Deborah Goleman Wolf, *The Lesbian Community with an Afterward* (Berkeley, California: University of California Press, 1980), 107, 177. According to Wolf, the Full Moon coffeehouse and bookstore, pseudonymously referred to "Demeter's Daughter" in her first edition of *The Lesbian Community* in 1979.
85. Ibid.
86. Within three years, the Full Moon closed because it could not renew its lease.
87. Started in Oakland in 1972, A Woman's Place was run as a collective. In 1982 some collective members locked out others as part of a conflict about "differing views of feminism" and charges of racism. Two years later the bookstore folded; its founders, Carol Wilson and Alice Molloy, started another bookstore called Mama Bears.
88. Sullivan, http://www.shapingsf.org/ezine/womens/bookstrs/main.html
89. Author's interview with Seajay
90. Ibid.
91. Sullivan, http://www.shapingsf.org/ezine/womens/bookstrs/main.html
92. Debra Michals, "Beyond 'Pin Money': The rise of women's small business ownership 1945–1980," 255.
93. Sullivan, http://www.shapingsf.org/ezine/womens/bookstrs/main.html
94. Ibid.
95. Seajay (August 1990), 59.
96. Ibid.

97. Ibid.
98. Analyzing political Black bookstores in London, UK, Beckles found they were relatively connected with each other there and persisted because of their own network. Anthony Colin Beckles, "PanAfrincan Sites of Resistance: Black Bookstores and the struggle to re-present black Identity," PhD dissertation, UCLA, 1995,183.
99. Such campaigns convinced Bantam to reprint Joanna Russ's lesbian-feminist science fiction novel, *The Female Man,* and also saved *The Well of Loneliness* from going out of print during the 50th anniversary year of its original publication. The bookstores also had a hand in keeping Toni Morrison's early novels (*Sula,* or *The Bluest Eye*) and Alice Walker's *Meridian* available, urging their mainstream publishers to get them into paperback. On another occasion, *FBN* subscribers helped Marge Piercy persuade Doubleday, the hardcover publisher of her second novel, *Dance the Eagle to Sleep,* to allow it to be published in paperback. See also *FBN* 2, no.1 (1978):9, *FBN* 2, no.2 (1979):2, *FBN* 3, no.2 (1979):11.
100. For some comments to feminist booksellers about priorities of publishers, see also "letters" of *FBN* 1, no. 4 (1976):1,6; *FBN*1, no.9 (1977):3, *FBN* 2, no.1 (1978):5,7.
101. "Carol Seajay" in *Outstanding Lives: Profiles of Lesbians and Gay Men,* ed. Brelin, Christa and Michael J. Tyrkus (Detroit, MI: Visible Ink Press, 1997), 344. *FBN* 1, no. 1 (1976): 1.
102. *FBN* informed feminist booksellers what was available and what was in print and out of print. It also brought their attention to new materials on special subjects. *FBN* 1, no. 3 (1977): 7–9. Kathryn Adams also pointed out that the important role of Carol Seajay and *FBN* in building feminist publishing communities. Adams, 180–156.
103. Lynn Taylor, "letters," *FBN* 4, no.3 (1980): 5.
104. Sister Moon, "This is what we like about FBN," *FBN* 2, no.1 (1978): 3
105. Lori Louise, "Letters (ClaireLight Women's Books), "*FBN* 10, no.2 (1987): 6.
106. Adams, 232.
107. Ibid.
108. *Emergency FBN* 3, no.3 (1979): 2.
109. "More on WIND closing," *FBN* 3, no.3 (1979): 3.
110. Ibid. The Wanderground: Stories of the Hill Women written by Sally Miller Gearhart in 1978. This science fiction tells of a world in which men and women are separated, with women in the hills while men remain in the cities.
111. Ibid., 2.
112. Andre,"(frontpage)," *FBN* 1, no. 1 (1976): 1.
113. Streitmatter, 181.
114. Anthony Colin Beckles, "PanAfrincan Sites of Resistance: Black Bookstores and the struggle to re-present black Identity," 1995, 183.
115. Brandt, 146.
116. Seajay (August 1990), 59.

117. "A Room of One's Own, special order receipt and forms," *FBN* 4, no.1 (1980):12–13; "Things you always wanted to know . . . ," *FBN* 2, no.2 (1978): 9.
118. Adams, 227.
119. Brandt, 46.
120. Ibid.
121. Sadhbh Neitar "Letters," *FBN* 4, no.4 (1980):4.
122. Karyn London, "This is what we like about *FBN*," *FBN* 2, no.1 (1978): 3.
123. Brandt, 141.
124. Sullivan, http://www.shapingsf.org/ezine/womens/bookstrs/main.html.
125. Seajay (1995), 79.
126. Brandt, 146

NOTES TO CHAPTER FIVE

1. For discussions of the backlash against feminism, see Susan Faludi, *Backlash: The Undeclared War Against American Women* (New York: Crown, 1991), Juliet Mitchell and Ann Oakley, *Who's Afraid of Feminism? Seeing Through the Backlash* (New York: New Press, 1997). For discussions about the defeat of the ERA, Myra Marx Ferree and Beth B. Hess, *Controversy and Coalition: The New Feminist Movement* (Boston: Twayne Publishers, 1985); Jane J. Mansbridge, *Why We Lost the ERA* (Chicago: University of Chicago Press, 1986); Steven M. Buechler, *Women's Movements in the United States: Woman Suffrage, Equal Rights, and Beyond* (New Brunswick: Rutgers University Press, 1990); Suzanne Staggenborg, *The Pro-Choice Movement: Organization and Activism in the Abortion Conflict* (New York: Oxford University Press, 1991).
2. David Armstrong, *Trumpet to Arms: Alternative Media in America* (L.A.: J.P.Tarcher, Inc., 1981), 356.
3. Robert C. Liebman and Robert Wuthnow, *The New Christian Right* (New York: Aldine, 1983). For New Right, see also Rebecca Klatch, *Women of the New Right* (Philadelphia: Temple University Press, 1987), David Frum, *How We Got Here: The Seventies* (New York: Basic, 2000).
4. Verta Taylor, "The Future of Feminism in the 1980's: a social movement analysis" in *Feminist Frontiers: rethinking sex, gender, and society,* ed. Laurel W. Richardson and Verta Taylor (Reading, MA: Addison-Wesley, 1983).
5. Teresa L. Amott, *Caught in the Crisis: Women and the US Economy Today* (New York: Monthly Review Press, 1993).
6. Ferree and Hess, 173.
7. Becki L. Ross, *The House That Jill Built: A Lesbian Nation in Formation* (Toronto: University of Toronto Press, 1995), 268.
8. Katheleen M Weston and Lisa B Rofel, "Sexuality, class and conflict in a lesbian workplace," in *The Lesbian Issue: Essays from Signs,* ed. Estelle B Freedman (Chicago: University of Chicago Press, 1985), 205.

9. Joan Gibbs and Sara Bennett, *Top Ranking: A Collection of Articles on Racism and Classism in the Lesbian Community* (NY: Come! Unite Press, 1980), 28.
10. Dana Shugar, *Separatism and Women's Community* (Lincoln: University of Nebraska Press, 1995), xiii-xiv, 187. Bonny Zimmerman finds "separatism's primary goal to be the creation of political theory and alternative institutions designed to bring about sociopolitical change; cultural feminism, on the other hand, is characterized by its goals to define a 'uniquely female nature, vision, and artistic expression." Bonnie Zimmerman, *The Safe Sea of Women: Lesbian Fiction, 1969–1989* (Boston, Mass.: Beacon Press, 1990), xiv. Alisa Margaret Klinger, "Paper Uprisings: Print Activism in the Multicultural Lesbian Movement," 81.
11. Pam Wilson-Race, "letters," *FBN* 2, no.4 (1978): 1,2.
12. Carol Seajay, "Our Words in Our Hands: a brief history of women's presses and bookstores" in Loraine Edwalds and Midge Stocker ed., *The Woman-Centered Economy* (Chicago : Third Side Press, 1995), 85
13. Ibid.
14. Dorothy Holland and Jackie Sparks, "Bookstore Profile: Doing It In Wyoming," *FBN* 14, no.1 (1991): 23.
15. Alisa Solomon, "Too Special for Words? Women's bookstore stiffed by SBA," *The Village Voice* (January 26, 1988). LHA collection, bookstore subject file.
16. "SBA refuses Grand Books," *FBN* 11, no.1 (1988): 12.
17. See also Gregory B. Mills and John L. Palmer, *Federal Budget Policy in the 1980s* (Washington, D.C.: Urban Institute Press, 1984); Flora Davis, *Moving the Mountain: The Women's Movement in American since 1960* (Urbana: University of Illinois Press, 1999), Susan Faludi, *Backlash: The Undeclared War Against American Women* (New York: Crown, 1991), Barbara Ryan, *Feminism and the Women's movement: Dynamics of Change in Social Movement Ideology and Activism* (New York: Routledge, 1992).
18. For discussions about Phyllis Schlafly, see Carol Felsenthal, *The Sweetheart of the Silent Majority: The Biography of Phyllis Schlafly* (Garden City, N.Y.: Doubleday, 1981), Susan Marshall, "Confrontation and Co-optation in Antifeminist Organizations," in *Feminist Organizations: Harvest of the New Women's Movement,* ed. Myra Marx Ferree and Patricia Yancey Martin (Philadelphia: Temple University Press, 1995), 323–338.
19. Marshall, 328.
20. Ibid.
21. Cheryl Hyde, "Feminist Social Movement Organizations: survive the New Right," in *Feminist Organizations: Harvest of the New Women's movement,* ed. Myra Marx Ferree and Patricia Yancey Martin (Philadelphia: Temple University Press, 1995), 313.
22. Ibid., 314.
23. Ibid.
24. Ibid.

25. Ibid., 315. See also, Suzanne Staggenborg, "Can Feminist Organizations Be Effective?" in *Feminist Organizations: Harvest of the New Women's movement,* ed. Myra Marx Ferree and Patricia Yancey Martin (Philadelphia: Temple University Press, 1995), 339–355.
26. According to American Civil Liberties Union, as of 2004, the federal Medicaid program mandates abortion funding in cases of rape or incest, as well when a pregnant woman's life is endangered by a physical disorder, illness, or injury. Currently only seventeen states fund abortions for low-income women on the same or similar terms as other pregnancy-related and general health services. "Public Funding for Abortion," ACLU: Reproductive Freedom (July 21, 2004) available online: http://www.aclu.org/ReproductiveRights/ReproductiveRights.cfm?ID=9039&c=146
27. Faludi, 418.
28. Rita Ciolli, "Grant for Women's Shelter Attacked," *Newsday* (June 1985):14.
29. Roberta Spalter-Roth and Ronnee Schereiber, "Outsider Issues and Insider Tactics: Strategic Tensions in the Women's Polity Network during the 1980s," in *Feminist Organizations: Harvest of the new women's movement,* ed. Myra Marx Ferree and Patricia Yancey Martin (Philadelphia: Temple University Press, 1995), 120.
30. In early 1977, after the Dale County Florida City Council had passed a "pro-gay" ordinance. In August, John Briggs, a California State Assemblyman, announced to put an anti-gay Proposition on the 1978 California ballot.
31. Suan Cavin, "The Invisible Army of Women: lesbian social protest, 1969–1988," in *Women and Social Protest,* ed. Guilda West and Rhoda Blumberg (NY: Oxford University Press, 1990), 325. A record high of 7,008 anti-gay violence incidents were reported to the National Gay and Lesbian Task Force (NGLTA) in 1987, compared with 4,946 incidents in 1986 across the US. For further information, see NGLTF Anti-Gay Violence, *Victimization and Defamation in 1987* (Washington, D.C.: NGLTF, 1987).
32. In 1970s FBI had already investigated feminist institutions. For example, Timothy Redfearn, an FBI informer, confessed to the August 1975 break-in in the *Big Mama Rag,* a Denver feminist newspaper to investigate the interconnections between lesbians or feminists and the radical community. "The FBI and Big Mama," *FBN* 1, no. 9/10 (1977): 5.
33. Howard Field, "Moral Moral Everywhere," *FBN* 5, no. 1 (1981): 14.
34. "Confidential" (January 1981). NW Collection, Box 4.
35. Calyx, a publisher was refused to bind the journal. *FBN* 14, no.4 (1991) reports the increase of censorship of publishers, and were refused to print. "Feminist & Gay Publishing: facing censorship at the printer," *FBN* 14, no.4 (1991): 15.
36. Ibid.
37. "TRI-STATE Bookstore coalition," *FBN* 5, no.3 (1981): 6.
38. "DJUNA BOOKS BUGGED," *FBN* 5, no.3 (1981): 5.
39. "Fire in Vancouver Women's Bookstore," *FBN* 4, no.4 (1980): 4.

40. "They Went That-a-Way," *FBN* 12, no.1 (1989): 28–29.
41. "They Went That-A-Way," *FBN* 2, no.4 (1978); "They Went That-A-Way," *FBN* 12, no.1 (1989): 28.
42. "Emma: Women's Bookstore in Buffalo," *FBN* 4, no.3 (1980): 5.
43. Quoted in Cavin, 325. According to the 1987 report of the National Institute of Justice, "the most frequent victims of hate violence today are Lesbians, Gay Men, Blacks, Hispanics, Southeast Asians, and Jews. Lesbians and gay men are probably the most frequent victims." See also Peter Finn, and Taylor McNeil, *The Response of the Criminal Justice System to Bias Crime: An Exploratory Review* (Cambridge, MA: Abt Associates, 1987).
44. "Facing down Censorship," *FBN* 14, no.5 (1992): 18.
45. "News from the Bookstore," *FBN* 15, no.5 (1993): 19.
46. As for the ideas of connection, sisterhood of other women with similarities in lifestyle and politics, see Jo Freeman, *The Politics of Women's Liberation* (New York: Longman, 1975).
47. Ibid.
48. According to "Transsexual, Transgender and Intersex History," since Olivia Records was on the edge of profitability, Olivia eventually crumpled beneath the separatists demands, asking for Sandy's resignation "Gay, Lesbian and Feminist Backlash." in *Transsexual, Transgender and Intersex History*. Available online: http://www.transhistory.org/history/TH_Backlash.html
49. Zuelma, "Zuelma Responds," in *Plexus* (April 1980). OWT collection.
50. Ibid.
51. Joan and Bennett, 1.
52. Ferree and Hess, 89.
53. Barbara Smith, "Black Feminism," in *The Reader's Companion to US Women's History*, eds. Wilma Mankiller, et al. (Boston: Houghton Mifflin Co., 1998), 202–204.
54. Ibid.
55. Combahee River Collective, "The Combahee River Collective: A Black Feminist Statement," in *Capitalist Patriarchy and The Case for Socialist Feminism*,ed., Zillah Eisenstein (New York: Monthly Review Press, 1979), 365–367. Combahee River Collective had begun as a chapter of National Black Feminist Organization (NBFO). In 1973 NBFO was formed by a group of Black feminists in NY, and it held a conference that drew hundreds of Black feminists from all over the country.
56. Catherine Mitchell, "Historiography: a new direction for research on the women's rights press" *Journalism History* 19 (summer 1993):59–63. This is because the editors of the woman's rights press at that time, like Elizabeth Cady Stanton and Susan B. Anthony, were themselves "privileged, white, and financially comfortable.
57. Louise Michele Newman, *White Women's Rights: The Racial Origins of Feminism in the United States* (New York, Oxford: Oxford University Press, 1999), 4.
58. In the 19th century there were some publications published by a working-class women or a Black woman. For example, *Lowell Offering* (1840–1845) was

published by women working in the textile mills of Lowell, Massachusetts. Josephine Ruffin, African American woman founded the *Woman's Era* (1890–1897), the country's first journal published by and for African-American women, which advocated women's suffrage and equal civil rights.

59. Mitchell, 59–63.
60. Doris Davenport, "The Pathology of Racism: A Conversation with Third World Wimmin," in *This Bridge Called May Back: Writings by Radical Women of Color,* eds. Cherrie L. Moraga and Gloria Anzaldua (New York: Kitchen Table Press, 1983), 85.
61. Ellen Gruber Carvey, "Out of the Mainstream and into the Streets: small press magazines, the underground press, zines, and artists' books" in *Perspectives on American Book History,* ed. Scott E. Casper (Amherst: University of Massachusetts Press, 2002), 368.
62. Barbara Smith, *Toward a Black Feminist Criticism* (Brooklyn, N.Y.: Out & Out Books, 1986): 172.
63. Barbara Smith, "A press of Our Own-Kitchen Table: Women of Color Press," *Frontiers: A Journal of Women Studies* 10 (1989):13. Harris claimed that Daughters was "strictly a business" for "profit-making" and wanted to "publish novels with both literary merit and commercial appeal." By 1979, when it went out of business, all titles abruptly went out of print; rights reverted to the authors. "June and Parke severed their connections with feminism and their authors, and retired to an insulated haute-bourgeoise life in Houston, June's home town," she said. At the time, June was fifty-three and Parke was forty-five or forty-six. She "hoped never to see either of them again." Bertha Harris, Lover (NY: New York University Press, 1993), xxxii- xxxiv.
64. Erlene Stetson, "Black Women in and out of Print," in *Women in Print,* ed. Joan E. Hartman and Ellen Messer-Davidow (NY: The Modern Language Association of America, 1982)
65. Terri Jean, "Selling Native Spirituality," in *The Native Truth: a column dedicated to historical truth and human rights activism of the American Indian,* Available online: http://www.bluecorncomics.com/newage.htm
66. "Trivia," *FBN* 13, no.4 (1990): 79.
67. Smith, 13.
68. Joan and Bennett, 28.
69. Smith, 13.
70. Denyse Lockard, "The Lesbian Community: An Anthropological Approach," *Journal of Homosexuality* 11 (Summer 1986): 92.
71. Linnea A. Stenson, "From Isolation to diversity: Self and Communities in *Sexual Practice/Textual Theory: Lesbian Cultural Criticism,* eds., Susan J. Wolfe and Julia Penelope (Cambridge, M.A.: Blackwell, 1993), 222.
72. Lockard, 92. Lockard does not reveal where the community is, but mentions it is in a large city in the Southwest with a population of over a quarter million at that time. Lockard, 89.
73. Dana Shugar, *Separatism and Women's Community* (Lincoln: University of Nebraska Press, 1995), 179–181. She also points out during the mid-1970s, a new genre of separatist literature emerged, it was hoped them to encour-

age women to join or form collectives, But the high rate of internal discord and collective failure described in these narratives worked to produce nearly the opposite effect. See Shugar, 181.

74. Barbara Smith, "Women of Color: Our Stories," *New Statesman* 8 (Jun 1984): 24.
75. Presphone Press collapsed into bankruptcy in May 1983, when Smith's own edited collection *Home Girls* was due to go to Persephon's printers. For Smith's experiences in white feminist press, see Barbara Smith, "Coming to the Table: The Differential Politics of This Bridge Called My Back" in *Eroticism and Containment: Notes form the Flood Plain,* eds., Carol Siegel and Ann Kebbey (New York: New York UP, 1994).
76. Barbara Smith, "Changing the World: Kitchen Table: Women of Color Press" in *Happy Endings,* ed. Kate Brandt (Tallahassee, FL: Naiad Press, 1993), 112.
77. Ibid.
78. Author's interview with Carol Seajay
79. Carol Seajay, "Women in print . . . extravaganza issue," *FBN* 5, no.2 (1981): 2.
80. Smith (1998), 336–337.
81. Norma Alarcon, "The Theoretical Subject(s) of This Bridge Called My Back and Anglo American Feminism," in *Making Face, Making Soul: Creative and Critical Perspectives by Women of Color,* ed Gloria Anzaldua (San Francisco, Aunt Lute Foundation Books, 1990), 357.
82. Tricia Lootens, "Third National Women In Print Conference," *Off Our Backs* 15.8 (Aug/Sep 1985): 23.
83. Barbara Smith, "A Press of Our Own: Kitchen Table: Women of Color Press," in *Communications at the Crossroads: The Gender Gap Connection,* eds. Ramona R. Rush and Donna Allen (Norwood, N.J: Ablex Publishing Corp., 1989), 207.
84. Jaime M. Grant, "Building Community-Based Coalitions from Academe: the union institute and the Kitchen Table: Women of Color Press Transition Coalition," *Signs: Journal of women in culture and society* (summer 1996): 1024.
85. In 1993 Toni Morrison won a Nobel Prize for literature.
86. Smith (1998), 336–337.
87. Quoted in Alisa Margaret Klinger, "Paper Uprisings: print activism in the multicultural lesbian movement," 188.
88. Author's interview with Carol Seajay.
89. "Flourishing At Last," *FBN* 11, no.1 (1988): 24. For example, a manager of Red & Black Books told books about not only feminist politics but politics in general "sit there like dust," Ibid.
90. "Six Years Old (OWT annual birthday statement) 1982," OWT collection, Box 2 2/14.
91. "Lammas 1984 Bestsellers," *FBN* 7, no.6 (1985): 39.
92. Ibid.

93. Rebecca Gordon, "More from A Woman's Place-Portland," *FBN* 2, no.3 (1978): 2–3. In another instance in the early 1990, Full Circle, a women's bookstore in Albuquerque, New Mexico, found a racist short story in the local feminist periodical, and returned the issue with a note explaining why. However, women of the periodical accused Full Circle of being "censors," and sent "racist death threats" to one of its staff members. Mary Morell in Full Circle said, "We've been at the center of controversy, nothing new in that." Mary Morell, "Letters," *FBN* 15, no.5 (1993): 7.
94. "Amazon bookstore," *FBN* 4, no.1 (1980): 7.
95. "The 1986 Statement," NW collection.
96. "The 1988 Statement," NW collection.
97. Old Wives Tales started "community-oriented events series" to educate the community through promotion of women's writing and publishing since December 1976. It later became the "Women's Voices" (four times a month) series which was made possible by the collective members and volunteers from the community, who carried out planning, publicity, and staffing, and never made a profit.
98. Store events calendars from 1979 to 1988, OWT collection, Box 1. For example, when applying for sponsored project status for the "Women's Voices," Old Wives' Tales reported six month loss on series is $2027.00 in total. OWT collection, Box 2/2/13.
99. Two letters from Alice Walker (August 26, 1993; September 23, 1993). OWT collection, Box 1 /3.
100. Cherrie Moraga, "Interview with Cherrie Moraga," *Third Woman* 3 (1986): 127–134. Furthermore, not surprisingly, in general 75% to 100% of Black residential areas have extremely few bookstores. According to Glenwood Ross, percentage (supply of retail, personal, and professional services by racial composition of zip codes) indicates less than 25% of African American residential areas have 82 bookstores, on the other hand, 75 to 100 % of African American residential areas have only 4 bookstores. Glenwood Ross, "Are Black Communities truly underserved?: an analysis of retail and professional services in the Atlanta Metropolitan Area," 4.
101. Linda Steiner, "History and Structure of Women's Alternative media," in *Women Making Meaning: New Feminist Directions in Communication* (New York: Routledge, 1992), 126.
102. Kristen Grimstad and Susan Rennie, *The New Woman's Survival Catalog* (New York: Coward, McCann & Geoghegan, 1973), 21.
103. For example, a flyer announcing an opening ceremony of Old Wives' Tales says "women only." Later it also welcomed male customers, while from time to time it had events exclusively for women or lesbians. OWT collection.
104. Secombe-Eastland (1988), 265.
105. Secombe-Eastland points out Twenty Rue Jacob served as what Sasha Gregory Lewis refers to as a "workshop of separatism." However, there was no consensual meaning how to meet the goal of "providing a separate place for woman," the contradiction emerged most clearly in the process of

defining the clientele in Twenty Rue Jacob. Secombe-Eastland (1988), 265, 259. See also Sasha Gregory Lewis, *Sunday's Women: A Report on Lesbian Life Today* (Boston: Beacon Press, 1979), 165.

106. Ibid.
107. "In the June issue of Womanews," *FBN* 5, no.1 (1981): 35.
108. "Notes from the Women at Bloodroot," *FBN* 5, no.2 (1981): 8.
109. Ibid.
110. Niobeh Erebor, "Dear Sisters," *FBN* 3, no.2 (1979): 1.
111. Andy Smith, "For all those who were Indian in a former life": Available online: http://ishgooda.nativeweb.org/racial/fem1.htm. This article first appeared in *Women of Power* (winter 1991). Andy Smith is a Cherokee woman, a co-founder of Women of All Red Nations (WAEN).
112. Steiner, 126.
113. "New Words Celebrates 15 years!" FBN 12, no.1 (1989): 9.
114. Ibid., 9–11.
115. See, for example, Pierre Bourdieu, Outline of a Theory of Practice (NY, Cambridge: Cambridge University Press, 1991): 171–97.
116. Lesbians, in particular needed a space, an alternative to the bars, which was regarded by some lesbians as the most obvious and often the only place to get in touch with their community. However, it was apparent that many women could not feel comfortable in such an environment. Moreover, only a small segment of the community like very young working-class women patronized such bars. Furthermore, as Lynette Secombe-Eastland points out, for those who are trying to maintain some secrecy in their lives, or going to through the emotional transition of "coming out," a women's bar is often regarded as frightening or threatening. She also notes that Twenty Rue Jacob women's bookstore in Salt Lake City, Utah, was created to alleviate a sense of social isolation and to identify a community—especially for those who would otherwise have only limited social connections. Lynette Secombe-Eastland, "Ideology, Contradiction and Change in a Feminist Bookstore," 32, 36.
117. Seccombe-Eastland, 64.
118. Gibbs and Bennett, 28.
119. Ibid., 90.
120. Quoted in Sally Munt, *Lesbian Nation, Community Space Heroic Desire; Lesbian Identity and Cultural Space* (NY: New York University Press, 1998):150
121. "Feminist Bookstore Days," *FBN* 15, no.2 (1992): 20; "Feminist Bookstores Day, 1991," *FBN* 14, no.2 (1991): 26. For example, the visibility of lesbians and lesbian materials in some stores was more apparent than in others. Mama Bears is one of the former stores; at the same time, the owners, Carol Wilson and Alice Molly told that they were "feminist first." They called their bookstore a "feminist bookstore" because they "wanted to do something for the women's movement." (Jean Tepperman, "Words as Gifts," *San Francisco Bay Guardian* (December 21, 1994): 24–5. OWT collection, Box 1:1/2.

122. McKey Koivisto and Elise Matthesen, "Honoring Women Who Honor Women: Amazon Turns 25!" *FBN* 18, no.4 (1995): 28. According to Jill Diane Zahnizer, lesbians dominated the scene: "The lesbians at Amazon wanted to co-exist amicably [with heterosexual women], but tended to think 'that's how it feels to be a minority!'" Zahnizer, 119.
123. Carol Seajay, "The Backlash and the backlist," *The Women's Review of Books*12 (1994): 18.
124. Rebecca Cragin, "Post-Lesbian-Feminism: Documenting 'Those Cruddy Old Dykes of Yore,'" in *Carryin' On in the Lesbian and Gay South,* ed. John Howard (New York: New York University Press, 1997), 286.
125. Seccombe-Eastland (1998), 64.
126. Ibid.,263.
127. Ibid., 67, 68.
128. Rebecca Gordon, "More from A Woman's Place-Portland," *FBN* 2, no.3 (1978): 2–3.
129. "The 1986 statement," NW collection.
130. "This is Not a Job," OWT collection, Box 1:1/2.
131. "1985 Old Wives' Tales Birthday Statement," OWT collection, Box 2 :2/14.
132. Untitled letter (October 26), OWT collection, Box 1:1/2
133. In addition to letters regarding racism in Old Wives' Tales, there are letters protesting that its carrying "heavily pro-Zionist, which is itself anti-Semitic," and asking it to carry books about pro-Palestinian materials, or complaining diet books displayed in the store because they were "anti-fat literature." OWT collection, Box 1
134. Resignation letter (February 10, 1992), OWT collection, Box 1:1/2.
135. After that, a massive "Debt-Free by 20 [20 years anniversary]" campaign was held. In 1994 February the "Women's Voices" event series there was awarded a grant for $8550 by the Women's Foundation. Untitled letter (Feb 4, 1994). OWT collection, Box 2/13.
136. In May 1995, the Board of Supervisors of the City and County of San Francisco issued a "Certificate of Honor" to Old Wives' Tales in "appreciative public recognition of distinction and merit for outstanding service to a significant portion of the people of the city and county of San Francisco." The Board especially emphasized Old Wives' Tales' "continuing commitment of the feminist movement . . . for 19 years of providing a safe meeting place for women to share their thoughts, dreams and inspiration." "Certificate of Honor (May 18, 1995 by Carole Migaen,)" OWT collection, Box 2, 2–35.
137. Quoted in David Armstrong, *Trumpet to Arms* (LA: J.P.Tarcher, Inc., 1981), 357.
138. Koivisto and Matthesen, 28.
139. Thomas J. Scheff, *Microsociology: Discourse, Emotion and Social Structure* (Chicago: University of Chicago Press, 1990), 4.
140. Reger, 613.
141. Shugar, 3.

142. Patricia Hill-Colllins, *Black Feminist Thought* (Boston: Unwin Hyman, 1990), 227.
143. Terri Jewell, "Barbara Smith and Kitchen Table Women of Color Press," *Hot Wire* 6 (May 1990): 20.

NOTES TO CHAPTER SIX

1. Myra Marx Ferree and Beth B. Hess, *Controversy and Coalition: The New Feminist Movement* (Boston: Twayne Publishers, 1985), 193.
2. "An excerpt from a letter to publishers from G. Roysce Smith, executive director of the American Book Association," *FBN* 3, no.5 (1979): 12.
3. Gail E. Hudson, "Bookstacks: the final chapter," *Vanguard Press* (July 1984). LHA collection, bookstore subject file.
4. Jill Diane Zahnizer, "Feminist Collectives: the transformation of women's business in the counterculture of the 1970s and 1980s," 3. The term collective may have been used originally by Spanish anarchists and Soviet or Chinese radicals and, in the late 1960s, came into vogue in the U.S.
5. Stephanie Riger, "Challenges of Success: stages of growth in feminist organizations," *Feminist Studies* 20 (1994): 2.
6. Nancy Ferro, Coretta Reid Holcomb, and Marilyn Saltzman-Webb, "Statement of Purpose" in *Women in Media: A Documentary Source books,* eds. Maurine Beasley and Sheila Silver (Washington, DC: Women's Institute for Freedom of the Press, 1977), 117.
7. "Touring Western Canadian Bookstores (Vancouver Women's Bookstore)," *FBN* 10, no.3 (1987): 13.
8. See also Joyce Rothchild-Whitt, "The Collectivist Organization: an alternative to rational-bureaucratic models," *American Sociological Review* 44 (August 1979): 509–27, Lois Ahrens, "Battered Women's Refuges: Feminist Cooperatives vs. social Service Institutions," *Radical America* 14, no.3 (1980): 41–47, Susan Schechter, *Women and Male Violence: The Visions and Struggles of the Battered Women's movement* (Boston: South End Press, 1982), Noelie M. Rodrigues, "Transcending Bureaucracy: feminist politics at a shelter for battered women," *Gender & Society* 2 (1988): 214–27.
9. As Davis and Kennedy point out, "butch-femme" relationships were explored mainly among working class lesbians in the lesbian bars before the 1950s; thus these lesbians formed their community around the lesbian bars and in the context of this particular community. However, just as the Daughters of Bilitis, a middle-class lesbian organization of the 1950s, had rejected butch/femme roles and bar culture, lesbian feminists of the 1970s challenged such roles and implied that those who engaged in them were not real feminists. The Daughters of Bilities, a lesbian organization of the 1950s, attempted to make lesbianism respectable by rejecting butch/femme roles and bar culture. In doing so, they showed discrimination against working class lesbians and their culture. Madeline D. Davis and Elizabeth Kennedy, *Boots of Leather, Slippers of Gold: The History of*

a Lesbian Community (New York: Penguin Books, 1994). See also Joan Nestle, *A Restricted Country* (Ithaca, NY: Firebrand Books, 1987).

Women who started Full Moon met in the Women's Studies programs at the local university. See Deborah Wolf, *Lesbian Community* (Berkeley: University of California Press, 1979), 123.

10. Davis and Kennedy also point out that the concept of butch-fem roles actually reduces butch-fem behavior to role playing and does not take into account the depth and complexity of butch and fem as an organizing principle which pervades all aspects of working-class lesbian culture. Davis and Kennedy:153–4.
11. Wolf, 123.
12. Susan Kriegar shows clear differences between "bar women" and "political women" in the late 1970s lesbian community in Urbana-Champaign, IL. Political women, mainly middle class and well educated, did not wear make-up, wore casual clothing (jeans etc.), or hiking boots as well as work shirts. On the other hand, bar women were "a lot more like working class." For political women, bar women seemed to make a big deal about getting a new car or new clothes," and were "into [gender] roles [like butch/femme roles]," but they "felt out of place with political women." For them, political women seemed not "having enough fun." They called political women "right on women." Susan Krieger, *The Mirror Dance: Identity in a women's community* (Philadelphia: Temple University Press, 1983), 16, 125.
13. Jo Freeman, "Tyranny of structurelessness," *Berkeley Journal of Sociology* 17 (1972/73): 151–164.
14. "Collective Crisis and Legal Struggles at ICI-A Women's Place," FBN 6, no.3 (1982): 13.
15. A feminist mediator used the techniques of collective decision-making with both sides. Wolf, 112.
16. "Basis of Unity," *FBN* 2, no.2 (1978):
17. "Closing," *FBN* 12, no.1 (1989):28.
18. For difficulties in the collectives, see Jane J. Mansbridge, *Beyond Adversary Democracy* (New York: Basic Books, 1980); Joyce Rothchild-Whitt, "The Collectivist Organization: an alternative to rational-bureaucratic models," *American Sociological Review* 44 (August 1979):509–27.
19. Linda Steiner, "The History and Structure of Women's Alternative Media," in *Women Making Meaning: New Feminist Directions in Communication* (NY: Routledge, 1992),127.
20. For difficulties of alternative way of working in the feminist institutions, see Susan Schechter, *Women and Male Violence* (Boston: South End Press, 1982); Carol Wharton, "Establishing Shelters for Battered Women: Local Manifestations of a Social Movement," *Qualitative Sociology* 10, no.2 (1987): 146–63; Noelie M. Rodrigues, "Transcending Bureaucracy: feminist politics at a shelter for battered women," *Gender & Society* 2 (1988): 214–27.
21. "Common Woman Books," *FBN* 10, no.2 (1987): 4.

22. Ibid.
23. "Burn Out," *FBN* 5, no.4 (1982):7.
24. Seajay (1995), 80.
25. "Staffing," *FBN* 5, no.4 (1982): 5.
26. Wolf, 111.
27. "They Went-That-a-Way," *FBN* 12, no.1 (1989): 28, 29.
28. Toni Armstrong, "Playing to the highest common denominator," in *The Woman-Centered economy : ideals, reality, and the space in between,* eds. Midge Stocker and Loraine Edwards (Chicago : Third Side Press, 1995), 224.
29. "Common Woman's Closing," *FBN* 14, no.6 (1992):41.
30. "Amazon Bookstore Celebrate the Tenth Year," *FBN* 4, no.1 (1980):7.
31. Volunteers of Crazy Ladies Bookstore formed "book brigade" so that the "human chain" extended across the street to the new building, a half block away could pass down books, bookshelves, the counter and other furnishings. Karen Beiser et al, eds., *Crazy Ladies: Vision and Venture: the History of Crazy Ladies Center, 1979–94* (Cincinnati: The Center, 1994), 11–12.
32. McKey Koivisto & Elise Matthesen, "Honoring Women Who Honor Women: Amazon Turns 25!" *FBN* 18, no. 4 (1995): 27.
33. "Amazon Bookstore Celebrate the Tenth Year," *FBN* 4, no.1 (1980):7.
34. "News from the Bookstores," *FBN* 12, no.6 (1990):7.
35. "Touring Western Canadian Bookstores," *FBN* 10, no.3 (1987): 11.
36. "Letters," *FBN* 10, no.2 (1987): 4.
37. "Womanboks Closes," *FBN* 10, no.3 (1987):24.
38. For example, The Book Garden in Denver, Colorado was founded by two female partners. However, one left and the other had to raise $17,500 within eight weeks to buy her share of the store. "Book Garden," *FBN* 10, no.3 (1987):27. A partner of the Women's Bookstore in Worcester, MA, also left while planning it. Another owner sent a letter to *FBN,* looking back upon her beginning, struggle and success. She noted, "The hardest lesson I had to earn was the saddest—don't trust anyone! No one cares about you as much as you do! Friends, lovers, and money just don't mix. . . . I had to start all over again." Sllen J. Gardner, "letter," *FBN* 4, no.2 (1987): 6.
39. Sullivan, http://www.shapingsf.org/ezine/womens/bookstrs/main.html
40. Ibid.
41. Lucille Pauline Frey, "One Woman, One Women's Bookstore: Case Study and Comments in the place of a woman's bookstore in a community," 133.
42. Karen Voltz, "Staffing," *FBN* 5, no.4 (1982): 5.
43. "The Thirty-first Street Bookstore, Baltimore," *FBN* 12, no.2 (1989): 41.
44. "Alaska Women's Bookstore," *FBN* 10, no.2 (1989):19.
45. "Tucson Business: close-up," *Tucson Lifestyle* (May 1996): 42–44. ATG collection
46. Cheryl Kohout, "Evolution of a bookstore," *Clarion* (Spring, 1993): 3,8. ATG collection.
47. Ibid., 3.

48. Kohout, 8. ATG collection
49. Carol Seajay, "Our Words in Our Hands: a brief history of women's presses and bookstores" in *The Woman-Centered Economy,* eds. Loraine Edwalds and Midge Stocker (Chicago : Third Side Press, 1995), 84.
50. Frey, 133.
51. For discussions over changes of forms of women's shelters, see also Susan Schechter, *Women and Male Violence* (Boston: South End Press, 1982).
52. Deborah R. Lewis, "The Original Womyn's Woodstock: Michigan Womyn's Music Festival."
53. Later, Bluestockings: Women's Bookstores and Cafe in New York City became a "radical bookstore, fair trade cafe, and activist center in the Lower East Side of Manhattan." Available online: http://www.bluestockings.com/
54. Marian Lydrooke, "We're Not Perfect Yet," *Rumbles* 1 (1980), reprinted in *FBN* 5, no.2 (1981): no page number.
55. Robert D. Hirsch, "Women Entrepreneurs: Problems and Prescriptions for Success in the Future," in *Women-Owned Businesses,* eds. Oliver Hagan, Carol Rivchun, and Donald Sexton (NY: Praeger, 1989), 5,8.
56. Lois Therrien, "What Do Women Want? A company They Can Call Their Own," *Business Week* (December 1986): 60.
57. Debra Michals, "Beyond 'Pin Money': The Rise of Women's Small Business Ownership 1945–1980," 253. Michals explains the increase of women entrepreneur by pointing out feminists' efforts toward gender equality along with the recession of the 1970s, and says that "Many feminist also became unwitting entrepreneurs . . . as the quest for their personal independence or a distinct women's culture led many to form feminist collective, cooperative and communal businesses designed to support the movement's agenda and provide an income for individual members. . . . Without the emergence of second wave feminism, then, such dramatic growth in women's business ownership would not have been possible." Michals, 254. See also Jo Freeman, *The Politics of Women's Liberation: A Case Study of an Emerging Social Movement and Its Relation to the Policy Process* (NY: David McKay, 1975).
58. The Boston Women's Health Book Collective, *Our Bodies, Ourselves* (New York: Simon & Schuster, 2nd Ed., 1976), 11.
59. Ann Harrison, "Big Business," in *The Woman-Centered Economy,* eds. Midge Stocker and Loraine Edwards (Chicago: Third Side Press, 199), 117.
60. Brooke William and Hannah Darby, "God, mom & apple pie: 'feminist' business as an extension of the American dream," *Off Our Backs* 5 (February 1976):18. See also Brooke Williams, "The Retreat to Cultural Feminism," *Feminist Revolution,* ed. Redstockings of the women's Liberation Movement (NY: Random House, 1978), 79.
61. Diana Press, "Letter to Editors and Publishers of the Feminist Press, Oakland, California, November 1977," quoted in " Diana Press Vandalized," *Big Mama Rag* (November/December 1977): 4, Coletta Reid and Kathy Tomyris, " A Statement from Diana Press: Press Suspends Women's Publications," *Big Mama Press* (June 1979): 25–26.

62. "Diana Press invaded/attacked by vandals (Press release from Diana)," *FBN* 1, no.9/10 (1977):3.
63. Laurie and Mary Anne, "Letter from Amazon Reality," *FBN* 2, no.1 (1978):1.
64. "Diana Press: An overview 1972–1979, " *FBN* 3, no.2 (1979): 5–8.
65. Ibid.
66. Armstrong, 230.
67. Seajay (1995), 80. As Karen Rudolph describes in "Feminist Fundraising Phobia," "all effective fundraisers have negative implications" because "despite our progressive politics, the feminist community is not immune to all the mixed-up feelings that revolve around money in this society, nor are we immune to greed or envy." On the other hand, women's "great expectations" of getting financial support from their community often turned out to be an "unrealistic expectation." Karen Rudolph, "Feminist Fund Raising Phobia," in *The Woman-Centered Economy,* eds. Midge Stocker and Loraine Edwards (Chicago: Third Side Press, 1995), 116, 95.
68. Ann Harrison, "Big Business," in *The Woman-Centered economy : ideals, reality, and the space in between,* eds. Midge Stocker and Loraine Edwards (Chicago: Third Side Press, 1995), 117.
69. Blush. LHA collection, bookstore subject file.
70. Claire Reinelt, "Moving onto the Terrain of the State," in *Feminist Organizations: Harvest of the New Women's movement,* ed. Myra Marx Ferree and Patricia Yancey Martin (Philadelphia: Temple University Press, 1995), 88, 89.
71. This did not happen only to feminist booksellers. As Phyllis Chesler points out, "Other feminist pioneers are–or are about to become homeless . . . Neither is independently wealthy, has a tenured position, or a pension; they remain dreadfully, bravely poor . . ." See Phyllis Chesler, "All We Have Is Each Other," in *The Woman-Centered Economy,* eds. Midge Stocker and Loraine Edwards (Chicago : Third Side Press, 1995), 108.
72. Amanda LeRougetel, "Edmonton's Feminist History Closes Chapter on Bookstore," *Herizons: women's news and feminist views* 6, no.2 (1992): 9.
73. "Womansplace Closes, Humanspace Opens," *FBN* 7, no.6 (1985):17.
74. Moonyean Grosch, *FBN* 7, no. 6 (1985).
75. The Boston Women's Health Book Collective, *The New Our Bodies, Ourselves: A Book By and For Women* (New York: Simon & Schuster, 1984), 14.
76. Ibid.
77. Mary Gebhart, "The Michigan Womyn's Music Festival," MA thesis, Michigan State University, 1998, 94.
78. Nett Hart, "Taking a slide," in *The Woman-Centered Economy,* eds. Midge Stocker and Loraine Edwards (Chicago: Third Side Press, 1995). 87.
79. "Letters," *FBN* 1, no.4 (1977): 2
80. Ibid.
81. Newsletter of *First Things First-Books for Women* (March 1975). LHA collection, bookstore subject file.

82. Theresa Corrigan, "Feminist Bookstores at the Root of Lesbian /Gay Books Success, " *FBN* 16, no.4 (1993):21–23.
83. Rebecca Gordon, "(letters)," *FBN* 2, no.2 (1978): 12.
84. "The Oracle Collective, Hayward, California: Feminist Bookstore Closes," *FBN* 4, no.4 (1980): 5.
85. Lynette Secombe-Eastland, "Ideology, Contradiction and Change in a Feminist Bookstore."
86. "1976 Old Wives Tales San Francisco statement," OWT collection.
87. "Old Wives Tales statement," OWT collection
88. Womanbooks, "What Can We Do?" (March 18, 1986). LHA collection, bookstore subject file.
89. "Womanbooks closes," *FBN* 10, no.3 (1987): 24.
90. D.M "Profile:Crazy Ladies," *FBN* 8, no.1 (1985): 8 (originally published in *Dinah* (the Cincinnati lesbian magazine). Carol Seajay also wrote in her 1985 conference report that "there seemed to be more emphasis on skills sharing workshops than theoretical and political analysis." *FBN* 8, no.1: 3.
91. "A Celebrate 10th Anniversary," *FBN* 4, no.1 (1980):7.
92. Carol Seajay, "Women in print: extravaganza issue," *FBN* 5, no.3 (1979) :2
93. "New Words Celebrates 15 years," *FBN* 12, no.1 (1989):9–11.
94. Amanda LeRougetel, "Edmonton's Feminist History Closes Chapter on Bookstore," *Herizons* 6, no.2 (1992):9.
95. "The Lamma Guide to Computer Purchase," *FBN* 10, no.3 (1987):24.
96. "Alaska Women's Bookstore," *FBN* 10, no.2 (1987):19.
97. "Training & Skills Sharing," *FBN* 5, no.1 (1981): 8.
98. Mary Farmer, et al, "The Lammas Guide to Computer Purchase," *FBN* 7, no.6 (1985): 26–28.
99. Lee Copeland, "Bookseller Fears Buyers Will Be Bound in Chains," Bookselling This Week (June 18, 2002): Available online: http://news.bookweb.org/news/573.html
100. Ann Morse,"Paradigm: women's bookstore," *FBN* 13, no.6 (1991): 21
101. Paula Wallace left Old Wives Tales, and started a women's bookstore, Full Circle in Albuquerque. Carol Wilson and Alice Molloy, who left A Woman's Place bookstore in Oakland, also started Mama Bears.
102. Pam Hicks, "(letters)," *FBN* 6, no.3 (1982).
103. She described it was a "straight job," and "quite a shock sometimes" for her. *FBN* 8, no.6 (1986).
104. Ibid., 84.
105. Gail E. Hudson, "Bookstacks: the final chapter," *Vanguard Press* (July 1984). DCT collection.
106. Susan Cavin noted that the attacks from the right wing had a positive effect on efforts to mobilize members and supporters. For example, large numbers of closet-apolitical lesbians and gays, who heretofore felt no need to join, apparently became active participants so that the annual lesbian/gay marches to commemorate the Stonewall riot grew larger every year in the 1980s. Susan Cavin, "The Invisible Army of Women, lesbian social protest,

1969–1988," in *Women and Social Protest,* ed. Guilda West and Rhoda Blumberg (New York: Oxford Univ. Press, 1990), 325.

107. Judith Rosen, "New Words: the collective works," *Publishers Weekly* (April 21, 1989):58.
108. For further discussions about the relationship between the rise of Black bookstores and Black student movement, the rise of Black studies courses and educational politics, see Donald Franklin Joyce, *Gatekeepers of Black Culture: black-owned book publishing in the United States, 1817–1981* (Westport, Conn.: Greenwood Press, 1983), 141 and Colin Anthony Beckles, "Pan African Sites of Resistance: Black Bookstores and the Struggle to Re-present Black Identity," 83.
109. Ibid.
110. Ferree and Hess, 80.
111. National Center for Education Statistics, *Digest of Education Statistics 1977/78* (Washington, DC: US Government Printing Office, 1978), 108, table 110.
112. Flora McMartin, "The Institutionalization of Women's Centers and Women's Studies Programs at three research universities," 18.
113. Florence Howe, *Seven Years Later: Women's Studies program in 1976, Report of the National Advisory Council on Women's Educational Programs* (Washington, DC: The department of Health, Education and Welfare, 1977), 15.
114. McMartin, 18.
115. Mari Jo Buhle, "Introduction," in *The Politics of Women's Studies: Testimony from 30 Founding Mothers,* ed. Florence Howe (NY: The Feminist Press at the City University of New York, 2000), xxii.
116. According to Mari Jo Buhle, the first Women's Studies programs were established at the end of the 1960s. Buhle, xv. McMartin, 26.
117. Howe, 15.
118. Elizabeth Lapovsky Kennedy, "Dreams of Social Justice: Building Women's Studies at the State University of New York, Buffalo," in *The Politics of Women's Studies: Testimony from 30 Founding Mothers,* ed. Florence Howe (NY: The Feminist Press at the City University of New York, 2000), 248.
119. Howe, 23.
120. Buhle, xi
121. Buhle, xv.
122. Marilyn Boxer, *When Women Ask the Questions: Creating Women's Studies in America* (Baltimore and London: The Johns Hopkins University Press, 1998), 28.
123. Boxer, 30.
124. Ibid.
125. Ibid., 106.
126. Lynn Rosen, "Women's Books Profitable," *New Directions for Women* (July/August, 1988): 18. For instance, at that time Routledge & Kegan Paul established specialized women's press divisions, and commercial publishers

also brought out anthologies making feminist articles that originally appeared in the alternative press available in mass-market paperbacks. They were collections of articles that had first been produced on mimeograph machines in the early days of feminist publishing such as *Sexual Politics, Rubyfruit Jungle, The Work of A Common Woman and Sisterhood is Powerful.* On the other hand, small publishers often lost authors to larger houses, which potentially offered greater financial rewards. Rosen, 18. See also Linda Steiner, "The History and Structure of Women's Alternative Media," in *Women Making Meaning: New Feminist Directions in Communication* (NY: Routledge, 1992), 134.

127. Rosen, 18.
128. Ferree and Hess, 81.
129. Mary MacKay, "Feminist Lit New Boom for Publishers," *IRIS: A Journal About Women* (Fall/Winter 1990):34. Moreover, university presses have played a leading role in shaping scholarly writings in each discipline. For discussions about the roles of university publishing houses, see also Paul Parsons, *Getting Published: The Acquisition Process at University Press* (Kansville: University of Tennessee Press, 1989).
130. Linda Garber, *Lesbian Sources: A Bibliography of Periodical Articles, 1970–1990* (NY: Garland Publishing, Inc., 1993), xxxiii-xlii.
131. Rose Norman, "Support Your Feminist bookseller: She Supports You!" *WSAction* 13 (1) (Fall 2001):32.
132. Sandi Torkildson , "Selling Textbooks, " *FBN* 15, no.4 (1992):29.
133. Ibid.
134. Ibid., 29–33.
135. Ibid.
136. Norman, 32. Norman also pointed out such "unarticulated fears" toward feminism kept many women who knew the existence of the stores away from women's bookstores.
137. "Women's Studies and Antigone Books Threatened by Conservatives," *FBN* 22, no.6 (2000):7.
138. Ibid. Author's interview. October 2001. ATG collection.
139. Audre Lorde criticized the intstitutionalization of feminism, claiming "The Master's Tools Will Never Dismantle the Master's House." Audrey Lorde, *Sister Outsider: Essays and Speeches* (Trumansburg, NY: Crossing Press, 1984), 112. She also claimed "The failure of academic feminists to recognize differences as a crucial strength is a failure to reach beyond the first patriarchal lesson. To use each other's difference to enrich our visions and our joint struggles. As white women ignore their built-in privilege of whiteness and define woman in terms of their experience alone, then women of color become "other," the outsider whose experience and tradition is too "alien" to comprehend. Refusing to recognize difference makes it impossible to see the different problems and pitfalls facing us as women." Audre Lorde, "Our Difference Is Our Strength," in *Identity Politics in the Women's movement,* ed. Barbara Ryan (NY: New York University Press, 2001), 317.

140. Carol Seajay said that feminist theory was not "people's theory," and did not look at "common people's lives." (Author's interview with Seajay) Mev Miller also pointed out textbooks became hard to read for common women. Mary Ellen Kavanaugh faulted feminist writers for producing texts that are either "too scholastic or too tepid." Ashlea Halpern, "Sisters in Struggle," *Punk Planet Magazine* (May/June 2003): 102.
141. Rosen,18.
142. Ibid.
143. MacKay, 34.
144. Ferree and Hess, 81.
145. Rosen, 18. Rosen reported that by 1981 the six largest feminist bookstores in the US grossed $300,000 to $400,000.
146. Ibid.
147. Norman, 32.
148. Claire Reinelt, "Moving on to the Terrain of the State," in *Feminist Organizations: Harvest of the New Women's movement,* ed. Myra Marx Ferree and Patricia Yancey Martin (Philadelphia: Temple University Press, 1995), 101.
149. Ibid.
150. Seajay (1995), 84.
151. Carol Seajay, "Feminist Publishing in the US," *259: An Introduction to a World of Women's Books,* ed. Feminist Book Fair Group (London: Feminist Book Fair Groups, 1984), 30.
152. Ibid.

NOTES TO CHAPTER SEVEN

1. *In a Different Voice* by Carol Gilligan was one of 1984 bestsellers in Lammas Women's Shop in Washington DC in 1984. "Lamma, 1984 Bestseller," *FBN* 7, no.6 (1985): 39.
2. Linda Alcoff, "Cultural Feminism versus Post-Structuralism: the identity crisis in feminist theory," *Sings: Journal of Women in Culture and Society* 13 (1988): 405–36.
3. Alice Echols, "The New Feminism of Yin and Yang," in *Powers of Desire: The Politics of Sexuality,* ed. Ann Snitow (NY : Monthly Review Press, 1983), 455.
4. Ibid.
5. Brooke William and Hannah Darby, "God, mom & apple pie: 'feminist' business as an extension of the American dream," *Off Our Backs* 5 (February 1976): 18.
6. Ibid.
7. Claude S. Fischer, "Ambivalent Communities: How Americans Understand Their Localities," *America at Century's End,* ed., Alan Wolfe (Berkeley: University of California Press, 1991), 79–80.
8. "A bookstore celebrates her tenth year," *FBN* 4, no.1 (1980): 7. Amazon announces its lending library.

9. Wolf, 120.
10. Judith Rosen, "New Words: the collective works," *Publishers Weekly* (April 21, 1989): 56.
11. Ibid.
12. "Notes from the computer table, " *FBN* 8, no.1 (1985): 1. *FBN* reports sidelines reach over 40% during December in some stores.
13. Ibid.
14. Seccombe-Eastland (1988), 261.
15. "Bookstore Skills Questions," Womanbooks (n.d.) NW collection.
16. Ibid.
17. Thomas J. Linneman, "Representing Social Movements: Advocacy and activism in Northwest Bookstores," *Sociological Perspectives* 42 (Fall 1999): 459.
18. Mev Miller, "Reading materials & engagement," (May 15, 2001): Available in Fifl-womenlit@literacy.nifl.gov.
19. Elizabeth Long, "Textual Interpretation as Collective Action," *The Ethnography of Reading,* ed. Jonathan Boyarin (Berkeley, CA: University of California Press, 1993), 180–211.
20. Frey, 43.
21. Ibid.
22. "Judith's Room," *FBN* 12, no.4 (1989): 11. Charis Books and More in Atlanta, GA, also organized bookstore events, inviting a number of feminist artists including Minnie Bruce Pratt, bell hooks, and Shay Youngblood.
23. Jane Addams Bookstore later closed its doors in Chicago to move to Champaign, IL.
24. "Women & Children First: Anniversaries," *FBN* 12, no.4 (1989): 13.
25. Lisa C. Moore, "Turning the Tables in Texas," Lambda Literary Foundation (2004). Available online: http://lambdalit.org/resources/resources-bookwoman.html
26. "Amazon Bookstore, " *FBN* 16, no.4 (1993): 17.
27. "Saturday seminar," *FBN* 18, no.4 (1995): 19.
28. Linda Bryant, "Bookstore program for girls & young feminists," *FBN* 21, 3 (1998): 29.
29. "News from the bookstores," *FBN* 15, no.3 (1992): 35. Full Circle (Albuquerque, NM) were taking the "register more voters" campaign. One of their staff took the training to become a qualified to register voters.
30. Old Wives' Tales event calendars 1977 to 1994, OWT collection.
31. When Old Wives' Tales faced financial crisis, it applied for sponsored project status to the San Francisco Women's Center for the "Women's Voices." "Women's Voices," (n.d.) OWT Collection, Box 2/2/13
32. "Charis Circle," *FBN* 19, no.6 (1997): 17.
33. Ibid.
34. Jennifer S. Croft, "Store Newsletters: Do they really work?" *FBN* 15, no.1 (1992): 37–39.
35. Soon after *Our Bodies, Ourselves* was published, some activists began practicing "self-help gynecology." According to Rosen, Carol Downer was

one of them, and she started the first self-exam at Every Woman's Bookstore in Los Angels on April 7, 1971.According to Rosen, within a year of Carol Downer's first self-exam, over two thousand women had attended such self-help women's clinic." Ruth Rosen, *The World Split Open* (N.Y: Viking, 2000), 176–177.

36. Many scholars consider that "bra-burning" typically represent the intention of main media at that time. For example, Joanna Foley Martin describes how the myth (bra-burning) was developed. Joanna Foley Martin, "Confession of a Non Bra Burner," *Chicago Journalism Review* 4 (July 1971):11.
37. Seajay (1995), 80.
38. Author's interview with Carol Seajay.
39. Author's interview with Carol Seajay.
40. "Crazy Ladies Customer Survey," *FBN* 16, no.2 (1993): 20.
41. Seajay (1995), 80.
42. Susan Cavin, "The Invisible Army of Women: lesbian social protest, 1969–1988" in *Women and Social Protest,* ed. Guida West and Rhoda Blumberg (NY: Oxford Univ. Press, 1990), 331.
43. Jo Reger, "Emotions, objectivity and voice: an analysis of a "Failed" participant observation," *Women's Studies International Forum* 24 (2001): 608–609.
44. John Lelan, "Homophobia," *Newsweek* (Feb 1994): 42–45.
45. Author's interview with Linda Bubon
46. Lucy Shumpert Brewster, "On Every Atom," *Blackstripe* Available online: http://www.blackstripe.com/archives/discussion/mothers/oneveryatom.htm l.
47. Secombe-Eastland (1988), 73.
48. Mary R. Somerville, "The New World of the American Public Library." in Gordon Graham and Richard Abel, ed., *The Book in the United States Today* (New Brunswick and London: Transaction, 1997), 37–48.
49. "Alaska Women's Bookstore," *FBN* 10, no.2 (1987): 19. See also Lucille Pauline Frey. "One Woman, One Women's Bookstore: Case Study and Comments in the place of a woman's bookstore in a community (movement, feminist, literature, art, music, history)," 1985.
50. 72% of customers in Crazy Ladies Bookstore agreed that they used the store to find out what was appealing in the community. Karen Beiser, et al, eds.,*Crazy Ladies: Vision and Venture: the History of Crazy Ladies Center, 1979–94* (Cincinnati: The Center, 1994), 15.
51. Chesnut and Gable, 273.
52. Seajay (1995), 84.
53. "Womanbooks Bookstore Skills Questions (1983)," NW collection.
54. Ibid.
55. Donna Niles, co-manager of Amazon Bookstore in *A Labor of Love: A 25 year history of Feminist and lesbian bookstores and publishing,* which Mev Miller produced a one-hour documentary for a radio program in 1995. MMC collection. This documentary was made for celebrating 25 years

anniversary of feminist publishing pioneers such as *Off Our Backs,* Feminist Press, and Amazon Bookstore. It includes interviews with Barbara Grier (Naiad), Barbara Smith (Kitchen Table), Jamie Lee Evans (Aunt Lute), Teresa Corrigan (Lioness Books), Pokey Anderson (Inklings), Carole Ann Douglas (Off Our Backs), Donna Niles (Amazon & Lammas), Marj Schneider (Womyn's Braille Press), Florence Howe (Feminist Press), Carol Seajay (Feminist Bookstore News), Linda Bubon (Women & Children First), Gilda Bruckman (New Words), Selma Miriam (Bloodroot), and Barb Wieser (Iowa Women's Press). Mev Miller also maintains web page, Women In Print: Central Source Networking, Keeping Women's Words in Circulation (The most comprehensive and current listing of women-owned & women-centered bookstores and publishers). Available online: http://www.litwomen.org/WIP/#biblio. (a one-hour documentary on cassette tape).

56. Secombe-Eastland (1998), 73.
57. "But what do you do all day, Dear?" *FBN* 3, no.4 (1979): 13.
58. Margaret De Ritter, "Staying with for the long howl," *FBN* 13, no.5 (1991): 28.
59. Theresa Corrigan, "Feminist Bookstores: Part of an Ecosystem," *Sojourner: The Women's Forum* 16.4 (1993):6B-7B.
60. The sales of New Words were $177,655. Net sales were $67,295 and net profit was $3,635. "New Words, Inc. Income Statement: Fiscal Year 1979," NW collection, Box 3.
61. "Contribution to consider (1981)," NW collection, Box 3.
62. "The Balkan Women's Book Drive Project, " *FBN* 16, no.5 (1994): 7.
63. "News," *FBN* 16, no.2 (1993): 15. See also Nancy Whittier for an example of a strong bond maintained between Fan the Flames Feminist Bookstore and a women's community in Columbus, Ohio in the1970s and 80s. Nancy Whittier, *Feminist Generations: The Persistence of the Radical Women's movement* (Philadelphia: Temple University Press, 1995).
64. Reinelt, 88, 89.
65. Seajay (1995): 77–86.
66. Ibid.
67. Kansas City Women, "Letters," *FBN* 9, no.6 (1987): 7–8.
68. Leonard Shatzkin, *In Cold Type: Overcoming the Book Crisis* (Boston: Houghton Mifflin Company, 1982), 9.
69. Gail E. Hudson, "Bookstacks: the final chapter," *Vanguard Press* (July 1984). DCT collection.
70. Shatzkin, 9.
71. Ibid., 2; Total sales of the entire book publishing industry in 1980 was 6 billion as much as or less than the sales of the Philip Morris (6.2billion). It might be said that book publishing industry was small and very complicated industry.
72. Corrigan: 6B-7B
73. Chesnut and Gable, 273.

74. Corrigan: 6B-7B.
75. Ginny Daley, "Women and Publishing in North Carolina," March 1992. Available online: http://scriptorium.lib.duke.edu/women/ncwwpub.html.
76. Elizabeth Long, "Women, Reading, and Cultural Authority: some implications of the audience perspective in cultural studies," *American Quarterly* 38 (Fall 1986): 600.
77. Mary Ellen Kavanaugh, "Letters," *Holt Uncensored* 277 (October 2001). Available online at http://www.holtuncensored.com/members/column277.html. However, in November 2003 My Sister's Words closed the door.
78. Women & Children First flyer (May 1980). It says "June is Kitchen Table: Women of Color Press month. Look for their new imprints and paperbacks and purchase them at a 10% discount!"
79. Corrigan, 6B-7B.
80. Ibid.
81. On the other hand, according to Carol Sejay, the debate that raged in the 70s about whether feminist authors should publish solely with feminist publishers to strengthen our publishing or was commercial publishing 'selling out' the movement, settled into the practical reality that everyone should publish as often and wherever possible. Carol Seajay, "Feminist Publishing in the US," *259: An Introduction to a World of Women's Books,* ed. Feminist Book Fair Group (London: Feminist Book Fair Groups, 1984), 30.
82. Nina Barrett, "Women & Children First: the evolution of a specialty market," *Publishers Weekly* (March 1987): 26. WCF collection.
83. Ann Christophersen, "Talking about the Basics: What is Feminist Writing and Why Do We Need Feminist Publishing?" *The Feminist Writers Guild* 8. 3 (1985–86): 6. WCF collection.
84. Author's interview with Linda Bubon and Ann Christophersen.
85. Martina Clarke, "20 years and going strong," *CLOUT!* (October 1999): 14. WCF collection.
86. Lisa Neff, "Independent's Day: Women & Children First feminist bookstore celebrates two decades," *Chicago Free Press* (November 1999): 1, 6–7. WCF collection.
87. Neff, 7. WCF collection.
88. For example, at Women & Children First, Sara Paretsky gave her first reading at their store, and Sandra Cisneros gave one of her earliest. They also hosted figures such as Gerda Lerner, Margaret Atwood, Gloria Steinem, Alice Walker, Bharati Mukherjee, Gwendolyn Brooks, Julia Alvarez, Susan Mnot, Barbara Kingsolver, Edwidge Danticat, and Hillary Rodham Clinton. Kyoko Mori, Lynne Sharon Schwartz, Louis Edrich, April Sinclair, Jonetta Cole, Moly Ivins, Barbara Smith, Clarissa Pinkola Estes, and Anna Quindlen, It was the only bookstore in the city of Chicago that asked Susan Faludi to speak when she published *Backlash*. Clarke, 14.
89. Neff, 6–7.
90. Clarke, 14.

91. One-third who answered my questionnaires, which was conducted in April and May in 1999, used words such as diversity and multicultural, and half of them used a word, community when they explained the importance of Women & Children First.
92. Barrett, 26.
93. Ibid.
94. Interview with Linda Bubon.
95. Interview with Ann Christophersen.
96. This award was given by Independent Gay and Lesbian Caucus of the Independent Voters of Illinois-Independent Precinct Organization in Chicago, Illinois. WCF collection.
97. Neff,10.
98. *FBN* 1, no. 1 (1976): 1.
99. Corrigan, 6B-7B.
100. Saralyn Chesnut and Amanda C. Gable," Women Ran It: Charis Books and More and Atlanta's Lesbian-Feminist Community, 1971–1981,"in *Carryin' On in the Lesbian and Gay South,* ed. John Howard (New York: New York University Press, 1997), 273. For example, Shay Youngblood, who first publicly appeared as a writer at Charis, says, "Charis isn't just a bookstore. It's been a kind of home/community for me for over 15 years. . . . Charis has been great for my social and intellectual life." Ibid., 273.
101. Miller, *A labor of love: A 25 year history of Feminist and lesbian bookstores and publishing,* 1995. MMC collection.
102. Ibid. Teresa Corrigan said women's bookstores brought one to three percent profit, very small profit, but they would do because they were "committed" and believed in what they did and continued to do so and it was a "labor of love." Ibid.
103. "Bookstore Profile: A Room of One's Own: interview with Sandi Torkildson," *FBN* 9/10 (1987): 43.
104. Klinger (1996), 68.
105. "Food for Thought: a bookstore profile," *FBN* 10, no. 4 (1987): 34.
106. "(editorial)," *FBN* 16, no.1 (1993): 3.

NOTES TO CHAPTER EIGHT

1. Nancy Boutilier was struck by how many women in Outwrite 93: Gay and Lesbian Writers Conference in 1993 made the effort to define themselves as feminists. She noted that their effort to stress their status as feminists was in response to the difficulty of the times. Nancy Boutilier, "The Feminist Mystique," *FBN* 16, no.4 (1993): 29.
2. Anti-gay Amendment 2 was an initiative that would have nullified gay rights laws in three communities and prohibited the passage of any gay rights laws in the entire state of Colorado. "Suspects folded guilty in the Closet bombing," *FBN* 15, no.6 (1993): 11.

3. Becca Cragin, "Post-Lesbian-Feminism: Documenting 'Those Cruddy Old Dykes of Yore' in John Howard, ed., *Carryin' On: in the Lesbian and Gay South* (New York: New York University Press, 1997), 285–327.
4. Susan Bates, owner of Alaska Women's Bookstore, was uncomfortable with an article about her store in *The Anchorage Times* in 1986. This is because "This 'gentleman' that interviewed me made his own decision to leave the category of books on lesbianism and homosexuality out of his article. A drastic oversight on his part!" "Alaska Women's Bookstore," *FBN* 10, no.2 (1987):19.
5. "Notes from the Computer," *FBN* 13, no.5 (1992):2.
6. For discussions over women of color in feminist publishing, see Simone Murray, "'Books of Integrity': The Women's Press, Kitchen Table Press and Dilemmas of Feminist Publishing" in *The European Journal of Women's Studies* 5.2 (1998): 171–93.
7. Jayna Brown, "Racism: Who has the last word? Women of color and feminist publishing," *FBN* 16, no.2 (1993):27.
8. Ibid.
9. Untitled memo (n.d.). NW collection, Box 5.
10. Heterosexual women also felt isolated from some women's bookstores. For example, women of color as well as heterosexual women often felt excluded and stated that Crazy Ladies Bookstore in Cincinnati, OH, was perceived as overwhelmingly white and lesbian and/or that they did not feel welcome at events at the building. "Feminist Bookstore Days," *FBN* 16, no. 2 (1993): 20
11. "Correspondence" (n.d.). OWT collection, Box 1.
12. For example, when I conducted a survey conducted in My Sister's Words in 1998, I received 60 responses. Two responses were from women of color.
13. *FBN* 15, no.2 (1992):19. There might be some Hispanic women, but no African American women as well as no Asians were in the photograph.
14. Corrigan, 7B.
15. Notes from the computer," *FBN* 12, no. 3 (1989): 1
16. "Red & Black Books," *FBN* 11, no.1 (1988):18. For example, Rooms of One's Own reported books on recovery accounted for 13% of the best seller books sales (188 books $1450) 4 titles of 30 bestsellers in lesbian titles. Lesbian books accounted for 25% of the total income from all books that sold 5 plus copies. "Rooms of One's Own," *FBN* 9, no.5 (1987). Along with the recovery movement, many books about recovery were published and sold well. Carol Wilson of Mama Bears who opened the store in 1983 said that particularly materials about recovery as well as lesbians helped the store open. Deonne Kahlerh, "A New Feminist Face Takes the Helm at Mama Bears Bookstore," in *Bay Area Business Woman* (March 2003): Available online: http://www.rightbrainleft.com/art-mama-bears.htm. As for alcohol problems among lesbians and gays, it was pointed out that many of them were heavily relied on the lesbian/gay bars or other public or private drinking settings to socialize and to be out. Therefore, it was identified as a potential risk factor which encouraged

alcohol abuse among lesbians and gay men. Later so-called twelve-step meeting for recovery alcohol and chemical dependency was offered by a number of lesbians and gay men's institutions in the 1980s. For discussions about recovery movement among lesbians, see also Kathleen O'Halleran Glaus, "Alcoholism, Chemical Dependency and the Lesbian Client," in *Loving Boldly: Issues Facing Lesbians,* ed. Esther D. Rothman and Ellen Cole (NY: Harrington Park Press, 1989), 133. For discussions concerning alcoholism and lesbianism, see, for example, Deborah L. Diamond and Sharon C. Wilsnack, "Alcohol Abuse Among Lesbians: a descriptive study," *Journal of Homosexuality* 4, no. 2 (1978): 123–142; Sandra C. Anderson and Donna C. Henderson, "Working with Lesbian Alcoholics," *Social Work* 30 (1989):518–525; Brenda Weathers, "Alcoholism and the Lesbian Community," in *Alcoholism in Women,* ed. Christen C. Eddy and John L. Ford (Dubuque, Iowa : Kendall/Hunt Publishing Company, 1980), 142–49, and Wiliam F. Skinner and Melanie Otis, "Drug and Alcohol Use Among Lesbian and Gay People in a Southern US Sample: Epidemiological, Comparative, and Methodological Findings From the Trilogy Project," *Journal of Homosexuality* 30, no.3 (1996): 59–92.

17. Ashlea Halpern, "Sisters in Struggle," *Punk Planet Magazine* (May/June 2003): 102.
18. Mev Miller, "Feminism and Literacy for Women: Politics and Resources," *Feminist Collection* 21 (Fall 1999): 17.
19. "Notes from the computer," *FBN* 13, no. 2 (1990): 11.
20. Carol Seajay, "Our Words in Our Hands: a brief history of women's presses and bookstores," in *The Woman-Centered Economy: Ideals, Reality, and the Space in Between,*ed. Loraine Edwalds and Midge Stocker (Chicago : Third Side Press, 1995), 77–86.
21. Nelle Oosterom, "Are Women's Bookstores Getting Squeezed Out?" *Herizons* 8, no.2 (1994): 16.
22. Feminist booksellers started to meet for a day of meetings and workshops in the Friday before ABA convention in 1984. *FBN* 14, no.2 (1991): 26.
23. Reports of Feminist Bookstore Day in each year in *FBN* 12, no.2 (1990): 14, *FBN* no.2 (1991): 2, *FBN*15, no.2 (1992):19. Three of the oldest and thriving women's bookstores reported their sales were record high: New Words reached $570,000 (1989), Amazon Bookstore $360,000 (1990) which was $241,000 in 1985, and Old Wives' Tales $391,000 (1991). *FBN* 13, no. 2(1990); "Balance sheets [of New Words]," NW collection, "Financial records [of Old Wives' Tales]," OWT collection.
24. "The March on Washington," *FBN* 16, no.2 (1993): 21.
25. Eric Hunter, "Learning from Loss," *CityBeat: Gay & Lesbian Issues* (April 5, 2001). Available online: http://www.citybeat.com/2001-04-05/ gayles.shtml
26. Carol Seajay, "Carol Seajay: Spreading the Word: Keeping Connected with Feminist Bookstore News" in *Happy Endings: Lesbian Writers Talk About Their Lives and Work,* ed. Kate Brandt (Tallahassee, Florida: The Naiad Press, Inc., 1993), 147.
27. Ibid.

28. Tolli, 28.
29. Ibid., 6B-7B In 1995, the Borders-Walden Group is renamed Borders Group, Inc. See the history of Borders Group, available online: http://www.bordersgroupinc.com/about/history.htm
30. "Invasions of the Chains," *FBN* 15, no 3 (1992): 27. The chains and superstores carried, on average, over 100,000 books in each location. For example, New Words carried in 1989 just 8,000 titles in a 1,143 square foot space. The total square feet of women's bookstores usually ranged from around 1,000 to 2,500. Judith Rosen, "New Words: the collective works," *Publishers Weekly* (1989): 56 Kathy Sharp, "1991 FB Financial Survey," *FBN* 15, no5 (1993): 55. Corrigan, 7B.
31. Anita Lahey, "Between the Pages: making a business of books," *Herisons* 10 (1996): 4.
32. Ibid.
33. Ibid.
34. Corrigan, 6B-7B. Corrigan also points out most lesbian authors who established their carrier through the feminist presses and feminist bookstores now publish their works from mainstream publishers, however, when they went mainstream, "the lesbian sexual content is absent, and lesbian characters are presented as nonsexual friends or as obsessed and dangerous," and they "destroy the source of literature that reflects the richness and diversity of lesbian lives."
35. Ibid.
36. Author's interview with Carol Seajay
37. Corrigan, 6B-7B.
38. "Open Letter to the Community [from My Sisters' Words]," (1994). LHA collection, bookstore subject file.
39. In 1986 the booksellers won the antitrust suit. *FBN* 9, no.3 (1987).
40. "Short Stories," *FBN* 11, no.4 (1988): 17.
41. Ibid. The anti-trust suit filed in the US district court in Philadelphia by American Booksellers Association in 1994.
42. Carolyn Gage, "Amazon Questions," *Feminista!* 4, no.2 (2000). Available online: http://www.feminista.com/v4n2/gage.html
43. Harriet L Schwarts, "Superstores vs. the Independents," *Philadelphia Gay News* (1998): Available online: http://www.pnpa.com/foundation/contests/keystone98/stories/schwartzstore.htm.
44. Corrigan, 6B-7B.
45. Audreay Eaglen, "Book Publishing: Past & Present, " in *Buying Books* (NY & London: Neal-Schuman Publishers, INC, 1989).
46. Andrea Fleck Clardy, "Somebody Else's Crisis: Feminist Publishers and Midlist Books, " *Book Research Quarterly* (1986): 5–9.
47. Carol Seajay, "Books as Wallpaper? An explanation for returns," *Publishers Weekly* 243, no. 46 (1996): 30.
48. Ibid.
49. Ibid. In fact, between 1960 and 1989, 573 mergers and acquisitions of publishers were made.(Albert N. Greco, *The Book Publishing Industry*

(Boston: Allyn and Bacon, 1996), 53.) Such waves of mergers and acquisitions have increased concentration in the publishing industry.(For discussions about a publishing industry treatment of corporate chains' superstores, notorious in the 1980s for introducing mass-market sales technology, particularly aggressive book remaindering, to mainstream publishing, see John F. Baker's "The 80s: Reaching New Heights," *Publishers Weekly* 5 (1990):19–20, Daily Maryles, "A Decade of Megasellers," *Publishers Weekly* 5 (1990): 24–26.) Ben Bagdikian warned that these actions would hurt the whole industry, particularly in terms of its diversity—specifically, the number of titles published. Ben Bagdikian, *Media Monopoly* (Boston: Beacon Press, 1983). At the same time, it is not the case that there are fewer publishers than before; on the contrary, there has been a tremendous increase in small presses during the last three decades. There were 12,000 publishers in 1985, compared to approximately 1000 in 1958. (Michael R. Gabriel, "The Astonishing Growth of Small Publishers 1958–1988," *Journal of Popular Culture* 24 (1990): 61–68. More and more people published in special interest fields such as those of feminist and lesbian publishers. Small houses emerged in various regions outside New York and, therefore, they produced more regional titles. Not all of these publishers were very active; some produced only one or two titles altogether, and some of them could not survive more than a year. But, the large number of new titles produced was not necessarily widely distributed. According to Milliot, the top ten trade publishers' share of 1993 trade and mass market book sales at sixty-two percent. Jim Milliot, "Sales Increase at Top 10 Trade Houses to $3.9 billion," *Publishers Weekly* 241, no.47 (1994): 10. According to Laura Miller, only about one in seven American presses continue to publish more than one new title each year. Laura Miller, "Merchandising to the Mind: The Cultural and Economic context of Book retailing and Wholesaling in the United States," 160.

50. Rose Norman, "Frequently asked questions about the problems facing feminist publishers and booksellers," *Women in Print.* Available online: http://mortonweb.uah.edu/wip/faq.html
51. Ibid.
52. 1.5 million titles listed in the 1994/95 version of *R.R.Bowker's Books in Print,* but in the fiction arena, brand name authors dominated all sales categories. Michael Normal points out "American publishers insist they 'support' literary fiction, but their record suggests something else." Michael Normal, "A book in search of a Buzz: the marketing of a first novel," *New York Times Book Review* 30 (1994): 3.
53. Rose Norman, "Shrinking shelves," *The Women's Review of Books* XIX, no.3 (2001):11–13.
54. Clardy, 5–9.
55. Carol Seajay, "The Backlash and the Backlist," *The Women's Review of Books* 12 (1994):18.
56. "Letters," *FBN* 15, no. 6 (1993): 26.

57. "Open Letter to the Community [from My Sisters' Words]," (1994). LHA collection, bookstore subject file. My Sisters' Words sent the letter to 2800 people in the community in 1994.
58. "Notes from the Computer, "*FBN* 15, no.5 (1993):3. "Finances, News from the Bookstores," *FBN* 15, no. 6 (1993): 25. "Feminist bookstores financial survey," *FBN* 25, no. 6 (1993):24.
59. Harriet Schwartz, "Superstores vs. the Independents," *Philadelphia Gay News* (1998). LHA collection.
60. "ABA '94 What a Scene!" *FBN* 17, no.1 (1994): 18.
61. Thee sales of Southern Sisters were $34,208 (Aug. 88 to Dec. 88), $85,141 (1989), $98,987 (1990), $111,532 (1991), $108,336 (1992), $103,768 (1993). It closed the doors in 1995. DCT collection.
62. Ibid. When Feminist Bookstores Day was planned, a definition of feminist bookstores were established: 1. They are owned (entirely) by women or by one woman (and that, of a board of directories exists, it is composed entirely of women), 2. 80% of the stock is written by women, 3. Primary commitment of the store is to feminism, 4. There is a strong commitment to feminist (including lesbian) publishing. After a year, however, some definitions changed. For example, percentage of the stock which must be written by/about women decreased from 80% to 51%, and a definition was added that 51% of the staff members must be women. "Feminist Bookstores Day," *FBN* 15, no2 (1992):19. This change reflects the increase of mix gender bookstores among feminist bookstores which include transgender people and gay men. Bluestocking in New York was one of them, and later the primary focus changed from "feminists" to "lesbian/gay/bisexual/transgender people" in 2004.
63. "Feminist Bookstores Day," *FBN* 14, no.2 (1991): 26.
64. "News from the Bookstores," *FBN* 14, no 4 (1991): 11. According to Seajay, Mary Morrell proposed the creation of a formal national network. *FBN* 14, no. 2 (1991): 26. FB-Net committee is made up of Joan Denman (Rubyfruit Books), Anne Frost (Full Circle), Barb Wieser (Amazon Bookstore), Kate Randall (Antigone), Linda Bubon (Women and Children First), Alison Cunningham (Golden Thread) and Theresa Corrigan (Lioness). "Feminist Bookstores Network," *FBN* 15, no.2 (1992): 21.
65. Christa Brelin and Michael J. Tyrkus, "Carol Seajay," in *Outstanding Lives: Profiles of Lesbians and Gay Men* (Detroit, MI: visible Ink Press, 1997), 344.
66. "The education committee in action," *FBN* 16, no.2 (1993): 19.
67. Tolli, "Invasions of the Chains," *FBN* 15, no. 3 (1992): 28.
68. Stephanie Poggi, "If We Want Women's Bookstores To Be There, We Have To Support Them," *Sojourner: the women's forum* 14, no.4 (1998): 29.
69. Elena Rutter, " A warm welcome is not a line item," *FBN* 17, no. 2 (1994): 33.
70. Seajay (1995): 73.
71. Bookstores, which attended the sessions, were Herland, Amazon, Lammas, Lioness, Full Circle, Book Garden, Women & Children First, Reader's Feast, My Sister's Words, A Room of One's Own, Brigit Books, Meristem, Inklings, Textures, Dreams & Swords, New Words, etc. Experiences in

bookselling varied, and it ranged from one and half year to almost twenty years. DCT collection.

72. "Feminist Bookstore strengths, weaknesses, opportunities and threats," (1994), DCT collection.
73. "FBNetwork launched Fall and Spring Catalog," *FBN* 18, no.1 (1995):13.
74. "Success," *FBN* 18, no.1 (1995):14.
75. Carol Seajay, "Feminist Bookstores Fight Back," *Ms.* (May/June 1995): 73.
76. Beth Morgan, "NY FB Week: Success stories," *FBN* 18, no.2 (1995): 35–40.
77. Feminist writers who wrote pledge were Dorothy Allison, Michelle Cliff, Ruth Hubbard, Irena Klepfisz, Robin Morgan, Margaret Rundall, Adrienne Rich, Sonia Sanchez and Alice Walker. Flyer of feminist writers pledge (n.d.), DCT collection. Bob Summer, "Bookselling as cultural politics; gay and lesbian bookstores." *Publishers Weekly* 27(1994): 29–31.
78. Poggi, 29.
79. "Women's Press Resolution," *FBN* 17, no.1 (1994): 18.
80. "Notes from the computer table," *FBN* 19, no.2 (1996):1.
81. Ibid.
82. Susan Raffo, "The Battle of the Amazons," *Z magazine.* Available online: http://www.zmag.org/Zmag/articles/raffo.htm 1995 Although the sales of Amazon.com were impressive in its initial year, its net losses were also huge. Jim Millot, "Amazon: sales, losses up, acquisitions, a stock split," *Publishers Weekly* 245 (1998):37.
83. "To Website or not to Website," *FBN* 19, no. 5 (1997). In 1996 Amazon bookstore launched an online bookstore, but in the early stages it reported confusion with Amazon.com. See "Amazon vs Amazon," *FBN* 22, no. 6 (2000):17.
84. "Correspondence," OWT collection, Box 1: 2/1
85. Ibid.
86. Vicky Greenbaum, "Old Wives Tales Going Strong," *Bay Area Reporter* (Aug 29, 1991): 1–10. OWT collection.
87. OWT collection, Box 1
88. Val C. Phoenix, "Old Wives' Tales facing closure, " *San Francisco Bay Times* (July 29, 1993). OWT collection.
89. Ibid.
90. Ibid.
91. Untitled letter (n.d.), OWT collection, Box 1:1/2. Old Wives' Tales reported to women in the community about what the store did and how they helped, and thanked them for what they did.
92. Phoenix, (page number unavailable).
93. "The Debt-Free By 20th [anniversary] Campaign," (n.d.). OWT collection, Box 2–26.
94. Untitled letter from Jeanne Adleman (n.d.), OWT collection, Box 1–2.
95. Untitled letter from Adienne Lauby (August 2, 1993), OWT collection, Box 1–2.

96. Daneel Buring, *Lesbian and Gay Memphis: Building Communities behind the Magnolia* (NY: Garland, 1997), 236.
97. Sally Munt, *Heroic Desire: Lesbian Identity and Cultural Space* (NY: NY University Press, 1998), 152.
98. Ibid., 153.
99. Barbara Ryan, *Identity Politics in the Women's Movement* (NY: NYU Press, 2001), 325.
100. Rosemary Hennessy, *Materialist Feminism and the Politics of Discourse* (New York: Routledge, 1993), 964.
101. According to Arlene Stein, in the mid-1980s, lesbian joined predominantly gay male organizations as ACT UP (AIDS Coalition to Unleash Power). ACT UP "engaged in public actions to fight for a more effective response to the AIDS epidemic." Arlene Stein, *Sex and Sensibility: Stories of a Lesbian Generation* (Berkeley: University of California Press, 1997), 145. However, Stein also points out chapters of ACT UP and Queer Nation in many cities "were marred by gender (and racial) conflicts." She says, "This recurrent problem underscored that while the new queer politics asserted the sexual difference that could not be assimilated into feminism, gender, too, resisted being completely subsumed within sexuality. Ibid.,194.
102. Rebecca Cragin, "Post-Lesbian-Feminism: Documenting 'Those Cruddy Old Dykes of Yore,'" in John Howard, ed., *Carryin' On in the Lesbian and Gay South* (New York: New York University Press, 1997): 287.
103. For discussions about popular culture and lesbianism, see Danae Clark's "Commodity Lesbianism" in Henry Abelove, et al ed., *The Lesbian and Gay Studies Reader (*New York: Routledge, 1993), 186–201, Sasha Torres' "Television/Feminism: Heart Beat and Prime Time Lesbianism," in Henry Abelove, et al., ed., *The Lesbian and Gay Studies Reader* (New York: Routledge, 1993), 176–185; Diane Hamer and Belinda Budge, *The Good, The Bad and The Gorgeous: Popular Culture's Romance with Lesbianism* (San Francisoc, CA: Pandora/Harper San Francisco, 1995).
104. Cragin, 289.
105. Arlene Stein, *Sex and Sensibility: Stories of a Lesbian Generation* (Berkeley: University of California Press, 1997), 194–195.
106. Ibid.
107. Untitled letter (July 17, 1993), OWT collection, Box 1–2.
108. Ibid.
109. Untitled fax (Sept 22, 1993), OWT collection Box 1–2.
110. "ABA Las Vegas, Feminist Bookstore Day," *FBN* 12, no.2 (1990): 27.
111. Barbara Wilson, "On leaving Seap Press—reflections, recollections, and the call of the muse," *FBN* 17, no.5 (1995): 31.
112. "Obituary of Nanci Stern," *FBN* 15, no.2 (1992); "Obituary of Audre Lord, *FBN* 15, no.4 (1992).
113. "Taking Care of Business: marketing to young feminist," *FBN* 16, no.2 (1993): 23.

114. For example, the number of books My Sister's Words sold in 1992 consisted of 929 volumes of general fiction, 928 of lesbian fiction, 866 of women's studies, 499 of lesbian non-fiction, 281 of recovery, 275 of psychology/self-help, 256 of spirituality, 206 of children, 200 of bio/autobiography, and others. (Categories of books below two hundred were omitted.) Ellen Kavanaugh, "My Sisters' Words," *FBN* 16, no.1 (1992): 29.
115. Jennie Boyd Bull, "*FBN* 17, no.4 (1994).
116. "National Lesbian and Gay Book Month," *FBN* 16, no.1 (1992): 33.
117. "Book-of-the Month Club launches Lesbian and Gay series," *FBN* 16, no.1 (1992): 15.
118. For example, the number of books My Sister's Words sold in 1992 consisted of 929 volumes of general fiction, 928 of lesbian fiction, 866 of women's studies, 499 of lesbian non-fiction, 281 of recovery, 275 of psychology/self-help, 256 of spirituality, 206 of children, 200 of bio/autobiography, and others. (Categories of books below two hundred were omitted.) Kavanaugh, 29.
119. Clairelight in Santa Rosa CA in 1993, Smedley's Bookshop, Ithaca NY after 18 years in 1994, Judith's Room closed in January 1995.
120. One customer, who used to go to Old Wives' Tales at least twice a week to make purchases and check the bulletin board, said, "Old Wives' Tales was much more than a bookstore; it served as an unofficial clearing house of information about the women's community. I also enjoyed the company of other shoppers. . . . Please understand that you were a remarkable and integral part of the SF women's community for many years. Your contributions were experienced by many and appreciated by all." Letter (Sept 23, 1993), OWT Collection, Box 1/1/2.
121. "1996 holiday sales," *FBN* 19, no.6 (1997):18–20.
122. "Where Have All the Book Sales Gone?" *FBN* 21, no.2 (1998):13.
123. Rose Norman, "Frequently asked questions about the problems facing feminist publishers and booksellers" *Women in Print* Available online: http://mortonweb.uah.edu/wip/faq.html
124. Karen Angel, "Are Independents Making a Comeback?," *Publishers Weekly* 243 (1998):21
125. When compared to the statistics for independent bookstores in general, which fell by 40% (5200 to 3300), women's bookstores (75%) did far better. Pat Holt, "When Feminist Bookstores Fight Back," *Holt Uncensored* 78(July 1999). Available online: http://www.holtuncensored.com/members/column78.html
126. Pat Holt, "When Feminist Bookstores Fight Back," *Holt Uncensored* 78(July 1999). Available online: http://www.holtuncensored.com/members/column78.html
127. Simone and Adele, "Sisterhood's Ultianatum," *FBN* 22, no.1 (1999): 19.
128. Andre Schiffrin, *The Business of Books* (Verso, 2000), 125.
129. Interview with a worker in Crazy Ladies Bookstore. Schwarts, available online: http://www.pnpa.com/foundation/contests/keystone98/stories/schwartzstore.htm.

130. Katheleen Wilkinson, "The Closing of the Feminist Press: thirty years after the revolution, feminist publishers are feeling the crunch," *Girlfriend* (March 2001): 33.
131. Julie Ford, "Fallen Leaves: Will Canadian feminist book publishing bloom again?" *Siren Magazine* (Oct/Nov 2000). LHS collection.
132. Carol Seajay, "The Backlash and the Backlist," *The Women's Review of Books* 12 (1994):18. In the same article, Seajay also points out lesbian literature published by mainstream publishers is "replete with lesbian characters who are mentally ill, who are battered and/or engage in truly brutal sex or, alternately, desexed or asexual lesbian characters," and warns it is a "very dangerous mirror for contemporary lesbians to peer into."
133. Rose Norman listed some of books which became no longer in print in her online *Women in Print* page. For example, books which were published Kitchen Table: Women of Color Press, and were no longer in print including *The Third Wave: Feminist Perspectives on Racism* by M. Jacqui Alexander, et al, *Voices Against Women and the Ongoing Challenge to Racism* by Angela Davis, *A Gathering Spirit* by Beth Brant. For more list of out of print feminist materials, see Rose Norman, "Books We Wouldn't Have Without These Feminist Publishers, " *Women in Print.* Available online: http://mortonweb.uah.edu/wip/faq.html
134. Ibid.
135. "FBN Crisis," *FBN* 22, no.2 (1999): 2.
136. Ibid.
137. Wilkinson, 33
138. Ibid.
139. Marie Kuda, "Feminist Bookstore News Closes," *Outlines: The Voice of Chicago's Gay and Lesbian Community* (July 2000). Available online: http://www.outlineschicago.com/0outlines/2000726/fembooks.html
140. Wilkinson, 33.
141. Kuda, http://www.outlineschicago.com/0outlines/2000726/fembooks.html.
142. Wilkinson, 33.
143. Deonne Kahlerh, "A New Feminist Face Takes the Helm at Mama Bears Bookstore," *Bay Area Business Woman* (March 2003). Available online: http://www.rightbrainleft.com/art-mama-bears.htm
144. Kuda, http://www.outlineschicago.com/0outlines/2000726/fembooks.html. After closing *Feminist Bookstore News,* Carol Sejay is still vigorously working to spread women's words starting together with her friend to issue Books To Watch Out For e-newsletters, which include short reviews of 20 to 30 new books, particularly lesbian and gay books and publishing news to help subscribers decide which books they want to read. Information on Books To Watch Out For is available online: http://www.btwof.com
145. Ibid.

NOTES TO CHAPTER NINE

1. Charlotte Bunch, *Passionate Politics: Feminist Theory in Action, Essays 1968–1986* (New York: St. Martin's, 1987), 220.
2. Ann Snitow, "Introduction," in *Powers of Desire: The Politics of Sexuality,* ed. Ann Snitow (NY: Monthly Review Press, 1983), 439. According to Ann Snitow, feminist learned to maintain a free and safe cultural space separated from mainstream from other minority group, especially taking their initial cues from black separatists.
3. Katie King, "Producing sex, theory and culture: gay/straight remappings in contemporary feminism in *Conflicts in Feminism,* eds., Marianne Hirsch and Evelyn Fox Keller (New York: Routledge, 1990), 92. King claimed that "Many alternative cultural institutions and much cultural activism in feminism became tarred with the brush of this narrowed pejorative vision of "cultural feminism." Ibid.
4. Patricia Hill Collins, *Black Feminist Thought* (New York: Routledge, 1991): 227.
5. According to Ferree and Hess, to greater or lesser extent depending on specific location, local "women's communities" provide an alternative way of actually living out these ideas, and the feminist culture such as women's studies programs and other "bounded environments" promoted feminist subculture. Myra Marx Ferree and Beth B. Hess, *Controversy and Coalition: The New Feminist Movement* (Boston; Twayne Publishers, 1985), 213.
6. Linda Christianse-Ruffman points out the importance of "a broad, complex, and expanding concept of the political" to understand "relations of ruling and women's struggles to change the agenda." Linda Christianse-Ruffman, "Women's Conception of the Political: Three Canadian Women's Organizations," in *Feminist Organizations: Harvest of the New Women's Movement,* ed. Myra Marx Ferree and Patricia Yancey Martin (Philadelphia: Temple University Press, 1995), 390. Ferree and Hess also indicate the concept of the "political" includes women's community and cultural organizations. Ferree and Beth B. Hess , 29. See also Roxana Ng, *The Politics of Community Services, Immigrant Women, Class, and State* (Toronto: Garamond Press, 1988).
7. Jo Reger, "Emotions, objectivity and voice: an analysis of a "failed" participant observation," *Women's Studies International Forum* 24 (2001): 613.
8. Alice Molly, "Letters," *FBN* 16, no.3 (1998): 9.
9. Ibid.
10. Anne Swidler, "Culture in action: symbols and strategies," *American Sociological Review* 51 (April 1986):273. Ann Swidler says, culture influences not by providing the ultimate values toward which action is oriented, but by shaping a repertoire or "tool kit" of habits, skills, and styles from which people construct "strategies of action."
11. Carol Seajay, "Our Words in Our Hands: a brief history of women's presses and bookstores," in *The Woman-centered Economy: Ideals, Reality, and*

the Space in Between, ed. Loraine Edwalds and Midge Stocker (Chicago: Third Side Press, 1995), 79.

12. Corrigan, 6B-7B.
13. Marie Kuda, "Feminist Bookstore News Closes," *Outlines: The Voice of Chicago's Gay and Lesbian Community* (July 2000). Available online: http://www.outlineschicago.com/0outlines/2000726/fembooks.html.
14. Figures of 2001 is from "Overview: the 'Women In Print' Movement and its Status Today," *Media Report to Women* 31, no.2 (Spring 2003): Available online: http:www.mediareportowomen,com/312.htm. Figures for 2002 are from "The State of Emergency in Feminist Publishing," *Off Our Backs* (Aug/Sep 2000): 5–6. In 2001, Rose Norman reported that from 1999 to 2000, one-third of the country's feminist bookstores closed their doors. Rose Norman, "Support Your Feminist bookseller: She Supports You!" *WSAction* 13, 1 (Fall 2001):30. However, many women still believe in the need for women's bookstores. As of December 2003, the number of women's bookstores had slightly increased, to 47 in the US. Feminist bookstore list (December 2003) in *Women in Print* maintained by Mev Miller. Available online: http://www.litwomen.org/WIP/stores.html#stores
15. Kathyrin McGrath. "Pushed to the Margins: the slow death and possible rebirth of the feminist bookstores," *Bitch* (July 2003): Available online: http://www.bitchmagazine.com/archives/07–03margins/margins.shtml
16. Kuda (July 2000). Available online: http://www.outlineschicago.com/0outlines/ 2000726/ fembooks.html.
17. Rose Norman, "Support Your Feminist bookseller: She Supports You!" *WSAction* 13 (1) (Fall 2001): 31. She also says, "All of these women demonstrate . . . 'the passions and motivations" other than money that drive feminist bookstore owners and staff.'" Ibid.
18. Brigit Books closed in 2003.
19. In 1999, Bluestockings in New York City, which was run as a collective with one paid staff person and 90 female and transgender volunteers, mostly in their 20s and early 30s. Their mission statement says that the store "promotes the empowerment of women through words, art and activism. We work to be an intersection of dialogue and information exchange, providing women-focused books, events, workshops, and a meeting and gathering place." Although Kathryn Welsh left Bluestocking and it closed for a while, it re-opened and served the community as a bookstore focused on lesbian/gay/bisexual/transgender people's needs and interests in 2004. http://www.soapboxinc.com/bio_welsh.html
20. Norman, 31.
21. Karen Kawaguchi, "Feminist Feast and Famine: after three decades, feminist bookstores are going through transitions to stay viable," *Publishers Weekly* (July 2000).
22. Ibid.
23. "About Us!" Change Makers (2004). Available online: http://www.changemakersforwomen.com/aboutus.html

24. Rachel Corbett, "Women's Bookstores Dwindle to Stalwart Few," in Women's eNews (8/15/05). Available online: http://www.womensenews.org/article.cfm/dyn/aid2413/context/archive.
25. A list of women's bookstores in 2005 is available in Appendix E.
26. "Broad Vocabulary." Available online: http://www.broadvocabulary.com
27. "Still Alive at Twenty-Five!" Available online: http://www.gcwrc.org/
28. Ibid.
29. "Center for New Words: Where Women's Words Matter!" in *Center For New Words:* Available online: http://www.centerfornewwords.org/
30. Carol Gilligan, "Voices for New Words," Available online: http://www.centerfornewwords.org/
31. McGrath. Available online: Available online: http://www.bitchmagazine.com/archives/07–03margins/margins. .shtml
32. Ibid.
33. As Mary Ellen Kavanaugh of My Sister's Words suggests, women's bookstores which were and are "a kind of public institution" might be "*deserving of public charity*" to greater and lesser extent. Mary Ellen Kavanaugh, "10 years of My Sisters' Words," *Gay and Lesbian Bookselling* 4, no.4 (Dec. 1997):1.
34. Wilkinson, 40.

Bibliography

Abel, Richard, and Gordon Graham. *The Book in the United States Today.* New Brunswick and London: Transaction Publishers, 1997.

Abelove, Henry, Michele Alina Barale, and David M. Halperin, eds. *The Lesbian and Gay Studies Reader.* New York: Routledge, 1993.

Ackelsburg, Martha. "Communities, Resistance, and Women's Activism: some implications for a Democratic Polity." In Ann Bookman, and Sandra Morgan, eds., *Women and the Politics of Empowerment,* 297–313. Philadelphia: Temple University Press, 1988.

Adam, Barry D. *The Rise of A Gay and Lesbian Movement.* New York: Twayne Publishers, 1995.

Adam, Margie. "Margie Adam's Lifetime Achievement Award Acceptance Speech May 31,1997." Margie Adam Homepage. Available online: http://www.margieadam.com/info/nwmfs.htm.

Adams, Kate. "Built out of books: lesbian energy and feminist ideology in alternative publishing." *Journal of Homosexuality* 34 (1997): 113–129.

Adams, Tracy Kathryn. "Paper Lesbians: Alternative Publishing and the Politics of Lesbian Representation in the United States, 1950–1990." Ph.D. diss., The University of Texas, Austin, 1994.

Ahrens, Lois. "Battered Women's Refuges: Feminist Cooperatives vs. Social Service Institutions." *Radical America* 14, no.3 (1980): 41–47.

Alarik, Soctt. "Two music pioneers remember the struggle." *Boston Globe Correspondent* (Oct 1, 2000): Available online: http://www.criswillamson.com/news.htm.

Albertine, Susan, ed. *A Living of Words: American Women in Print Culture.* Knoxville: University of Tennessee Press, 1995.

Alcoff, Linda. "Feminist Theory and Social Science: new knowledge, new epistemologies." In *Body Space: Destabilizing Geographies Gender and Sexuality,* ed. Nancy Duncan. New York: Routledge, 1996.

———. "Cultural Feminism versus Post-Structuralism: The Identity Crisis in Feminist Theory." *Signs: Journal of Women in Culture and Society* 13, no. 3 (1988): 405–36.

Allen, Donna. *Media Report to Women*. Washington, DC: Women's Institute for Freedom of the Press, 1978.

Allen, Jeffner, ed. *Lesbian Philosophies and Cultures*. Albany, NY: State University of New York Press, 1991.

Allen, Martha L. *The Development of Communication Networks Among Women, 1963–1983*. Ann Arbor: University Microfilms International, 1989.

———"Women's Media: The Way to Revolution." *Off Our Backs* (February 1990): Available online: http://www.wifp.org/oobarticle.html.

Allen, Pamela. *Free Space: A Perspective on the Small Group in Women's Liberation*. New York: Times Change Press, 1970.

Almanzer, Richardo, et al. "Is the Political Personal? Everyday Behaviors as Forms of Environmental Movement Participation." *Mobilization* 3.2 (Oct 1998): 185–205.

Altbach, Philip G. *Perspectives on Publishing*. Philadelphia: American Academy of Political and Social Science, 1975.

Altman, Dennis. *Homosexual: Oppression and Liberation*. New York: Discus, 1973.

Anderson, Charles, ed. *Bookselling in America and the World: Some Observation & Recollections*. NY: The New York Times Book Co., 1975.

Anderson, Sandra C. and Donna C. Henderson. "Working with Lesbian Alcoholics." *Social Work* 30 (1989): 518–525.

Anderson, Charles. *Bookselling in America and the World: Some Observation & Recollections*. NY: Quardrangle/The New York Times Book Co.,1975.

Anderson, Margaret. *Thinking About Women: Sociological Perspectives on Sex and Gender*. New York: Macmillan Publishing Co., 1988.

Angel, Karen. "NYC's only Feminist Store to Close." *Publishers Weekly* (1995): 313.

———. "Getting in the door: the small presses." *Publishers Weekly* 144 (1997): 32.

———. "Are Independents Making a Comeback?" *Publishers Weekly* 243 (1998): 21.

Anne, Sheila. "Lesbian Separatism." *Off Our Backs* 22 (6) (June 1992): 17.

Anzaldua, Gloria, ed. *Making Face, Making Soul Haciendo Caras: Creative and Critical Perspectives by Women of Color*. San Francisco: Aunt Lute Foundation Books, 1990.

Apatheker, Bettina. *Tapestries of Life: Women's Work, Women's Consciousness and the Meaning of Daily Existence*. Amherst: University of Massachusetts Press, 1989.

Apostol, Jane. "Vroman's Pasadena: A Century of Books, 1894–1994." *Southern California Quarterly* 78 (1996): 91–93.

Armstrong, David. *A Trumpet to Arms: Alternative Media in America*. LA, California: J.P Tarcher, Inc., 1981.

Armstrong, Toni. "Playing to the highest common denominator." In *The Woman-Centered Economy: Ideals, Reality and the Space in Between*, eds. Midge Stocker and Loraine Edwards. Chicago: Third Side Press, 1995.

Armstrong, Elizabeth. "Multiplying identities: identity elaboration in San Francisco's Lesbian/Gay organizations, 1964–1994." Ph.D. diss., University of California, Berkeley, 1998.

———. *The Retreat from Organization: US Feminism Reconceptualized.* New York: SUNY Press, 2002.

Arnold, June. "Feminist Presses and Feminist Politics." *Quest* 3 (1975): 18–26.

Bagdikian, Ben H. *The Media Monopoly.* Boston: Beacon Press, 1990.

Bailey, Beth. "The Women's Movement: Liberation for Whom?" In David Farber, and Beth Bailey, eds., *The Columbia Guide to America in the 1960s,* 125–133. NY: Columbia University Press, 2001.

Baker, John F. "The 80s: Reaching New Heights." *Publishers Weekly* 5 (1990):19–20. Daily Maryles. "A Dacade of Megasellers." *Publishers Weekly* 5 (1990): 24–26.

Baldacci, Leslie. "Carving a niche: Feminist bookstore bucks odds." *Chicago Sun Times* (1 March, 1998): 21.

Banner, Lois W. *Women in Modern America, A Brief History.* New York: Harcourt Brace Jovanovich, Inc., 1974.

Barr, Roseanne. *Roseanne: My Life as a Woman.* NY: Harper & Row, 1989.

Barrett, Nina. "Women & Children Firs: the evolution of a specialty market." *Publisher's Weekly* (27 March 1987): 26–27.

Bates, Eric. "Chaining the Alternatives: what started a movement has become an industry." *Nation* 266 (June 29, 1998):11–18.

Baxandall, Rosalyn, Linda Gordon, and Susan Reverby, eds. *America's Working Women.* New York: Random House, 1976.

Beam, Joseph. "Introduction: Leaving the Shadows Behind." In Joseph Beam ed., *The Life: A Black Gay Anthology,* 13–18. Boston: Alyson, 1986.

Bechdel, Alison. *Dykes to Watch Out For.* Ithaca, NY: Firebrand Books, 1986.

———. *The Indelible Alison Bechdel: Confessions, Comix, and Miscellaneous Dykes to Watch Out For.* Ithaca, N.Y.: Firebrand Books, 1998.

Beck, Evelyn Torton. "The Politics of Invisibility." *NWSA Journal* 1 (1988):93–102.

Beiser, Karen Phebe,et al, eds. *Crazy Ladies: Vision and Venture: the History of Crazy Ladies Center, 1979–94.* Cincinnati: The Center, 1994.

Beck, Evelyn Toton. *Nice Jewish Girls: A Lesbian Anthology.* Watertown, Mass.: Persephone, 1982.

Beckles, Colin A. "Pan African Sites of Resistance: Black Bookstores and the Struggle To Re-present Black Identity." Ph.D. diss., University of California, Los Angeles, 1995.

———. "Black Bookstores, Black Power, and the F.B.I.: The Case of Drum and Spear." *Western Journal of Black Studies* 1996 20(2): 63–71.

Beemyn, Brett, ed. *Creating a Place for Ourselves: Lesbian, Gay, and Bisexual Community Histories.* New York: Routledge, 1997.

Beidler, Philip D. *Scriptures for a Generation: What We Were Reading in the '60s.* Athens: University of Georgia Press, 1994.

Belenky, Mary. *Women's Ways of Knowing: The Development of Self, Voice and Mind.* New York: Basic Books, 1988.

Bellah, Robert N., Richard Madsen, William M. Sullivan, Ann Swidler, and Steven M. Tipton, eds. *Habits of the Heart: Individualism and Commitment in American Live.* New York: Perennial Library, 1986.

Bender, Thomas. *Community and Social Change in America.* Baltimore: Johns Hopkins University Press, 1982.

Berkeley, Kathleen C. *The Women's Liberation Movement in America.* Westport, CT: Greenwood Press, 1999.

Bernstein, Elizabeth. "A Woman's Spirit Launches Web Store." *Publishers Weekly* 4 (August 1997): 39.

Berry, Faith. "A Question of Publishers and a Question of Audience." *Black Scholar* 17 (1986): 41–49.

Berry, Mary Frances. *Why the ERA Failed: Women's Rights and the Amending Process of the Constitution.* Bloomington: Indiana University, 1986.

Berube, Allan, and John D'Emilio. "The Military and Lesbians During the McCarthy Years." *Signs* 9 (1984):759–75.

Bird, Jon, et all., eds. *Mapping the Futures: Local Cultures, Global Change.* London: Routledge, 1993.

Bitonti, Tracy Simmons. "Twentieth-Century American Women Writers and the Literary Marketplace." Ph.D diss. University of South Carolina. 1997.

Blush, Bonnie. "Empty Shelves at Labyris," *Majority Report* (April 5, 1975).

Boardman, Edna M. "The art & science of book reviewing." *The Book Report* 12 (Jan. 1994): 17.

Boaz, Martha Terosse. "A Qualitative analysis of the criticism of best sellers; a study of the reviews and reviewers of best selling book from 1944–1953." Ph.D. diss., The University of Michigan, 1955.

Bogus, Diane. "The 'Queen B' Figure in Black Literature." In Karla Jay and Joanne Glagow, eds. *Lesbian Texts and Contexts: Radical Revisions,* 2275–290. New York: New York University Press, 1990.

Bolotin, Susan. "Voices from the Post-Feminist Generation." *New York Times Magazine* (October 7, 1982): 28–31.

Bonn, Thomas L. *Heavy Traffic and High Culture: New American Library as Literary Gatekeeper in the Paperback Revolution.* Carbondale: Southern Illinois University Press, 1989.

"Book reviewing comes of age." *Library Journal* 121 (July 1996): 64.

Boston Women's Health Book Collective. *Our Bodies, Ourselves: A Book by and for Women.* New York: Simon and Schuster, 1973.

Bourdier, Pierre. *Distinction: A Social Critique of the Judgment of Taste.* Cambridge, MA: Harvard University Press, 1984.

Boutell, Cleve. "More than a store." *Small Press* (1995): 25.

Boxer, Marilyn. *When Women Asked the Questions: Creating women's studies in America.* Baltimore: Johns Hopkins University, 1999.

Boyte, Harry C. *The Backyard Revolution: Understanding the New Citizen Movement.* Philadelphia: Temple University Press, 1980.

Brady, Maureen, and Judith McDaniel. "Lesbians in the Mainstream: Images of Lesbians in Recent Commercial Fiction." *Conditions* 7 (1980): 82–105.

Brandow, Karen, Jim McDonnell, and Vocations for Social Change. *No Bosses Here: A Manual on Working Collectively and Cooperatively.* Boston, MA: Alyson Publications, 1981.

Brandt, Kate ed. *Happy Endings: Lesbian Writers Talk About Their Lives and Work.* Tallahassee, Fla.: Naiad Press, 1993.

Brandt, Kate, "Carol Seajay: Spreading the Word." In Kate Brandt ed. *Happy Endings: Lesbian Writers Talk About Their Lives and Work,* 141–150. Tallahassee, Florida: The Naiad Press, Inc., 1993.

Brelin, Christa and Michael J. Tyrkus. *Outstanding Lives: Profiles of Lesbians and Gay Men.* Detroit, MI: Visible Ink Press, 1997.

Brody, Michael. *Are 'We There Yet?': A Continuing Story of Lavender Woman, A Chicago Lesbian Newspaper, 1971–1976.* Iowa City, IA: Aunt Lute Book Company, 1985.

Brondine, Karen. "Politics of Women Writing." *The Second Wave* 5 (1979): 6–13.

Brotman, Barbara. "A Street of one's Own." *Chicago Tribune* (3 December 1992): 1–2.

Broude, Norma, and Mary Garrard, eds. *The Power of Feminist Art.* New York: Abrams, 1994.

Brownmiller, Susan. *In Our Time: Memoir of a Revolution.* New York: Dial, 1999.

Buechler, Steven M. *Women's Movements in the United States: Woman Suffrage, Equal Rights, and Beyond.* New Brunswick, N.J.: Rutgers Univ. Press, 1990.

Bulkin, Elly, Minnie Bruce Pratt, and Barbara Smith, eds. *Yours in Struggle: the Feminist Perspectives on Anti-Semitism and Racism.* New York: Long Haul Press, 1984.

Bunch, Charlotte. "Learning from Lesbian Separatism." *Ms.* (November 1976): 60–61, 99–100, 102.

———. *Passionate Politics: Feminist Theory in Action, Essays, 1968–1986.* New York: St. Martin's, 1987.

Bunch, Charlotte and Sandra Pollack, eds. *Learning Our Way: Essays in Feminist Education.* Trumansburg, N.Y.: Crossing Press, 1983.

Buring, Daneel. *Lesbian and Gay Memphis: Building Communities Behind the Magnolia Curtain.* New York: Garland, 1997.

Burks, William. "Glynn Sudbery Awards." *Windy City Times* (29 May 1986): 5.

Burnett, Gary, Michele Besant and Elfreda A Chatman. "Small Worlds: normative behavior in virtual communities and feminist bookselling." *Journal of the American Society for Information Science and Technology* 52 (7) (2001): 536–547.

Butler, Judith. *Gender Trouble: Feminism and the Subversion of Identity.* New York: Routledge, 1990.

Cadman, Eileen, Gail Chester, and Agnes Pivot. *Rolling Our Own: Women as Printers, Publishers and Distributors.* London: Minority Press Groups, 1981.

Cahn, Susan. *Coming on Strong: Gender and Sexuality in Twentieth-Century Women's Sport.* New York: Free Press, 1994.

Calusen, Jan. *Books & Life.* Columbus : Ohio State University Press, 1989.

Caplette, Michele Kathleen. "Women in book publishing: a study of careers & organizations." MA thesis, The State University of New York at Stony Brook, 1981.

———. "Book Publishing: A Study of Careers and Organizations," Ph.D diss., State University of New York at Stony Brook, 1981.

Carabillo, Toni, and Jidith Meuli. *Feminist Chronicles, 1953–1993.* Los Angels: Women's Graphics, 1993.

Caraway, Nancie. *Segregated Sisterhood: Racism and the Ppolitics of American Feminism.* Knoxville: University of Tennessee Press, 1986.

Carrier, Esther Jane. *Fiction in Public Libraries, 1900–1950.* Littleton, Colo. : Libraries Unlimited, 1985.

Carvey, Ellen Gruber, "Out of the Mainstream and in to the Streets: small press magazines, the underground press, zines, and artists' books." In Scott E. Capser, et al eds., *Perspectives on American Book History.* Amherst: University of Massachusetts Press, 2002.

Case, Donald O. "Book Reviewing." *Journal of the American Society for Information Science* 46(1995): 325.

Casper, Scott E, Joanne D. Chaison, and Jeffrey D. Groves, eds. *Perspectives on American Book history: Artifacts and Commentary.* Amherst: University of Massachusetts Press, 2002.

Castells, Manuel. *The City and the Grassroots.* Berkeley, CA: University of California Press, 1983.

Castro, Ginette. *American Feminism: A Contemporary History.* New York: New York University Press, 1990.

Cavin, Susan. "The Invisible Army of Women: lesbian social protest, 1969–1988." In Guida West, and Rhoda Blumberg, eds., *Women and Social Protest,* 321–332. NY: Oxford University, 1990.

Certeau, Michel de. *The Practice of Everyday Life. Berkeley,* CA: University of California Press, 1983.

Chafe, William. *The Unfinished Journey.* New York: Oxford, 1995.

Chambers, Ian. "A Strategy for Living." *Cultural Studies* (Summer 1975): 161.

Champion, Dean J, and Michael F. Morris. "A Content Analysis of Book Reviews in the AJS, ASR, and Social Forces." *American Journal of Sociology* 78 (Mar., 1973): 1256–1265.

Charles, Debbie. "Revolution NOW! Alternatives in Music," *Paid My Dues* (October 1974):10–11

Cheney, Joyce, ed. *Lesbian Land.* Minneapolis, MN: Wordweavers, 1986.

Chesler, Phyllis. "All We Have Is Each Other." In *The Woman-Centered Economy,* ed. Loraine Edwalds and Midge Stocker. Chicago: Third Side Press, 1995.

Chesnut, Saralyn, and Amanda C. Gable. "'Women Ran It: Charis Books and More and Atlanta Lesbian Feminist Community, 1971–1981," In *Carryin' On in the Lesbian and Gay South,* ed. John Howard, ed., New York: New York University Press, 1997.

Christina, Barbara. "The Race for Theory." *Feminist Studies* 14 (1988): 67–79.

Christianse-Ruffman, Linda. "Women's Conception of the Political: Three Canadian Women's Organizations." In *Feminist Organizations: harvest of the new women's movement,* ed. Myra Marx Ferree and Patricia Yancey Martin, 372–396. Philadelphia: Temple University Press, 1995.

Christophersen, Ann. "Talking about the Basics: What is Feminist Writing and Why Do We Need Feminist Publishing?" *The Feminist Writers Guild* 8. 3 (1985–86): 6.

Clardy, Andrea Fleck. "Creating the Space: Feminist Publications Outside the Mainstream." *Women's Studies International Forum* 6 (1983): 545–546.

———. "Feminist Presses." *Ms.* (August 1985): 65–68.

———. "Somebody Else's Crisis: feminist publishers and midlist books." *Book Research Quarterly* (Sprint 1986): 5–9.

———. *Words to the Wise: A Writing Guide to Feminist and Lesbian Periodicals and Publishers.* Ithaca, N.Y.: Firebrand Books, 1986.

Clark, Danae. "Commodity Lesbianism." In *The Lesbian and Gay Studies Reader,* Henry Abelove, et al ed., 186–201. New York: Routledge, 1993.

Clarke, Martina. "20 Years and going strong." *CLOUT!* (October 1999): 14–19.

Clausen, Jan. "The Politics of Publishing and the Lesbian Community." *Sinister Wisdom*1.2 (1976): 95–115.

———. "A Movement of Poets: Thoughts on Poetry and Feminism." Part 1. *New Women's Times Feminist Review* (November/ December 1981): 8–11; Part 11. (January/February 1982):407, 13–14, 16; Part III. (March/April 1982): 8–11.

———. "A Craving for Community." *Women's Review of Books* 9 (March 1992): 8–9.

Clement, Richard W. *The Book in America with Images from the Library of Congress.* Golden, Colorado: Fulcrum Publishing, 1996.

Cohen, Ralph. "Reviewing Criticism." In *Literary Reviewing,* James O. Hoge, 1–18. Charlottesville: University Press of Virginia, 1987.

Collins, Patricia Hill. *Black Feminist Thought.* New York: Routledge, 1991.

Combahee River Collective, "The Combahee River Collective: a black feminist statement." In *Capitalist Patriarchy and the Case for Socialist Feminism,* ed. Zillah Eisenstein, 365–367. New York: Monthly Review Press.

Conover, Pamela Johnston and Virginia Gray. *Feminism and the New Right: Conflict Over the American Family.* New York: Praeger, 1983.

Cooter, Margaret et al. *Reviewing the Reviews: A Woman's Place on the Book Page.* London: Journeyman, 1987.

Corigan, Theresa. "Feminist Bookstores: Part of an Ecosystem." *Sojourner: The Women's Forum* 16. 4 (1993): 6B-7B.

Corson, Suzanne. "New Waves in Lesbian Publishing." *Alternative Library Literature* (Phoenix, AZ: Oryx Press, 2000/2001):29–31.

———. "Our Books, Our Shelves." *Girlfriends* (Sep 2000): 10.

Coser, Lewis A. "Publishers as Gatekeepers of Ideas." *Annals of the American Academy of Political and Social Science* 421 (1975): 14–22.

———. *Books: The Culture & Commerce of Publishing.* N.Y.: Basic Books, 1982.

Couch, W.T. "A Case History in Book Publishing." *American Quarterly* 1 (4) (Winter 1949): 302–313.

Cragin, Becca. "Post-Lesbian-Feminism: Documenting 'Those Cruddy Old Dykes of Yore.'" In *Carryin' On,* ed. John Howard, 285–327. New York: New York University Press.

Creekmur, Corey K, and Alexander Doty, eds. *Out in Culture: Gay, Lesbian and Queer Essays on Popular Culture.* Durham, NC: Duke University Press, 1995.

Creelman, Janet and Roma M. Harris. "Coming Out: The Information needs of lesbians." *Collection Building*10 (3/4) (1990): 37–41.

Cruikshank, Margaret. *The Gay and Lesbian Liberation Movement.* N.Y.: Routledge, 1992.

———. "Foreword." In *The New Lesbian Studies,* ed. Bonnie Zimmerman and T. McNaron, xi-xii. New York: Feminist Press, 1996.

Culligan, Glendy. "Born free but not liberated." *Saturday Review* 54 (1971): 25–28,41.

Curtis, Anthony. *Lit Ed: On Reviewing and Reviewers.* U.K. Manchester: Carcanet Press, 1998.

Daines, Guy. "Wide Impact Overall." *Library Association Record* 96 (Jan. 1994): 37.

Daley, Ginny. "Women and Publishing in North Carolina" (March 1992). Available online: http://scriptorium.lib.duke.edu/women/ncwwpub.html.

Daly, Mary. *Gyn/ecology: The Metaethics of Radical Feminism.* Boston: Beacon Press, 1978.

Dana, Robert. "An Interview with Lawrence Ferlinghetti." *Midwest Quarterly* 24(1983): 412–440.

Darnovsky, Marcy, Barbara Epstein, and Richard Flacks, ed. *Cultural Politics and Social Movements.* Philadelphia: Temple University Press, 1992.

Davenport, Doris. "The Pathology of Racism: A Conversation with Third World Wimmin." In *This Bridge Called My Back: Writings by Radical Women of Color,* eds. Cherrie L. Moraga and Gloria Anzaldua, 85–90. New York: Kitchen Table Press, 1983.

Davidson, Cathy. *Revolution and the Word: the Rise of the Novel in America.* New York: Oxford University Press, 1986.

Davis, Flora. *Moving the Mountain.* New York: Simon & Schuster, 1991.

Davis, Kenneth C. *Two-Bit Culture: The Paperbacking of America.* Boston: Houghton-Mifflin. 1984.

De Lauretis, Teresa. "Queer Theory: Lesiban and Gay Sexualities-An Introduction." *Differences: A Journal of Feminist Cultural Studies* 3 (1991): iii-xviii.

De Muth, Danielle M. "Carol Seajay, American publisher, activist and writer." In *Gay & Lesbian Biography,* ed. Michael J. Tyrkus. Detroit; London : St. James Press, 1997.

Deckard, Barbara. *The Women's Movement: Political, Socio-Economic and Psychological Issues.* New York: Harper and Row Publishers, 1979.

Delaney, John ed. *The House of Scribner, 1931–1984.* Detroit: Gale Research, 1998.

Dell, Richards. *Lesbian Lists: a Look at Lesbian Culture, History, and Personalities.* Boston: Alyson Publications, 1990.

D'Emilio, John. *Sexual Politics, Sexual Communities: The Making of a Homosexual Minority in the United States, 1940–70.* Chicago: University of Chicago Press, 1983.

D'Emilio, John, and Estelle Freedman, *Intimate Matters: A History of Sexuality in America.* New York: Harper Collins Publishers, Inc., 1988.

———. *Making Trouble: Essays on Gay History, Politics, and the University.* Chicago: University of Chicago Press, 1992.

Dennis, Everette E, Craig LaMay, and Edward Poare eds. *Publishing Books.* New Brumswick & London: Transaction Publisher, 1997.

Dessauer, John P, Paul Doebler, and Wayne Nordberg, eds. *Book Industry Trends.* Darien, CT: Book Industry Study Group, 1978.

Dessauer, John P. *Book Publishing: What It Is, What It Does*. NY: R.R. Bowker Company, 1981.

———. "US Retail Book Sales by Subject: A First Estimate." *Book Research Quarterly* 2 (1986–87): 15–17.

Diamond, Deborah, and Sharon C. Wilsnack. "Alcohol Abuse Among Lesbians: a descriptive study." *Journal of Homosexuality* 4, no. 2 (1978):123–142.

Dirks, Nicholas B, Geoff Eley, and Sherry B. Ortner, eds. *Culture/ Power /History*. Princeton, NJ: Princeton University Press, 1993.

Dong, Stella. "Kitchen Table: Publishing for Third World Women." *Small Press* 2 (January/February, 1985): 26–31.

Donnelly, Nisa. "The Sound of Two Rocks." *Lambda Book Review* 4/2 (Jan/Feb 1994). Available online: http://www.english.uiuc.edu/maps/poets/g-l/grahn/intexcerpts.htm.

Donoghue, Frank. *The Fame Machine: Book Reviewing and Eighteenth-Century Literary Careers*. Stanford, Calif.: Stanford University Press, 1996.

Donovan, Debbie. "Identity beyond the Community: the making of suburban lesbian friendship networks." Ph.D.diss., State University of New York at Albany, 1999.

Doughty, Frances. "Frances Doughtly Talks to Charlotte Bunch about Women's Publishing." *Sinister Wisdom* 13 (1980):71–77.

Douglas, Carol Ann, and Fran Moira. "*Off Our Backs:* the First Decade 1970–1980." In *Voices from the Underground,* ed. Ken Wachsberger, 107–123. Tempe, AZ: Mica Press, 1993.

Douglas, Susan. *Where the Girls Are: Growing up Female with the Mass Media*. New York: Random House, 1994.

Downing, John. *Radical Media: the Political Experience of Alternative Communication*. Boston: South End Press, 1984.

Drewry, John E. *Book Reviewing*. Boston : The Writer, Inc, 1946.

Duberman, Martin. *Stonewall*. New York: Dutton, 1993.

DuBois, Ellen et al., eds. *Feminist Scholarship: Kindling in the Groves of Academe*. Chicago: University of Illinois Press, 1985.

———. *Unequal Sisters: a Multicultural Reader in U.S. Women's History*. New York: Routledge, 2000.

Duggar, Lisa, and Nana D. Hunter, eds. *Sex Wars: Sexual Dissent and Political Culture*. New York: Routledge, 1995.

Duncan, Nancy, ed. *Body Space: Destabilizing Geographies of Gender and Sexuality*. New York: Routledge, 1996.

Dynes, Wayne R. *Lesbianism*. New York and London: Garland Publishing, Inc, 1992.

Dzwonkoski, Peter, ed. *American Literary Publishing Houses, 1900–1980: Trade and Paperback*. Detroit: Gale, 1986.

Eagle, Audrey. *Buying Books*. New York and London: Neal-Schuman Publishers, INC.,1989.

———. "Publishing for Women." *WLW Journal* 16. 2 (1993): 3–4.

Eastland, Lynette. "Ideology, Contradiction, and Change: A Study of a Lesbian Feminist Bookstore." Ph.D.diss., The University of Utah, 1985.

Eastman, Dale. "Ann Christophersen and Linda Bubon." *Today's Chicago Woman* (April 1990): 64.

Echols, Alice. "The New Feminism of Yin and Yang." In *Powers of desire: the politics of sexuality,* Ann Snitow et al., eds. New York: Monthly Review Press, 1983.

———. "The Taming of the Id: Feminist Sexual Politics, 1968–1983." In *Pleasure and Danger: Exploring Female Sexuality,* ed. Carole S. Vance, 50–72. Boston: Routledge & K. Paul, 1984.

———. *Daring to Be Bad: Radical Feminism in America, 1967–75.* Minneapolis : University of Minnesota Press, 1989.

———. "We gott get out of this place: notes toward a 'remapping' of the sixties." In *Cultural Politics and Social Movements,* Marcy Darnobsky, Barbara Epstein, and Richard Flacks. Philadelphia: Temple University Press, 1992.

Eder, Donna, Suzanne Staggenborg, and Lori Suderth. "The National Women's Music Festival: collective identity and diversity in a lesbian feminist community." *Journal of Contemporary Ethnography* 23 (4) (Jan., 1995): 485.

Eisenstein, Hester. *Contemporary Feminist Thought.* Boston: G.K. Hall & Co., 1983.

Eisenstein, Zillah. *The Radical Future of Liberal Feminism.* New York: Longman, 1981.

———. *Feminism and Sexual Equality: Crisis in Liberal America.* New York: Monthly Review Press, 1984.

"End of an Era: will the feminist bookstore soon be a thing of the past?" *Off Our Backs* (2003):18.

Endres, Kathleen L, and Therese L. Lueck. *Women's Periodicals in the U.S: Social, Political Issues.* Westport, Connecticut: Greenwood Press, 1996.

Enke, Anne. "Locating Feminist Activism; women's movement and public geographies, Minneapolis and St. Paul, 1965–80." Ph.D. diss., University of Minnesota, 1999.

Epstein, Jason. *Book Business: Publishing: Past, Present and Future.* New York: W.W. Norton, 2001.

Esterberg, Kristin G. "From Accommodation to Liberation: A Social Movement Analysis of Lesbians in the Homophile Movement." *Gender & Society* 8 (Sep. 1994): 424–443.

Evans, Jamie Lee. "Aunt Lute Books: Theory and Practice in Action." In *Woman-Centered Economy,* ed. Loraine Edward, 299–303. Chicago: Third Side Press, 1995.

Evans, Sara and Harry Boyte. *Free Spaces: The Source of Democratic Change in America.* New York: Harper and Row, 1986.

Evans, Sara. *Personal Politics: The Roots of Women's Liberation in the Civil Rights Movement and the New Left.* New York: Knopf, 1979.

———. *Born For Liberty: A History of Women in America.* New York: Free Press, 1989.

———. "Women's History and Political Theory: toward a feminist approach to public life." In *Visible Women: New Essays on American Activism,* ed. Nancy Hewitt and Susan Lebsock, 119–139. Urbana, IL: University of Illinois Press, 1993.

Faderman, Lillian. *Surpassing the Love of Men*. New York: William Morrow, 1981.

———. *Odd Girls and Twilight Lovers: a History of Lesbian Life in Twentieth Century America*. New York: Columbia University Press, 1991.

———. *Chloe plus Olivia: An Anthology of Lesbian and Bisexual Literature from the 17th Century to the Present*. New York: Viking, 1994.

———. *To Believe in Women: What Lesbians Have Done for America—A History.* Boston: Houghton Mifflin Co., 1999.

Fantasia, Rick. *Cultures of Solidarity: Consciousness, Action, and Contemporary American Workers*. Berkeley, L.A.: University of California Press, 1988.

Farber, David and Beth Bailey. *The Columbia Guide to American in the 1960s*. New York: Columbia University Press, 2001.

Farmanfarmaian, Roxane. "Behind the Times: an Old Wives Tale." *Publishers Weekly* 246(1996): 30.

Farnham, Christie. *The Impact of Feminist Research in the Academy.* Bloomington, Indiana: Indiana University Press, 1987.

Fauldi, Susan. *Backlash: The Undeclared War Against American Women*. New York: Crown Publishers, Inc., 1991.

Feinberg, Leslie. *Stone Butch Blues*. Ithaca: Firebrand, 1993.

Felsenthal, Carol. *The Sweetheart of the Silent Majority: the Biography of Phyllis Schlafly.* Garden City, NY: Doubleday, 1981.

Ferguson, Ann. "Is there a Lesbian Culture?" In *Lesbian Philosophies and Cultures*, ed. Allen Jeffiner, 63–88. New York: SUNY Press, 1991.

Ferkenhoff, Eric. "Women and Children First: Bookstore offers viewpoints on life and politics." *Chicago Sun-Times* (11 January 1996).

Ferree, Myra Marx, and Patricia Yancey Martin, eds. *Feminist Organizations: Harvest of the New Women's Movement*. Philadelphia: Temple University Press, 1995.

Ferree, Myrna Marx, and Beth B. Hess. *Controversy and Coalition: The New Feminist Movement*. Boston : Twayne Publishers, 1985.

Firestone, Shulamith and Anne Koedt. *Notes from the Second Year.* New York: N.Y. Radical Women, 1968.

Firestone, Shulamith. *The Dialectic of Sex: The Case for Feminist Revolution*. New York: William Morrow, 1970.

Fischer, Claude S. "Ambivalent Communities: How Americans Understand Their Localities." In *America at Century's End*, ed. Alan Wolfe, 79–90. Berkeley, CA: University of California Press, 1991.

"Fortress in a changing landscape." *Small Press* 14 (1996):10.

Foucault, Michel. *History of Sexuality, Volume 1: An Introduction*, trans. Robert Hurley. New York: Random House, 1978.

Franchild, Marina. "Just What Can Feminist Afford?" Part 1. *Big Mama Rag* 6 (April 1978): 5–8, 12. Part II. *Big Mama Rag* 6 (May 1978):6–7, 10.

———. "Franchild Responds." *Big Mama Rag* 6 (September 1978):2–12.

Franzen, Trisha, "Differences and Identities: feminism and the Albuquerque Lesbian Community." *Signs: Journal of Women in Culture and Society* 18 (1993): 891–906.

———. *Spinsters and Lesbians*. New York: New York University Press, 1996.

Freedman, Estelle. "Separatism as Strategy: Female Institution Building and American Feminism, 1870–1930." *Feminist Studies* 5 (1979) : 512–552.

———. *Lesbian Issue: Essays from Signs.* Chicago: University of Chicago Press, 1985.

Freedman, Estelle and John D'Emilio. *Intimate Matters: A History of Sexuality in America.* New York: Harper & Row, 1988.

Freeman, Jo. "Tyranny of Structurelessness." *Berkeley Journal of Sociology* 17 (1972/73): 151–164.

———. *The Politics of Women's Liberation.* New York: David McKay, 1975.

———. "Separatism as Strategy: female institution building and American feminism." *Feminist Studies* 5 (Fall 1979): 512–528.

Freeman, Jo, ed. *Social Movements of the Sixties and Seventies.* New York: Longman, 1983.

Freeman, Jo, and Victoria Johnson, eds. *Waves of Protest: Social Movements Since the Sixties.* Lanham: Rowman and Littlefield, 1999.

Freeman, Lisa. "The University Press in the Electronic Future." In *Scholarly Publishing: The Electronic Frontie* , ed. Robin Reak, 147–64. Cambridge, Mass.: The MIT Press, 1996.

Frey, Lucille Pauline. "One Woman, One Women's Bookstore: Case Study and Comments in the place of a woman's bookstore in a community (movement, feminist, literature, art, music, history)." Ph.D. diss., The Union for Experimenting Colleges and Universities, 1985.

Friedan, Betty. *The Feminine Mystique.* New York: Norton, 1963.

Frye, Marilyn. *The Politics of Reality: Essays in Feminist Theory.* Trumansburg, New York: The Crossing Press, 1983.

Frum, David. *How We Got Here: The Seventies* (New York: Basic, 2000).

Fulton, Len, and Dick Higgins. *Whole COSMEP Catalog.* CA: Dustbooks,1974.

Fuss, Diana, ed. *Inside/Out: Lesbian Theories, Gay Theories.* New York: Routledge, 1991.

Gabriel, Michael R. "The Astonishing Growth of Small Publishers, 1958–1988." *Journal of Popular Culture* 24(3) (Winter 1990): 61–68.

———. "Gains for industry stocks in 1999." *Publishers Weekly* 247 (Jan 10, 2000): 10.

Gage, Carolyn, "Amazon Questions." *Feminista!* 4 (2000). Available online: http://www.feminista.com/v4n2/gage.html

Garber, Linda. *Lesbian Sources: A Bibliography of Periodical Articles, 1970–1990.* NY: Garland, 1993.

Gardiner, Judith Kegan. *Provoking Agents: Gender and Agency in Theory and Practice.* Urbana, IL: University of Illinois Press, 1995.

Garnham, Nicholas. "Political Economy and Cultural Studies: reconciliation or Divorce?" *Critical Studies in Mass Communication* 12 (March 1995): 62–71.

Gates, Charles E. "Children's Books: 500 Million a Year: Where to Go from Here?" In *The Book in the United States Today,* ed. Gordon Graham and Richard Abel, 11–22. New Brunswick and London: Transaction Publishers, 1997.

Gebhart, Mary Alice. "The Michigan Womyn's Music Festival." M.A thesis, Michigan State University, 1998

Geoffrey Nunberg, ed. *The Future of the Book*. Berkley: University of California Press, 1996.

Gere, Anne Ruggles. *Intimate Practices: Literacy and Cultural Work in US Women's Clubs, 1880–1920*. Urbana, IL: University of Illinois Press, 1997.

Gibbs, Joan and Sara Bennett. *Top Ranking: a Collection of Articles on Racism and Classism in the Lesbian Community*. New York: Come! Unite Press, 1980.

Gick, Andrea. "Meeting with the 'enemy.'" *School Library Journal* (Sept. 1997): 97.

Gillon, Margaret. *Lesbians in Print: A Bibliography of 1500 Books with Synopses*. Irvine, CA : Bluestockings Books, 1995.

Gomez, Jewelle. "A Cultural Legacy Denied and Discovered: Black Lesbians in Fiction by Women." In *Home Girl: a Black Feminist Anthology*, ed. Barbara Smith, 110–123. New York: Kitchen Table: Women of Color Press, 1983.

Gould, Lois. "Creating a Women's Culture." *New York Times Magazine* (Jan., 1977): 10–12.

Graham, Gordon and Richard Abel, ed. *The Book in the United States Today*. New Brunswick and London: Transaction Publishers, 1997.

Grand, Wayne. *Book Reviewing*. NY: London: A. A. Knopf, 1928.

Grant, Jaime M. "Building Community-Based Coalitions from Academe: The Union Institute and the Kitchen Table Women of Color Press Transition Coalition." *Signs* (Summer 1996): 1024–33.

Graubard, Stephan, ed. *Reading in the 1980s*. New York: Bowker, 1983.

Greco, Albert N. "U.S. Book Returns, 1984–1989." *Publishing Research Quarterly* 8 (1992): 46–61.

———. *The Book Publishing Industry*. Boston: Allyn and Bacon, 1996.

Green, Jack. *Fire the bastards*. Normal, IL : Dalkey Archive Press, 1992.

Greenbaum, Vicky. "Old Wives Tales Going Strong." *Bay Area Reporter* (Aug 29, 1991): 1–10.

Grimstad, Kirsten and Susan Rennie, eds. *The New Woman's Survival Catalog*. New York: Berkeley Publishing Corporation, 1973.

———. *The New Woman's Survival Sourcebook*. New York: Knopf, 1975.

Grimstad, Kirsten, Valerie Harms, Elana Klugman, and Terry Wolverton. "Catalog of Feminist Publishing, Part 1. " *Chrysalis* 2 (1977):101–111.

Groschwitz, Nancy. "Practical Economies for a Women's Community." In *Lavender Culture*, eds. Jay, Karla, and Joanne Glasgow, 477–483. NY: Jove Publications, 1979.

Gross, John J. *The Rise and Fall of the Man of Letters: Aspects of English Literary Life since 1800*. Chicago: I.R. Dee, 1992.

Gusfield, Joseph R. *Community: A Critical Response*. NY: Harper & Row, 1975.

Gutin, JoAnn C. "Becoming a book reviewer." *The Writer* 109 (Oct 1996): 18.

Hacker, Jeffrey. *Publishing Books for Consumers: Market Trends and Forecasts, 1985–88*. White Plains, N.Y.: Knowledge Industry Publications, 1985.

Hall, David D. "A History of the Book in American Culture." *Book Research Quarterly* 6(1990): 63–69.

Hall, Gloria, Patricia Bell Scott, and Barbara Smith, eds. *All the Women are White, All the Blacks are Men, But Some of Us are Brave: Black Women's Studies.* Old Westbury, NY: Feminist Press, 1982.

Halpern, Ashelea. "Sisters in Struggle." *Punk Planet Magazine* (May/June 2003): 100–105.

Hans, Elizabeth A. "Librarians & Booksellers working together in the Year of the Young Reader."*School Library Journal* (Jan. 1989): 24–7.

Harmon, Katharine. *From Publisher to Reader: the Increased Availability of Books Through Specialty Retail Outlets.* NY: Book Industry Study Group, 1992.

Harris, Bertha. *Lover.* Plainfield, VT: Daughters, 1976.

Harris, Laura and Elizabeth Crocker. *Femme: Feminists, Lesbians, and Bad Girls.* New York: Routledge, 1997.

Harris, Michael H. "No Love Lost: Library Women vs. Women who use Libraries." *Progressive Librarians* 5 (1992): 1–18.

Harrison, Ann. "Big Business." In *The Woman-Centered Economy: Ideals, Reality and the Space in Between,* eds. Midge Stocker and Loraine Edwards. Chicago: Third Side Press, 1995.

Harrison, Cynthia Ellen. *Women's Movement Media: a Source Guide.* New York: R.R.Bowker Company, 1975.

———. *On Account of Sex: the Politics of Women's Issues, 1945–1968.* Berkeley: University of California Pres, 1988.

Hartman, Joan E., and Ellen Messer-Davidow, eds. *Women in Print.* New York: The Modern Language Association of America, 1982.

Hass, Elizabeth A. "Libraries and Booksellers: Working Together in the Years of the Young Reader." *School Library Journal* 35 (Jan. 1989): 24–27.

Haugland, Ann. "Defining the book: culture and commerce in the New York times book review." Ph.D. diss., University of Iowa, 1992.

———. "Books as culture, books as commerce: an analysis of the text and format of the New York times book review." *The Journalism Quarterly* 71 (1994): 787–799.

Heim, Kathleen M. *On Account of Sex: an Annotated Bibliography on the Status of Women in Librarianship, 1977–81.* Chicago: American Library Association, 1984.

Helen Tierney, ed. *Women's Studies Encyclopedia.* Westport, CT: Greenwood Press, 1999.

Henderson, Bill. "Independent Publishing: Today and Yesterday." In *Perspectives on Publishing,* eds. Philip G. Altbach, and Sheila McVey, 217–230. Philadelphia: American Academy of Political and Social Science, 1975.

Hennessy, Rosemary. *Materialist Feminism and the Politics of Discourse.* New York: Routledge, 1993.

Hewitt, Nancy A. "Beyond the Search for Sisterhood: American Women's History in the 1980s." In *Unequal Sisters: a Multicultural Reader in U.S. Women's History,* ed. Ellen C. Dubois, 1–4. New York: Routledge, 1990.

Hewitt, Nancy and Susan Lebsock, eds. *Visible Women: New Essays on American Activism.* Urbana, IL: University of Illinois Press, 1993.

Heywood, Leslie, and Jennifer Drake, eds. *Third Wave Agenda; Being feminist, Doing Feminism.* Minneapolis: University of Minnesota, 1997.

Hilgartner, Stephen and Charles L. Bosk, "The Riser and Fall of Social Problems: a public arenas model." *American Journal of Sociology* 94 (July 1988): 53–78.

Hill-Collins, Patricia. *Black Feminist Thought.* Boston: Unwin Hyman, 1990.

Hilts, Paul. "Or Do They Need a Place of Their Own? " *Publishers Weekly* (24 Feb.1997): 39.

Hirsch, Marianne, ed. *Conflicts in Feminism.* New York: Routledge, 1990.

Hirsch, Walter, and Ronald T. Potter-Efron. "Book Reviews and the Status of Authors and Reviewers." *Contemporary Sociology* 9 (July 1980): 520–522.

Hodgins, Jane. "Fresh Ink: Spinsters Ink marks 20 years of feminist publishing." *Minnesota Women's Press* (Sep 1998): Available online: http://www.womenspress.com/newspaper/1998/spinstersink.html.

Hogan, Kristen A. "Defining Our Own Context: the past and future of feminist bookstores." *Thirdspace* 2, no. 2 (March 2003): Available online: http://www.thirdspace.ca/articles/hogan.htm

Hogan, Steve, and Lee Hudson, eds. *Completely Queer.* New York: Henry Holt, 1998.

Hoge, James O. *Literary Reviewing.* Charlottesville: University Press of Virginia, 1987.

Hoggart, Richard. *Speaking to Each Other.* New York: Oxford University Press, 1970.

Holt, Pat. "Facing the Worst: the bad news." *Holt Uncensored* 28 (Jan 12, 1999): Available online: http://www.holtuncensored.com/members/column28.html.

———. "Letter from Adrienne Rich." *Holt Uncensored* 29 (Jan 15, 1999): Available online: http://www.holtuncensored.com/members/column29.html.

———. "Then Strange Statistics." *Holt Uncensored* 61 (May 18, 1999): Available online: http://www.holtuncensored.com/members/column61.html.

———. "When Feminist Bookstores Fight Back." *Holt Uncensored* 78 (July 23, 1999): Available online: http://www.holtuncensored.com/members/column78.html.

———. "Book Brawl." *Whole Earth* 97 (Summer 1999): 64–67.

Hole, Judith. *Rebirth of Feminism.* New York: Times Books, 1973.

Hones, Margaret. "Homelessness: a bookselling issue?: social responsibilities of book retailers." *Publishers Weekly* (Apr. 27 1990): 38–9.

hooks, bell. *Ain't I a Woman: Black Women and Feminism.* Boston, MA: South End Press, 1981.

———. *Talking Back: Thinking Feminist, Thinking Black.* Boston, MA: South End Press, 1989.

———. "Black students who reject feminism." *The Chronicle of Higher Education* (13 July 1994): A44.

———. *Feminist Theory: From Margin to Center.* Cambridge, MA: South End Press, 2000.

Horowitz, Daniel. *Betty Friedan and the Making of the Feminine Mystique: the American Left, the Cold War, and Modern Feminism.* Amherst: University of Massachusetts Press, 1999.

Horowitz, Irving Louis. *Communicating Ideas: The Politics of Scholarly Publishing.* New Brunswick, NJ: Transaction Publishers, 1991.

Horvath, Stephen. "The Rise of the Book Chain Superstore." In *The Book in the United States Today,* eds. Gordon Graham and Richard Abel, 63–76. New Brunswick and London: Transaction Publishers, 1997.

Howard, Gerald. "The Cultural Ecology of Book Reviewing." *Media Studies Journal* 6 (Summer 1992): 90.

Howard, John, ed. *Carryin' on in the Lesbian and Gay South.* New York: New York University Press, 1997.

Howe, Florence. *Seven Years Later: Women's Studies program in 1976, Report of the National Advisory Council on Women's Educational Programs.* Washington, DC: The department of Health, Education and Welfare, 1977.

Howell, Kevin. "Changes Hit Gay/Lesbian Businesses." *Publishers Weekly.com* (July 24, 2000).

Hudak, Leona. *Early American Women Printers and Publishers 1639–1820.* Metuchen, NJ & London: The Scarecrow Press, Inc., 1978.

Hunter, Eric. "Learning from Loss." *CityBeat: Gay & Lesbian Issues* (April 5, 2001).

Hyde, Cheryl. "Feminist Social Movement Organizations: Survive the New Right." In *Feminist Organizations: Harvest of the new women's movement,* eds. Myra Marx Ferree and Patricia Yancey Martin, 306–322. Philadelphia: Temple University Press, 1995.

Jackall, Robert and Henry M.Levin. *Worker Cooperatives in America.* Berkeley, CA: University of California Press, 1984.

Jacobs, William Jay. *Women in American History.* New York: MacMillan Publishing Company, 1976.

Jaggar, Alison M, and Paula S. Rothenberg. *Feminist Frameworks: Alternative Theoretical Accounts of the Relations Between Women and Men.* New York: McGraw-Hill,1993.

Jay, Karla, and Allen Young. *Lavender Culture.* New York: Jove/HBJ Book, 1979.

Jay, Karla, and Joanne Glasgow, eds. *Lesbian Texts and Contexts Radical Revisions.* NY: New York University Press, 1990.

Jenkins, Jerrold R. *Inside the Best Sellers.* Mich.: Rhodes & Easton, 1997.

Jensen, Mike, and Pat Holt. "Feminist bookstore unfriendly to men." *Holt Uncensored* 79 (1999): Available online: http://www.holtuncensored.com/members/column79.html.

Jesudason, Melba. "Building Women's Studies Reading Area Collection: University of Wisconsin-Madison, College Library Experience." *Reference Services Review* 20. 1 (1992): 81–93.

Jewell, Terri L. "Barbara Smith and Kitchen Table Women of Color Press." *Hot Wire* 6 (1990): 20–22, 58.

Joan, Polly and Andrea Chesman. *Guide to Women's Publishing.* Paradise, CA: Dustbooks, 1978.

Johnson, Gayle. "Women in Publishing." In *Perspectives on Publishing,* eds, Philip G. Altbach, and Sheila McVey, 259–272. Philadelphia: American Academy of Political and Social Science, 1976.

Johnston, Hank and Bert Klandermans., eds. *Social Movements and Culture.* Minnesota: University of Minnesota Press, 1995.

Johnston, Hank, Enrique Larana, and Joseph R. Gusfield. *New Social Movements: from Ideology to Identity.* Philadelphia: Temple University Press, 1994.

Jones, Jeffery Alan, "Hidden Histories, Proud Communities: multiple narratives in the queer geographies of Lexington, Kentucky, 1930–1999." Ph.D. diss., University of Kentucky, 2001.

Jones, Tim. "The bind of small booksellers." *Chicago Tribune* (19 March 1998): 1,4.

Joyce, Donald F. *Gatekeepers of Black Culture: Black-Owned Book Publishing in the United States, 1817–1981.* Westport, Conn.: Greenwood Press, 1983.

———. "Reflections of the Changing Publishing Objectives of Secular Black Book Publishers, 1900–1986." In *Reading in America: Literature and Social History,* ed. Cathy Davidson, 226–239. Baltimore, MD: Johns Hopkins University Press, 1989.

———. *Black Book Publishers in the United States: A Historical Dictionary of the Press, 1817–1990.* New York: Greenwood Press, 1991.

Kahlerh, Deonne. "A New Feminist Face Takes the Helm at Mama Bears Bookstore." *Bay Area Business Woman* (March 2003). Available online: http://www.rightbrainleft.com/art-mama-bears.htm

Kaminer, Wendy. *A Fearful Freedom: Women's Fight from Equality.* Reading, MA: Addison-Wesley, 1990.

Kato, Reiko N. "Lesbians of color conference: the politics of 'sisterhood.'" In *Voices of Color,* eds. Yolanda Alaniz and Nellie Wong, 30–34. Seattle: Red Letter Press, 1999.

Katz, Jonathan. *Gay American History: Lesbians and Gay Men in the USA.* New York: Thomas Y. Crowell, 1976.

Kauffman, Linda, ed. *American Feminist Thought at Century's End: A Reader.*
Cambridge, MA: Blackwell, 1993.

Kavanaugh, Mary Ellen. "10 years of My Sisters' Words." *Gay and Lesbian Bookselling* 4, no.4 (Dec. 1997): 1.

Kawaguchi, Karen. "Feminist Feast and Famine: after three decades, feminist bookstores are going through transitions to stay viable." *Publishers Weekly.com.* (July 24, 2000).

Kaye, Melanie. "Culture Making: Lesbian Classics in the Year 2000?" *Sinister Wisdom* 13 (1980):23–34.

Keener, Karen M. "Out of the archives and into the academy: opportunities for research and publication in lesbian literature." In *Women in Print,* eds. Joan E. Hartman, and Ellen Messer-Davidow, 71–86. New York: The Modern Language Association of America, 1982.

Keith, Michael. *Places and the Politics of Identity.* London: Routledge, 1993.

Keller, Nicole. "Feminist Bookstores Celebrate First Week." *Publishers Weekly* (15 May 1995): 19.

Kennedy, Elizabeth. "Dreams of Social Justice: Building Women's Studies at the State University of New York, Buffalo." In *The Politics of Women's Studies: Testimony from 30 Founding Mothers,* ed. Florence Howe, 243–263. NY: The Feminist Press at the City University of New York, 2000.

Kennedy, Elizabeth, and Madeline Davis. *Boots of Leather, Slippers of Gold: the History of a Lesbian Community.* NY: Penguin, 1993.

Kerber, Linda, Kathryn Sklar, and Alice Kessler-Harris, eds. *U.S. History as Women's History.* Chapel Hill: University of North Carolina Press, 1996.

Kerr, Mark. "Bookselling and the Internet." *Multimedia Information and Technology* 25 (Feb 1999): 67–71

Kessler, Lauren. *The Dissident Press: Alternative Journalism in American History.* Beverly Hills: Sage Publications, 1984.

King, Katie. "Producing sex, theory, and culture." In *Conflicts in Feminism,* ed. Marianne Hirsch. New York: Routledge, 1990.

Kirkpatrick, David. "Quietly, Booksellers Are Putting and End to the Discount Era." *The New York Times* (Oct 9, 2000). Available online: http://www.nytimes.com/2000/10/09/business/09BOOK.html

Klinger, Alisa Margaret. "Paper Uprisings: Print Activism in the Multicultural Lesbian Movement." Ph.D. diss., The University of California, Berkeley, 1995.

———. "Writing Civil Rights: the political aspirations of lesbian activist-writers." In *Inventing Lesbian Cultures in America,* ed. Ellen Lewin. Boston : Beacon Press, 1996.

Koedt, Anne, Ellen Levine, and Anita Rapone. *Radical Feminism.* New York: Quadrangle, 1973.

Kotha, Suresh. "Competing on the Internet: the Case of Amazon. com." *European Management Journal* 16 (1998): 212.

Kramer, William J. "Independent Bookselling: A Frontline Dispatch." In *The Book in the United States Today* , eds. Gordon Graham and Richard Abel, 49–62. New Brunswick and London: Transaction Publishers, 1997.

Krieger, Susan. "Lesbian identity and community: recent social science literature." *Signs: Journal of Women in Culture and Society* 8 (1982): 91–108.

———. *The Mirror Dance: Identity in a Women's Community.* Philadelphia: Temple University Press, 1983.

Kuda, Marie. "Feminist Bookstore News Closes." *Outlines; the Voice of Chicago's Gay & Lesbian Community* (July 26, 2000).

Lahey, Anita, "Between the Pages: Making a Business of Books." *Herisons* 10, no.4 (October 1996): 26–29.

Lamm, Donald. "Two Decades of Publishing: The 1920s and 1980s." *Library Chronicle of the University of Texas at Austin* 25 (1995): 88–95.

Lane, Michael. "Shapers of Culture: the editor in book publishing." *Annals of the American Academy of Political and Social Science* 421 (Sep. 1975): 34–42.

Laude, Jan. "Folklore as an Instrument of Stigma: Folklore as an Instrument of Liberation: The Case of Lesbian Coding." Ph.D. diss., Indiana University, 1991.

Lauret, Maria. *Liberating literature: feminist fiction in America.* London: Rougledge & Kegan Paul, 1994.

Leghorn, Lisa and Katherine Parker. *Woman's Worth: Sexual Economics and The World of Women.* Boston: Routledge & Kegan Paul, 1981.

Lehmann, Chris. "Burning down the House: The Collapse of an Intellectual Publisher." *Lingua Franca*7 (Sept. 1997): 48–52.

Leland, John. "Homophobia." *Newsweek* (Feb 14, 1994): 42–45.

Lev, Benjamin. "The Process of Book Reviewing." *Interfaces* 22 (Sept. 1992): 85.

Levart, Shery. "Independent publishing for the multiracial community." *Interracial Voice*. Available online: http://www.webcom.com/^intvoic/sheryl.thml.

LeVay, Smith. *City of Friends: a Portrait of the Gay and Lesbian Community in America*. Cambridge, MA: MIT Press, 1995.

Levin, Jennifer. "Good News/Bad News—The Penguin Book of Lesbian Short Stories edited by Margaret Reynolds." *Lambda Book Report* 4 (Jan. 1994): 15.

Levin, Martin P. "The Positive Role of Large Corporations in U.S." In *The Book in the United States Today* , eds. Gordon Graham and Richard Abel, 225–244. New Brunswick and London: Transaction Publishers, 1997.

Lewin, Ellen, ed. *Inventing Lesbian Cultures in America*. Boston: Beacon Press, 1996.

———, eds. *Out in Theory*. Urbana: University of Illinois, 2002.

Lindholm-Romantschuk, Ylva. *Scholarly Book Reviewing in the Social Sciences and Humanities: The Flow of Ideas Within and Among Disciplines*. Westport, CT: Greenwood press, 1998.

Linneman, Thomas J. "Individual Action and the Diffusion of Social Movement Ideology: Gay and Lesbian Studies in Northwest Bookstores." *Sociological Perspectives* 42 (1999): 459.

———. "Representing Social Movements: advocacy and activism in northwest bookstores." *Sociological Perspectives* (Fall 1999): 459.

Little, Suzanne. "Pressing Women's Issues: Four Feminist Presses." *Small Press* 5 (1988): 23–27.

Lightfoot, Martin. "The Distribution of Books: weak link in the publishing chain." In *Perspectives on Publishing* , ed. Philip G. Altbach, 71–82. Lexington, MA: Lexington Books, 1976.

Lockard, Denyse. "The Lesbian Community: An Anthropological Approach." *Journal of Homosexuality* 11 (summer) 1986: 83–96.

Lofland, John. *Protest: Studies of Collective Behavior and Social Movement*. New Brunswick, N.J.: Transaction Books, 1985.

Long, Elizabeth. "Women, Reading, and Cultural Authority: some implications of the audience perspective in cultural studies." *American Quarterly* 38 (Fall 1986): 591–612.

Lootens, Tricia. "Third National Women In Print Conference." *Off Our Backs* 15.8 (August-September 1985): 8–26.

Lorde, Audre. Our Difference Is Our Strength." In *Identity Politics in the Women's Movement,* ed. Barbara Ryan, 315–319. New York: New York University Press, 2001.

———. *Sister Outsider: Essays and Speeches*. Trumansburg, NY: The Crossing Press, 1984.

Lorimer, Rowland and Paddy Scannell, "Editorial." *Media, Culture and Society* 15 (April 1993): 163–166.

Luey, Beth. "The 'Book' on Books- Mammon and the Muses." In *Publishing Books,* eds. Everette E. Dennis, Craig LaMay, and Edward Poare, 141–150. New-Brumswick & London: Transaction Publisher, 1997.

Lynn Witt, ed. *Out in All Directions: the Almanac of Gay and Lesbian America*. New York: Warren Books, 1995.

Lynn, Susan. "The Politics of feminism." *Reviews in American History* 19 (1991): 593–598.

MacKay, Mary. "Feminist Lit New Boom for Publishers." *IRIS: A Journal About Women* (Fall/Winter 1990): 34.

Macphail,Bruce. "Book Reviews and the Scholarly Publisher." In *Literary Reviewing* , ed. James Hoge, 101–111. Charlottesville: University Press of Virginia, 1987.

Mairs, Nancy. "Response and responsibility." *The Women's Review of Books 11* (Jan 1994): 7.

Mankiller, Wilma et al., eds. *The Reader's Companion to U.S. Women's History.* N.Y., Houghton Mifflin Company, 1998.

Mann, William J. "The Gay and Lesbian Publishing Boom." *The Harvard Gay and Lesbian Review* 2 (Spring 1995): 24–27.

Mansbridge, Jane J. *Why We Lost the ERA.* Chicago: University of Chicago Press, 1986.

Marcoux, Alex. "The Passion Within" (Women's Work Press) *OutLook Press* (February 2002). Available onlie: http:www.outlookpress.com/featuresmain.htm.

Marcus, Eric. *Making Gay History: the Half-Century Fight for Lesbian and Gay Equal Rights.* NY: Perennial, 2002.

Marks, Jim. "Community or Commodity?" *Lambda Book Report* 6 (May 1998): 8–10.

Marotta, Toby. *The Politics of Homosexuality.* Boston: Houghton Mifflin, 1981.

Marx, Bill. "The decline of book reviewing." *Publishers Weekly* 240 (Oct. 25, 1993): 36.

Maryles, Daisy. "A Decade of Megasellers." *Publishers Weekly* 5 (Jan. 1990): 24–26.

———. *Space, Place and Gender.* Minneapolis, Minnesota: University of Minnesota, 1993.

Mather, Anne. "A History of Feminist Periodicals." *Journalism History* 1, no.4 (1974/1975): 108–11; *Journalism History* 1, no.3 (1974):82–85 ; *Journalism History* 2, no.1 (1975):19–23, 31.

McCombie, Brian. "Breaking Into Book Reviewing." *The Writer* 109 (Jun. 1, 1996): 17.

McCormack, Thomas. "Super Stores." *Publishers Weekly* (Jun. 1998): 27.

McDermott, Patrice. *Politics and Scholarship: Feminist Academic Journals and the Production of Knowledge.* Urbana and Chicago: University of Illinois Press, 1994.

McDowell, Linda. "Spatializing Feminism." In *Body Space: Destabilizing Geographies, Gender and Sexuality,* ed. Nancy Duncan, 28–44. New York: Routledge, 1996.

McElroy, Wendy. "You Are What You Read?" *Zetetics* (June 29, 2000). Available online: http://www.zeteics.com/mac/rockwell/mcelroy000629.html.

McGrath, Kathyrin. "Pushed to the Margins: the slow death and possible rebirth of the feminist bookstores." *Bitch* (July 2003): Available online: http://www.bitchmagazine.com/archives/07–03margins/margins. .shtml

McMartin, Flora. *The Institutionalization of Women's Centers and Women's Studies Programs at Three Research Universities.* Berkley, CA: University of California Berkeley, 1993.

McRobbie, Angela. *Postmodernism and Popular Culture.* London: Routledge, 1994.

Melucci, Alberto. "The Symbolic Challenge of Contemporary Movements." *Social Research* 52 (1985): 789–816.

———. *Nomads of the Present: Social Movements and Individual Needs in Contemporary Society.* Philadelphia: Temple University Press, 1989.

———. *Challenging Codes: Collective Action in the Information Age.* New York: Cambridge University Press, 1996.

Merritt, LeRoy C, Martha Boaz, and Kenneth S. Tisdel. *Reviews in Library Book Selection.* Michigan : Wayne State University Press, 1958.

Merton, Robert K. *The Sociology of Science.* Chicago: University of Chicago Press, 1973.

Michals, Debra. "Beyond Pin Money: the rise of women's small business ownership 1945–1980." Ph.D. diss. New York University, 2002.

Miller, Laura Jean. "Merchandising to the Mind." Ph.D. diss., University of California, San Diego, 1998.

———"Shopping for Community: the Transformation of the Bookstore Into a Vital Community Institution." *Media, Culture and Society* 21 (1999):385.

Miller, Mark Crispin. "The Crushing Power of Big Publishing." *Nation* 264 (Mar. 17, 1997): 11–18.

Miller, Mev. "Feminism and Literacy for Women: Politics and Resources." *Feminist Collection* 21 (Fall 19999): 17–20.

———. "Independent Women's Bookstores." In *Out in All Directions: the almanac of gay and lesbian America,* Lynn Witt, ed., 598–599 (New York: Warren Books, 1995).

———. "Labor of Love: A 25 year history of Feminist and Lesbian Bookstores and Publishing." 1995 (one-hour documentary on cassette tape recording)

———. "Fortress in a Changing Landscape." *Small Press* 14 (1996): 10.

———. "Shopping at independent bookstores." In listserv nifl-womenlit@literacy.nifl.gov (May 7, 2001).

Milliot, Jim. "Amazon: sales, losses up: acquisitions: a stock split." *Publishers Weekly* (4 May, 1998): 37.

———. "Publishers optimistic about spread of technology." *Publishers Weekly* (3 Jan , 2000): 19.

Mills, C. Wright. *White Collar: The American Middle Classes.* New York: Oxford University Press, 1951.

Miner, Valerie and Helen Longino, eds. *Competition: A Feminist Taboo?* New York: The Feminist Press, 1987.

Mitchell, Catherine. "Historiography: A New Direction for Research on the Woman's Rights Press." *Journalism History* 19 (1993): 59–63.

Mitchell, Juliet and Ann Oakley, eds. *Who's Afraid of Feminism? Seeing through the Balcklash.* New York: New Press, 1997.

Mizruchi, Ephraim H. *Regulating Society.* NY: Free Press, 1983.

Mohanty, Chandra Talpade, Ann Russo, and Lourdes Torres, ed. *Third World Women and the Politics of Feminism.* Bloomington: Indiana University Press, 1991.

Mohanty, Chandra Talpade." Our Race and Voice: challenges for liberal education in the 1990s." *Cultural Critique* 14 (1989/90): 179–200.

Moore, Lisa C. "Turning the Tables in Texas." *Lambda Literary Foundation* (2004) Available online: http://.ambdalit.org/resources/resources_book-woman.html.

Moore, Steven. "Introduction." In *Fire the Bastards,* Jack Normal Green, v-xiv. Normal, IL : Dalkey Archive Press, 1992.

Moraga, Cherrie and Gloria Anzaldua, eds. *This Bridge Called My Back: Writings by Radical Women of Color.* New York: Kitchen Table Press, 1983.

Moravec, Michelle. "Building Women's Culture: feminism and art at the Los Angels Women's Building." Ph.D. diss., University of California, Los Angels, 1998.

Morgan, Robin, ed. *Sisterhood is Powerful: An Anthology of Writings from the women's Liberation Movement.* New York: Random House, 1970.

Morris Rosenberg, and Rulph Turmen, ed. *Social Psychology, Social Perspectives.* New York: Basic Books, 1981.

Morris, Aldon and Cedric Herring. "Theory and Research in Social Movements: A Critical Review." *Annual Review of Political Science* 2 (1987): 137–198.

Morris, Aldon D. and Carol Mclung Mueller. *Frontiers in Social Movement Theory.* New Haven, CT : Yale University Press, 1992.

Mudd, Karen. "Lesbian Separatism: Then and Now." *Off Our Backs* (August/September 1983): 10.

Munt, Sally, ed. *New Lesbian Criticism: Literary and Cultural Readings.* New York: Columbia University Press. 1992.

———. *Heroic Desire; Lesbian identity and cultural space.* New York: New York University Press, 1998.

Murray, Simone. "Books of Integrity: The Women's Press, Kitchen Table Press and Dilemmas of Feminist Publishing." *The European Journal of Women's Studies* 5 (1998): 171–193.

———. "Live Authors, Live Issues: dilemmas of race and authenticity in feminist publishing." In *Alternative Library Literature, 1998/1999, A Biennial Anthology,* eds. Sanford Berman, and James P. Danky, 46–54. Jefferson, North Carolina and London: McFarland & Company, Inc., Publishers, 2001.

Mutter, John. "The Changing Face of Bookselling." *Publishers Weekly* (5 Jan. 1990): 28–29.

———. "Bookstores fighting for sale." *Publishers Weekly* 239 (1992): 9.

Muter, John and Maria Heidkamp. "Booksotres Fighting For Sales: Bargain Books a Bright Spot." *Publishers Weekly* (10 August 1992): 9.

Myron, Nancy and Charlotte Bunch, eds. *Lesbianism and the Women's Movement.* Baltimore: Diana Press, 1975.

National Library. "Positive Opinion Poll: LA Survey on library usage and satisfaction." *Library Association Record* 96 (Jan. 1994):34–36.

Natowitz, Allen and Paula Wheeler Carlo. "Evaluating review content for book selection: An analysis of American history reviews in *Choice, American Historical Review,* and *Journal of American History.*" *College & Research Libraries* 58 (Jul. 1997): 323–336.

Neavill, Gordon. "Role of the Publisher in the Dissemination of Knowledge." In *Perspectives on Publishing,* eds. Philip G. Altbach, and Sheila McVey, 47–58. Philadelphia: American Academy of Political and Social Science, 1975.

Neff, Lisa. "Independent's Day: Women & Children First feminist bookstore celebrates two decades." *Chicago Free Press* (10 Nov.1999): 1, 6–7.

Nestle, Joan and Brett Beemyn. *Creating a Space for Ourselves: Lesbian, Gay and Bisexual Community Histories.* NY: Routledge, 1997.

New York Radicalesbians, "The Woman-Identified Woman." In *Lesbians Speak Out,* ed. the Women's Press Collective. New York: The Women's Press Collective, 1971.

Newitt, Nancy A. "Beyond the search for sisterhood: American Women's History in the 1980s." In *Unequal Sisters: A Multicultural Reader in U.S. Women's History,* ed. Ellen Carol Dubois, 1–4. New York: Routledge, 1990.

Newman, Louise Michele. *White Women's Rights: The Racial Origins of Feminism in the United States.* New York, Oxford: Oxford University Press, 1999.

Newton, Esther. *Cherry Grove, Fire Island: Sixty Years in America's First Gay and Lesbian Town.* Boston: Beacon Press, 1993.

Ng, Roxana. *The Politics of Community Services, Immigrant Women, class, and State.* Toronto: Garamond Press, 1988.

Nicholson, Catherine. "The Rape of Diana." *Sinister Wisdom* 5 (1978): 73–76.

Norman, Rose. "Support Your Feminist Bookseller: She Supports You." *NWSA Action.* 13.1 (Fall 2001): 30–32.

———. "Shrinking Shelves: What's Happening to Feminist Bookstores?" *Women's Review of Books.* 19.3 (December 2001): 11–13.

———. "Books We Wouldn't Have Without These Feminist Publishers." *Women in Print.* Available online: http://mortonweb.uah.edu/wip/faq.html

———. "Frequently asked questions about the problems facing feminist publishers and booksellers." *Women in Print.* Available online: http://mortonweb,uah.edu/wip/faq.html

———. "Feminist Publishers on Issues in Feminist Publishing." *Women in Print.* Available online: http://mortonweb.uah.edu/wip/interview_publishers, html

O'Connor, Jill. "What makes a feminist bookstore special?" *Ms.* (1983): 12, 79–82.

Oliver, Pamela, "Bringing the Crowd Back In: the nonorganizational elements of social movements." *Research Social Movements, Conflilct and Change* 11 (1989): 1–30.

Olson, Mancur. *The Logic of Collective Action: public goods and the theory of groups.* Cambridge, MA: Harvard University Press, 1965.

Onodera, Midi. "Untitled. ." In *Piece of My Heart: A Lesbian of Colour Anthology,* ed. Makeda Silvera, 199–203. Toronto: Siter Vision, 1991.

O'Sullivan, Gerry. "Against the Grain." *Humanist* 50 (November 1990) : 43–45.

Palumbo-Liu, David. *The Ethnic Canon: Histories, Institutions, and Interventions.* Minneapolis: University of Minnesota Press, 1995.

Parini, Jay. "The Disappearing art of reviewing books." *The Chronicle of Higher Education*45 (Jul 23, 1999): B4-B5.

Parsons, Paul. *Getting Published: The Acquisition Process at University Press.* Kansville: University of Tennessee Press, 1989.

Patter, Robert L. "Reviewing Reviewing: From the Editor's Desk." In *Literary Reviewing,* ed. James Hodge, 88–100. Charlottesville: University Press of Virginia, 1987.

Peck, Abe. *Uncovering the Sixties: The Life and Times of the Underground.* New York: Random House, 1985.

Pena, Terri de la. "Eco de una Amistad/ Echo of a Friendship." In *Lesbian Friendship: For Ourselves and Each Other,* eds. Jacqueline S. Weinstock and Esther D. Rothblum, 31–38. New York and London: New York University Press, 1996.

———. *Latin Satins.* Seattle, Wash.: Seal Press, 1992.

Penelope, Julia, and Susan Wolfe. *Lesbian Culture: An Anthology—The Lives, Work, Ideas, Art, and Visions of Lesbians Past and Present.* Freedom, Calif. Crossing Press, 1993.

Penelope, Julia. "Consciousness as style; style as aesthetic." In *Language, Genders and Society,* ed. Barrie Thorns, 125–139. Cambridge, MA: Newbury Publishing, 1983.

Peterson, Andrea L.T., "Something Not So Odd: Odd Girls Press shuts down after just six years." *Woman's Monthly* (January 2003). Available online: http://www.womo.com/oddgirls.htm#top

Phelan, Shane and Mark Blasius, eds. *We Are Everywhere: a Historical Sourcebook in Gay and Lesbian Politics.* New York: Routledge, 1997.

Phelan, Shane. "Identity and community: lesbian-feminism as political theory." Ph.D. diss., University of Massachusetts at Amherst, 1987.

———. *Identity Politics: Lesbian-Feminism and Limits of Community.* Philadelphia: Temple University Press, 1989.

Pheterson, Gail. "Alliances Between Women: Overcoming Internalized Oppression and Internalized Domination." *Signs* 12 (1986): 146–160.

Phillips, Lee Anne, "Gay and Lesbian Words in Danger Today." Available online: http://www.qrd.org/qur/www/media/print/bookstores/glbrnets.html

Pitchard, Sarah. "Feminist Thought and the Critique of Information Technology." *Progressive Librarian* 8 (1993): 1–9.

Pochoda, Phil. "Universities Press On." *The Nation* 265 (Dec. 1997): 11.

Poggi, Stephanie. "If We Want Women's Bookstores To Be There—We Have To Support Them." *Sojourner: The Women's Forum* 24 (1998): 29.

Polletta, Francesca. "Cultural Politics and Social Movements & Social Movements and Culture." *Contemporary Sociology* 25 (July 1996): 483–85.

Potter, Clare. *The Lesbian Periodicals Index.* Tallahassee, FL: Naiad Press, 1986.

Potter, Clarkson. *Who Does What and Why in Book Publishing.* New York : Carol Publishers Group, 1990.

Powell, Walter W. *Getting into Print: The Decision-Making Process in Scholarly Publishing.* Chicago: University of Chicago Press, 1985.

Powell, Walter. "Whither the Local Bookstore?" In *Reading in the 1980s,* ed. Stephen Graubard, 51–64. New York: R.R. Bowker Company, 1983.

Postrel, Virginia. "The Big Uneasy: nothing upsets stasis-loving social critics more than new institutions for buying and selling." *Forbes* 158 (August 1996): 32.

Quindlen, Anna. *How Reading Changed My Life.* New York : Ballantine Pub. Group, 1998.

Raffo, Susan."The Battle of the Amazons." *Zmagazine.* Available online: http://eee.zmag.org/Zmag/articles/raffo.htm

Ragan, Sandra. *The Lynching of Language: Gender, Politics & Power in the Hill-Thomas Hearings.* Urbana: University of Illinois Press, 1996.

Rakow, Lana F. *Women Making Meaning: New Feminist Direcrions in Communication.* New York: Routledge, 1992.

———, ed. *The Revolution in Words: Righting Women 1868–1871.* NY: Routledge, 1991.

Rather, Lois. *Women as Printers.* Oakland, California: The Rather Press, 1970.

Reagon, Bernice Johnson. "Coalition Politics: Turning the Century." In *Home Girl: A Black Feminist Anthology,* ed. Barbara Smith, 356–368. New York: Kitchen Table: Women of Color Press, 1983.

Reese, Debbie. "Authenticity & sensitivity." *School Library Journal* 45 (Nov 1999): 36–37.

Reger, Jo. "Emotions, Objectivity and Voice: an analysis of a 'Failed' participant observation." *Women's Studies International Forum* 24 (2001): 605–616.

Reid, Calvin. "Third World Press: 25 years fighting for empowerment." *Publishers Weekly* 240 (Jan. 1993): 22.

———. "Houses with No Doors." *Publishers Weekly* 241(May 1994): 62–66, 83.

Reid, Coletta. "Taking Care of Business." *Quest* 1(Fall 1974): 6–23.

Reinelt, Claire. "Moving onto the Terrain of the State." In *Feminist Organizations: Harvest of the new women's movement,* ed. Myra Marx Ferree and Patricia Yancey Martin, 84–104. Philadelphia: Temple University Press, 1995.

Rennie, Susan and Kirsen Grimstad, ed. *The New Woman's Survival Sourcebook.* New York: Knopf, 1975

Retter, Yolanda. "On the Side of Angels: Lesbian Activism in Los Angels, 1970–1990." Ph.D. diss., University of New Mexico, 1999.

Rich, Adrienne. *On Lies, Secrets and Silence.* New York: Norton, 1979.

———. "Compulsory Heterosexuality and Lesbian Existence." *Signs* 5 (Summer 1980): 631–660.

———. "Notes for a Magazine: What Does Separatism Mean?" *Sinister Wisdom* 18 (1981): 83–91.

Riger, Stephanie. "Challenges of Success Stages of Grown in Feminist Organizations." *Feminist Studies* 20 (July 1994): 275–277.

Risman, Barbar, and Donald Tomaskovic-Devey. "The Solemn responsibility of book reviewing; Take Two." *Contemporary Sociology* 27 (July 1998): vii.

Rix, Sara E. *The American Woman 1988–89: A Status Report.* New York: W.W. Norton & company, 1989.

Roback, Diane. "Children's Bookstores: Applying the brakes." *Publishers Weekly* (Jan. 11, 1993): 31

Robnett, Belinda. *How Long? How Long? African-American Women and the Struggle for Freedom and Justice.* New York: Oxford University Press, 1997.

Rochon, Thomas R. *Culture Moves: Ideas, Activism, and Changing Values.* NJ: Princeton, 1998.

Rogers, Everett M. *Diffusion of Innovations.* New York: Free Press, 1983.

Rose, Lynn. "Women's Books Profitable." *New Directions for Women* 17 (1988):18.

Rosen, Judith. "New Words: The Collective Works." *Publishers Weekly* (April 21, 1989): 56.

———. "Women's Bookstores: 20 years and thriving." *Publishers Weekly* 239 (May, 1992):18.

———. "Women's Bookstores: surviving in a changing retail climate." *Publishers Weekly* (April 1997) : 23.

———. "Women's Books for Profitable." *New Directions for Women* (July/August 1988): 18.

Rosen, Ruth. *The World Split Open*. New York: Viking, 2000.

Rosenwein, Rifka, "The Power Behind the Stacks." *Brill's Content* (August 1998): 116–121.

Rosoff, Ilene. *Woman Source Catalog & Review: Tools for Connecting the Community of Women*. Berkeley, CA: Celestial Arts, 1995.

Ross, Becki L. *The House That Jill Built: A Lesbian Nation in Formation*. Toronto: University of Toronto Press, 1995.

Ross, Glenwood II. "Are Black Communities Truly Underserved? An analysis of retail and professional services in the Atlanta Metropolitan Area." Ph.D. diss., Georgia State University, 1998.

Roth, Moira, ed. *The Amazing Decade: Women and Performance Art in America 1970–80*. Los Angeles: Astro Arts, 1983.

Rothchild-Whitt, Joyce. "The Collectivist Organization: an alternative to rational-bureaucratic models." *American Sociological Review* 44 (August 1979):509–27.

Rudy, Kathy. "RADICAL FEMINISM, LESBIAN SEPARATISM, AND QUEER THEORY." *Feminist Studies* (Spring 2001): 194.

Rupp, Leila. *Surviving in the Doldrums*. New York: Oxford, 1987.

Rush, Ramona R. *Communicating at the Crossroads: the Gender Gap Connection*. Norwood, New Jersey : Ablex Publishing company, 1989.

Russon, Ann, and Cheris Kramarae, eds. *The Radical Women's Press of the 1850s*. NY: Routledge, 1991.

Rust, Paul. *Bisexuality and the Challenge to Lesbian Politics: Sex, Loyalty and Revolution*. New York: New York University Press, 1995.

Rutledge, Leigh W. *Gay Decades: From Stonewall to the Present*. New York: Plume, 1992.

Ryan, Barbara. *Feminism and the Women's Movement: Dynamics of Change in Social Movement, Ideology and Activism*. New York: Routledge, 1992.

———. *The Women's Movement / References and Resources*. New York: G.K. Hall & Co., 1996.

———. *Identity Politics in the Women's Movement*. New York: New York University Press, 2001.

Sale, Kirkpatrick. "A Matter of Influence." In *Sixties Without Apology*, eds. Sohnya Saryers et al, 331–345. Minneapolis, MN: University of Minnesota Press, 1984.

Sameh, Catherine. "Women's Space, contested terrain." *Against Current* 12 (1997): 6.

Sandoval, Chela. "U.S. Third World Feminism: The Theory and Method of Oppositional Consciousness in the Postmodern World." *Genders* 10 (1991): 1–24.

Sarton, May. *The Education of Harriet Hatfield*. New York: W.W. Norton, 1989.

Scheff, Thomas J. *Microsociology: Discourse, Emotion and Social Structure.* Chicago: University of Chicago Press.

Schiffrin, Andre. *The Business of Books: How International Conglomarates Took Over Publishing and Changed the Way We Read.* NY: Verson, 2000.

Schneider, David Philip. *Aging Political Activists: Personal Narratives from the Old Left.* Westport, CT.: Praeger, 1995.

Schulman, Sarah. *The Sophie Horowitz Story.* Tallahassee, Fla.: Naiad Press, 1984.

———. *My American Story : Lesbian and Gay Life during the Regan/Bush Years.* New York: Routledge, 1994.

Schwartz, Harriet L. "Superstores vs. the Independents." *Philadelphia Gay News* (1998).

Scott, Alan. *Ideology and the New Social Movements.* London: Unwin Hyman, 1990.

Seajay, Carol. "Feminist Publishing in the US." In *250: An Introduction to a World of Women's Books,* ed. the Feminist Book Fair Group, 28–30. London: Feminist book Fair Groups, 1984.

———. "The Backlash and the Backlist." *The Women's Review of Books* 12 (1994): 18.

———. "Feminist bookstores Fight Back." *Ms.* (May/June 1995): 68–73.

———. "Our Words in Our Hands: a brief history of women's presses and bookstores." In *The Woman-Centered Economy: Ideals, Reality, and the Space in Between,* eds. Loraine Edwalds and Midge Stocker, 77–86. Chicago : Third Side Press, 1995.

———. "Books as Wallpaper? An explanation for returns." *Publishers Weekly* 243 (1996):30.

———. "Feminist Presses, Publications, and Bookstores." In *The Reader's Companion to U.S. Women's History.,* ed. Wilma Mankiller, 224–226. Boston: Houghton Mifflin Co., 1998.

Secombe-Easland, Lynette. "Ideology, Contradiction and Change in a Feminist Bookstore." Ph.D. diss., University of Utah, 1985.

See, Lisa. "Sisterhood Discovers Powerful Benefit: Feminist Bookstore Turns to Community Outreach to Fight Slipping Sales." *Publishers Weekly* 18 (Mar. 1996): 26.

Seeley, Christopher, "Two Foremothers of Lesbian Folk Rock Combine Voices for Histories." *Southern Voice* (October 25, 2002). Available online: http://www.criswillamson.com/news.htm

Seller, Maxine Schwartz, ed. Women Educators in the United States, 1820–1993: A Bio-graphical sourcebook. Westport, Conn.: Greenwood Press, 1994.

Senson, Linnea A. "From Isolation to Diversity: Self and Communities in Twentieth-Century Lesbian Novels." In *Sexual Practice/Textual Theory: Lesbian Cultural Criticism*, ed. Susan Wolfe and Julia Penelope, 208–225. Cambridge, MA : Blackwell, 1993.

Shatzkin, Leonard. *In Cold Type: Overcoming the Book Crisis.* Boston: Houghton Mifflin Company, 1982.

Shields, Rob. *Lifestyle Shopping: The Subject of Consumption.* London: Routledge, 1992.

Short, Kayann. "Publishing feminism in the feminist press movement, 1969–1994." Ph.D. diss., The University of Colorado, 1994.

Shugar, Dana R. *Separatism and Women's Community.* Lincoln: University of Nebraska Press, 1995.

Shulman, Sarah. *My American Story: Lesbian and Gay Life During the Reagan/ Bush Years.* N.Y.: Routledge, 1994.

Sidel, Heike. "The 'Invisibles': Lesbian Women as Library Users." *Progressive Librarian*14 (Spring 1998): 41–43.

Silvera, Makeda, ed. *Piece of My Heart: A Lesbian of Color Anthology.* Toronto: Sister Vision, 1991.

Simon, Daniel. "Keepers of the Word." *The Nation* (December 25, 2000): 25–32.

Simon, Linda. "The Pleasures of Book Reviewing." *Scholarly Publishing* 27 (1996): 237.

Simonds, Wendy. *Women and Self-Help Culture: Reading Between Lines.* New Brunswick: Rutgers University Press, 1992.

Simons, Judy. "Women, Publishing and Power." In *In Writing: A Woman's Business: Women, Writing and the Marketplace,* eds. Judy Simons and Kate Fulbrook, 183–192. Manchester, U.K.: Manchester University Press, 1998.

Skinner, William, and Melanie Otis, "Drug and Alcohol Use Among Lesbian and Gay People in a Southern US Sample: Epidemiological, Comparative, and Methodological Findings From the Trilogy Project," *Journal of Homosexuality* 30, no.3 (1996):59–92.

Smith, Barbara "Toward a Black Feminist Criticism." *Conditions* 2 (1977): 25–44.

———. "Notes for Yet Another Paper on Black Feminism, or Will the Real Enemy, Please Stand Up? " *Conditions* 5 (1979): 123–127.

———. "Across the Kitchen Table: A Sister to sister Dialogue." *Sinister Wisdom* 18 (1981):63–75.

———. "Response." *Sinister Wisdom* 20 (1982):100–104.

———, ed. *Home Girl : a Black Feminist Anthology.* New York: Kitchen Table: Women of Color Press, 1983.

———. "A Press of Our Own—Kitchen Table: Women of Color Press." *Frontiers: A Journal of Women's Studies* 10 (1989): 11–13.

———. "Between a Rock and a Hard Place: Relationships Between Black and Jewish Women." In *Yours in Struggle: the Feminist Perspectives on Anti-Semitism and Racism* , eds. Elly Bulkin, Minnie Bruce Pratt, and Barbara Smith, 67–87. New York: Long Haul Press, 1984.

———. "Changing the World: Kitchen Table: Women of Color Press." In *Happy Endings,* ed. Kate Brandt, 109–118. Tallahassee, Florida: The Naiad Press, Inc., 1993.

Smith, Michael Peter. *Breaking Chains: Social Movements and Collective Action.* New Jersey: Transactional Publications, 1991.

Smitherman, Geneva, ed. *African American Women Speak Out on Anita Hill-Clarence Thomas.* Michigan: Wayne State University Press, 1995.

Snitow, Ann. *Powers of Desire: The Politics of Sexuality.* NY: Monthly Review Press, 1983.

Snowdon, Shane. "Why Support Feminist Publishing? " *Sojourner: The Women's Forum* (December 1988): 40–41.

Somani, Indira. "Bookstore gives women a voice." *Monitor* (Winter 1993): 16.

Somerville, Mary R. "The New World of the American Public Library." In *The Book in the United States Today* , eds. Gordon Graham and Richard Abel, 37–48. New Brunswick and London: Transaction Publishers, 1997.

Sommers, Christina Hoff. *Who Stole Feminism? : How Women Have Betrayed Women.* New York: Touchstone/Simon & Schuster, 1995.

Spalter-Roth, Roberta and Ronnee Schreiber. "Outsider Issues and Insider Tactics: Strategic Tensions, the Women's Policy Network During the 1980s." In *Feminist Organizations,* eds. Myra Marx Ferree and Patricia Yancey Martin, 105–127. Philadelphia: Temple University Press, 1995.

Spender, Dale. "The Gatekeepers: a feminist critique of academic publishing." In *Doing Feminist Research* , ed. Helen Roberts, 186–202. Boston: Routledge & Kegan Paul, 1981.

———. *The Writing in the Sex?* NY: Pergamon Press, 1989.

———."Electronic Scholarship: Perform or Perish." In *Women, Information Technology and Scholarship,* ed. Jeannie Taylor, Cheris Kramarae, and Maureen Ebber, 28–43. Urbana: University of Illinois, 1993.

Spender, Lynne. "The Politics of Publishing: Selection and Rejection of Women's Words in Print." *Women's Studies International Forum* 1983 6(5): 469–473.

———. *Intruders on the Rights of Men: Women's Unpublished Heritage.* London: Pandora, 1983.

Staggenborg, Suzanne. "Women's Movements in the US." *American Journal of Sociology* 97 (91): 214–216.

Stall, Susan J. "Feminist Organizations." *Gender and Society* 11. (1997): 372–74.

Stearns, Peter. "Social history update: a little problem about bookstores." *Journal of Social History* 31 (Winter 1997): 501.

Stein, Arlene. *Sisters, Sexperts, Queers: Beyond the Lesbian Nation.* New York: Plune, 1993.

———. "All dressed up, but no place to go?" In *Out in Culture: Gay,Lesbian and Queer Essays on Popular Culture,* eds. Corey K.Creekmur and Alexander Doty, 476–483. Durham, NC: Duke University Press, 1995.

———. *Sex and Sensibility: Stories of a Lesbian Generation.* Berkeley: University of California Press, 1997.

Steiner, Linda. "History and Structure of Women's Alternative media." In *Women Making Meaning: New Feminist Directions in Communication,* ed. Rakow, Lana F, 121–143. New York: Routledge, 1992.

Stenson, Linnea A. "From Isolation to Diversity: Self and Communities in Twentieth-Century Lesbian Novels." In *Sexual Practice/Textual Theory : Lesbian Cultural Criticism* eds. Susan J. Wolfe and Julia Penelope, 208–225. Cambridge, MA: Blackwell, 1993.

Stillman, Teery A. "The Internet and the romance of bookselling." *AB Bookman's Weekly* 101 (Mar. 1998): 657–8.

Stocker, Midge and Loraine Edwards. *The Woman-Centered Economy: Ideals, Reality, and the Space in Between.* Chicago: Third Side Press, 1995.

Stowe, Steven. "Thinking about Reviews." *The Journal of American History* 78 (Sep., 1991): 591–595.

Strainchamps, Ethel. *Rooms with No View: A Woman's Guide to Man's World of the Media.* NY: Harper & Rowe, 1974.

Streitmatter, Rodger. *Unspeakable: The Rise of the Gay and Lesbian Press in America.* Boston: Faber & Faber, 1995.

———. *Voices of Revolution: The Dissident Press in America.* New York: Columbia University Press, 2001.

Stryker, Susan. *Gay by the Bay: A History of Queer Culture in the San Francisco Bay Area.* San Francisco, Calif.: Chronicle Books, 1996.

Sullivan, Elizabeth. "Carol Seajay, Old Wives Tales, and the Feminist Bookstore Network: I came to San Francisco with a ray of hope about living life as a lesbian woman." *Shaping San Francisco on the Web.* Available online, http://www.shapingsf.org/ezine/womens/bookstrs/main.html

Summer, Bob. "Bookselling as cultural politics; gay and lesbian bookstores." *Publishers Weekly.* (June 27 1994): 29–31.

Sutherland, John. *Bestsellers : Popular Fiction of the 1970s.* London: Routledge & Kegan Paul, 1981.

Swidler, Ann. "Culture in Action : Symbols and Strategies." *American Sociological Review* 51: 273–86.

———. "Talking About the Basics: What is Feminist Writing and Why Do We Need Feminist Publishing?" *The Feminist Writers Guild* 8 (Winter 1985): 1–11.

———. *Talk of Love: How Culture Matters.* Chicago: The University of Chicago Press, 2001.

Taylor, Verta and Leila J. Rupp. "Women's Culture and Lesbian Feminist Activism: A Reconsideration of Cultural Feminism." *Signs* (Autumn 1993): 32–61.

Taylor, Verta and N. Raeburn. "Identity politics as high-risk activism: career consequences for lesbian, gay and bisexual sociologists." *Social Problems* 42(1995): 252–273.

Taylor, Verta and Nancy. Whittier. "Collective Identity in Social Movement Communities." In *Frontiers in Social Movement Theory,* ed. Aldon D. Morris. New Haven, CT: Yale University Press, 1992.

———. "Analytical Approaches to Social Movement Culture: The Culture of the Women's Movement." In *Social Movement and Culture,* eds. Hank Johnston and Bert Klandermans, 163–188. Minnesota : University of Minnesota Press, 1995.

Taylor, Verta and Nancy Whittier and Cynthia Fabrizio Pelak. "The Women's Movement: Persistence through transformation." In *Feminist Frontiers 5*, eds. Laurel Richardson, Verta Taylor, and Nancy Whitter, 559–574. Boston, MA: McGraw Hill, 2001.

———. "The New Feminist Movement." In *Feminist Frontiers IV,* ed. Laurel Richardson, 544–561. New York: McGrow Hill, 1997.

Taylor, Verta, "The Continuity of the American Women's Movement." In *Women and Social Protest,* eds. Guilda West and Rhoda Lois Blumberg, 277–301. NY: Oxford University Press, 1990.

———. "Social Movement Continuity: The Women's Movement in Abeyance." *American Sociological Reviews* 54 (1989): 761–775.

———. "The Future of Feminism in the 1980's: a social movement analysis." In *Feminist Frontiers: Rethinking Sex, Gender, and Society,* eds. Laurel W. Richardson and Verta Taylor. Reading, MA: Addison-Wesley, 1983.

Tebbel, John. *A History of Book Publishing in the United States, Volume I: the creation of an industry 1630–1865.* New York: R.R. Bowker, 1972.

———. *A History of Book Publishing in the United States, Volume II: the expansion of an ainustry 1865–1919.* New York: R.R. Bowker, 1975.

———. *A History of Book Publishing in the United States, Volume III: the golden age between two wars 1920–1940.* New York: R.R.Bowker, 1978.

———. *The Media in America.* New York: Mentor Books, 1974.

———. *Between Covers: The Rise and Transformation of Book Publishing in America.* New York & Oxford: Oxford University Press, 1987.

Tebbel, John, and Mary Ellen Zuckerman. *The Magazine in America, 1741–1990.* New York: Oxford University Press, 1991.

Terris, Virginia. *Woman in America: A Guide to Information Sources.* Detroit, Mich.: Gale, 1980.

"The Astonishing Growth of Small Publishers 1958–1988." *Journal of Popular Culture* 24 (Winter 1990): 61–68.

"The State of Emergency in Feminist Publishing." *Off Our Backs* 30 (8) (Aug/Sep 2000): 5–6.

The Women's Review of Books. Pilot Issue, Wellesley Massachusetts. Summer, 1983.

"Third World Press: 25 years fighting for empowerment." *Publishers Weekly* 240 (Jan 4, 1993): 22.

Thom, Mary. *Inside Ms.: 25 Years of the Magazine and the Feminist Movement.* New York: Holt, 1997.

Thorpe, Rochella. "The changing face of Detroit's lesbian bars, 1940–1975." In *Creating a Place for Ourselves: Lesbian, Gay, and Bisexual Community Histories* ed. Brett Beemyn, 77–86. New York: Routledge, 1997.

Tierney, Helen, ed. *Women's Studies Encyclopedia.* Westport, Connecticut : Greenwood Press, 1999.

Tillman, Lynne. *Bookstore: The Life and Times of Jeannette Watson and Books & Co.* New York: Harcourt Brace & Company, 1999.

Torres, Sasha. "Television/Feminism: HeartBeat and Prime Time Lesbianism." In *The Lesbian and Gay Studies Reader*, eds. Henry Abelove, Michele Aina Barale, David M. Halperin, 176–185. New York : Routledge, 1993.

Travis, Molly Abel. *Reading Cultures : The Construction of Readers in the Twentieth Century.* Carbondale : Southern Illinois University Press, 1998.

Tuchman, Gaye. *Making News: A Study in the Construction of Reality.* New York: Free Press, 1978.

Turner, Anne M. "Opinion polls: a savvy tool to raise library value." *Library Journal* (Oct. 1997): 40.

Tyrkus, Michael J, ed. *Gay & Lesbian Biography.* Detroit; London: St. James Press, 1997.

Vaid, Urvashi. *Virtual Equality: The Mainstreaming of Gay and Lesbian Liberation.* New York: Anchor Books, 1995.

Valeska, Lucia. "The future of female separatism." In *Building Feminist Theory from Quest,* ed. Charlotte Bunch, 20–31. New York: Longman, 1981.

Valk, Anne. "Separatism and sisterhood: race, sex and women's activism in Washington, D.C., 1963–1980." Ph.D., diss., Duke University, 1996.

Van den Berghe, Pierre. *Academic Gamesmanship*. New York: Abeland-Schuman, 1970.

Van Dyke, Elizabeth Artemis. "A Woman's Place is in History: communicating and preserving the culture of minority groups of women and their organizations in an archival format. " Ph.D. diss., The Union Institute, 1991.

Van Gelder, Lindsy and Pamela Brandt. *The Girls Next Door.* New York: Touchstone Press, 1997.

Van Hook, John. "The Indexes to Current Work on the History of the Book." *Analytical & Enumerative Bibliography* 6(1992): 10–19.

Vance, Carole S., ed. *Pleasure and Danger: Exploring Female Sexuality.* Boston: Routledge & K. Paul, 1984.

Vanderbilt II, Arthur T. *The Making of a Bestseller from Author to Reader*. N.Y: McFarland & Co., 1999.

Vita, Ginny, ed. *Our Right to Love: A Lesbian Sourcebook*. New York: Prentice-Hall, 1978.

Wachsberger, Ken, ed. *Voices from the Underground.* Tempe, AZ: Mica Press, 1993.

Walker, Scott. "A Review in the Times?! Oh, no!." *Publishers Weekly* 250 (1993): 41–45

Wandersee, Winifred. *On the Move: American Women in the 1970's.* Boston: Twayne Publishers, 1988.

Warner, Michael. *Fear of a Queer Planet: Queer Politica and Social Theory.* Minneapolis: University of Minneapolis Press, 1993.

Warren, Patricia Nel. "Has the Gay Publishing Boom Gone Bust?" *Harvard Gay and Lesbian Review* 6 (1999): 7.

———. "Starter Kit for New GLBT Writers." *Wildcat: International* 2001. Available online: http://www.wildcatintl.com/partners/secrets/pat_se36.html

Watkins, Bonnie and Nina Rothchild. *In the Company of Women: Voices from the Women's Movement.* St. Paul, Minnesota; Minnesota historical Society Press, 1996.

Weathers, Breanda. "Alcoholism and the Lesbian Community." In *Alcoholism in Women,* eds. Christen C. Eddy and John L. Ford, 142–149. Dubuque, Iowa : Kendall/Hunt Publishing Company, 1980.

Weeks, Jeffrey. *Sexuality and its discontents' meanings, myths, and modern sexualities* (New York: Routledge, 1985)

———. *Making sexual history*. Malden, Mass. : Blackwell, 2000.

Weightman, Barbara A. "Gay bars as private places." *Landscape* 24:1 (1980):9–16.

Weisbard, Phyllis Holman. "Reviews and their afterlife." *The Women's Review of Books* 12 (Jan. 1995): 16–17.

Weiss, Andrea, and Greta Schiller. *Before Stonewall: The Making of Gay and Lesbian Community.* Tallahassee, FL: Naiad, 1988.

Weitz, Rose. "From Accommodation to Rebellion: The Politicization of Lesbianism." In *Woman-Identified Woman,* ed. Dart and Sandee Potter, 238. Palo-Alto, CA: Mayfield Publishing Co., 1984.

Weller, Marilyn. "Women's Own Media." *Equal Times* (October 13–26, 1980): 1.

Weller, Sam. "Women and Children First is #1 with Authors and Customers." *Publishers Weekly. Com (Jul. 1999).*

West, Celest. *The Passionate Perils of Publishing.* San Francisco: Booklegger Press, 1978.

———. "The Literary Industrial Complex." *Chrysalis* 8 (Summer 1979):95–103.

———, ed. *Words in Our Pockets : The Feminist Writers' Guild Handbook on How to Gain Power, Get Published & Get Paid.* Paradise, CA: Dustbooks, 1985.

West, Guilda and Rhoda Lois Blumberg, ed. *Women and Social Protest.* NY: Oxford University Press, 1990.

West, James L.W., III. "Blockbusters, Basketball, and the Book Industry." *Harvard Library Bulletin* 30 (1982): 336–348.

———. *American Authors and the Literary Marketplace Since 1900.* Philadelphia: University of Pennsylvania Press, 1988.

Weston, Kathleen M. ed. *Long Slow Burn: Sexuality and Social Science.* New York: Routledge, 1998.

———. "Sexuality, class and conflict in a lesbian workplace." In *The Lesbian Issue: Essays from Signs,* ed. Estelle B. Freedman. Chicago: University of Chicago Press, 1985.

Whalen, Jack and Richard Flacks. *Beyond the Barricades: The Sixties Generation Grows Up.* Philadelphia: Temple University Press, 1989.

Wharton, Carol. "Establishing Shelters for Battered Women: Local Manifestations of a Social Movement." *Qualitative Sociology* 10, no.2 (1987): 146–63

Whisler, Sandra M. "Electronic Publishing and the Indispensability of Publishers." In *The Book in the United States Today,* eds. Gordon Graham and Richard Abel, 213–224. New Brunswick and London: Transaction Publishers, 1997.

Whiteside, Thomas. *The Blockbuster Complex: Conglomerates, Show Business, and Book Publishing.* Middletown, CT: Wesleyan University Press, 1981.

Whittier, Nancy. "Persistence and Transformation: Gloria Steinem, the Women's Action Alliance, and the Feminist Movement, 1971–1997." *Journal of Women's History* 14 (Summer): 148–150.

———. "Turning It Over: Personnel Change in the Columbus, Ohio, Women's Movement." In *Feminist Organizations,* ed. Myra Marx Ferree and Patricia Yancey Martin, 180–198. Philadelphia: Temple University Press, 1995.

———. *Feminist Generations: The Persistence of the Radical Women's Movement.* Philadelphia: Temple Univ. Press, 1995

"Why Women's Bookstores?" *Lesbian.com* (November 12, 2002): Available online: http://www.lesbian.com/marketplace/bookstores_why.html

Wiley, Mark. "How to read a book : Reflections on the Ethics of Book Reviewing." *Journal of Advanced Composition* 13 (Fall 1993): 477.

Wilkinson, Kathleen. "The Closing of the Feminist Press: thirty years after the revolution, feminist publishers are feeling the crunch." *Girlfriends* (March 2001): 31–33, 40.

Willamson, Jane, Diane Winston, and Wanda Wooter. *Women's Action Almanac.* New York: William Morrow & company, INC., 1979.

Willett, Charles. "Starting an Alternative Library." *Librarians at Liberty* 1 (1994): 6–7.

Williams, Brooke, and Hannah Dorby. "God, Mom & Apple Pie." *Off Our Backs* 5 (February 1976): 18.

Williams, Brooke. "The Retreat to Cultural Feminism." In *Feminist Revolution* , ed. Redstockings of the Women's Liberation Movement. New York: Random House, 1978.

Williams, Kathie Denise. "Louisville's lesbian feminist union: a study in the development of a local lesbian-feminist organization and its effect on the city's entire homosexual community." M.A thesis, University of Louisville, 1995.

Willis, Ellen. "Radical Feminism and Feminist Radicalism." In *The '60s Without Apology,* eds. Sohnya Sayres, Anders Stephanson, Stanley Arnowitz, and Fredric Jameson, 91–118. Minneapolis: University of Minnesota, 1984.

Willis, Holly. "Books Inc." *The Reader* (November 1995): Available online: http://www.msbooks.com/msbooks/booksInc.html

Wilma Mankiller, ed. *The Reader's Companion to U.S. Women's History.* New York: Houghton Mifflin Company, 1998.

Wilson, Carol, et al., eds. *Lesbians Speak Out.* San Francisco: Free Women's Press, 1971.

Wilson, John K. "In Print: The politics of book reviewing." *In These Times* 19 (November 28, 1994):34.

Wilson, Midge and Kathy Russell. *Divided Sisters: Bridging the Gap between Black Women and White Women.* New York: Anchor Books, Doubleday, 1996.

Wingfott, Alana. "Big Stores, Small Stores, and Knee-Jerk." The 3rd WWWave: feminism for the new millennium (November 2002): Available online: http://www.io.com/~wwwave/books/alnarant.html

Wittmer, Jill Lisa. "Learning our lives: lesbian existence and experience in Washington, D.C." Ph.D. diss., The American University, 1994.

Wolf, Deborah Goleman. *The Lesbian Community.* Berkeley and Los Angeles, CA: University of California Press, 1980.

Wolfe, Alan. "The Solemn responsibilities of book reviewing." *The Chronicle of Higher Education* 44 (1998): B4-B5.

Woloch, Nancy. *Women and the American Experience.* New York: McGraw-Hill, 1994.

Women in Publishing: 9 to 5 organization. *Women in the Boston Area Publishing Industry. A Status Report.* Boston March 1975.

Women's Committee at Harper and Row. *Report on the Status of Women at Harper and Row.* NY: March 1975.

Women's National Book Association. *Women's National Book Association Honors Book Women: 70 who have made a difference: on the occasion of its 70th anniversary, 1917–1987, and the Year of the Reader.* New York: WNBA, 1987.

Wrenn, Jenny. *Guide to Women Book Publishers in the United States for 1990.* LA, California: Clothepin Fever Press, 1990.

———. "Visibility through Book Publishing : The Story of Clothespin Fever Press." *Collection Building* II (1991) : 32–34.

Yaffe, Deborah. "Feminism in Principle and in Practice: Everywomans Books." *Atlantis: A Women's Studies Journal* 21.1 (Fall 1996): 154–157.

Zahniser, Jill. "Feminist Collectives : the transformation of women's business in the counterculture of the 1970s and 1980s." Ph.D. diss., The University of Iowa, 1985.

Zboray, Ronald and Mary Saracino Zboray. *A Handbook for the Study of Book History in the United States.* Washington, DC: Library of Congress, 2000.

Zboray, Ronald J. "Book Distribution and American Culture: A 150-Year Perspective." *Book Research Quarterly* 3 (1987): 37–59.

Zimmerman, Bonnie. *The Sage Sea of Women: Lesbian Fiction, 1969–1989.* Boston: Beacon Press, 1990.

———. "What Has Never Been: an overview of lesbian feminist literary criticism." In *Lesbianism,* ed. Wayne R. Dynes. New York and London: Garland Publishing Inc., 1992.

———and Toni A.H.McNaron, eds. *The New Lesbian Studies: Into the Twenty-first Century.* New York: Feminist Press, 1996.

———. "'Confessions' of a lesbian/feminist." In *Cross-Purposes: Lesbians, Feminists and the Limits of Alliance,* ed. Dana Heller, 157–168. Bloomington: Indiana University Press, 1997.

———. *Lesbian Histories and Culture: An Encyclopedia.* New York: Garland Publisher, 2000.

Zinkhan, George, M and Terry Clark. "The role of books and book reviews in the knowledge dissemination process." *Journal of Marketing* 59 (Jan 1995): 106.

Index

O

P

Q

R

S

T

U

V

www.ingramcontent.com/pod-product-compliance
Lightning Source LLC
Chambersburg PA
CBHW071455110726
47908CB00003B/615

* 9 7 8 0 4 1 5 8 8 2 6 0 6 *